In praise of Myra Hess - National Treasure

I loved reading this affectionate, elegant and informative biography of one of the greatest figures in British musical history.
Sir Stephen Hough

Jessica Duchen writes with a great depth of musical understanding and genuine empathy for the neglected National Treasure that is Myra Hess. At last here is the biography she so richly deserves as Jessica Duchen gives Myra Hess a concert platform for a new audience. It's a terrific achievement. Surely Hess, who did so much in wartime London to bolster courage and culture by giving concerts at the National Gallery, should now be on the fourth plinth opposite the Gallery?
Anne Sebba - Author, presenter & lecturer

An engrossing read bringing fresh perspectives on a remarkable musician and on the 20th century cultural backdrop from which she emerged.
Fiona Maddocks - Author and music critic

Myra Hess was not only a major artist and a riveting personality; she also lived through uniquely fascinating times. In this eminently readable biography, Jessica Duchen brilliantly evokes both a powerful and attractive character, and the eras she inhabited. A sympathetic and thoroughly researched study of a musical legend.
Steven Isserlis

Packed with colourful anecdotes and musical insight, this biography is a tour-de-force, revealing the real Myra Hess beyond the myths.
Tasmin Little

Jessica Duchen's biography of Myra Hess restores to us a great pianist in all her complex glory, complete with her dedication, her struggles with nerves, her probing musicianship, her personal courage in the face of illness, her gift for friendship, and her sense of fun. A sympathetic, balanced and rounded portrait.
Susan Tomes - Pianist, writer and educator

MYRA HESS

NATIONAL TREASURE

MYRA HESS

NATIONAL TREASURE

Jessica Duchen

Foreword by Stephen Kovacevich

KAHN & AVERILL • LONDON

Published by Kahn & Averill
2-10 Plantation Road
Amersham, Buckinghamshire, HP6 6HJ
United Kingdom

www.kahnandaverill.co.uk

First published in hardback in 2025 by Kahn & Averill

A CIP record of this book is available from the British Library

Cover design by Økvik Design
Set and printed in Great Britain by Halstan UK, Amersham
www.halstan.co.uk

For Product Safety Information please contact our EU representative:
Halstan Deutschland GmbH, Johannes-Kepler-Straße 5, 55129 Mainz, Germany.
info@halstan.de

ISBN 978-1-0687762-0-5

To the memory of my mother,
Myra Duchen
(1932-1994)

When Death Came Near

By John Masefield
(In honour of Dame Myra Hess, 1945)

When death came flying near, accustomed joys
Seemed the illusions of a sickened sense,
Effort to ring a fever out of noise,
Fever, to drive a flying minute hence.
A scale went roaring down in violence.
The gassy catchwords rose, as counterpoise.
Then, this musician, with the link that binds
Spirits to spirit and the mind to minds,
Brought to the jangled hearts a unison,
Touching the notes that make one everyone,
Bringing a world where every seeker finds
The beauty and joy of service to the sun.

Contents

Author's Note

I WAS ABOUT SIX YEARS OLD when my mother parked the car outside Dame Myra Hess's former home at 48 Wildwood Road, London NW11. We were going for a walk on the Heath Extension, directly opposite. She pointed out the blue plaque.

My mother's name was also Myra. Born into an orthodox Jewish South African family in Johannesburg, she had been a talented pianist and had won the opportunity to study at the Royal Academy of Music in London. Her father refused to let her go.

As a piano-mad music student in the 1980s, I was lucky enough to experience the upswing of interest in the 'golden age', as historical recordings began to be remastered and reissued on CD. I feasted on the playing of Artur Schnabel, Sergei Rachmaninoff, Alfred Cortot and many others, but I loved few quite as much as Myra Hess's, which shone out with humanity, insight and immediacy, as well as a sense of humour rare at that time. Learning about her National Gallery concerts and their impact – which proved beyond a doubt the significance, indeed the necessity, of music to the human spirit – I was thrilled to find she was a national heroine. A national treasure.

Each part of her life story held a different fascination: first, the Edwardian rebel, Bohemian and, of necessity, feminist; then the young superstar embraced by America in the Roaring Twenties. As time went by, she experienced shattering emotional betrayals, mutilating medical horrors, disapprobation from critics expecting 'feminine charm', and some thinly veiled anti-Semitism. Amid all this, she created one of the most popular piano pieces of her day: her transcription of Bach's *Jesu, Joy of Man's Desiring*.

Then came World War II and the National Gallery concerts, which she devised, then ran every weekday for six and a half years notwithstanding the Blitz. Gradually the toughness she had been forced to develop in her youth morphed into indomitability, mingling her musicianship with qualities literary and theatrical. She was seemingly fearless. She would stand up to anybody and speak out whenever necessary. Few dared reciprocate in kind. After the war, she resumed her American tours, this time keeping diaries full of delicious detail; and after a conglomeration of medical issues, she spent her last few years teaching in London. The agonising process that led to her retirement from performing is all too human.

It is a great privilege to write the biography of one of my lifelong 'heroines'. I was born two days before Myra's memorial service was held at St Paul's Cathedral, and grew up in Hampstead, treading the same pavements that she would have known and walking daily past Tobias Matthay's former home. I share with Myra a profound love for our home city, London, the distanced background of Orthodox Judaism and its emotional legacies, a physical height – five foot three – and the pianistic conundrum of small hands. I hope that this book may help to preserve her memory and to release her real personality from behind the myths, with all her generosity, affection, wit and abrasiveness intact.

When I met the actress Patricia Routledge, who incarnated Myra magnificently in Nigel Hess's show *Admission One Shilling* with the pianist Piers Lane, she instructed me: 'Honour her.' I've tried to do so.

Jessica Duchen

Acknowledgements

INNUMERABLE PEOPLE HAVE been vital to the creation of this book. Please forgive me any inadvertent omissions.

First, members of the Hess family granted me access to and permission to quote from a treasure-trove of documents that have never been published before: Nigel Hess, Libbie Foster and Alan Hess have my boundless thanks. Jane Camilloni kindly gave me access to Myra's letters to Jelly d'Arányi, her duo partner for over two decades. Myra's ex-pupils have been invaluable presences: Stephen Kovacevich, John and Richard Contiguglia and Ann Schein. The screenwriter Judy Meewezen generously allowed me to use interviews she conducted some years ago with individuals who have since passed away, notably Yonty Solomon and Colin Hess. Arnold Griller, son of Sidney Griller, talked to me about his father and the Griller Quartet's relationship with Myra, and sent me copies of Myra's letters to Sidney. Tobias Matthay's biographer, Stephen Siek, emeritus professor of music at Wittenberg University, Springfield, Ohio, and a former president of the American Matthay Association, has been the kindest and most generous of sounding-boards, as well as an extraordinary fount of first-hand knowledge about some of Myra's close friends.

Jerry Butson of Oxford University Press dug out archive material pertaining to *Jesu, Joy*. Lewis Foreman, biographer of Arnold Bax, let me bombard him with questions and lent me some rare materials. Mike Spring of APR Records invaluably shared with me his discography of Myra's 78rpm early recordings. Tully Potter sent me his articles interviewing some key string players in Myra's life. Hugh Cobbe kindly provided images of some unpublished letters of Myra's that he has now placed in the British Library's collection.

I am deeply grateful to the staff of the British Library and the National Gallery Archives for their help, and to the Gallery's artistic director, Gabriele Finaldi, for his moral support and enthusiasm. I am also indebted to the late Marian McKenna's book *Myra Hess: A Portrait*.

My heartfelt thanks to wonderfully helpful and supportive friends and colleagues, including Mark Ainley, Mark Berry, Richard Bratby,

Leah Broad, Robin Cherry, Michael Church, James Eggleston, Helen Fry, Trudy Gold, Michael Haas, Andrew Keener, Nadia Lasserson, Rex Lawson, Jeremy Nicholas, Mike Oldham, Jamie Pass, and the pianists Piers Lane (who ran a series of Myra Hess Days at the National Gallery in the 2000s) and Sir András Schiff (who lent me Myra's volumes of Schubert piano music, given to him by Howard Ferguson). I have enjoyed interviews about Myra and her associates with Fiona Fraser, Myra's great-niece Diana King, Nick Logie and Diana McVeagh, among others. Further Hess family members, Dominic Lawson and Louise Barder, have provided invaluable pointers, contacts and moral support. I am grateful to Helen Stern and Tim Masters for information about Myra's assistance for Kindertransport children.

A veritable army of friends and family have put up with my obsessiveness, scattiness, high stress and endless pleas for chocolate. Roxanna Panufnik, Tasmin Little, Amanda Hurton, Eric Wen, Stellaria Ciampolini-Vukelic, Henrietta Foster, Erica Worth, Joanna Pieters, my brother Michael and his family, and many more, I owe you all. And I couldn't have done anything without the patience (and culinary skills) of my husband, Tom.

Finally, this book wouldn't exist without the devoted support of Kahn & Averill – Leslie East, Sidney Buckland and Christopher Smith. Christopher's parents courted in the National Gallery Concerts queue. In which light, the ultimate thanks must go to Myra herself.

Introduction

I WAS ONLY TWELVE when the news reached our family home in Somerset that 'Auntie' Myra had died. I had met her a couple of times during infrequent trips to London, the most recent at her home in St John's Wood when she was already suffering badly from the cruel arthritis in her hands which prevented her from playing in her final years. I remember I had the temerity to play to her myself. Her review was that I made a 'nice noise' – a comment which I've cherished ever since. The house backed on to Lord's cricket ground and she enjoyed hearing the applause at the end of each over, reminding her of a lifetime of concerts, while the back lawn (an indelible memory from all those years ago) was in the shape of a grand piano. Her sense of humour was as much a part of her as the grit and determination she used to make her way in a man's world and achieve so much.

As I grew older and started to make my own way in the precarious music business I became more conscious of Dame Myra's extraordinary legacy – and in particular those years for which she is most remembered during the Second World War when she organized the life-affirming lunchtime concerts at London's National Gallery. We told that story in a show called *Admission: One Shilling* with Dame Patricia Routledge and Piers Lane which played to many audiences both in the UK and abroad who were often hearing about Myra's courage and emotional sacrifices for the first time.

Myra was my great-aunt – her brother Herbert was my grandfather. I wish I had known her better. I remember thinking, when we all attended her memorial service in a packed St Paul's Cathedral, that she must have been considered a national treasure. She would, of course, have hated the idea – down-to-earth Myra had no time for such things. But through her recordings, her writings, the lasting impression she made on those who were fortunate enough to hear her play, and now this definitive new biography, we can know Myra a little better and feel the warmth and humanity that made her who she was, and which captivated listeners all over the world.

Nigel Hess

Preface

I CAME TO BRITAIN to study with Myra Hess when I was 18, after the Griller Quartet had introduced me to her in California. I can promise you that she was not the girl next door, she was not auntie pouring tea and she was not the Queen Mother. Her Beethoven took no prisoners. It's nearly 50 years since the last biography of her was published and now it is high time for another one, allowing new aspects of her personality to come to light. There is much here from her letters and diaries that has not been published before – and hers was not a common voice.

Myra's legacy is very much alive; her recordings are still listened to, appreciated and valued – but people don't play like that today. Therefore the more insight we can have into her life, what she thought of other musicians and what they thought of her, the better. Her concerts at the National Gallery throughout the Second World War have become the stuff of legend: she had the initiative and the heroism to see that through in extremely dangerous circumstances.

The British made her into the pianistic equivalent of the Queen Mother, but in America she was a different kind of artist; there her performances seemed much more exciting. I heard her first in San Francisco, where I grew up: she played the Mozart D minor Piano Concerto, which was positively demonic. The US released something in her, whether because of the cultural atmosphere or because of the American Steinway pianos that she loved.

I knew her best as a teacher, and the main thing that I studied with her was Beethoven. You can count on the fingers of your hands the number of musicians who have a deep appreciation of late Beethoven, a category of music on its own, and I can't think of anyone I'd rather have worked with on it. She was never dogmatic. She would interrogate your musicianship deeply and, like that beer advertisement of a few years ago, she got to places that others did not reach. And she had a wicked sense of humour – I remember that some of her remarks had quite a snarl to them.

She had a deep aversion to using speed as a main ingredient in all circumstances – and like many Americans, I had previously had a liking for it. She showed me that although speed can be exciting, sometimes it is less so, depending on the passage or the character of the music. In her own way, she was as unique a pianist as Vladimir Horowitz, though her approach was completely different; nobody else, certainly not among British pianists, had such warmth in the sound. She had one of the richest sounds of any pianist; it came from deep within her.

Myra Hess opened up new profundity, understanding, range of expression and more in my playing. To this day I am increasingly grateful for the time I spent with her.

Stephen Kovacevich

A London Jewish Childhood
(1890–1902)

Dame Myra Hess's niece, Libbie, loved as a little girl to brush out her aunt's luxurious hair. Myra's locks reached almost to her waist. Afterwards she would wind it up and pin it into place, with soft side wings framing her face. The lavish extent of those tresses was strictly controlled and hidden from view.

Myra was five foot three, but on stage she seemed much taller. Audience members sometimes described her as a giant, rock-like presence. With dark hair, fair complexion and heavy-lidded grey-green eyes, she looked magnificent in the concert dresses of 'splendid colour' she chose in her youth[1]. Later she preferred plain black, adorned only with a jade amulet – but sometimes she wore red velvet. Her favourite colour nevertheless was powder blue, which she chose for her stationery, and her favourite flower was the delicate, sweet-scented freesia[2].

She moved with a light, strong, springy step. At home or visiting her siblings, she was not one to tiptoe around. 'When she came to stay,' Libbie recalls, 'you knew somebody was in the house.'[3] She would clown about, sometimes making orange-peel teeth to startle the children with a surprise grin. She loved crosswords, Scrabble and card games; when she was due at their Birmingham home, Libbie's father, John, would make sure to organise Bridge or Canasta evenings.

She adored her nieces and nephews and delighted in hearing them play their piano pieces. They adored her in return. They knew she was a famous pianist: sometimes they would be taken to one of her concerts, where they could watch her with mingled pride and astonishment. To them, she was just Auntie Myra. Yet there was a side of herself that was kept back, away from them, and possibly from everyone else.

The symbolism of long hair goes back millennia. The Biblical story of Samson and Dalila apportions Samson's strength to his hair; and in Orthodox Judaism, in which community distant generations of the Hesses had lived, upon marriage a woman would be expected to shave her head and wear a wig, to cease attracting any man but her husband.

Myra's immediate family were Orthodox, if selectively so. Religious traditions lingered in their South Hampstead household: the Friday night Kiddush ritual, blessing a cup of wine, bread, salt and candles at sundown, signals the onset of Shabbat and the expectation that for the ensuing 24 hours one would not work or travel, let alone give a concert. Myra's profession was not compatible with this, but she always tried to avoid performing on the important Jewish festivals – mostly to avoid upsetting potential concert-goers – and would often ring family members to check on the correct dates[4]. Her great-niece, Diana King, recalled discovering with surprise that her grandmother, Myra's sister Irene, could read Hebrew fluently; probably all the Hess siblings had learned as children.

'It is, of course, impossible for an artist to keep the Orthodox faith strictly,' Myra told an interviewer. 'Besides, one's ideas change and I look at life a bit differently now. But I shall always look back on those religious times in my home with peace and happiness. Despite the strict rules to which we all had to conform, we were all happy.'[5]

She once reflected that her strict Orthodox upbringing 'has always been my saving'. She carried with her, consciously or not, its intense self-discipline, its sense of ritual and perhaps some of its moral codes.

From Spitalfields to Hampstead

Julia Myra Hess was born at 86 Alexandra Road, London NW8, on 25th February 1890. Myra would have preferred to be called Julia. Over the years, various people, including herself, nicknamed her Missie, the Dame, Auntie, Pishkosz, and sometimes Hyra Mess.

South Hampstead, between Hampstead Village and St John's Wood, was a prime slice of Victorian north London suburbia; the ravages of two world wars and some 1960s architects lay far in the future. The locale was dominated by stucco-fronted houses with generous gardens. Along the tree-lined thoroughfares, horse-drawn, open-topped buses would carry passengers towards the West End. Alexandra Road was relatively modest, backing on to the railway that ran between Euston and Watford Junction.

The Hesses had not always lived in this area. Myra's father, Frederick Solomon Hess, had inherited his family's factory at 28 Spital Square, Spitalfields: his father, Samuel Hess, had founded the textile firm in 1847, manufacturing peaks for uniform caps worn by the London Police, the Beefeaters, the St John's Ambulance Corps and the military, among others. The company had once controlled silk looms that wove material for cuffs and even for church altar cloths. It situates the family broadly in what was termed 'the *schmatter* trade' – clothing – which was flourishing in the East End.

Myra as a small child

Three of Myra's grandparents were East End natives, their families having settled there well before the substantial influx of Jewish immigrants fleeing pogroms in the Pale of Settlement in the late 19th century. Samuel was the exception, born in 1824 in Merzig, Saarland. Close to today's French border, it was a small Prussian town roughly equidistant between Saarbrücken and Luxembourg. Hess remains a common surname in the area, which extends up to Mannheim, Mainz and beyond.

The 1851 census found Samuel living at 8 Crispin Street, Spitalfields. He had honed his trade in Germany before seeking a more liberal environment in England; he and his Amsterdam-born housemate, Solomon Harris, are listed as 'cap peak manufacturers, employing 5 hands'. Thirty years later, they had 40 employees and Samuel and his wife, Alice Cantor, had eight children. Frederick Solomon was the eldest, born in 1855 in Finsbury, Bishopsgate. Samuel's brother, Morris, married Alice's sister, Kate, and the two families settled next door to each other at 55 and 57 Grosvenor Street, Islington.

Frederick's wife, Lizzie Jacobs, was the third of seven children of John and Julia Jacobs. A petite, dark, vivacious young woman, she had grown up at 32 Finsbury Square, where her large family was listed in the 1871 census along with two nurses, a housemaid, a needlewoman and a cook. That suggests some significant social progress: when Julia Cohen met John Jacobs around 1851, the latter and his widowed mother were probably her parents' lodgers at Tripes Yard, Spitalfields, near Petticoat Lane. The great violist Lionel Tertis, a chamber music partner of Myra's, spent his childhood in the vicinity some 30 years later; it was so squalid, he recalled, that he thought himself lucky to have survived.[6]

This warm, ambitious family had only a slight musical connection: Lizzie was a good singer and loved to accompany herself at the piano. Many musicians of the time came from East End backgrounds, often following in the footsteps of their parents and siblings. Samuel Kutcher, leader of the Kutcher Quartet and the London Chamber Orchestra, was a sweet-toned violinist from a large family devoted to the profession. Tertis was the son of a synagogue cantor from Minsk; his passion for music was inspired by his father's tenor voice. The Hesses, however, had no such professions; nor, at first, such aspirations for their smallest daughter.

A Few Victorian Values

Benjamin Disraeli stood down as Britain's prime minister ten years before Myra was born. In certain ways he symbolised the changing fortunes of the British Jewish community. During his political career, spanning the mid-19th century, the British Empire had arguably reached its apex, with galloping industrial development. Disraeli, a favourite of Queen Victoria and a cultured, intellectual, ambitious thinker, represented to many the pinnacle of Jewish emancipation; in Britain parliament had been barred to Jews until 1858. Nevertheless, he – like the Queen's earlier musical favourite, Felix Mendelssohn – was a convert to Christianity, which put a slightly different slant on the matter.

The Hesses substantially mirrored the values and structures of the Victorian era. It was an age full of paradoxes. Its society liked to emulate the monarch and her consort's enthusiasms, including music and literature, yet despite the Queen being an all-powerful figurehead, ordinary women were supposed to stay at home, produce babies and leave professions and politics to their husbands. The writer Oscar Wilde skewered the atmosphere with lines like: 'I hope you have not been leading a double life, pretending to be wicked and being good all the time. That would be hypocrisy.'[7] A respectable front often masked private excess.

Performing in public was not considered a suitable activity for middle-class women, even as serious artists; many were those whose husbands insisted they surrender upon marriage the very gifts that might have attracted the men in the first place. Yet women who did build high-profile careers, such as the actresses Sarah Bernhardt and Ellen Terry or the pianist Clara Schumann, enjoyed tremendous veneration. Intriguingly, some of the best-known British-born pianists before Myra were women, among them Arabella Goddard (1836-1922) and Fanny Davies (1861-1934), a pupil of Clara Schumann.

All male homosexual activity was made a criminal offence in Britain in 1885 – though 'buggery' had been illegal since 1533, with the last hanging for sodomy taking place in 1835. Wilde, imprisoned in 1895, and later Sir John Gielgud fell victim to 'sexual indecency' laws, which were not liberalised until 1967. Gay women, however, were not included; and 'intense friendships' between women were nothing unusual. Maybe they were seen as less of a threat to one another's physical safety; or perhaps male lawmakers simply could not believe that such things went on, so did not legislate against them. But go on they did, and without constrictive 'identity' pigeonholes. Eugenie Schumann, youngest daughter of Robert and Clara Schumann, lived for decades with her female partner, the singer Marie Fillunger. The British composer Ethel Smyth pursued relationships with both men and women, citing Virginia Woolf as her last great love.

Nevertheless, middle-class prudery tended to keep young people, especially girls, in the dark about sex until they married. Innocence often extended to cluelessness; confusion about feelings or actions could result; a wedding night could be a shock. The knowing populace more than a century later tend to assume that everybody was 'at it', but the chances are that at first they had no idea what 'it' was. Some may never have found out.

The Great British Musical Amateur

In music, the great British amateur reigned supreme. Queen Victoria and Prince Albert were eager, accomplished musicians in their spare time. Musicianship was a desirable social accoutrement, especially for young women of marriageable age; many, if not most children were therefore given music lessons. Amateur choruses flourished around the country, a tradition that had begun with Handel's 18th century oratorios and was rejuvenated by Mendelssohn, who in 1846 created *Elijah* for premiere by a Birmingham chorus 271 strong.

At professional level, however, music was ill-supported. Although the Royal Academy of Music had been founded in 1822, a survey in 1870 found that only some ten per cent of professional orchestral musicians in the country had studied there. The Royal College of Music was founded 60 years later by the Prince Consort, replacing a National Training School for Music that had failed to thrive under the leadership of the composer Arthur Sullivan. Music education was often church-oriented – the one respectable direction for a life in this art, according to the well-to-do family of Ralph Vaughan Williams, who opposed his dream of becoming an orchestral viola player.

In 1872 a Church Choral Society and College of Church Music were established in London, merging three years later to become Trinity College of Music. By 1877, it was running external exams so popular that within two years they spread to 200 different centres around the UK and later to India, Australasia and South Africa.

British instrumentalists of the time could reach impressive standards through their capacity for hard work, involving studies with European professors in Britain, going abroad or autodidacticism. Tertis, the violinists Isolde Menges and Marie Hall, and the cellist Felix Salmond were all fine examples. The pianist Harold Bauer (1873-1951), later a friend and sometime sparring partner of Myra's, was the son of a German-Jewish violinist in Kingston-upon-Thames. He found the atmosphere of his native country so depressing that he left Britain for Paris at the first opportunity. Maurice Ravel dedicated his 'Ondine' to him.

With a lack of native role-models, it was widely thought that only a foreign training, preferably German, could turn English musicians into top-level professionals. The Leipzig Conservatory, founded by Mendelssohn, was a magnet; Smyth, Sullivan and Charles Villiers Stanford all studied there. Stanford became London's most important composition professor, teaching Gustav Holst, Ralph Vaughan Williams, Rebecca Clarke (a close friend of Myra's), Samuel Coleridge-Tayor, Frank Bridge, John Ireland and Leopold Stokowski.

Britain's music lovers tended to revere foreigners. When Ignaz Paderewski, Camille Saint-Saëns and Anton Rubinstein arrived on tour, respectively from Poland, France and Russia, they brought virtuoso piano techniques honed by tutelage with pupils of Beethoven and Liszt, from whom they also inherited a view that music is a sacred art bestowed by God, not just a genteel parlour pastime. These larger-than-life personalities held an exotic fascination for British audiences (what marvellous accents they had!), who tended to undervalue anyone home-grown. Painters and poets depicted the flame-haired Paderewski as an archangel. Myra herself loved his playing above all. The quality of his sound fascinated her so much that she once caught the train to Manchester and queued all afternoon outside the Free Trade Hall in order to hear him again.

Family Values

Myra was the Hesses' fourth child; after she was born they needed more space. They moved to 78 Boundary Road, a long street that crosses Abbey Road and Finchley Road, marking the boundary between Hampstead and St John's Wood. Photographs show No. 78 (which was later demolished) as a typical stucco-fronted house, with a little path separating it from the street and a short flight of stairs up to the front door.

The Hess siblings in 1896: Myra, John, Herbert and Irene

The siblings were close in age and close growing up. Alice Irene ('Reenie') was born in 1884, followed by John Frederick in January 1886, Samuel Herbert in 1888 and, of course, Myra. Libbie recounted that her father John and Myra were the naughty ones. They saw little of Frederick; he would leave for the office in Spitalfields early in the morning and return after their bed-time. In Lizzie, however, they had a devoted and loving mother and Myra, as the youngest, was the apple of her eye. Lizzie had her hands full, running a household of four bright, argumentative children, while her husband spent scant time at home, but was adamant about the exactitude of mealtimes when he did.

The children were kept in check by a fastidious nanny. What with primary school at Oak Hill Park, walks on Hampstead Heath, regular spoiling and cuddles from her aunts (Lizzie was from a large family) and games in the garden room with her siblings – though she once flung a book at John, who had been teasing her, and broke a window – the small Myra's every minute was accounted for. And for summer holidays the Hesses would choose the Isle of Wight, a popular destination favoured by Queen Victoria, who had a royal residence at Osborne.

Earliest Lessons

The little quartet all had music lessons. The elder three began ahead of Myra, with two teachers by the wonderful name of the Misses Reason. The boys learned the violin and all of them the piano. Aged five, Myra was given a cello. Even a quarter-size cello is not much smaller than a petite five-year-old, and she struggled with it. But she would go to the upright piano in the garden room to pick out tunes by ear and invent accompaniments. Here she found her natural habitat.

She envied the attractive pieces that Herbert was playing – he was the most musical of the other three – while she, as a beginner, was stuck with endless scales. Such was her progress that after two years, Florence Reason advised Lizzie that she needed a more advanced teacher.[8] (An artist named Florence Reason, who became well known, was then living with her sister Kathleen, a governess, in Alexandra Road, the street where Myra was born. It's possible that they were the Hesses' Misses Reason.)

To assess her aptitude, the Hesses took Myra, aged seven, to Trinity College of Music, which awarded certificates of proficiency in performance. She became the youngest child yet to receive one. While she would never have described herself as a prodigy ('*Gott sei dank, nein!*' she said[9] – '*Thank God, no!*'), she stood out from the crowd.

When she was eight, her father insisted that she perform at a charity concert. She played Gurlitt's *Rondo alla Turca* and a study by Stephen Heller as encore. So uncomfortable was she about being on a stage that she trotted as fast as possible up to the instrument and forgot to sit down until she was halfway through the first piece.[10] It was not a particularly positive introduction to performing. Throughout her long career, Myra suffered so much from pre-concert nerves that her friend Rebecca Clarke later described her as 'almost the most pathologically nervous person' she knew.[11]

The family spent the winter of 1900-01 in Brussels, their doctor having advised them to quit London to ease Herbert's attacks of asthma, which were exacerbated by the cold, damp climate and sooty pollution. The spell abroad was a happy time for the youngsters. They made excellent progress in music and languages – Myra attended a school that taught in French and German – and Herbert's condition did improve.

While they were gone, the Victorian age came to an end. Queen Victoria died on 22nd January 1901, to be succeeded by the 59-year-old Edward VII. Her state funeral drew together myriad representatives of European royalty, among them Emperor Wilhelm II of Germany, the Archduke Franz Ferdinand, heir presumptive to the Austro-Hungarian throne, and Grand Duke Mikhail Alexandrovich, representing the Russian Emperor. Their fates proved inextricable from the world events of the next two decades.

Back in London, Myra was taken next to the Guildhall School of Music. Less than 20 years old, founded by the Corporation of London in 1880, it was in a grand 19th century pile in John Carpenter Street, between the Inner Temple gardens and Blackfriars Bridge. Here she had lessons with several enthusiastic young pianists and composers, Julian Pascal, Orlando Morgan, and the pianist Leonhard Emil Bach. Having taught in London since 1882, Bach had studied in Berlin and composed numerous chamber works and several operas. A photograph shows him at a piano with the elderly Franz Liszt – giving Myra a slight but pleasing connection to that legendary virtuoso. She progressed well and in 1902 won the college's Steinway medal and scholarship. But Emil Bach died that same year, aged 52, leaving Myra in urgent need of a mentor.

Around this time, Frederick became secretary-treasurer of the Playgoers Club, which he had co-founded. He and Lizzie often went to theatrical opening nights and their growing children could sometimes get passes for second nights; Herbert and Myra would go along together. But the club also presented performing opportunities, which Frederick pounced on for his gifted daughter.

Participating in a 'Ladies Cigarette Concert' in the grand ballroom of the Hotel Cecil by the Thames Embankment, she played nothing less than a Liszt Hungarian Rhapsody. The *Jewish Chronicle* reported hearing 'clever Miss Myra Hess, who was enthusiastically encored for an exquisitely rendered pianoforte solo'. Myra was just 11 and the sight and sound of a prim little schoolgirl playing such demanding repertoire would have turned heads.

The *JC* continued noting her activities, mentioning her performances in Jewish charity concerts, winning the Guildhall's Steinway Scholarship – and a reporter once spotted her selling programmes at the Playgoers' Club's charity concert for the Children's Pantomime Fund at Her Majesty's Theatre. By 30th December 1904, the paper was terming her 'one of the most talented young pianists in London'.

Myra, Irene and Harriet

Another of the most talented young pianists in London was Myra's closest friend. Irene Scharrer was two years Myra's senior and attended the same primary school, St Leonard's; Lizzie was friends with her mother, Ida Scharrer. The two girls shared not only a passion for music, but also an irrepressible sense of humour. As children they became piano duo partners and they worked together right through to Irene's farewell performance in 1958. Myra's friend Mabel Reynolds dubbed their concerts 'Myrene' recitals, and the label stuck[12].

At the Royal Academy of Music, Irene was studying with the piano professor Tobias Matthay, who had also taught her mother. Irene had won the Ada Lewis Scholarship Competition for free tuition at the Academy; as Myra needed a new teacher, she encouraged her to apply for it too. Myra won it hands down and duly enrolled in autumn 1903 to become Matthay's pupil. Soon the two girls were spotted by the budding composer Arnold Bax, giggling together in their Academy classes[13]. Though some years older, born in 1883, he had joined the Academy on the same day as Irene in 1901.

The girls' contrasting pianistic personalities oddly made them ideal partners: each brought a different and complementary range of colours to their joint performances. Myra's touch was rounded and songful, with an earnest approach that predisposed her to Bach, Mozart and Beethoven. Irene had a brighter sound and a mesmerising way with glittery fingerwork, along with rhapsodic expression that suited Chopin and Liszt. Hearing her at one of Matthay's house concerts, the pianist Vladimir de Pachmann was 'enraptured' by her Chopin études; afterwards, he told Irene: 'I could not play them better myself – certainly I could not play them faster.'[14]

Myra and Irene have often been described as cousins. This was not the case. Irene's great-grandfather, the watchmaker Moses Samuel from Liverpool, was patriarch to a large family which did not include the Hesses but did count among its members the founders of the H.Samuel chain of jewellery stores.

Myra Hess and Irene Scharrer – 'Myrene' – prepare for a sack race in 1925

The pianist to whom Irene *was* related was Harriet Cohen. Born in December 1895 (not 1896, as she said in her autobiography), she shared a great-great grandfather with Irene. As Myra and Irene went through their teens, the much younger Harriet hung on to their coat-tails, looking up to them, longing to do what they did; she and her sister Olga especially adored the brilliant and beautiful Irene. It was also Irene who was the youngest pupil yet accepted by the Academy, although Harriet claimed, inaccurately, that that accolade was her own. A group photo of Matthay's students in the pedagogue's garden shows Myra, Irene and Harriet sitting together, but with the two elder girls leaning away from the youngest.

Later, Harriet recalled how she had hero-worshipped the duo as they were growing up; she volunteered to serve as their errand-runner in chief, entailing many tumbles from her bicycle, but also welcome meals at all times of day. She remembered Irene 'spoiling' her, but was rather in awe of Myra, who could be 'severe'.[15] These very different young women impacted upon each others' lives in ways they could never have anticipated.

Irene, tall and charismatic, was distressed by the way Myra suppressed her own fine looks and exhorted her to free her lavish hair from its tight controls. But Harriet cultivated her own exceptional appearance – dark, slender, fey – and soon discovered what an advantage it was.

She had tiny hands, even smaller than Myra's. Myra could stretch a ninth, but Harriet could scarcely manage an octave; she claimed to have webbing between her fingers which prevented a greater extension. It is an unusual condition, but not unknown. Harriet turned her difficulty into a fascination for others; she proved adept at transforming disadvantage into victimhood which won attention and sympathy.

Small hands, however, do not have to be a problem for pianists. As usual, it's not what you've got, it's what you do with it; the individual player needs to devise ways to circumvent such difficulties. That Myra played copious quantities of Brahms, including both the piano concertos, and that Harriet could take on the challenging pieces Arnold Bax later created for her, rather proves the point.

An unforgettable image jumps out from Matthay's wife Jessie's memoirs. At their Hampstead home, a red-brick Victorian villa on the steep hill of Arkwright Road, with views clear across London, Matthay would hold student concerts to accustom his pupils to performing. The youngsters would wait upstairs until it was time to play for their audience on the ground floor. 'Your turn now, Myra.' And Myra – in her white organza concert dress, with her hair loose as Irene had suggested – arrived by sliding down the banister.

1 C. Mackail in *Myra Hess by her Friends*, p7
2 Letter to Edith Frank, 1963
3 Author interview with Libbie Foster
4 Author interview with Diana King
5 D. Ewen, 'Myra Hess, a Poet in Tones', *The American Hebrew*, October 1928, p688
6 L. Tertis, *My Viola and I*, p5
7 O. Wilde, *The Importance of Being Earnest*
8 M. McKenna, *Myra Hess*, p9
9 *The Cincinnati Post*, 7 December 1938
10 CBS Radio interview with J. Fassett, 10 Feb 1952
11 R. Sherman interview with Rebecca Clarke, *A Rebecca Clarke Reader*, p165-6
12 I. Scharrer in *Myra Hess by her Friends*, p5
13 A. Bax, *Farewell My Youth*, p19
14 J.H. Matthay, *The Life and Works of Tobias Matthay*, p43
15 H. Cohen, *A Bundle of Time*, p31

'Uncle Tobs'
(1903–1907)

Myra remembered:

> At the age of thirteen I thought I was an accomplished pianist. But then I became a pupil of Tobias Matthay and discovered that I was just beginning to learn about music. I immediately discovered that I had merely touched the fringe of musical art. I had a startling awakening to all the beauties of music of which I had not even dreamed....life began all over again. Till then I had just played; now I began to think.[1]

Myra with her mentor, Tobias Matthay, towards the end of his life

When she began studying with him, Matthay was about 45 and an eminent professor at the Academy. Six foot tall, bespectacled and imposing, with an intent gaze and an impressive moustache, he became one of the most influential people in Myra's life, and she in his. His students nicknamed him 'Uncle Tobs'; Myra, Denise Lassimonne and Frank Mannheimer, who were not just pupils but honorary family to the Matthays, called him 'Punky' – Denise's mix of 'Papa' and 'Uncle'.

Making notes for an interview with John Amis in the early 1960s, Myra jotted down her thoughts about Matthay's significance:

> He was one of the great teachers of all time. Although he plumbed the depths of the mechanical science of technique, he was not interested in anyone who just played the piano well. He insisted on the musical intention and significance of every sound one made, and all his vast knowledge was directed towards one goal: the true expression of music. He was completely broad-minded in outlook, and if one gave a really convincing interpretation, he never tried to impose his own idea of the work. He begged his students for creative and original thought and the only times I ever saw him depressed after a lesson was when a pupil had shown no imagination. Before a performance, he always said 'enjoy the music', and this maxim has helped me through many a nervous hour before a concert. He was also a great human being, and his influence on those around him extended far beyond music. He was beloved and revered as 'Uncle Tobs' by all his friends and pupils.

In the 1940s the historian Jacques Barzun remarked that Matthay's students could be identified by their sound even in a dark room. That sound was, according to Matthay's biographer Stephen Siek, 'devoid of harshness, and characterised by extraordinary beauty, resonance and range of tonal colour'.[2] It could almost be a description of Myra's own distinctive piano 'voice'.

'Enjoy the Music'

Matthay was born in Clapham, south London, where his parents had settled after leaving northern Germany; they continued to speak German at home and kept their name's German pronunciation ('tt', not 'th'). His legacy has faded somewhat, even become controversial, yet this remarkable figure exerted a vast influence over British pianism around the time that Myra first slid down his banister. Many of the UK's finest pianists passed through his studio – besides Myra, Irene and Harriet, they included Moura Lympany, Clifford Curzon, Eileen Joyce and Harold Craxton. But also, Matthay's teaching was vital in the developing consideration of piano playing's physical mechanisms. This had long been underestimated, with sometimes hellish results for pianists.

Many listeners bask in the impression that musical performance is an exalted art, something spiritual that happens as if by magic while a performer channels the soul of Beethoven, Brahms or whoever. The endless hours, days, months and years of preparation, the sweat and the nerves, the self-doubt and stage-fright, the pains in the shoulders, arms, wrist, lower back, neck and more, all this goes unseen, deliberately, to preserve that blessed illusion.

Nevertheless, playing a musical instrument is a physical business. Sometimes, when everything is 'working', it represents a fine balance of mind, body and spirit. On the one hand, a musician's understanding of a composition and the imagining of its ideal sound goes nowhere without the technique to play it. On the other hand, what use is physical ability without real artistic vision? The price for pianists' intense dedication is often injury (there are other prices too), but for decades, for centuries, it was common for professional musicians to balk at admitting any problem, from physical discomfort to serious illness, for fear of reputational damage and loss of work, yet sometimes doing themselves greater damage in the long run.

In the 21st century, musicians' occupational hazards have gained wider recognition and support from doctors and professional bodies such as the Musicians' Union and the British Performing Arts Medicine Trust. Previously, however, musicians suffering tennis elbow, tendinitis, carpal tunnel syndrome or other conditions could find themselves dismissed as 'neurotic' (a common slander against 'artistic' people), or even 'spoilt' and 'entitled', never mind that their livelihood is at risk. These problems can result from poor posture and excessive tension in a vicious cycle between mind and body.

When Matthay was building his piano school, the medical profession had not even begun to catch up with the musical one. That was where his principles came into play.

Old School Ties

In Myra's youth, 'schools' of piano playing were much more defined than they have been since long-distance air travel became ubiquitous. Lineage – a family tree of who had studied with whom – could often be a factor in building an artist's reputation.

The French school, centred on the Paris Conservatoire, developed over the 19th century through pianists such as Louise Farrenc, Antoine François Marmontel and Élie-Miriam Delaborde. Its hallmarks included a bright and edgy sound, rigorous clarity and *jeu perlé* (pearled touch). In Germany and central Europe, the approach was more intellectual and involved meatier tone, projecting the music's structures ahead of surface colours. Here Clara Schumann was an abiding influence. She loathed Liszt's flamboyant showmanship; her pupils cultivated a high-minded, rather self-effacing approach.

Liszt himself had been inspired by the mesmerising violinist Niccolò Paganini and modelled his image along similar lines. He was a pupil of Carl Czerny, who had studied with Beethoven; and Liszt's numerous pupils carried on, as far as possible, his grand romantic style. The teaching of Theodor Leschetizky, likewise a Czerny pupil, was also influential in this central European strand.

The Russian school was honed by Anton Rubinstein, founder of the St Petersburg Conservatory, whom Matthay revered. Among its greatest exponents were Sergei Rachmaninoff, Alexander Scriabin and later Josef Lhévinne, Josef Hofmann, Alexander Goldenweiser (pupil of Alexander Siloti and Ferruccio Busoni) and Heinrich Neuhaus (who taught Sviatoslav Richter and Radu Lupu). It was the last word in virtuosity, cultivating great colouristic range, the control of texture and voicing to create sonic perspective, and an uncompromising work ethic.

A large network of music schools across Russia trained pupils from early childhood to develop advanced abilities. In the UK, serious musical studies tended to begin a few crucial years later. Therefore it was, arguably, hard for students who had missed rigorous early drilling to reach a level at which they could compete with such formidably-schooled performers.

Where did Matthay fit in? His became a type of English school and his trademark was the special sound quality, full and warm, that can result from playing with a relaxed arm. He expounded his ideas in a large, systematic – maybe over-systematic – treatise in 1903, *The Act of Touch*, plus a series of shorter volumes afterwards.

He carried strong influences from the German and Austrian strands that emphasised freedom of movement throughout the body. Czerny, Beethoven's protégé, penned a treatise in the form of letters to a fictional pupil, 'Cecilia', outlining matters such as the role of good posture in freeing up the arms and therefore the expressiveness of the playing. Adolph Bernard Marx (1795-1866), a professor of musicology in Berlin, wrote about the inseparability of physicality and interpretation; and his pupil, Ludwig Deppe, Matthay considered the finest teacher of his time. Tone production, Deppe wrote, develops 'solely through the weight of the hand, through simple movements of lifting and falling, with quiet, relaxed fingers'. This made the sound 'not only more refined, but also more intense in character.'[3]

Matthay and the Royal Academy

A portrait of Tobias Matthay in 1923

Matthay entered in 1871 London's first music college, the Royal Academy of Music, which occupied two rambling, interconnected 18th-century houses at nos. 4 and 5 Tenterden Street, just off Oxford Circus. Dreaming of becoming a composer, he studied with William Sterndale Bennett and Arthur Sullivan, the opera-writing partner of W.S. Gilbert, who was a stickler for accuracy and clarity.

The youthful Matthay soon fell under the spell of Wagner. He glimpsed him in person in 1877, when Wagner intended to conduct his music at the Royal Albert Hall but ultimately, due to illness, shared the duties with Hans Richter. Matthay's friend Frederick Corder, later 'curator' (deputy principal) of the Academy, was likewise enthralled. Among Corder's achievements were translations, in collaboration with his wife, Henrietta, of the Ring cycle and *Parsifal*; they were used for English performances for decades.

Like Matthay, Corder was of German Jewish origin and lived in Hampstead, in Albion Road (later renamed Harben Road, Swiss Cottage). Largely thanks to him, the Academy developed a name for encouraging the 'progressive' strand of romantic and post-romantic composition, cultivating eclectic talents from the adventurous impressionism of Arnold Bax to the high-spirited 'light music' of Eric Coates. At the Royal College of Music, Charles Villiers Stanford's teaching preferred a more traditional approach where Brahms rather than Wagner was most venerated; Vaughan Williams, Holst and Coleridge-Taylor were among its alumni. Critics would accuse the easygoing Corder's pupils of being undisciplined and the ferocious Stanford's of lacking confidence.

Neither institution, however, encouraged 'modern music'. At the Academy, Corder and the principal, Sir Alexander Campbell Mackenzie, had little time for such dubious new approaches. Mackenzie had grown up and performed in Germany and was amenable to the avant-garde when it meant Liszt, Berlioz and Wagner. But compared to the work of Debussy in France, Schoenberg in Vienna, and in Russia Rachmaninoff, Scriabin and the first stirrings of Stravinsky, British musical creativity was lagging behind.

Matthay's piano professors at the Academy included William Dorrell, a friend of Bennett's, and Walter Macfarren, who found Matthay's taste for contemporary music suspect. Dorrell set him Mendelssohn's Piano Concerto No. 2 – written in 1837 – supposedly as a modern and revolutionary work. And when he brought Macfarren Liszt's Piano Concerto No. 1, the professor thought he was 'going to the dogs'.[4] But in London Matthay heard Liszt perform, Anton Rubinstein too, and he hung on every note of Hans von Bülow, whose playing left him awestruck.

Several years later, Matthay began to teach his first Academy class, in harmony. At first, as his wife Jessie remembered, the facilities were so basic that Matthay found his pupils sitting on the floor and had to source a wooden bench for them. Most students at the time were female, which added a layer of insult to the situation; it seems that among the professors Matthay was unusually gallant.

He rapidly took to teaching, starting aged 16 at his parents' home. By 1879, as the family needed cash for the education of his sister, Dora, he was advertising for pupils:

> PIANOFORTE, Harmony – Mr. TOBIAS A. MATTHAY, R.A.M., will have a few hours DISENGAGED after Easter. Address 40 Manor-street, Clapham.[5]

By 1880 he was an associate professor at the Academy. After five years he began to attract 'first study' piano students.

Figures of Speech

Matthay greatly admired the philosophies of Herbert Spencer (1820-1903), an advocate of Charles Darwin and of the primacy of science and psychology. This gave him the attitude that 'valid' art required both a scientific approach and the musician's understanding of how listeners would respond to their work[6] – a question of cause and effect. Spencer's 1857 essay, *On the Origin and Function of Music*, discussed its basis in language and speech patterns. Matthay too associated music with speech; and Jessie, whom he married in 1893, became the most sought-after elocutionist of her day. Actors who consulted her included Alastair Sim and John Gielgud; the latter used to go to the Tobias Matthay Pianoforte School (TMPS) premises in Wimpole Street for sessions with her.[7]

Born Janet Henderson Kennedy, Jessie – 'Auntie Jessie' to Myra and her friends – was the daughter of the Scottish folksinger David Kennedy. Matthay considered that 'she was also quite a fine pianist and musically could have held her own with any of my artists':

> On my advice, however, she seriously took up verse speaking and with her wonderfully sympathetic tone, keen rhythmical sense, and intense love for the beautiful and the true in poetry, she eventually made a great name for herself as an interpreter of poetry; probably she was the most subtle artist of her time – the Myra Hess of her profession![8]

Jessie's recitals always included piano interludes from her husband's pupils, not least Myra, Harriet and Gertrude Peppercorn. Myra's eloquent phrasing has some intriguing common ground with the recitations of actors such as Gielgud, Laurence Olivier and Peggy Ashcroft. They infuse their words with musical undulation, creating a mesmerising narrative of contrasts and controlled cadences to wrap up a sentence or a thought. Similarly, Myra's phrasing not only sings, but also speaks, complete with intakes of breath and a sense of ebb and flow. Two of her lifelong passions were literature and theatre; as for elocution, her own cut-crystal accent could perhaps have been cultivated through Jessie's expert advice.

The art of acting was always an inspiration to Myra. As she told the pianist Denis Matthews, who had consultation lessons with her during World War II, 'as a nation we [the British] tend to produce much better actors than musicians, because we lose our self-consciousness when we put on grease-paint and adopt someone else's personality!'[9] She was only half-joking. Critics commented that, like an actor, Myra could change the character of her sound from composer to composer and from piece to piece. As for walking on stage, for someone who suffered from nerves as much as she did, the ability to act proved invaluable. 'She could have been a great actress,' her friend Bruce Simonds remembered.[10]

Fading Fashions

Myra remained close to Uncle Tobs for the rest of his life and was one of the executors of his will. Nevertheless, her attitude to his approach changed over the years. Her former student Stephen Kovacevich remarks on an incident that Myra had related to him: 'She was at a party and heard Arthur Rubinstein playing Brahms's Piano Quintet,' he says, 'and it was so wonderful and so natural. She said: "I realised then that Matthay's method did not have to be the be-all and end-all."'[11]

Generally in the long term, a backlash against Matthay appeared. What caused the reversal?

First, Matthay's founding of his own school, separately from the Academy, created bad feeling at the latter. Perhaps that was unsurprising, especially if both were chasing the same sources of financial support; but after John Blackwood McEwen became the Academy's principal in 1924, the situation deteriorated. McEwen was so much in conflict with Matthay – notably, insisting that Matthay's teaching of rubato was deeply flawed – that in 1925 the professor resigned, feeling unable to stay if the Principal was publicly attacking his work.

Myra felt that the reaction against Matthay was due to misunderstandings that worsened over time. She considered his approach to the science of piano playing far less dogmatic than some believed. 'What made him a great man and a great teacher is that he never once lost sight of music, despite his scientific leanings,' she said. His ideas were never 'categorical', but had become crudely exaggerated; for example, he emphasised relaxation in the wrist as an antidote to old notions of playing with a wrist so firm that a penny could be balanced on it. But he would never have endorsed the 'flabbiness' that some players adopted, imagining he would approve.[12]

Sometimes a focus on beauty of sound and arm relaxation has been clumsily equated with sacrificing 'fast fingers'. Yet many of Matthay's students had great facility, among them Irene Scharrer, Eileen Joyce and Moura Lympany, besides Myra herself – her aesthetic preferences for slower, quieter, more detailed and reflective playing were not typical of Matthay pupils. Indeed, Matthay's teaching had proved that technical ability was not incompatible with a sense of physical ease – and therefore he probably did a great deal of good.

He did not reject the brilliance of Liszt, Godowsky et al; he was trying to understand and explain them, mingling artistic questions with analysis. But as the remainder of Romanticism went up in flames with World War I and the final dregs with World War II, it became fashionable to repudiate even the notion of scientific answers, on the grounds that there could be none.

In his fall from musical vogue, then, Matthay may have been nothing more than a useful scapegoat.

Rhapsodies Out of Everything

At 12, Myra was young for the Academy and Jessie Matthay warmed to her: 'a demure little girl ... inclined to shyness; but when that shyness gave place to a very subtle and infectious sense of humour she proved herself the most delightful comrade to the rest of the class.' Jessie was also impressed by her partnership with Irene: 'While waiting for their lessons, they would often indulge in high-jinks on the two student pianos, extemporising simultaneously in a wildly exciting manner, making rhapsodies out of everything.'[13]

Together with Arnold Bax, Felix Swinstead, York Bowen, Harold Craxton, Frederick Moore, Hilda Dederich, Vivian Langrish and later Harriet Cohen, Irene and Myra became members of the Tobias Matthay Pianoforte School. When his Arkwright Road home proved inadequate, he and Jessie acquired more suitable premises at 96 Wimpole Street; they had to fight regulatory battles to have a piano school there at all and even to put up a small brass plaque identifying it. Myra gave the school's opening recital on 25th February 1905 – her 15th birthday.

High Marley: the house that Matthay built

There was one more crucial element in the TMPS: Uncle Tobs' country house, High Marley, not far from Haslemere and Fernhurst. On holiday in 1906 he came across what Jessie described as 'the hilltop of his dreams', overlooking the soft green hills of the South Downs and the Sussex Weald. Having secured two acres of land (which he later expanded to six), he designed the house himself to make the most of the sun. 'To watch the building of the house,' Jessie wrote, 'was like following the development of the symphony.'[14]

High Marley's several sun-catching facets boasted corner turret rooms to one side, and to the other, a big wooden first-floor balcony. A piano made for and gifted to Matthay by the firm of Carl Bechstein took up residence in his second-floor study, under the gabled roof above the entrance. He taught in the large sitting room, overlooking the garden.

There was ample space for visitors and the students would often join Uncle Tobs and Jessie there for weekends or holidays, mingling piano study, socialising, fresh air and country walks, or trots, as Myra called these short excursions – she was not a great walker. Much-loved Christmas gatherings there would feature games of charades (they nicknamed it 'dumb crambo'), for which Matthay planned his clues in minute detail.

Right up until Matthay's death at the end of World War II, Myra loved to spend time at High Marley with him and her fellow students – and if she became a substitute daughter for the childless Matthays, they were also substitute parents to her. The moment he heard Myra's car toot on the drive, Matthay, in his Irish country tweeds, would drop everything and go to the door, ready to embrace her. Then the pair would head straight for the piano.

The evenings extended into the wee hours, as Myra's friend Frank Mannheimer recalled. Frank – who was from Dayton, Ohio, and had studied briefly in Germany before coming to London and Matthay – was blessed with a warm, benevolent character that later made him a beloved professor. Myra would encourage him to stay up late playing card games, her favourite end-of-day wind-down, and after midnight, Matthay, who loved a late-night snack at 2 or 3am, might emerge in his nightcap and dressing gown to provide a feast of apples, raisins and biscuits, or sometimes a bottle of whisky and a soda siphon.

The Labyrinth of Tenterden Street

In the Academy's Tenterden Street premises, Mackenzie, the principal, occupied a sunny room overlooking Hanover Square. Those ushered into his presence would be struck by his imposing personality, his emphatic Scottish accent and his disconcerting way of pacing up and down while interviewing a quaking prospective pupil.[15] Matthay, by contrast, taught in the semi-subterranean Room 19, which was so chilly that he kept an old steamer rug over his knees. Here, however, his piano became the centre of his students' lives.

Student concerts ('fortnightlies') took place every two weeks. Myra would sometimes play in a line-up that might also include new pieces by Arnold Bax or York Bowen, a song from Clara Butterworth and elocution students' recitations of Shakespeare or Ibsen. She and Irene performed often as a duo, as inseparable at their pianos as they were in class (Corder once threw them out of the room for excessive giggling). At an end-of-year Academy concert in July 1904, they performed Weber's *Invitation to the Dance* in an arrangement Corder had made especially for them.

Eric Coates, a composition and viola student who entered the Academy in 1906, found the curriculum demanding, but with hilarious moments, notably the compulsory sight-singing classes. He witnessed Myra being asked to sing a melody in the bass clef and trying to pretend she was a baritone[16]. She was taking singing lessons, but used her skills to indulge in merciless mimicry. She could sing a pious song, 'The Rosary' a semitone flat while somehow keeping a straight face, imitate Queen Victoria with a lace doily atop her head, or deliver a send-up of Gounod's 'Jewel Song' from *Faust* that became legendary. With her keen ear, she caricatured everything from royalty to East End Cockneys to a plethora of dramatic foreign accents.

At the piano, she had a party trick of playing Chopin's 'Black Keys' Etude by rolling an orange, concealed in her right hand, across the eponymous notes.[17] Just before the final cascade of octaves she would throw the fruit to a willing (and fore-warned) member of her audience.

Once the pianist Harold Samuel, a good friend of Myra's, was adjudicating a competition at the TMPS and fell prey to another of her practical jokes. She put on a set of protruding false teeth and some heavy spectacles and let down her hair. Then she plodded onto the stage when everyone else had played, handed him her candidate number and began to thud out some Bach. Samuel listened until enough time had elapsed for him to stop her, upon which Myra revealed her hoax in peals of laughter. On the marking sheet, Samuel had written: 'Not quite up to it!'

Myra's piano studies, however, were deeply serious and encompassed a wide repertoire, from the baroque intricacies of JS Bach to contemporary music such as Debussy, Granados and Szymanowski. Her recital programmes often included the likes of a Liszt Hungarian Rhapsody, a

Chopin sonata or group of waltzes or mazurkas, alongside works by her friends, colleagues and teachers: Matthay, Corder and Benjamin Dale, a fellow Academy student, whose gigantic Piano Sonata in D minor became his best-known work thanks to Myra's determined championing.

Her journey to the Academy from Boundary Road involved a horse-drawn bus, which took a clopping, rattle-ridden half hour to reach Oxford Circus. Coming back, Irene and Myra took different buses but were often so busy chatting on their way from the Academy to their respective stops that they would walk between them together several times. Eric Coates lived nearby on Kilburn High Road and left a colourful description of his bus rides, trying to keep dry on rainy days with an unwieldy umbrella and the vehicle's meagre waterproof apron, to say nothing of the chaos on icy mornings in winter. Fortunately the upstairs room of the Blenheim Restaurant, round the corner from the Academy on New Bond Street, became an unofficial students' club, all day offering welcome and affordable hot tea and currant buns.[18]

Rebecca Clarke

Among the lifelong friends Myra made at the Academy was Rebecca Clarke, two years her senior. They shared a sense of humour and Rebecca noted Myra's charming way of hunching her shoulders when she laughed, something the pianist retained all her life.[19] They also had in common challenging relationships with their philandering yet ultra-controlling fathers.

Rebecca, who grew up in Harrow, was the daughter of an American father and German mother. Tall, stylish and more independent than many of her peer group of young women, she was a violin student, though was already beginning to write music. When her theory professor fell in love with her and proposed marriage, however, it was not the rather sweet-natured young teacher who was forced to leave the Academy, but the blameless student.

Her move to the Royal College of Music proved fruitful: she became Stanford's sole female composition pupil and, on his advice, switched from violin to viola, so that she could play in the middle of orchestral textures and understand them from within. Lionel Tertis was her mentor on the instrument. When she fell out with her father over his extra-marital affairs, he refused to continue funding her studies.The College's principal, Hubert Parry, discreetly paid her fees himself, telling her that he had found her a scholarship.

Myra took part in various concerts devoted to Rebecca's music, in both Britain and the US. After Rebecca settled in New York, the touring Myra would often meet up with her and her husband, the pianist James Friskin, whom Rebecca married in her fifties. Despite considerable successes in her youth, she stopped writing soon after her marriage and her excellent music fell into neglect. It was only when Robert Sherman interviewed her about Myra, when she was nearly 90, that her stacks of compositions came to light. Thereafter she began to gain renewed acclaim.

At first, Myra herself showed some bent for composing. She won the Hine Prize at the Academy in 1905 for writing the best English ballad; she also penned her own cadenzas for Mozart piano concertos. Talking about her cadenzas in a radio broadcast in 1962, however, she reported with great relish that they were 'long ago destroyed and burnt'.[20] Asked what she would now find they were like, she responded, laughing: 'I should probably be very, very ill! I have a visual memory of masses and masses of arpeggios and the most terrible modulations...' Although she jettisoned the idea of composing, her ability to write well for her instrument stood her in good stead. Matthay encouraged his students to make transcriptions of their own, and she was no exception.

Two Matthay Friends

Tobias Matthay with Denise Lassimonne in 1937

Myra made many friends – and one enemy – in Matthay's class. Among the former was the American pianist Bruce Simonds, who headed a transatlantic upsurge of interest in Matthay's methods. The pianist John Kenneth Adams described Simonds as an engaging personality:

"He was a small man, very precise in every way ... physical movement, speech, humor, directness ... all these were blended together with a superb sense of living for the moment. There was a twinkle in his eye, even if it sometimes clouded over when he became really serious.[21]"

Five years younger than Myra, Simonds came to Britain in 1920, disillusioned with the piano tuition he had experienced in Paris and eager to investigate the exciting things he had heard about Matthay. He took to the professor like a family member, while enchanting his classmates with his unflappability. Adams recalled that he 'came in to our Beethoven class and sat down at 9am and played the whole of the "Hammerklavier" from memory'.[22]

In 1921 Simonds was appointed a professor at Yale; he settled in Hamden, Connecticut, close to New Haven, with his wife, Rosalind Brown, a fellow pianist. He was the first Matthay student to take the professor's methods, reputation and legacy across the Atlantic and in 1925 became the first president of the newly founded American Matthay Association. When Myra began touring in the US, Bruce and Rosalind welcomed her with open arms. Myra's celebrity in the US much enhanced Matthay's repute there and resulted in many more students heading for London to join his disciples.

Another young pianist became almost an adopted child for Uncle Tobs and Auntie Jessie: the half-French Denise Lassimonne, who was in the Hess inner circle from the start. They could not formally adopt her after her father's death as her mother was still alive, but aged about 18, she went to live with them at High Marley and was as happy to find their support as they were to find her. Jessie would sign cards to her as 'Mummy II'.[23]

Since Denise and Myra were both honorary Matthay daughters, their relationship became sisterlike, if unevenly so; Denise looked up to Myra, indeed hero-worshipped her, almost too much. She was a complex character, sometimes described as nervous and emotionally needy, but she became a superb pianist and teacher; Stephen Siek was among her pupils, and she made a recording of all the Bach Two-Part Inventions (sadly never released - possibly because of the shortage of shellac in wartime). She remained one of the closest of those who were drawn increasingly to Myra's brightening star.

The Bizarre Multiverse of Arnold Bax

Arnold Bax, in his memoir *Farewell My Youth*, recalled the Academy's chaotic layout and noted that Room 27, the most remote, was commonly used for romantic assignations. Eric Coates, however, remembered plenty going on in Room 14, thanks to the encouragement of Mr Hallett, a warden, who could give lovelorn youngsters a word of advice or a delivery of a note, then forget to check the room's occupancy at lock-up time.[24]

Arnold Bax

Bax was emerging as one of the Academy's most interesting young composers. He was a Matthay student and a fine pianist, as his recordings attest (his performance of his own Viola Sonata with Lionel Tertis is a striking example). Born in Streatham in 1883 into a well-to-do family, he never had to earn a living from composing; likewise, his father, a barrister, thanks to a private income did not need to practise law.

The family moved during Bax's childhood to a magnificent house, Ivybank, on Haverstock Hill, between Hampstead Village and Belsize Park – a steep uphill march from South Hampstead where the Hesses lived. Its sprawling gardens and tennis court gave Arnold and his younger brother, Clifford, the space and freedom to develop their abundant imaginations. Arnold attended the Hampstead Conservatoire, run by the folksong expert Cecil Sharp, which awakened his fascination with traditional music, poetry and legends, particularly Irish ones. Photographs of him as a young man show deep-set eyes, bushy eyebrows and high cheekbones, plus a pronounced, pointed chin. In few of these images is there even a hint of a smile.

Bax seems to have taken his various selves very seriously. In time he developed not just one identity, but several. His passion for all things Celtic led him to live for several years in Dublin, publishing poetry under the pseudonym 'Dermot O'Byrne', and he could travel at whim, including to Russia and Ukraine. Developing his musical career (under his real name) he benefited from the championship of his pianist friends from the Academy – especially two female pianists. One was Myra. The other was Harriet.

His virtuoso juggling of multiple egos extended to his personal relationships. For those close to him, his mix of complex imagination and calculating attitudes had a far-reaching impact.

Music On and Off the Stage

Myra's musical activities beyond the Academy were increasing, thanks to her parents' soirées at which she and her friends would play chamber music. Often these were on Friday evenings, when Frederick Hess would invite his friends to dinner; the family seems to have jettisoned rules about not playing musical instruments on Shabbat.

Among their guests was the Hungarian violinist Joseph Szigeti, a friend and colleague of Bela Bartók's, but then just 15, fresh from studies in Budapest with Jenö Hubay and taking lessons at the Academy. Bax would sometimes come along and bring his latest pieces. Myra also played cello sonatas with Walton O'Donnell, whom her first biographer, Marian McKenna, suggested was an early romance or crush.[25]

An article from the *Belfast Telegraph* in 1937 described O'Donnell's 'personal charm, his breezy directness, and his obvious hatred of sham', which would have made him and Myra a good musical match. They performed the Brahms F major Cello Sonata in an Academy concert at the Queen's Hall in February 1907. O'Donnell, following an intensive army training, became a teacher of composition and conducting at the Academy, plus conductor of the BBC's Military Band. Myra performed his piece *Before the Dawn* in one of her first New York recitals in 1922.

Her solo appearances were gathering steam, often in charity concerts: her name appeared in a giant event at the Royal Albert Hall, a 'Grand Military and Popular Concert in Aid of Her Majesty the Queen's Fund for the Unemployed and Starving Poor' one December Tuesday afternoon in 1905. At the Playgoers' Club, she had been upgraded from programme seller to concerto soloist; in its annual charity concert, with the London Symphony Orchestra conducted by Mackenzie, she played the final two movements of the Grieg Concerto. That month, too, an Academy three-day bonanza of student performances caught the ear of *The Times*' critic, who said that it 'brought again to public attention a very richly-gifted pianist in Miss Myra Hess, who played Grieg's Piano Concerto quite superbly … the poetry of her interpretation of the slow movement and her spirit and energy in the first were in the highest degree praiseworthy and, as she played with obvious enjoyment and splendid self-possession, she should go far.'[26] The next summer, the Academy awarded Myra its Frederick Westlake Memorial Prize for female pianists.

Around then, Lizzie began to keep scrapbooks of her daughter's reviews. She seems at first not to have made the cuttings as a systematic record, let alone an aid to Myra's career; it took several years for her to start noting the reviews' sources. She was a proud mother, but not a 'prodigy mother'. When Myra was 17, Lizzie started meticulous notebooks chronicling her engagements, with a note of the repertoire, venue, date, fee, expenses and profit, when there was any. Myra and her assistants continued this practice for the rest of her life.

The first entry in the first notebook is Myra's official debut at the Queen's Hall with the New Symphony Orchestra under the baton of a young conductor named Thomas Beecham.

1 C. Saerchinger, 'A Lady in her Own Right', *Saturday Review of Literature*, Vol. 36, 28 February 1953, p56
2 S. Siek, England's Piano Sage: *The Life and Teachings of Tobias Matthay*, p32
3 Deppe, *Arm-leiden des Klavierspielers* (Problems of the Arm among Pianists), see Siek, op. cit.
4 Siek, op. cit., p99
5 Ibid., p103
6 Ibid., p135-6
7 Ibid., p383
8 T. Matthay obituary of Jessie Matthay, *Musical Opinion*, 1937
9 D. Matthews, *In Pursuit of Music*, p90
10 B. Simonds, 'Myra in America' in *Myra Hess by her Friends*, p47
11 Author interview with Stephen Kovacevich
12 R. Gelatt, *Music Makers*, p224
13 J. Matthay, *The Life and Works of Tobias Matthay*, p39-40
14 Ibid., p50
15 E. Coates, *Suite in Four Movements*, p57
16 Ibid., p64
17 MH first CBS interview with J. Fassett, 1952
18 E. Coates. op. cit., p68
19 Ed. L. Curtis, *A Rebecca Clarke Reader*, p164
20 MH BBC Radio interview with John Amis, 1962
21 J.K. Adams, *Bruce Simonds and the Power of Words*, American Matthay Association website, https://www.matthay.org/Bruce.htm
22 Ibid.
23 Author interview with Stephen Siek
24 Coates, op. cit., p112
25 McKenna, op. cit., p14
26 *The Times*, 16 December 1905

The Importance of Being Earnest
(1907–1910)

Queen's Hall Debut

WHAT DEBUT COULD SEEM MORE auspicious than performing two grand-scale concertos at the mighty Queen's Hall? It was London's premier venue for orchestral concerts, built in 1893 by the architect Thomas Knightley. On the corner of Langham Place and Upper Regent's Street, its curved, colonnaded façade displayed busts of the great composers; the portico welcomed audiences of up to 2,500. The horseshoe auditorium was painted the colour of 'the belly of a London house mouse' (though stories that Knightley kept pet mice in order to check the colour are probably apocryphal); it boasted ceiling murals, a magnificent organ and an enviable acoustic. This was the home of the Queen's Hall Orchestra, founded by the conductor Henry Wood; and here he first established the annual Promenade Concerts in 1895.

Myra around the time she made her debut

Now, on the front of the programme, there shone 17-year-old Myra's image, clad in a ballgown, her face serious and unsmiling. For the event, she later recounted, she borrowed a dress from her cousin Juliet. The superficial glamour of the occasion on 14th November 1907 concealed Myra's giant effort, plus some mysterious behind-the-scenes machinations.

Critical responses to her playing veered from mildly complimentary to somewhat patronising. *The Times*' critic wrote:

Mr Beecham is an adept in the art of making attractive programmes ... It is no wonder that he gets a large audience, even on a day like yesterday, when, between morning and evening, critics and the public have the opportunity of attending as many as 12 concerts. … Miss Hess happily had not to endure the severe ordeal of playing to empty benches, and her reading of Beethoven's pianoforte concerto in G and Saint-Saëns's in C minor was sound and musical. Her phrasing shows intelligence and her technical ability is very considerable, though the poetry she brings out in slow movements is not always apparent in louder and more rapid passages. In these, she sometimes sacrifices charm to mere brilliance. A hard and as it were glittering touch, though out of place in Beethoven, is quite appropriate to Saint-Saëns and the French concerto was the most successful thing Miss Hess did. She added a nocturne and a study by Chopin at the end of the concert…[1]

He spent many more lines on Beecham's premiere of Charles Woods' *Symphonic Variations on an Irish Air* than he did on dismissing with faint praise the soloist on whose account – artistic and financial – the whole event was taking place. For Myra had engaged the orchestra, conductor and venue herself. This was what it took to make an official London debut.

Beecham was heir to a pharmaceutical fortune and through a fortunate combination of hard cash, luck, entrepreneurship and a charismatic personality with famously barbed wit, he became one of the galvanising forces of classical music in Britain before World War II. Matthay, however, had little faith: 'Who is this fellow Beecham?' he said to Myra. 'If he doesn't accompany you properly, I shall come and do it myself!'[2]

According to Myra, the whole experience was an endurance test: under-rehearsed, chaotic and lonely. In a 1952 interview on CBS with the reporter Jim Fassett, she described it with her usual humour, noting that it was also Beecham's first appearance at Queen's Hall and that he had effectively put on a whole symphonic programme in addition to her two concertos: 'It was very long and I remember [Beecham] was so busy with his own rehearsal that I had to get to Queen's Hall an hour before this terrible concert began, to finish rehearsing my second concerto.'

Matthay tried to comfort the disappointed young pianist, who had hoped that the event would lead to more, or at least better, engagements. Besides, there were a number of other positive reviews, including one from Benjamin William Findon (a family friend), who wrote: 'A new star has arisen in the musical world, whose light should shine brilliantly for many years to come.'[3] And Jessie, in her memoir, declared the event 'brilliant, emphatic and memorable'.[4]

But how exactly did Myra fund it? Lizzie's notebook sets out the financial implications:

EXS: £87.18 (Powell) £90
Tickets sold £80
Loss £10

'Powell' was the concert manager Lionel Powell; part of the expenses went on advertising and on tickets for friends and family – so many that one critic took objection to a crowd that 'devotes the rest of the time to… discussing the prospects of the new Diabolo Club at Upper Tooting'.[5]

Ninety pounds in 1907 is equivalent to about £13,850 in 2023, while the £10 loss equates to a little bit over £1500 – problematic to someone in straitened circumstances. Myra did not have ready access to such amounts; and Frederick, according to McKenna, disapproved of the event and was either unwilling or unable to stump up. Three years later, the Hesses were in such a difficult financial position that in December 1910 Frederick filed for bankruptcy. Cruel rumour suggested that financing Myra's debut was to blame, but this turned out to be far from the truth.

Who, then? Beecham could possibly have found the funds, but at that point his access to the pharmaceutical fortune was restricted, and in any case his seemingly lackadaisical attitude suggests he was scarcely interested enough to have done so.

There was one person well off enough, generous enough and fond enough of Myra to have helped her: Uncle Tobs.[6] If he was her benefactor, he was also careful enough never to let anybody know.

Early Recitals

Myra later described the sluggish start to her career, in 1936 telling the *Radio Times*:

> It took me years before I was established. People think because I have a good time now, it all came easily. For years I had to earn my living by teaching. I had a very slow success. My reputation in England was built by giving a recital every season, and it took every penny I could save to pay for it.

Any publicity she could gain would not hurt, and in 1907 she wrote an article entitled *How to Play Beethoven*. Its tone is serious and its content revealing, despite its author's youth:

> … To render the works of any of the great masters satisfactorily, one must sink one's own personality in that of the composer, and play with perfect spontaneity and without any striving after individual effects. Where, in Chopin, the effects are purely pianistic, in Beethoven they are orchestral. The piano should be treated, more or less, as an orchestra. This enables one to get the necessary breadth and variety of tone colouring…
>
> Beethoven is my favourite composer, because his works seem to appeal most strongly to my own temperament, and I should certainly advise anyone who wished to excel in music … to choose works suited to his or her own temperament, and not to play this or that because 'one ought to' or because 'So-and-So does'; for, though that may be piano-playing, it certainly cannot be called music.

She finishes by advising that the pianist should never let him/herself be conquered by any 'difficult' passage:

> With perseverance, every difficulty can be overcome, and no trouble should be considered too great to obtain a really good technique. Expression, 'soul' and an intimate knowledge of the 'spirit' of the work will do much towards a perfect rendering of the same, but unless supplemented by a really perfect technique, much of the artistic effect will be hopelessly lost.[7]

Her concert life was building, step by step. She gave a recital in Louth Town Hall shortly after the Beecham concert, then performed with the violinist Aldo Antonietti in Chislehurst on 5th December, including two of the biggest sonatas in the repertoire, the César Franck and Beethoven's 'Kreutzer', Op. 47. A week later she was in Birmingham Town Hall, together with the soprano Gertrude Brooks, Winnie Udall, Frank Shale and Szigeti, contributing pieces by Chopin, Matthay, Liszt and the fiendish Rossini-Liszt Tarantella. She played in a concert at the Grafton Galleries for the Alliance Franco-Brittanique three days later, the Chopin C sharp minor Scherzo, and the following day an event at the Bechstein Hall included her in the Beethoven 'Moonlight' Sonata Op. 27 No. 2, two Brahms intermezzi and the Rossini-Liszt. Her first appearance of

1908 was Beethoven's Piano Concerto No. 4 in the Bournemouth Winter Gardens, for which she made a profit of one pound, eight shillings and sixpence.

Her debut recital at the Aeolian Hall took place on 25th January. For this, she performed Bach's Toccata and Fugue in D minor arranged by d'Albert, Schubert's 'Wanderer' Fantasy, Franck's Prelude, Chorale and Fugue, a selection of Brahms intermezzi, Chopin's Ballade No. 3 and two pieces, *Albumblatt* and *Elves*, by Matthay. Lizzie's notebook records that 312 people attended and it cost £33.

The Aeolian Hall, at 135–137 New Bond Street, which one entered through an elegant Grecian portico, was built as the Grosvenor Gallery by the artist Coutts Lindsay. Its first owners, the Grosvenor Club, sold it in 1903 to the Orchestrelle Company of New York, which became the Aeolian Company, manufacturers of musical instruments (Myra would later perform at their much larger New York venue). The London premises held showrooms, offices and a concert hall seating about 480: a shoebox-shaped auditorium with arched proscenium, a small balcony and alcoves along the walls.

The Times critic complained, again, about a 'hard edge' to Myra's tone, though he noted that the programme, 'exacting though it was, was given throughout with untiring energy and very little appearance of effort'. He went on to heap untrammelled praise upon the 'nobility' in the playing of another recitalist (male), who has scarcely been heard of since.[8]

Myra was able to perform a substantial amount of repertoire within a few weeks or even a few days, but had not much income to show for it. She had 25 concerts in 1908, at venues that ranged from the Bechstein Hall to the Royal Albert Hall and from Reigate to Paris, where she performed with the violinist Winifred Smith at the Salle Erard. Most significantly, she made her Proms debut at the Queen's Hall on 2nd September, playing the Liszt Piano Concerto No. 1 – very far from her typical repertoire – with Henry Wood conducting ('He was wonderful – he was so helpful and friendly,' she recalled)[9]. It was the first of around 90 appearances she would make at the Proms over the decades.

The Times' review was sniffy, but chiefly about the piece, '... the dreary wastes of Liszt's pianoforte concerto in E flat, which gave Miss Myra Hess ample opportunities of exhibiting her very considerable technique; any genuine musical feeling was precluded by the nature of the music. The rapturous applause with which the performance was greeted showed once again that the glamour of virtuoso playing is not yet a thing of the past.'[10]

Myra's fee for this glamorous virtuoso playing was 3 guineas, equivalent in the 2020s to about £550. The problem was not just that she had too few concerts; also her fees were too low, and options for moving things forward were frustratingly limited, even with awards, accolades and a strong CV. These were the days before a network of international competitions and BBC broadcasts existed to showcase young talent. Myra's only option was to pay her own way, booking the halls for her recitals, inviting influential decision-makers and hoping that one thing would, in due course, lead to another.

Even supposedly exotic and attractive foreigners found the British market sclerotic. That year a young pianist from Odessa arrived in London, fresh from studying with Leschetizky in Vienna. He was three days older than Myra and his name was Benno Moiseiwitsch. After the abortive Russian revolution of 1905, he and two of his brothers had decided, despite (or because of) their youth, to move abroad. Benno came to London with his brother John, where he auditioned for the Academy, only to be rejected on – allegedly – the grounds that he was too good and they could teach him nothing more. He turned instead to Leschetizky and by the time he made his London debut it seems that the great professor too had decided he could teach him nothing more.[11]

Benno, blessed with a nonchalant virtuoso facility and a hefty dose of onstage charisma, had the further advantage that his brother John and his uncle Sasha had no qualms whatsoever about pushing him into the limelight. Faced with intense competition from the likes of Paderewski, Rachmaninoff and Percy Grainger, besides less celebrated native recitalists, and turned away by several managers, Sasha and John sought another route in. They decided that Benno should make his debut alongside an existing star, as a type of supporting act. They chose the singer Nellie Melba, then made it happen. And it worked.[12]

Benno and Myra became lifelong friends. They were different enough artists not to be direct rivals – he was a full-on, extrovert romantic with a feel for both detail and flashiness – but they shared a joie de vivre and a wicked sense of humour. Benno's nephew described him as an appealing personality, 'tender, emotional and, at times, deeply perceptive'[13], as well as charming and lively. Legend has it that at some point he proposed to Myra. But such was his reputation as a Lothario that it would be no wonder if he made approaches to her, and equally unsurprising that she turned him down. They made a strong partnership nevertheless for lunches, games of Bridge and occasional duo performances.

There was, however, another man in Myra's life at the time: the violinist Aldo Antonietti.

'A Very Handsome Italian Violinist'

Myra was among a group of friends – literary, musical and thespian – whose meetings centred on Frederick Corder's house in Albion Road, South Hampstead, and on Hampstead Heath, where they pursued their fondness for tennis and cricket. The Bax brothers, Arnold and Clifford, were core members along with Paul Corder, Frederick's composer son. So were Aldo Antonietti and his three siblings, Olga, Hilda and Arturo, who were actors.[14]

Next there was the Farjeon family: Eleanor and Harry, the first a writer, the latter a composer and student, subsequently teacher, at the Academy, and their brother Herbert ('Bertie'), a writer and critic. Their father, Benjamin, was from the East End, a journalist, novelist and playwright who was friendly with Frederick Hess. Through Clifford Bax and the Farjeons, notably Eleanor's close friendship, from 1912, with the critic and poet Edward Thomas, literature also became part of the alliance between these musical and sporty Edwardian souls of the Hampstead set.

Eleanor recalled that the group extended to Arnold's closest friend Godwin Baynes, a popular young doctor and rowing 'blue', Paul Corder's sister Dorothea (Dolly) and the siblings Gertrude and Stacy Aumonier. Meeting several times a week, they played games, devised entertainments, discussed life, and thronged the theatre galleries 'to drink in Wagner, dote on the Russian dancers, and adore the Irish players'.[15] Myra and Irene would join in when they were not busy practising or performing. Little Harriet would sometimes tag along.

It was the type of group with which a writer like Rosamund Lehmann or Rebecca West would have had a field day: gifted young people whose emotional lives were bound up with their artistic vocations and who depended on one another, to various degrees, to feed their dreams. Aldo and Myra shared musical aspirations; Myra played Arnold's music; Eleanor, older in years but younger in spirit, hankered in vain for Edward, who was married; Clifford, a playwright, poet and translator of myriad song and opera texts, later had a passionate affair with Olga. And Myra and Aldo grew closer, although she was only 17 and he was nine years older.

Aldo, despite his Mediterranean name, was born in Kingston-upon-Thames. The four siblings were the children of Daniele Antonietti, an Italian opera director and professor of music, and his English wife Grace Emma Bolton, also a musician. When Aldo, the eldest, was a baby, they moved to Santiago, Chile, where Daniele was engaged to stage Italian operas at the Municipal Theatre. Here Arturo, Olga and Hilda were born, but the family beat a retreat to England in 1891, when the Chilean Civil War broke out.

Arturo, with the stage name 'Vernon Steele', appeared in dozens of Hollywood films between 1915 and 1949. Hilda, or 'Hilda Anthony', was a dark-eyed beauty with a dazzling smile; she was in several silent movies, but her passion was theatre, and she performed in vaudeville besides more serious works. Olga went with Arnold Bax to Russia in 1910 as chaperone-of-sorts when he elected, on a whim, to escort home a beautiful Ukrainian girl, Natalia Skarginska.[16] Since Natalia then became engaged to another man, Bax proposed to Olga. She turned him down, upon which he departed for Britain, abandoning her to solitary travel home.[17] Later Clifford left his wife for Olga, although the relationship proved short-lived.

As early as 1901, Aldo was making an impression on concert life. 'Signor Aldo Antonietti, the young violinist, who gave a most attractive recital in the Bechstein Hall on Friday, had some years ago acquired a remarkable degree of technical skill, during his state of pupilage at the Royal Academy of Music,' one review recounted, 'but a successful tour on the Continent has given him that breadth of style, confidence, and repose of manner which can be learnt only by experience.'[18]

It seems extraordinary, given the era and the restrictive atmosphere at the Hesses' home, that in 1910 Myra, aged 20, would take off abroad with an attractive young man, however well the families knew one another.[19] Yet off they went to Holland apparently as a couple in love. Remembering it years later in a recorded interview, Myra said simply: 'I fell in love with a very handsome Italian violinist and went on tour with him.'

They played in Amsterdam, Rotterdam and Haarlem to a warm reception. A review in the *Nieuwe Rotterdamsche Courant* on 5th October responded to their recital in the small hall of the Concertgebouw: 'It is a pleasure to listen to the singing of his rare Maggini. His technique is immaculate, and the only wish one continues to cherish on hearing him is that his delivery be a little less cerebral'. Myra is 'energetic and temperamental … works that can tolerate great playing, such as Franck's Prélude [Chorale and Fugue] and Chopin's Ballade [No. 3], enhanced the robust character of her playing.'

A piano accompanist, Mrs. Mussel-Belinfante, is credited too. Myra was not Aldo's 'accompanist', but an independent artist, sharing the concert on an equal footing. She performed solos (Chopin, Schumann and Matthay), and though she played the big sonatas with Aldo, the other pianist took over for the fiddle showpieces. This was standard practice.

Perhaps the second pianist was also chaperone, even by default, which might have made a difference to Myra's parents. Or perhaps Frederick and Lizzie knew that Aldo had 'honourable intentions'. Aldo's second wife, Mary Lediard (a relation of Gustav Holst, whose mother's name she shared), told McKenna in the 1970s that Aldo had wanted to marry Myra and that she seriously considered accepting; but Aldo wanted a family, which would have interrupted her career. On the one hand, we only have the second Mrs Antonietti's word for this, more than half a century after the event; on the other hand, Mary was a Matthay student just four years Myra's junior and would have known her well for years. It is also not impossible that Myra was deliberately defying her family. Other theories suggest that her head may have been turned by somebody else.

All or Nothing

Myra herself put the situation differently. In 1938, in an interview with Reed Hynds in St Louis, she responded:

> Do I believe that a woman could be married and carry on such a career as mine? I don't know, but I think it depends on the woman. If she took marriage lightly, or if she was a woman who liked to flit from one husband to another, doing concerts between, why then it might be possible. But I couldn't. I'm afraid I would be too earnest about marriage, and in this business there is only one thing one can be really earnest about. That is playing the piano. One sacrifices a great deal, but there are compensations.[20]

Given her exacting nature, if Myra had become a wife and mother, she would have applied the same all-in commitment to the role as she gave to her playing – and she felt unable to do both. It was all or nothing. She spoke in her usual twinkling way; but a serious point is hiding under the light touch (and the sideswipe at another, very real pianist, in whose case 'husband' is rather a euphemism).

The sacrifices were real too. Libbie Foster remembers Myra as a motherly aunt who loved children and would have liked some of her own[21]; Libbie's brother, Colin Hess, also described Auntie Myra as 'very loving'[22]. Perhaps the awareness of that sacrifice made her single-mindedness still more powerful.

When, in the same interview, Reed Hynds asked her if she would repeat her career if she had the choice, Myra gave 'a grimace' and replied: 'Yes, I'm afraid I would! But I always tell youngsters, "If you even hesitate to ask yourself whether or not you want a career, you should choose against it. Only those who are so dead sure that they think of no alternative are the ones for careers."'

Irene Scharrer was one of the first people to come up against Myra's uncompromising attitude on that score. She became established as a star soloist well before Myra was, making her debut in the Aeolian Hall in October 1904, aged barely 16. Soon afterwards, Henry Wood invited her to perform Liszt's Concerto No. 1 and Saint-Saëns's No. 2. 'Her touch,' observed *The Musical Times*, 'was delightfully sympathetic and delicate, and florid passages were rippled off with fascinating clearness and lightness.'[23] Her recordings – Scarlatti sonatas, Chopin studies, Mendelssohn Songs without Words and her signature piece, Litolff's Scherzo for piano and orchestra – demonstrate quicksilver passagework, wit, poetry and musical intelligence. Irene, however, had no intention of giving up her emotional and family life.

In 1915 she married Samuel Gurney Lubbock, a master at Eton and former classics scholar at King's College, Cambridge. He was a decade and a half her senior and resident at the school. Myra was not one to hold back when she saw people she loved risking damage to themselves or their reputations. She and Irene were a duo, and whether Myra was running backstage at the Royal Albert Hall to tell Irene that her dress was on back to front, or objecting to her decision to marry, she would always speak up. Irene wrote in her memoir for *Myra Hess by Her Friends* that 'her distress was genuine when it became clear that I could not rule out marriage and the desire for children, for she knew that they would inevitably come first in my life – and how right she was!' Myra, Irene noted, was willing to sacrifice everything for her music.

Perhaps Myra feared that Irene was making a still bigger mistake. Having witnessed her mother's long-suffering existence, she knew the pain that could result when things went wrong. Ultimately this happened to Irene too.

The agonising choice between marriage and vocation peppered films and fiction right up to the 1960s. Maybe the most famous is *The Red Shoes* (1948), in which a ballerina's conflict between her passion for dance and her love for a composer ends with her suicide. Even beyond the upsurge of feminism in the 1970s, female soloists often had private lives that were unconventional at best or turbulent at worst; the more famous the artist, the more public the scrutiny and the less stable the outlook.

The root of Myra's problem lay in Victorian familial attitudes. Less than a century earlier, Fanny Mendelssohn's father, having given her an elite musical education, told her when she was 14 that her destiny was domestic, and music a mere 'ornament'. Women's situation had eased remarkably little by the 1900s. Frederick had been thrilled to push his talented child onto the stage. But when she announced her intention to become a professional, he thought her London debut a foolish enterprise.

In 1912, Aldo Antonietti married the Dutch pianist Henriette Mossel, daughter of the violinist, teacher and impresario Max Mossel, and settled with her in the Netherlands, where they had two children. They later divorced and he married Mary in 1936.

Meeting Mengelberg

Myra's tours of the Netherlands were becoming annual events. The trip with Aldo had won her some important friends, notably the van Riemsdijk family, with whom she now regularly stayed in Amsterdam. The artist Jonkheer Barthold Willem Floris van Riemsdijk, renowned for his portraits, was director of Amsterdam's Rijksmuseum; his own paintings soon included one of a beautiful young English pianist.[24] His daughter, Maggie, was a university student about Myra's age and became a close friend, often going along on her Dutch tours as companion. She found Myra's extreme nervousness baffling. Myra had to explain that most performers suffered this way.[25] She had not yet found the card games and crossword puzzles that later helped her get through pre-performance anxieties or wind down at the end of a long day on the road, the stage or both.

On the concert platform, nobody would have guessed the agonies she was going through. A Dutch review in 1910 compared her to the Valkyrie heroine of Wagner's Ring cycle:

> During … Chopin's Sonata in B flat minor, we immediately felt … with how broad and pure a temperament this young woman

> experienced the 'drama'. Felt with awe for so much well-controlled power of expression, physical and psychological. But when, in the trio melody of the Scherzo, the sun broke through … there was suddenly in that sound a tenderness of such fine yet deep emotional shades as no man could sing out. This real feminine in Myra Hess's playing seems to us to be the most characteristic element of her talent … while heroism is by no means lacking, she is a keyboard 'Brünnhilde' in the pure sense of the word, and one who gives herself sincerely, without virtuosity…[26]

An influential figure in Amsterdam's cultural life, van Riejmsdijk had helped to propel Willem Mengelberg into the post of the Concertgebouw Orchestra's chief conductor. Mengelberg had been friendly with Gustav Mahler, whose symphonies he championed upon the international stage. He was not an easy man or musician to please. Doris Monteux (wife of the conductor Pierre Monteux) wrote that he was 'at the same time kind and generous, unkind and small, bombastic yet gentle, childishly naïve, foolishly proud and pompous yet ridden with a feeling of unworthiness, religious yet at times positively hedonistic. Truly a more complex character never lived.'[27]

Willem Mengelberg, photograph with inscription to Myra

Despite regular drip-feed calls from Mrs van Riemsdijk begging him to engage her young English house-guest, Mengelberg remained resistant – until one day his piano soloist fell ill. Myra was still asleep when the telephone rang around noon with an unexpected summons. Mrs van Rijmsdijk woke her; incredulous, she hid under the bedclothes. That gave her hostess the chance to say yes before Myra could possibly say no.[28]

Therefore on 10th February 1912 Myra made her surprise Concertgebouw debut in the Schumann Piano Concerto, navigating for the first time the long flight of stairs down onto the stage that has terrified generations of soloists, especially alarming for those in high heels and long dresses (Myra's was dark red). It was her first major international success and it transformed her fortunes. Mengelberg was bowled over; he would remain a vital musical partner for Myra as long as history allowed. The reviews were so good that Dutch audiences began flocking to her concerts and quickly took her to their hearts.

Her annual Dutch tours often propped her up financially for the rest of the year. In January 1912 she had performed the Schumann Piano Concerto with the New Symphony Orchestra conducted by Landon Ronald for the fee of three pounds and three shillings (about £300 in 2024). Two months later, a recital in The Hague including Chopin's Sonata in B flat Minor made her a profit of £15, more than four times the home concerto. In January 1913 she performed Beethoven's Piano Concerto No. 4 with Mengelberg and the Concertgebouw Orchestra in Amsterdam, for which she was paid £30 (equivalent to £2,900).

An additional performance of the work took place in The Hague at short notice, when she was asked to replace the pianist Carl Friedberg, who was unwell. She regarded this as 'a privilege and an honour'[29], given his popularity in Holland. She had no idea that one day he would become her friend and mentor in the US, while his sister would be her agent.

After that, it was back to the tight-fisted British music societies that paid Myra typically about ten pounds ten shillings for a recital. The upshot was that she spent a great deal of time teaching. She and her piano occupied a bedsit on the top floor of the Hess family's latest home, 50 Boundary Road. Here she welcomed numerous pupils, mostly for the TMPS.

Pianos at Parties

Not all great music-making was taking place in public. It was at private salons and parties that Myra and her colleagues had some of their most enjoyable experiences. Among these were the basement chamber music evenings at the home of Paul and Muriel Draper in Edith Grove, Chelsea. Paul, an American tenor, was well known for his Lieder singing, but also for his weak spots: gambling and alcohol. The Drapers' parties were Bohemian, rather seat-of-the-pants occasions, continuing despite Muriel's affair with the Polish pianist Arthur Rubinstein. Muriel's sister-in-law, Ruth Draper, was an actress and comedienne, inventor of the comedy monologue; she became a lifelong friend of Myra's.

Musicians Myra encountered there, besides the ubiquitous Rubinstein, included the cellist Pablo Casals and the pianist Harold Bauer, both of whom she adored, besides Fritz Kreisler, Lionel Tertis, the Polish composer Karol Szymanowski and the Russian bass Feodor Chaliapin, who occasionally turned pages for Rubinstein. Other guests might include Henry James and John Singer Sargent, who drew a charcoal portrait of Myra at the keyboard. Tertis recalled that the gatherings 'lasted as a rule from midnight to daybreak'[30]. It may have been at one of these that Myra observed Rubinstein playing the Brahms Piano Quintet, splendidly natural and at ease, and began to reflect that there were other ways besides Matthay's to play the piano.[31]

The American critic Irving Kolodin, chatting to Myra at Casals's festival in Perpignan in 1951, gleaned a favourite reminiscence. Late one night, after much music, the company paused for refreshments and cigars were ceremoniously brought out. Myra, 'impelled by some spirit of daring ... accepted one with a flourish. Fritz Kreisler, she relates, deftly snipped the end off, Feodor Chaliapin ... provided the match and Pablo Casals stood by in wonder as Hess managed enough puffs to qualify as a musical Amy Lowell!'[32]

The Drapers' parties foundered on Paul's gambling. In 1913, he lost everything. He went home and told Muriel. She offered him a cup of tea.

In late April 1913, the poet Edward Thomas and his family lent their country house at Wick Green, near Petersfield, to the Farjeon siblings and their Hampstead set for an Easter house party, with one proviso: 'Be careful not to dance the floors down.'[33] Bax, Olga, Godwin Baynes and his fiancée Rosalind Thorneycroft, Paul Corder, his sister Dorothea and Myra were among them, though Eleanor, writing about it later, could not remember all of the guests. Dorothea, the eldest, served as chaperone. Eleanor, Olga and Myra shared a room while the boys took the nursery.

One day Eleanor found Myra, who was a bookworm, reading in a patch of sunshine in the garden, convulsed and wailing – probably with laughter – over a volume by Lafcadio Hearn, an author equally known for introducing Japanese culture to the west and for his collections of ghost stories. Bertie Farjeon swiped the book from her and, Eleanor wrote, insisted upon reading out 'a ghastly incident about a lonely valley inhabited by evil things with faces as bald as eggs'. It left them all in hysterics, 'and Myra completely collapsed…'[34]

Arnold Bax was one of the first to arrive at the house and among the last to leave, having come straight from a holiday in Majorca with Clifford, Gustav Holst and Balfour Gardiner. He brought along an outsized cigar. Even when all the guests had taken ample puffs, it was left unfinished. They abandoned its remnants on Edward Thomas's mantelpiece.[35]

Given Bax's lengthy stay, he and Myra must have overlapped. And if there was a missing link in Myra's personal life, it may be that most elusive and self-willed of composers, Arnold Bax himself.

1 *The Times*, 15 November 1907
2 Siek, op. cit., p330
3 B.W. Findon in *The Referee*, November 1907, see also McKenna op. cit., p32
4 J. Matthay, op. cit., p44
5 Unlabelled cutting, Hess Scrapbook, see also McKenna op. cit., p33
6 Siek, op. cit., p330
7 MH, How to Play Beethoven, see McKenna op. cit., p277-8
8 *The Times*, 27 January 1908
9 MH BBC interview with John Amis, 1962
10 *The Times*, 5 September 1908
11 M. Moiseiwitsch, *Moiseiwitsch*, p46
12 Ibid., p49-50
13 Ibid., p195
14 L. Foreman, *Bax: A Composer and his Times*, p45
15 E. Farjeon, *Edward Thomas, The Last Four Years*, p2
16 Foreman, op. cit., p76
17 Ibid., p79
18 *The Times*, 17 June 1901
19 McKenna, op. cit., p43
20 *St Louis Star-Times*, 22 December 1938
21 Author interview with Libbie Foster
22 J. Meewezen interview with Colin Hess
23 Quoted in S. Siek booklet notes to APR 6010
24 McKenna, op. cit., p44
25 Ibid., p48
26 https://www.rijksmuseum.nl/nl/collectie/RP-F-F00667-AY
27 D. Monteux, *It's All in the Music*, see also Bloomfield, Arthur, *More than the Notes*, accessed online
28 McKenna, op. cit., p46
29 MH Introduction to J. Smith, *Master Pianist: The Career and Teaching of Carl Friedberg*, pviii
30 Tertis, op. cit., p45
31 Author interview with Stephen Kovacevich
32 *The Record*, 28 July 1951
33 E. Farjeon, op. cit., p 7
34 Ibid., p9
35 Ibid., p10

Rarely, rarely comest thou, Spirit of Delight
(1910–1915)

IF MYRA ENCOUNTERED a spirit of delight in the years that for many young women are their most exciting – the early twenties – it could well have been off the west coast of Scotland. The Matthays loved to visit the silvery seascapes of the Western Isles; and in 1912 Myra went with them and a collection of friends and like-minded fellow students to stay on the remote and magical Isle of Eigg. Jessie's friend Kenneth MacLeod, a folklorist whom she described as a poet-priest, was at the centre of the gathering; one evening, Jessie wrote, 'all these kindred spirits (of whom Myra Hess was one) assembled on a smooth green knoll overlooking the sweep of Laig Bay framed by the mountains of Rum and Skye, and sang and spoke out their hearts to one another'.[1] It would have been an unforgettable moment of escape amid Myra's increasingly stormy existence.

Father and Daughter

In the Hess household, conflict was brewing. The trouble went back to the collapse of the family's finances several years earlier: on 30th December 1910, Frederick had filed for bankruptcy.[2] They had been obliged to leave 78 Boundary Road and had to relocate several times. In 1911 they were at 176 Belsize Road and by 1914 50 Boundary Road, near their former, more impressive home.

Several factors had fed the downturn. First, Frederick was suffering from diabetes, which remained untreatable beyond following a low-sugar diet. McKenna attributes his violent outbursts to the illness and the recognition that he might not have long to live. This seems a generous interpretation. His business situation had much to answer for: the country was in a recession and the family firm had been losing profitability. By 1910, several years after the company moved to 44 Bethnal Green Road, Frederick no longer had a financial interest in it, but was employed as a manager by his former partner.

Myra's father, Frederick Hess

Frederick had once been a creative powerhouse. He was, according to a magazine report after his death, of 'an inventive nature'[3] and had developed a motorcyclists' racing helmet that saved lives and became compulsory headgear for competitors. He had also invented, among other things, the Cantor-Hess bamboo stretcher for field service and a dummy magazine rifle for the Church Lads' Brigades. These had all sold well.

But in the end, he was brought down by his extravagance with the Playgoers' Club and the theatrical world. He had a penchant for West End nightclubs, after-show parties and 'show girls', one of whom he reportedly brought home to meet the family. His attempts to recoup his losses via the stockmarket sent his finances up and down – mostly down.

Myra's fortunes were not flourishing either. She had not quite enough concerts – 24 in 1911 – and in the UK was not commanding fees commensurate with her abilities, whether because she did not wish to charge a higher rate, or because she did not realise that she could. Female performers still lacked the cachet – and the pay – of their male peers; and there could have been a toxic combination of naivety from Myra and Lizzie and cynicism from a music business ready to take advantage of a young woman with no battle-axe manager to fight her corner.

Her fees ranged from decent to lousy. A recital in 1911 for 'Mr Hambro' in Prince's Gate paid £10 (respectable), one for St Mary's Musical Society at 34 Lancaster Gate 2 guineas (not), and her annual self-funded Bechstein Hall recital, noted in her log-book with big curly letters, cost her £37 and made £10 profit. In 2023, those figures equated respectively to around £5375 and £1400. Investing that much in a recital represented a significant risk.

Myra, as one of the TMPS's top teachers, coached the pupils Uncle Tobs assigned to her both at its premises, 96 Wimpole Street, and at home, including four of the most advanced students. Her fee was typically less than 16 shillings per lesson. The Academy, which moved to an impressive new home on Marylebone Road in 1911, did not employ her, although she presided at its exams in 1916.

Her students included Maud Randle, who became a professional pianist in Leicester; Elizabeth Ivey Brubeck from the US, whose son, Dave, became a jazz legend; Muriel Lillie, sister of the actress Beatrice Lillie; Vera and Juliet (Judy) Compton-Burnett, younger sisters of the novelist Ivy; and Ruth Howard, later the aunt of the author Elizabeth Jane Howard, who based on Ruth the character of Rachel Cazalet in *The Cazalet Chronicles*. Ruth, Judy and Vera gravitated to Myra and became her inseparable friends.

Myra needed such friends, because home life was becoming untenable. The deepening rift between her and her father was not solely about a generational shift in attitudes. An autocratic Victorian patriarch was up against a career-minded daughter with Bohemian tendencies – performing, smoking, all-night parties, a bawdy sense of humour and no intention of marrying. But then the cash-strapped Frederick told Myra that if she had to play the piano, she should make some proper money for the family and go instead into music hall.[4]

This instruction was anything but innocent. It came after all Myra's years of high-level study, her debut with Beecham, her triumphs with Mengelberg, her Bechstein Hall recitals, the soirées with Szigeti and O'Donnell – all of which took place under Frederick's nose and sometimes, though not always, with his encouragement. But music was still an 'adornment' for a daughter, an accomplishment to enhance perceived marriageability. Heaven forfend that a young woman who had been steered towards serious music should suddenly wish to make it her life.

Music hall stars were by no means lacking in talent. Charlie Chaplin's father was among them and Chaplin himself started out there. The biggest names in this field could make good money by performing in several different venues per night. Still, its 'serio-comic' acting and singing, rooted in working class, Cockney songs full of saucy innuendo, was light years away from Myra's passion for Beethoven. And though extremely popular and increasingly marketed to the middle class, it was not altogether a respectable profession for young women – as Frederick's predilection for 'show girls' would have made him well aware. The hostile charge behind his demand is unmistakable: insult besides injury.

Matters came to a head when Myra was rehearsing upstairs for a recital with her violinist friend Winifred (Winnie) Smith. Dinner time came and went, but the musicians continued to work. Frederick lost his temper. He stormed up the stairs and manhandled Winnie out of the studio and out of the house, to her fury and Myra's desperate distress. The incident – witnessed by Myra's brothers and allegedly supported by at least one other family member – was the last straw. Myra decided that she had to leave home.[5]

As she implied in a letter to Ruth in which she poured out her feelings, she longed to help her mother through this horrible situation. 'I know "she" has had to fight too – and in so many ways has been so wonderfully understanding and patient,' she wrote. 'I always was sorry for ~~them~~ her – !!! having me. A little less so now – but a brick wall is always a sad affair.'

Her friends credited Winnie for helping to persuade Myra to escape. Myra told Ruth: '[Winnie] is one of those great-simple ones who make life "spin" on its right side – and who is never shaken by circumstances – however vicious they may be.'[6]

When Myra left Boundary Road for good, her Bechstein had to be winched out of the third-floor window. She could not bear to watch, and walked up and down Abbey Road with Ruth until it was over.

A wandering minstrel with no fixed address, Myra for a while used the TMPS's premises for her correspondence. Finding somewhere to live as a single woman of 24 with a grand piano in 1914 was no easy task. Perhaps that made it difficult for her to plan and book concerts; her diary for June to November 1914 remained devoid of engagements. Part of that could be attributed to the outbreak of World War I; but also, until then Lizzie had been helping her. Now they were no longer under the same roof with adequate ease of communication.

Myra found welcome respite in weekends at High Marley, especially an extended stay when Matthay's pupils gathered for the last time that academic year, weeks before the war broke out. Otherwise, she relied on short-term stays with connections facilitated by her Hampstead friends: possibly by the Corders, who were close to the Pre-Raphaelite circles; or possibly by Bax.

Enchanted Summers

Bax in 1910 had written his most ambitious work yet, *Enchanted Summer* for chorus and orchestra. It seems spellbound by Celtic pagan magic and the Pre-Raphaelite aesthetic. The impact late in that year of Diaghilev's Ballets Russes and the first London exhibition of Impressionism had brought the young century leaping into full colour; the composer, who had already seen the ballet company in Russia, soaked it up like a musical sea-sponge. Then on 28th January 1911 he married Elsa ('Elsita') Sobrino, the daughter of the Spanish pianist Carlos Sobrino, whose family and the Baxes were friends and neighbours. Bax's father gave the young couple a house: 11 Chester Terrace, in the cream-coloured Nash Terraces that line the Outer Circle of Regent's Park. In summer 1911, Bax acquired a country house in Wiltshire: Broughton Gifford, where he and Clifford hosted cricket-based parties.

Bax's material fortune was arguably his spiritual and moral misfortune. Having never had to take responsibility for earning a living, he had the luxury of acting on whim. He and Elsita, who was pregnant, could simply decamp to Rathgar, Dublin, where the composer immersed himself in Celtic culture and began to publish poetry under the pseudonym 'Dermot O'Byrne'. There, their children were born, Dermot on 22nd January 1912 and Maeve on 22nd January 1913.

In 1909 Myra had taken part in concerts and receptions at Novello's Hall in Wardour Street, for Jean Sibelius (16th February) and Vincent d'Indy (27th March), whose Piano Sonata she performed. Bax had been her escort for the latter event. He wrote that d'Indy was impressed and delighted that Myra, who was only 19, could get to grips with the complexities of the sonata.[7] Bax later claimed that he had gone along just because he wanted to meet the French composer[8]; this may or may not have been true.[9]

That spring Myra had played a good deal of new music: works by Ernö Dohnányi, the *Sea Pieces* by Edward MacDowell (1898) and pieces by Corder, Matthay and Felix Swinstead. On 18th March 1910 her performance diary included Bax's name for the first time: she played his Valse, which was dedicated to her, in a concert at the Society of British Composers, Broadwood Rooms, alongside Paul Corder's Four Studies. Bax's piece, the manuscript dated 16 February 1910, is listed by Lewis Foreman as his first work for solo piano; its dedication read: 'To Myra Hess, most poetical of pianists with admiration and sympathy'.[10] She continued to perform both compositions that season, plus extracts from Benjamin Dale's Sonata, including at Paris's Salle Erard in June.

Bax's *Romantic Tone Poem* was in her Bechstein Hall recital in April 1911; on her suggestion he changed the title to *Symphonic Phantasy* and ten years later it finally settled down into being his Piano Sonata No. 1. A work filled with glowing colour that exploits the instrument's subtle sonorities as well as its power, it would have suited Myra especially well – although if anything 'romantic' inspired it, it was Natalia Skarginska and the church bells of Kyiv.

In 1912 Myra took up his *May Night in the Ukraine* and *Gopak*, including them frequently in her programmes, from the Royal Academy Musical Union on 2nd November to the Bechstein Hall on 9th April 1913. The first is a nocturne, chromatic and tinged with Ukrainian folksong, Debussian sensuality and Bax's mystical fairy-dust; it is dedicated to 'Olga and Natasha'. The second is a stomping dance with a lighter-hearted middle section. In the months before she moved out of Boundary Road, she performed some Bax pieces at the Society of British Composers in March and part of his Violin Sonata with Winnie Smith at Steinway Hall in June 1914. If there was a devotion on her part, Bax was benefitting handsomely from it.

On 4th March 1913, Balfour Gardiner, who was championing Bax's orchestral music, put on at the Queen's Hall his latest work, *Christmas Eve on the Mountains*.[11] As the audience assembled, the 17-year-old Harriet Cohen caught the composer's eye and smiled.

Bax had been well aware of Harriet; she had been gaining accolades and prizes at the Academy, and he had written to her the year before. But now something about her 'small dryad face', as he recalled, turned into 'a flame of beauty burning through me, stinging my overwrought nerves'[12]. It was the beginning of a love affair that would change Harriet's life completely – and Bax's, to some degree.

Harriet was happy as 1913 went by to accept his invitations to the theatre or tea. She even sent him a gift of a tie. Bax was becoming obsessed with her, never mind that he had a one-year-old son and a new baby daughter. Under the spell of the Ballets Russes, he began to nickname Harriet 'Tania' and signed himself 'Arnolshka' in letters to her. When he and his young family left Ireland in 1914 for Marlow, Buckinghamshire, it was probably because he wanted to see more of the nubile pianist whose image he could not banish from his mind.

The Pre-Raphaelite Descendents

Musicians' biographies often confine themselves to the musical field, while those of artists and writers sometimes reduce music to a passing mention, from which you might think there was no overlap between these artistic worlds. Yet Myra's circles of friends drew in writers like Eleanor Farjeon, John Galsworthy, and later, in the US, Willa Cather and Thornton Wilder, and actors including Ruth Draper, Katherine Cornell, Joyce Grenfell and Ronald Colman. As for artists, the Bloomsbury Set did not play a large role in her life, but the Pre-Raphaelites – or rather their families – certainly did.

If Myra articulated melodies like an actor reciting and relishing a beautiful text – Jessie Matthay's expertise – or could fill a musical expanse with perspective, colour and logical drama just as a painter constructs a balanced canvas, it is not a coincidence. Her intellect, sharpened by hard graft, literature, theatre, travel and artistic friends, organically fed her musicianship.

It was through Bax that Myra found the practical help that she needed after leaving home. He introduced her to Lady Georgiana Burne-Jones, widow of the painter Edward Burne-Jones and aunt of Rudyard Kipling, who lived at The Grange, a cottage – or rather, three cottages linked together – on the green at Rottingdean, East Sussex. Myra adored her unreservedly. Myra did sometimes gravitate towards older women who perhaps represented substitute, protective mother figures (there was at least one more, in the US) and through the concert-free summer months of 1914 she and her Bechstein moved down to the coast to stay in lodgings nearby. In London, an insane rumour made out that she had fled town to have a baby. Her concert programmes for 1914-15 should be enough to scotch that notion: at liberty to practise for seven hours a day, she was learning and perfecting vast quantities of new repertoire, well away from the stresses, strains and quarrels of her family home.

Next, Lady Georgiana introduced her to her daughter, Margaret, and son-in-law, Jack Mackail, the Oxford Professor of Poetry from 1906-11 and William Morris's official biographer. Their third and youngest child, Clare, became a lifelong friend to Myra. At the Mackails' musical 'festivals' at their home in Pembridge Gardens, Holland Park, Myra could often be found giving impromptu performances; once they cobbled together a string orchestra to accompany her in the Bach D minor Concerto.

In true Pre-Raphaelite fashion, Clare was willowy with pale skin, huge eyes and long hair. Myra described her as 'a breathtaking beauty' and addressed her in letters as 'my angel'.[13] She had attended St Paul's Girls School, where Holst was director of music; later she took drawing courses at the Slade Art School. Her musical acquaintances included the ubiquitous Bax, Vaughan Williams and Holst himself; she probably sang in an informal world premiere of 'Neptune' from *The Planets*.

While her elder siblings, Denis Mackail and Angela Thirkell, became well-known authors, Clare never pursued a career, despite plentiful intellectual pursuits. Her history was far from straightforward. Allegedly, her brother-in-law, Angela's first husband from 1911 to 1917, sexually assaulted her[14]; she had had a nervous breakdown in her teens and may have suffered from anorexia nervosa.[15] She also had a thyroid complaint that was poorly understood at the time and entailed debilitating treatment, including some that was 'electrical'; at 32 she had an operation for it in Bavaria, for which she had to be escorted, heavily drugged, across the Channel. Eventually Clare adopted what her sister termed a 'dotty religion'. From the mid 1930s she lived in a house in Sussex named Four Winds with fellow members of a theosophical-ish collective, nicknamed simply The Group.

Clare's biographer, Tim McGee, writes that her friendship with Myra was one of the closest in her life (though he mistakes Myra for being Dutch). Writing for *Myra Hess by Her Friends*, Clare described the pianist's gift for empathy: 'this facility of identifying herself with others, which meant that she really felt their joys and sorrows as her own'. She recorded, too, that Myra on stage could create the illusion of being tall and slender: 'the noble and expressive brow and bearing, the swift grace of the walk on and off the platform, and the long, deep bow which was to remain characteristic all her life'.[16]

The Winged Victory of Samothrace, Myra's favourite statue

Clare was Myra's companion several times on her tours of the Netherlands. They also travelled together to Italy – Florence, Siena, Perugia, Assisi – and here Clare remembered Myra experiencing the surroundings and the art galleries with the receptiveness with which she listened to music. She contemplated her favourite paintings 'with the same veiled and inward concentration which always enveloped her when she began to play'.

From Italy they went to Paris, where Myra was playing at the Salle Erard; she borrowed a room with a small upright piano on which to practise. At the Louvre, Clare watched as Myra saw the Winged Victory of Samothrace for the first time: the ancient statue, a headless but magnificent portrayal of a robed woman with wings, that presides over the central staircase. Myra was overwhelmed, Clare wrote, 'often slipping in after the tourists had done and "letting it have its way" with her, listening to what it had to say'.

Closer to home, the two often went for weekends at High Marley, or to Larkbeare, Cumnor Hill, near Oxford, where dwelt in a specially designed Arts and Crafts house a remarkable couple: Mary Venables and Anne Wynne Thackeray ('Tandy'), a cousin of the novelist William Makepeace Thackeray. Tandy had helped to found the Cumnor Rise Hospital and she and Mary were keen supporters of women's suffrage.

Tandy's catchphrase was: 'If you want to have a friend, be a friend'.[17] And friends they had. Both accomplished musicians, they loved to hold bohemian musical evenings after Oxford concerts, attracting both students and budding professionals such as the conductor Adrian Boult and the organist Hugh Allen. Myra, at the upright piano, took requests from the partygoers, who included numerous undergraduates; over the years many would be in military training or on leave.

Allen's interest in the Bach cantatas - works little known at the time - brought to light No. 147, *Herz und Mund und That und Leben* (Heart and Mouth and Deed and Life). It ends with a chorale setting in which the theme is embedded, jewel-like, within a surrounding halo of triplets. Myra and Clare first heard it together in a service at New College Chapel. In German it is *Jesu bleibt meine Freude*. In English, with a new text provided especially for Allen by the poet laureate Robert Bridges, it became *Jesu, Joy of Man's Desiring*.

The former home of William Holman Hunt, 10 Tor Gardens in Kensington, was now owned by the engineer and businessman Thomas Blair Reynolds, whose wife, Mabel Edith Reynolds, was John Galsworthy's sister. She liked to invite young musicians in need to give house-concerts in her substantial studio. Myra had known the family for a while; Mabel's nephew's wife, Viola Sauter, reportedly helped dress her for her debut in 1907.[18]

Mabel, born in 1871, was a fine writer with an enquiring mind and a striking personality, author later of a biography of her brother (published in 1936) and a translation from the Dutch of Henri Borel's *The Rhythm of Life*, based on the philosophy of Lao Tse. Myra, like many others, nicknamed her 'Mother Mab'. She had two children, Veronica and Owen – the artist Owen Blair Reynolds – in her thirties, which would have been regarded as quite late for motherhood. The story went that she had been in love with the artist Georg Sauter, who then married her elder sister, Lilian, a poet and suffragist. The intellectual, cultured and politically minded sisters had rebelled against their mother's repressive Victorian outlook, much encouraged by their father.

Vera and Judy Compton-Burnett told McKenna of Mabel's 'erratic behaviour and strange moods'. McKenna's resulting account describes Mabel as having 'a robust and determined nature' and speaks of her being 'domineering, possessive, eccentric, even a bit frightening because she was so unpredictable. According to one of Myra's intimates, she had some of the characteristics of a vampire'.[19] This bizarre description makes it impossible not to wonder quite what was going on.

The Galsworthy family, from Devon, owned numerous houses both in London and in various areas of the countryside, especially the west country. Mabel often invited Myra to spend a summer month at her Cornish house near Trevose Head; Myra would go, along with Clare, Vera or Denise Lassimonne. Even Harriet went. According to her, Mabel once insisted, when Harriet had been describing the wonders of Bax's beloved Ireland, that she and Harriet travel there together; Harriet wrote of their resulting trip in purple prose in her autobiography *A Bundle of Time*.

Mabel frequently engaged Myra to give concerts at 10 Tor Gardens, paying her handsomely; and when Myra needed somewhere to live, she invited her to move in. The pianist would have had time and space there to practise to her heart's content. Yet she declined. Vera recalled a day in Cornwall, in summer 1915, when she spotted Myra alone on the cliffs, pondering the sea below, and hesitated to disturb a moment of intense solitary reflection. Denise remembered an episode when Mabel, listening to Myra playing Brahms after dinner, abruptly rushed out into the night and vanished.[20] This strange incident is all the stranger for resembling a scene in the 1946 movie *Humoresque* in which Joan Crawford, as a philanthropist in love with the violinist she sponsors, does something remarkably similar. The violinist on the soundtrack is Isaac Stern, who was also Myra's last duo partner. (Fortunately, unlike Joan Crawford's character, Mabel returned the next morning, having ended up at a friend's house nearby.)

End of an Era

'This year I am 24,' Myra wrote, early in 1914, 'and if I don't soon make a reputation for myself I may never have a career at all.'

The times were not making the prospect easier, for London was a city of seething unrest. Social and class divisions were rife: some 30 per cent of its population of about 7.2m was poverty stricken. Strikes were commonplace, from mining to construction work to trains, buses and trams. 'Suffragettes' were ever more active, their strategies including attacks on artworks in the Royal Academy, National Gallery and Tate and the planting of home-made bombs at St George's Hanover Square and St John's Smith Square.

These women, demanding the right to vote, were often chased down and viciously beaten by men or indeed by the police; and when arrested, they faced imprisonment. In jail, their hunger strikes were met with force-feeding in which no cruelty was spared. Ethel Smyth, who had written the anthem *March of the Women* in 1911, was among those involved with a campaign of window-smashing the following year; she served time in Holloway Prison alongside her friend Emmeline Pankhurst.

This ferment of anger, however, was soon overtaken by the calamity of the 'Great War' – which, with painful irony, made women's presence in professional and artistic life more significant than ever before.

On 28th June the Archduke Franz Ferdinand, heir presumptive to the Austrian Emperor Franz Joseph, was assassinated in Sarajevo by a Bosnian Serb student, Gavrilo Princip. By 28th July, Austro-Hungarian forces were at war with Serbia. Ructions spread across Europe; further declarations of war followed. In the last week of July, Londoners began to panic-buy coal, flour and foodstuffs, which soon caused shortages. A financial crisis was brewing; the London Stock Exchange closed and interest rates doubled to 8 per cent. By 1st August, prices were rocketing. As the dominos fell, Britain was drawn into the conflict by its obligation to defend Belgium, which Germany invaded on 3rd August. British citizens awoke on 4th August to find their country at war.

From the hills near High Marley, Myra, Irene, Uncle Tobs and the other Matthay students had recently observed a fleet of military aeroplanes, 'circling in the sunshine like a flight of silver birds over the Solent,' as Jessie put it. 'In less than four months the whole Sussex weald was one vast camp – "Kitchener's army".'[21]

The halcyon days of the Petersfield house party and the Drapers' musical nights were now, with hindsight, as tender as a piece that Ralph Vaughan Williams had written in summer 1914: *The Lark Ascending*, responding to the eponymous poem by George Meredith. The music captures an impression of the balmy air and a distant bird rising towards the heavens.

Edward Elgar, whose Hampstead home had been a magnet for the hero-worshipping Harriet on her bicycle, had sensed the world turning towards the shadows. Between his first and second symphonies – respectively 1907-8 and 1911 – a gulf had opened; the Second Symphony's ecstasies half-conceal an undertow of instability that seems to threaten imminent collapse. He attached an epigraph to the work. The words are from Percy Bysshe Shelley's cry to lost joys: 'Rarely, rarely comest thou, Spirit of Delight.'

1 J. Matthay, op. cit., p53
2 McKenna, op. cit., p53
3 Obituary of Frederick Hess, *Men's Wear*, December 1916
4 McKenna, op. cit., p55
5 Ibid., p56-7
6 MH letter to Ruth Howard, printed in McKenna, op. cit., p58-9, original stated as destroyed
7 Bax, *Farewell My Youth*, p60
8 Siek, op. cit., p322
9 Bax in *Farewell My Youth* identified the occasion as the London Music Club two years later, but this memoir is liberally peppered with inaccuracies and Siek has identified the real occasion.
10 Foreman, op. cit., p75
11 The concert is cited by Bax as the world premiere of his *Christmas Eve on the Mountains*. That concert also held the world premiere of Gustav Holst's *The Cloud Messenger*, which he does not mention; he does refer to a performance of the Schumann Piano Concerto, but this work does not appear in any of the reviews. This was one of Myra's signature works, though there is no performance of it listed in her notebook for that day. Perhaps Bax is conflating different events and issues.
12 Bax, op. cit., p84-86
13 T. McGee, *Barely Clare*, p20
14 Ibid., p 55-56
15 Orlando, Women's Writing in the British Isles from the Beginnings to the Present, accessed via https://orlando.cambridge.org
16 This and preceding extracts from C. Mackail, 'Early Days', in *Myra Hess by her Friends* pp6-16
17 https://users.ox.ac.uk/~djp/cumnor/remembrances/031.htm
18 McKenna, op. cit., p67
19 Ibid., p66
20 Ibid., p68
21 J. Matthay, op. cit., p55

The Great War
(1914–1918)

What's In A Name?

The Great War left no life unchanged. Myra could not help but be affected in every way: career, identity, home, independence and future development. Nevertheless, during the conflict's four years she was able to establish living arrangements that suited her well for two decades; she formed long-lasting musical relationships; and she built, finally, the firm reputation she needed and desired.

By the end of August 1914, around 30,000 men were enlisting every day, bolstering the small British army, 700,000 strong (France's was about 1.3m; Germany, within a week of hostilities breaking out, mustered 3.8m). The upbeat mood might have been different had people not believed that everything would be over in a few months. This was far from reality, and the new year brought a fresh source of alarm. On 19th January 1915 Britain had its first taste of the threat from air power when German Zeppelins, resembling giant airborne whales, bombed towns on the east coast, including Yarmouth, Sheringham and King's Lynn. Soon London, too, was targeted.

As the wartime atmosphere took hold, a virulent anti-German feeling arose in the British populace. The German community in London had been sizeable; it shrank by two-thirds. German citizens were interned en masse in locations including the Isle of Man and, in London, Alexandra Palace – among them Willy Strecker, London representative of the Mainz music publishing firm B Schott und Söhne, Johannes Joachim, son of the violinist Joseph Joachim, and Mabel's brother-in-law Georg Sauter, who was subsequently expelled back to Bavaria and never saw his wife again.

Mackenzie, the Academy's principal, was an enthusiastic Wagnerite, had spent much time in Germany and spoke the language well. Nevertheless, he brought the institution into line with the anti-German practices encouraged at government level. In contrast, Matthay, despite his German family background, resisted it all; he could be somewhat naive, often to his own detriment. At one point MI5 suspected him of being a German spy.[1]

The Bechstein piano firm – Matthay's preferred instruments, and at that time Myra's too – was in deep trouble. Its concert hall, designed by Thomas Collcutt and built in 1901 beside the company's showrooms on Wigmore Street, was the venue of choice for young recitalists, including Myra, but in due course the company's assets were seized, along with those of other German firms in Britain. Feelings ran so high that Nellie Melba was criticised for singing 'Land of Hope and Glory' to the accompaniment of a Bechstein piano. In 1916 the hall was sold to the Debenhams group, which reopened it the following year under a new name: Wigmore Hall.

Many families with German names changed them to avert the danger. An antiques dealer, Michael Siegenberg, who lived in Islington with his wife and their musical son, Clifford, adopted the surname Curzon. Three gifted Hungarian sisters – the violinists Adila and Jelly and pianist Hortense – had moved to Britain with their mother just before the war; they switched their surname, von Arányi, for a French version, d'Arányi. And in 1917 the Royal Family selected 'Windsor' as their own new name.

There was some irony in musicians assuming inconspicuous monikers; normally they did the opposite, since audiences appeared to value foreigners, especially Russians, more than local talent. The Texan pianist Lucy Hickenlooper, who married the conductor Leopold Stokowski, changed her name to Olga Samaroff. A Matthay student 25 years Myra's junior, Mary Gertrude Johnstone, later became Moura Lympany. Meanwhile in central Europe, Jewish musicians might change their names to evade the pernicious anti-Semitism that could hold back their progress. The conductor Bruno Walter, with whom Myra loved to work, had under some duress changed his surname from Schlesinger in 1896.

'Hess', to those in the know, was a German name, but Myra left it alone. There is no particular evidence that she struggled to find concerts because of it. The origins were probably not obvious enough to be the low-hanging fruit that the xenophobic press or public targeted; besides, she was a Londoner and her family had been British for generations. More than 20 years later, however, she would be fighting the perception that they were not.

The reachable fruit was splattered across papers such as the *Sunday Dispatch*, where the diary 'Dispatch Box' (on 23rd May 1915) reported with palpable glee: 'Mr Arnold Bax, whose vivid composition "In a Vodka

Shop" was played with such success at Miss Myra Hess's concert at the Bechstein Hall, was stricken the following day with German measles. And all because he devoted himself to a Russian theme.'

Sense and Sensibility

Myra's 1914 had started well with a major tour of the Netherlands and concerts at Steinway Hall, Bechstein Hall and Leighton House. Then came the four-month hiatus from June to November; when her performances resumed, she played at the Blackheath Conservatoire, then in a charity concert at the Langham Hotel in aid of Belgian refugees. Among venues for the autumn were the Grafton Galleries, for the Franck Piano Quintet with the London String Quartet, led by the violinist Albert Sammons. She visited the Bournemouth Winter Gardens, the Grand Hotel Birmingham and the Bechstein Hall again on 2nd December for the Classical Concert Society.

Her programmes included, among other things, the Schumann *Etudes symphoniques*, groups of Scarlatti sonatas and Chopin groups including the Nocturne in C minor, the A flat Impromptu and the F sharp minor Polonaise. Under her fingers, too, were old friends such as a selection of Brahms intermezzi from Opp. 117 and 119.

On 10th December at Max Mossel's Drawing Room Concerts, again at the Grand Hotel Birmingham, she jumped in to replace Percy Grainger, who was stuck in the USA due to the war. 'By this substitution, we had the pleasure of hearing a clever artist, who brought both novelty and individuality, as well as superior technique,' said the next day's *Birmingham Gazette*, which deemed her *Etudes symphoniques* 'a near perfect performance'. Indeed, Myra was attracting reviews that hailed her intelligence, individuality and poetic expressiveness. Few wittered about womanliness; none targeted her name, origins or long-established German repertoire.

She had developed a sensible system for introducing a judicious number of new pieces each season, putting them into programmes alongside works she knew inside out. Usually she would set aside six weeks of the summer to prepare. In 1913 new repertoire had included Brahms's Sonata No. 3 in F minor and Schumann's *Kinderszenen*; the first half of 1914 brought new Scarlatti sonatas in E major and C major and a selection of the Schubert German Dances. Her programmes in 1915 suggest she had made good use of her stay in Rottingdean: for instance, her Bechstein Hall recital on 18th May introduced Bach's Toccata and

Fugue in G minor, Ravel's Pavane, Debussy's 'Reflets dans l'eau' and 'Jardins sous la pluie', alongside Beethoven's 'Appassionata' Sonata, the Franck Prelude, Chorale and Fugue, O'Donnell's *Before the Dawn*, four pieces by Bax and Brahms's Waltzes.

Not everything in Myra's life was quite as sensible as her programme planning. Bax had been rejected for military service, partly due to his 'nervous temperament', but more seriously because of a heart condition. Among the copious letters between him and Harriet, the latter's biographer Helen Fry came across a note from Myra to Bax, dated 9th April 1915 (a Friday). It reads:

> I feel leagues nearer to you since Monday and Tuesday. It is too good to be real. I'd love to come and see you if not every other day – every day! But this confounded recital is going to tie me up a good bit for the next week or two. I hope to see you for a moment tomorrow – and perhaps you could come here one evening after dinner? My love to you, Myra.[2]

This does not quite amount to a love letter, and it makes clear, even when admitting that she would like to see him every day, that her preparation for concerts came first. But it appears to be the closest to such a thing from Myra that has been left intact. Towards the end of her life she insisted on destroying much personal correspondence.

A fuzzy legend exists, via several long-distance commentators, that Myra had fallen in love with a married musician and suffered great disappointment when the hope that he would leave his wife for her came to nothing. Antonietti had married only in 1912, well after their Netherlands tour. The behaviour sounds much more like that of Bax.

His marriage seemingly was not preventing him from stringing Myra along while simultaneously trumpeting his passion for Harriet, who reciprocated – although she was also busy with a catalogue of flirtations with famous men, from Sir Edward Elgar to George Bernard Shaw to D.H. Lawrence whom, despite knowing that he had tuberculosis, she once instructed to wade into a pond at a garden party to pick her a water-lily.

Bax had written a new piano piece, *The Maiden with the Daffodil,* inspired by Harriet; he had seen her at a soirée at the Corders' house wearing a dress patterned with a single flower. But it was Myra who gave the world premiere, at the Aeolian Hall on 24th March. The dedication was 'To Tania', Bax's private name for Harriet. Perhaps Myra did not even know this when she took on the performance.

On 29th April she also premiered *In a Vodka Shop* (another Ukraine-related piece), which he dedicated to her, perhaps in gratitude that she had introduced him to the publisher, Augener's, which printed it. It might otherwise seem a strange musical gift for a pianist who had never been into a vodka shop in her life. To Harriet, the composer made excuses over the dedication, saying that *The Maiden with the Daffodil* was coming out soon and he wished to avoid any resulting gossip. But weeks later, he wrote to Harriet including a remark that sounds like a vicious takedown of Myra, in the underhand guise of paying Harriet a compliment: 'It is rather pleasing aesthetically to be interpreted by some-one who (to put it vaguely) does not disgrace the human race in her appearance.'[3]

Myra Hess in her twenties

Photographs of Myra in her twenties show her deep eyes and forthright gaze, her severe expression tempered with spirituality. Her friends considered her beautiful and her 'comely' looks attracted compliments in reviews of her first US tours. It appears that the slippery Bax was playing the two pianists off against each other – so to speak, behind their backs.

Myra and Harriet had known each other since girlhood and at this point were still friends. Harriet, who had not yet given a London debut recital, told Bax that both she and Myra found his music extremely difficult, and that Myra had been coaching her on his new pieces. Harriet was consulting her weekly, in addition to her studies with Matthay.

By the autumn, however, Harriet's secret relationship with Bax had grown so intense that she longed for a safety valve. She decided to unburden herself to the supposedly empathetic Myra. Afterwards, she told Bax that Myra had revealed she had known for a long time about his feelings (how, exactly?), but had not been sure about Harriet's. She wrote that Myra was 'perfectly wonderful' about it, but also notes that she 'didn't seem too happy'. 'She said – She would love you whatever you did – but that you were very naughty! She said – "You [Harriet] are only 19 or 20 and have all your life to live yet".'[4]

Perhaps it was in a spirit of concern for Harriet's youth and wellbeing that Myra took the matter further. Harriet wanted to believe that Myra had her best interests at heart when she confronted Bax outright about the affair and tried to persuade him to break it off.

Soon afterwards, bitter notes crept into Harriet's letters when she mentioned Myra. At one point she envied a beautiful Bechstein grand that arrived for Myra at Mabel Reynolds' cottage, which Harriet was not permitted to touch. By spring 1916 she feared that Myra had turned against her; she wrote to Bax that she was jealous and believed Myra wanted him 'to fall in love with her and all her friends instead of me!!'[5] Moreover, the Matthays now knew about the relationship and Jessie, taking a dim view, was exhorting Harriet to extricate herself. All of this only persuaded the young pianist to throw herself in still deeper.

Bax's own priority was his music. He considered dividing up his existing piano pieces between the rival performers. On the back of the manuscript of his 1916 *Nereid*, he scribbled two columns. To Myra he assigned the two violin sonatas, *The Happy Forest*, Two Capriccios, *Moy Mell* (for two pianos, written in 1916 for Myra and Irene) and the *Symphonic Fantasy*. 'Tania''s list included *A Mountain Mood*, *Winter*

Waters, *Ideala* and the Quintet[6]. Myra's features the bigger repertoire, Harriet's the more personal music.

The rift between Myra and Harriet ran deep and did much damage. Myra's exacting standards for herself and her associates made her speak out, as usual, when she felt she could make a difference. She could be blunt, however, and her targets did not always take it in good spirit. Irene experienced this when she decided to marry rather than be single-minded about her career. Myra, who was generous-spirited and had plenty of charm when she wished to, maybe did not even realise the effect her words could have. Unused to forthright expression amid a culture known for its double-speak and euphemisms, those on the receiving end might feel intimidated, attacked and sometimes hurt beyond repair, especially if they looked up to her – as most people did.

But Harriet was the only one with whom the antagonism seemed mutual. Unlike her, Myra did not readily admit to jealousy; but as the years passed, she and her friends missed no opportunity to get in a dig, denigration or barbed joke at Harriet's expense. Nobody else she knew was targeted in such terms so consistently, or for so long.

8 Carlton Hill

In 1915, a solution emerged for Myra's living arrangements, thanks to Vera and Judy Compton-Burnett.

The seven Compton-Burnett siblings, their leanings ranging between literary, artistic, esoteric and musical, had lost their father in 1903 and mother in 1911. The youngest sisters, only 15 and 11 at the time, had therefore become the responsibility of the eldest, Ivy, who went on to be a celebrated novelist, chronicler of the tortured psychologies of family relationships in this time of turbulent social change. One brother, Guy, had died of pneumonia; another, Noel, apple of his sisters' eyes, had enlisted for World War I. They also had six older half-siblings from their father's first marriage.

Ivy's controlling nature made the family home in Hove a place of alarming silences and repression. Vera and Judy (respectively fourth and fifth of the seven) loathed it; they found release in music, becoming piano students first of Matthay and then of Myra. Ivy hated music – to the consternation of her sisters, who wished to practise at home. They became desperate to move out, together with the younger girls, Stephanie Primrose ('Baby') and Katherine ('Topsy'), a keen and gifted violinist.

Vera and Judy invited Myra to visit them in Hove. There, she was aghast at the fettered and emotionally fetid atmosphere in which her friends were not so much living as being forced to exist. Myra was equally in need of escape from her oppressive family. Thus the five young women resolved to share a house.

They took a lease on 8 Carlton Hill, a semi-detached, stucco-fronted villa in St John's Wood which Myra could not have contemplated otherwise; Ruth reported that her savings book showed a total of 14 shillings and sixpence. Together, the plan became feasible. An artist's studio extended into the back garden and was accessed down a small, erratic flight of stairs. This would be Myra's, along with a bedroom and the basement living area; the Compton-Burnetts divided the rest of the house between them.

Myra was officially their 'guest', since subletting was not permitted, but with a lease costing £98 per year plus rates, they shared the overheads. They all could rely on in-house companionship, but functioned as separate households; the Compton-Burnetts had their own housekeeper, while Myra employed a couple, John and Ethel Maul, to take care of her day-to-day needs. Ethel had formerly been nanny to Myra's sister Irene's three children. John was caretaker and driver, once Myra could own a car, while Ethel looked after domestic chores and meals. Myra was many things, but not a cook.

Mrs Maul would bring her dinner in an alcove that Myra called 'the glory hole', surrounded by her library of books and music. The pianist was a night owl and worked into the wee hours; interviewed by McKenna, the housekeeper recalled: 'She said if she did her practising at night and then went to bed with the music on her brain, she was sure it would help.'[7] As for mornings, the diligent Mrs Maul eventually began to bring Myra breakfast in bed.

Her annual tour of the Netherlands as yet unaffected by the war, Myra set off in late October, giving her first concert there on 1st November. She returned after two months to find that the Compton-Burnetts, with Mabel's help, had transformed the damp, draughty studio into a beautiful music room, with brocade curtains, gold-hued hessian coating the walls and a copper stove for heating. The space was soon home to her two Bechstein grand pianos and would be the scene of countless rehearsals, musical parties and impromptu house-concerts over the next two decades.

The Steiner Connection

Myra and the Compton-Burnetts established in 8 Carlton Hill a home that was everything Ivy's could not be: full of air, music, art, dance and friendship. At first, Ivy had considered moving in too. She would never have been able to stand it.

She disliked her sisters' circle of musical and spiritual friends, convinced that 'Mystical means muddle-headed'[8]; the four siblings were gravitating towards a burgeoning movement embracing esotericism and 'spiritual research'. Vera and Judy were attracted to the theosophical teachings of Annie Besant and the philosophies of Ralph Waldo Emerson's American disciples; Topsy and Baby were intrigued by 'New Thought', influenced by Ralph Waldo Trine's *In Touch with the Infinite*.

Vera and Judy later travelled to Switzerland to attend Rudolf Steiner's lectures at his Goetheanum in Dornach, a college he had founded in 1912 as a 'school of spiritual science'. As his disciples they translated many of his writings into English, including *Man as Symphony of the Creative World* and *The Foundations of Esotericism*; the latter was the text of his 31 lectures from 1905 that formed the basis of his Anthroposophical Society.

Some of Steiner's philosophies can seem extreme, even far-fetched, more than a century on (though perhaps no more questionable than some outlandish ideologies espoused in the 21st century). Nuggets of wisdom pepper his texts. His teachings advocated a path of inner spiritual development that rippled out into practical application in almost every discipline, from art and music to agriculture, economics and end-of-life care. He saw the human as a threefold being of spirit, soul and body, and believed in a spiritual perception that was independent of the senses; human consciousness needed training to reach beyond the material level. Judy and Vera's introduction to *The Foundations of Esotericism* speaks of 'the evolving figure of man', aiming for the development of the 'ego' towards the highest and most spiritual state.

Holst was an enthusiast: his popular suite *The Planets* was connected via his enthusiasm for Theosophy to Steiner's ideals of the soul's development, evolving from the war-like Mars towards the pure spirit of Neptune (and in Vera and Judy's introduction to the lectures, some of the spiritual development is mooted to take place on the planet – real or metaphorical – Jupiter). It was probably no coincidence that under the impact of war, both Anthroposophy and Theosophy became increasingly popular.

Steiner became influential via his network of schools, which persists into the 21st century. Vera and Judy later ran one: The Priory School at Kings Langley, where they taught music and eurythmy, Steiner's systematic form of dance that seeks to mirror the music's processes physically. They founded, too, the first eurythmy school in London. Judy continued to teach music at Kings Langley until her death aged 88. Ex-pupils recall Vera as a particularly warm personality, Judy as an excellent pianist even after losing most of her sight in later life, and both sisters as effective and charismatic teachers.[9]

Myra could scarcely have been insensible to her housemates' interests. Their father, Dr James Compton-Burnett, had been a homeopath and Myra embraced homeopathy for the rest of her life. Her doctor, a trusted confidant, was Dr Charles Yarrow Eccles, a medical physician turned homeopath. As for eurythmy, this physical embodiment of music could well have found an echo in Myra's deep-seated sense of rhythm and her vivid melodic articulation. Yet beyond these potential influences, there is little to suggest that Myra shared Vera and Judy's dedication to Anthroposophy. She was far too busy working.

Through 1915 the pages of Myra's engagements book became more crowded. She performed twice at the Proms – the Grieg Concerto, then Saint-Saëns No. 4 11 days later – and charity concerts were plentiful, including one at the Carlton Hotel for the War Emergency, with her fellow pianist Adelina de Lara.

The 1916 tour to Holland was her most substantial and profitable yet. She gave 25 concerts, including the Schumann Piano Concerto and Franck's Symphonic Variations (new to her repertoire) with Mengelberg in Amsterdam, Beethoven's Fourth Piano Concerto in Utrecht and the Grieg in an Arnhem charity concert. Her solo recitals drew in various combinations of the Mozart D minor Fantasy, a Scarlatti group, Schumann's G minor Sonata, Beethoven's 'Appassionata' Sonata, Brahms's Waltzes, a selection of Chopin Nocturnes, mazurkas, etudes, the Third Ballade and the Barcarolle, as well as his Sonata No. 2 in B flat minor (the 'Funeral March'), the Bach Toccata and Fugue in G minor, the Bax Nocturne and *Maiden with a Daffodil*, the Ravel Pavane, Debussy's 'Jardins sous la pluie', Matthay's 'Elves', Liszt's *Liebestraum* No. 3, and the Dutch Peasant Dances arranged by Julius Röntgen. Several concerts were shared with the cellists Thomas Camirez and Thomas Denys.

This is a more than substantial amount of music, but Myra was thriving on hard work and commensurate acclaim; and in another step forward, she was working with a manager, Ethel L. Robinson, who had been agent to the late Joseph Joachim and the pianist Fanny Davies. When she returned, she had a profit of about £230 after paying all expenses (the equivalent in the 2020s of over £29,000). During the rest of 1916 she gave a further 25 concerts – the same number that she had packed into less than two months away.

Triumphs and Tragedies

The start of 1916, though healthy for Myra financially, launched a year that mingled consolidation, loss and a major crisis. First, though, she made a vital new friend.

The first mention of the Hungarian violinist Jelly d'Arányi in Myra's engagements book is dated 30th March 1916 – 'Mr Reynolds [Mabel's home], with Jelly d'Arányi and Thelma Bentinck'. It was a programme of piano trios: Brahms's in C minor and the Ravel, written less than two years earlier. Jelly (pronounced 'Yelly') was to become the violinist with whom Myra worked most closely and for longest.

Over the years Myra had played with Szigeti, Aldo Antonietti, and Mischa Elman (whose proposal of marriage she is said to have turned down); much later she worked with Isaac Stern. Her duo with Jelly, however, lasted for over two decades, up to 1940. Jelly's biographer, probably referring to the date chez Reynolds, mentions their first meeting: 'Jelly recalls that [she and Myra] "eyed each other like dogs"'.[10] Jelly was three years Myra's junior. Her career, like her sister Adila's, was suffering from World War I xenophobia; Mabel's support for Jelly complemented her championship of Myra.

The war was raging. That year three million young men went into battle at the Somme between 1st July and 18th November; around 300,000 of them were killed, including the composers George Butterworth and Frederick Septimus Kelly. The latter had survived the horrors of Gallipoli the previous year, only to meet his death here. Jelly had been in love with him.

Kelly's portrait, drawn by John Singer Sargent, stood on the piano at Jelly's Chelsea home. When he left for Gallipoli, she and her mother were living with her middle sister Hortense, who had married the economist Ralph Hawtrey. Although there was no engagement, nor any sign that Jelly's affection was requited (Kelly may have been homosexual), her family continued to call him 'her only fiancé'[11]. He was Australian, Eton-educated and an Oxford blue whose rowing skills won him an Olympic gold medal in London 1908. Jelly never married, though her exotic beauty and dazzling playing won her many besotted admirers. Tall and willowy, with dark eyes, Slavic cheekbones and the charisma of a superstar, she was not short of opportunity; she probably had some affairs and when she rejected one infatuated suitor, the musicologist Donald Francis Tovey, she seems to have suggested she was waiting for another man, who was ill. But she never found anyone thereafter with whom she could contemplate settling down.

Common parlance had it not that there were too few men after the wartime slaughter, but instead that there were two million 'surplus women'. Those born between 1885 and 1895 were the worst affected by the lack of potential husbands. Myra and Jelly were born respectively in 1890 and 1893. None of the Compton-Burnett sisters and half-sisters married – and (as Ivy's biographer Hilary Spurling pointed out) this was not the exception for their generation, but the rule.[12]

The carnage took a great toll on the musical world. Orchestras needed years to recover from losing so many of their members; when in the 1920s a vogue for neo-classicism arose in new music, requiring smaller ensembles than were usual in the decade of Stravinsky's *Le sacre du printemps* and Ravel's *Daphnis et Chloé*, it was not least because fewer performers were available. At the same time, more opportunities were materialising for female musicians as the men disappeared in military service.

That summer the New Queen's Hall Orchestra's Proms began on 26th August, but its contents were not announced until the tenth of that month. *The Musical Times* noted that 'It is gratifying that these concerts are to be held this autumn,' then commented: 'Owing to calls to the Army, the orchestra is necessarily somewhat reconstituted, and it is stated that it will include some lady players.'[13] At the Academy, Mackenzie, in his speech at the end of year prizegiving, noted the increased numbers of female students: 'Why a greater preponderance prevails to-day, one need hardly answer. Every fit student or professor responded to the call [to arms].' This academic year had been, he said, 'the most exacting and difficult within the longest and ripest experience here'.

Moments of Crisis

On 21st September, Myra was playing the Mozart Piano Concerto in D minor K466 with Sir Henry Wood when she suffered a memory lapse. Most musicians have them now and then, and Wood was no stranger to such occurrences. He managed the orchestral part so that the audience remained oblivious. When Myra apologised afterwards, he joked, 'Why, heavens, that was nothing. Nothing at all. You might have gone into the wrong movement and *then* we would have had some fun!'[14]

Nevertheless, Myra had an Achilles heel: her debilitating pre-concert nerves. The strains were mounting up – the war and whatever emotional difficulties she was experiencing – and she was starting to wonder whether she could face spending her life under such extreme stress. She had several Proms that September and October; the next was on 20th October, the Schumann Piano Concerto conducted by Landon Ronald. Not long beforehand, she took a sharp knife and set out for the autumnal woods of Hampstead Heath. Her intention, as she later confided in Howard Ferguson, was to cut her own hands so severely that she would be unable to play.[15]

Whatever was she thinking? What would she have done in the aftermath, in the middle of the Heath? What if she had hit an artery? Fortunately, she had too little courage and too much sense to see it through. She managed to talk herself down and went home.

By November she was performing better than ever. *The Times* reviewed her at the Aeolian Hall, in three Bach Preludes and Fugues, Brahms's Sonata No. 3 in F minor, Debussy's prelude 'Minstrels', some etudes by Szymanowski and Bax's *Symphonic Phantasy.*

> Miss Hess belongs to the school which believes in dramatizing the incident of the moment by piling up, even engineering, vast crescendos, and leading the astonished hearer from rapture to rapture … It was natural that this method should be most successful with works which are nearest to our own time, and Debussy's 'Minstrels' was exactly suited to such exposition ... Szymanowski's Etudes … were also a success, and the Phantasy … gave a fine opportunity for a brilliant rather than solid technique. It seemed a pity that such unsuitable composers as Bach and Brahms should have been drawn upon for the programme.[16]

It is ironic that Myra later became legendary for her Bach and Brahms, while Debussy and Szymanowski vanished from her repertoire. As did Bax.

December 1916 took Frederick, Myra's father, aged 61. He was fortunate to have survived with diabetes for around 12 years. The pair had managed a degree of reconciliation on the sole occasion he visited

Carlton Hill, and she was able to see him in a nursing home before he fell into a coma. A press notice about his death in the trade magazine *Men's Wear* reported that he had still been at work a few days beforehand: 'It was only by the exercise of great will-power and determination that he had been able to bring himself month after month to continue at work, for he was not in a fit state of health to warrant so much continued exertion.' Myra's own extraordinary will power and work ethic did not come from nowhere. Perhaps she was more her father's daughter than she realised.

The Conflict Deepens

The year 1917 started in sombre mood under the vast impact of the Somme and its losses. More were to come. At the Battle of Arras, the poet Edward Thomas was killed, one of some 159,000 British soldiers left dead, injured or missing.

Myra could not go to the Netherlands in January. The Channel crossing was too dangerous, presenting the dual obstacles of British undersea mines and German U-boats. In March 1916, the composer Enrique Granados and his wife had been travelling from Folkestone to Dieppe when their boat, the Sussex, was torpedoed; the couple were among about 50 casualties. By early 1917 Germany had increased its U-boat fleet to 140, able to puncture the British blockade and resume unrestricted submarine warfare. In the Atlantic, their torpedoing of American vessels helped to propel the US away from neutrality; so, too, did the communist revolution in Russia, which caused international alarm lest others should follow suit. By April, the US had joined the war.

British musical life was increasingly dependent on its women, and Myra had an intense schedule. She gave just short of 50 UK concerts that year, which would be a respectable number even in peacetime. They took her to such diverse venues as Leighton House in Holland Park, Manchester's Free Trade Hall, Eton College, the Kinnaird Hall in Dundee, London's Aeolian Hall and the renamed Wigmore Hall, the Repertory Theatre, Birmingham, and, in Brighton, the Aquarium.

To her solo repertoire she had added Beethoven's 'Les Adieux' Sonata, Op. 81A; and some Rachmaninoff Preludes, Op. 32 No. 10 and Op. 33 No. 5, featured when she performed in December in a Slavonic Series at the Grafton Galleries, where a Russian exhibition was in full swing. In concertos, she was still playing the Schumann, the Grieg, Franck's Symphonic Variations and Saint-Saëns No. 4; at the 1917 Proms she also performed Mozart's A major Concerto K488. And in January 1918, the words 'Rachmaninoff Concerto No. 2' appeared for the first time in her schedule, in Leeds.

Reviews were welcoming, even comfortable. Commenting on her Symphonic Variations with Wood at the Queen's Hall on 9th February 1918, *The Times* noted: 'Miss Hess was...exactly suited with the César Franck. Her beautifully loose wrists kept the balance of each theme perfect and the tone was never forced'.

There was more chamber music too, with Jelly and the cellist Arthur Williams: not least, Schubert's Trio in B flat, Brahms's C major, Schumann's F major and one of Beethoven's in E flat (the records do not state which of the three it was); as a duo, she and Jelly relished Bach's heavenly Sonata in E major.

One year and two days after Frederick's death, an unimaginable calamity struck the idealistic household at 8 Carlton Hill.

The Compton-Burnetts' brother, Noel, had been killed on 14th July 1916, early in the Battle of the Somme. The news left the family shattered, Topsy and Baby in particular. Aged 22 and 18, they had alarmed their sisters by seeming to retreat from the world; Topsy had lost interest in her violin playing and her adored Shakespeare, and the pair were listless and disengaged. On 10th December 1917, they told the Compton-Burnetts' housekeeper that they were going away for a few days. They did not return.

Anxious investigations revealed that they had never reached their intended destination at West Wickham. On 27th December, alarm set in: it turned out that the door of the room they shared in 8 Carlton Hill was locked. Their half-sister Iris came round and forced it.

Inside, according to the inquest, the bodies of the two young women were lying on their right sides. The left hand of the second body was holding the dressing gown of the other. Near the bed were five empty bottles of 'veronal', a sleeping potion (barbital or diethylbarbituric acid) that both had used regularly – Topsy had been taking it for toothache. Although they had not been seen alive since 10th December, the post-mortem showed that they had been dead for only a few days. The coroner could not determine whether the outcome was accidental or deliberate.

Their traumatised housemates fled, with Winnie Smith, to sanctuary at Mabel Reynolds' house. After the funeral Myra summoned her own considerable strength to support Vera and Judy, telling them that she would quite understand if they wished to give up Carlton Hill and that they must not worry about her, but put themselves first. They nevertheless elected to stay. Later they redecorated the room in which Topsy and Baby had died; eventually Myra took it over as her bedroom. Faced with such memories, few housemates would have been tough enough to do that.

Ivy, in her elderly years, blamed her sisters' fate on the malign influence of 'all that music'.[17]

Harriet, horrified by the Compton-Burnetts' tragedy, was perturbed that Vera, to whom she had thought herself close, would not come to her place instead of Mabel's. She was still more upset that when the group headed to High Marley for a fortnight's refuge, she was not invited. She felt alienated from Myra's entire circle: Ruth, Clare, Mabel and, she feared, the Matthays themselves. She blamed Myra and Winnie for bad-mouthing her.[18] It did not seem to occur to her that her own actions – having an affair with a married man, living in a flat that he financed for her, defying her friends' advice and then expecting sympathy from them for the resulting pain – might carry some responsibility.

Harriet tended to believe that everybody loved her. Many did. Perhaps she intended to be a free spirit. Some of her friends, like the adoring Rebecca West[19], were magnetised by her cultural interests – she collected art, travelled widely, loved literature and held celebrity-studded bohemian parties – besides her beauty, vulnerability and expertise in winning sympathy. But others considered her little better than a tart; and for struggling musicians, nothing is worse than a rival artist whom they suspect is being given concert engagements for the wrong reasons.

Harriet's letters to Bax were full of narcissistic extremes. Twice that year she mentions thoughts of suicide, whether by swimming out to sea – when the Bechstein arrived at Mabel's cottage for Myra and Harriet was not allowed to touch it – or by throwing herself under a tube train. It was safe for Bax to assume that she would not.

An Enduring Partnership

In Myra's own life, a growing partnership was in the ascendant. On 4th October 1918, she wrote to Jelly:

> My dear Jelly,
>
> Clare told me she had met you the other day & that you had talked about playing at hospitals. Do let us do some together. I am hopelessly

busy this month, but after November 2nd I am very keen to play whenever I can at hospitals.

How are you?
I hope we shall meet soon.
With much love
Yours ever
Myra

I would willingly come to the 'Face' Hospital you mentioned.[20]

This was the Queen's Hospital in Sidcup, founded in 1917 by the New Zealand surgeon Harold Gillies, offering pioneering facial reconstruction surgery for people who had suffered battle injuries from burns or shrapnel. Jelly was ahead of her time in her passion for bringing the comfort of music into hospitals.

Jelly and Myra were building a real friendship based on their music-making, though their personalities were very different. Myra was industrious, determined, non-compromising; Jelly was glamorous yet ascetic, flirtatious yet other-worldly. A 1933 drawing by Myra's friend Marjorie Gunn caricatures Jelly radiating star quality in a magnificent gown while Myra sits plugging away at the piano in the background. Yet they shared a zest for life, great mutual respect and an irrepressible sense of fun, and from 1918 their connection deepened with their concerts.

After Jelly's mother died, and the Hawtreys left London for the US, Jelly moved in with her other sister, Adila, and her husband, the lawyer Alexander Fachiri, in nearby Netherton Grove. When the d'Arányi girls and their mother had first moved to London, they left their father behind in Hungary, where he was head of the Budapest police. They made their names in Britain as a trio of exotic teenage prodigies in the house-concerts of Edwardian high society, which often termed them 'those darling Hungarian sisters'.

They were more than that. They were the great-nieces of Joseph Joachim, the celebrated violinist and close friend of Johannes Brahms and Clara Schumann. Adila had been his last pupil. Jelly, seven years younger, had been too young to study with him, but had had lessons with Hubay.

Of course they attracted endless attention from men. Bela Bartók had had crushes first on Adila, then on Jelly, for whom he wrote his two violin sonatas. Jelly enjoyed a correspondence with Aldous Huxley in his student days and was the target of hopeless passions from Tovey, John Steuart Wilson, Julian Huxley and even George Mallory, to name but four. Aldous Huxley left a teasing caricature of her in his novel *Crome Yellow*, a satirical take on Lady Ottoline Morrel and Garsington: here a house-guest named Jenny wears her hair in coiled plaits over her ears – a style Jelly favoured – and consequently can hear nothing. She is, however, a talented musician…on the drums.

Myra and Jelly had affectionate nicknames for one another: Myra called Jelly by her family moniker, 'Sai', and sometimes addressed her letters to 'Darling gut-scraper' or 'My darling sister genius'. She signed herself 'Pishkosz' often with a Z extending into bouncy trails along the paper. In Hungarian the word means 'dirty'.

Although Myra's filthy sense of humour was often remarked upon, published examples are rare – presumably unprintable. One such arrived in a letter to Jelly at Christmas 1928 with a gift of handkerchiefs. Myra wishes her 'all the happiness you deserve in the New Year - & that when you wipe your arse on these hankies that you will think of your Peeeshkosh???'[21]

Jelly d'Arányi and Myra Hess at the BBC

The duo's high spirits sometimes got them into trouble. Once, after rehearsing at Repton School, they went out for some fresh air before the performance and Jelly tossed a shawl over her head for warmth. The material caught on something above her: a red-eyed head of a bison affixed to the wall. They laughed so much that Jelly had not managed to stop by the time they were on stage. Waiting for her to get a grip, Myra prepared the opening note, only to hit the wrong one, sparking Jelly into further uncontrollable fits.[22]

On another occasion they were playing at the North Devon Music Club when, in the middle of a Brahms sonata, the audience was transfixed by the sight of a uniformed postman walking up the aisle towards the platform. Here he waited until the movement was over, then handed Jelly a letter. When she could stop laughing, Jelly announced to the audience: 'It is not a love-letter, it is for the piano tuner.' Some time elapsed before they were able to finish the performance.[23]

Over the interwar years, Myra's letters to Jelly became increasingly free and lively, in handwriting more liberated than her later, rather formal and clear script. She was concerned when Jelly was ill and even rather possessive, telling her that she could not have 'my blessed partner' afflicted so much[24] (she never referred to any other musician that way), and being affronted – if mockingly so – when Jelly played with another pianist. They saw each other through difficult times, including the loss of both their mothers, and happy days, attending house-party, tennis-playing weekends. 'We must go abroad together,' Myra enthused to Jelly. 'It was so heavenly in Bavaria.'[25]

Even so, Jelly was a soloist and went her own way, trailing clouds of glory and male admirers. Myra, the more practical of the two, sometimes gently chivvied along the slightly absent-minded violinist if she needed an urgent response for programme planning or concert booking. Her inner circle of friends was very different. A note scribbled by Marjorie Gunn gives a list of guests at a dinner at 'Boulogne Restaurant' on Thursday 6th June 1918 'In Memoriam of a HAT … and a superb party'. The list is headed by 'Myra (very beautiful – reasonable as ever!)', then 'Marjorie Gunn' in florid writing; Sazzie (underlined), Clare [Mackail], Juliet [Judy] Compton-Burnett, Ruth [Howard], Vera [Compton-Burnett], Winnie [Smith].'[26]

Other than taking part in a performance in aid of the Red Cross of a Toy Symphony by the Victorian composer Richard Blagrove, with a group of prominent musicians playing toy instruments, Myra's next concerto was on 16th June at the Queen's Hall, the Saint-Saëns No. 4 in C minor. She had played concertos at the Queen's Hall many times since her debut, but now she was beginning to give recitals there too. In a 'Ballad Concert' on 27th October she performed short works by Poldini, Rachmaninoff and Chopin; another, on 18th February, included Chopin, Scarlatti and Brahms. The Wigmore Hall seated about 550. The Queen's Hall was triple the size.

1 Siek, op. cit., p373
2 H. Fry, *Music and Men*, p38
3 Bax to Cohen, 14 May 1915, BL, see Siek, op. cit., p472
4 Cohen to Bax, late 1915, BL, see Siek, op. cit., p473
5 Cohen to Bax, undated in 1916, BL, see Siek, op. cit., p473
6 Foreman, op. cit., p183
7 McKenna, op. cit., p75
8 H. Spurling, *Ivy*, p234
9 Author interview with Nicholas Logie
10 J. Macleod, *The Sisters d'Arányi*, p173
11 Author interview with Jane Camilloni
12 Spurling, op. cit., p237
13 *The Musical Times*, Vol. 57, No. 883 (1 September 1916), p420
14 Amis BBC interview with MH, 1962
15 McKenna, op. cit., p40
16 *The Times*, 3 November 1916
17 Spurling, op. cit., p236
18 Cohen to Bax, 30 December 1917, BL, see Siek, op. cit., p475
19 Rebecca West based her novel *Harriet Hume* on Harriet Cohen and Bax, without changing their first names.
20 MH to Jelly d'Arányi, private archive, d'Arányi family
21 MH to JdA, Christmas 1928
22 Macleod, op. cit., p159
23 *The Times*, letter from 'M. W. L.', 6 April 1966
24 MH to JdA, 1936, private archive, d'Arányi family
25 MH to JdA, 1928, Ibid.
26 Marjorie Gunn diaries, Medway Archives

Breakthrough
(1918–1924)

THE ARMISTICE WAS SIGNED on the eleventh day of the eleventh month, 1918. When the news came, Myra was rehearsing chamber music in her studio. The rehearsal quickly turned into a celebratory party.

Beyond the immediate joy, it was a time to take stock of a tragic wasteland in which millions were left dead, maimed, traumatised and bereaved; and 1919 brought little relief as a pandemic of Spanish flu ravaged an already exhausted population, killing around 50 million people worldwide. Bax fell ill with it early in 1918. Ivy Compton-Burnett was fortunate to survive when her attack turned into pneumonia.

Harriet had still worse: tuberculosis, possibly contracted from D.H. Lawrence. She had to go to a Swiss sanatorium to recover. Her optimism revived, however, when Bax left Elsita and moved out into a flat in Fellows Road, Hampstead. Here he would live through the interwar years – but without a divorce. He claimed, fairly or not, that as a Spanish Catholic, Elsita would not agree to one. In 1919, Harriet suffered a miscarriage.

Although Myra's name had appeared in the agency Ibbs and Tillett's brochure since the 1911-12 season, she had relied on Ethel Robinson to manage her Bechstein/Wigmore Hall concerts. From 1918 onwards, however, her UK management rested solely with Ibbs and Tillett, and now matters began to take off.

Not everything was smooth sailing; for instance, there was a run-in with the composer Joseph Holbrooke, for whose piano concerto Myra had been proposed as soloist. But in general, she was in the best possible hands. The company, founded in 1906 by Robert Leigh Ibbs and John Tillett, represented Kreisler, Casals, and many pianists from overseas who hoped to re-establish their careers in Britain following the war, among them Ferruccio Busoni, Moritz Rosenthal and Sergei Rachmaninoff. By 1920 the roster also included Irene Scharrer and Benno Moiseiwitsch.

A New Model of Management

The advent of powerful artist management companies was a major boon for the musicians who signed up with them. These organisations were rising to dominate the music business, topped by powerful figures with all the right connections, who would secure engagements, broker deals and plan suitable career paths for their charges, at least in theory. They were paid in commission, taking ten, 15 or 20 per cent of the artist's fee, justified by the fact that a musician working alone might not be sufficiently shameless to demand an adequate amount.

It was an era of grand personalities with ambitions and expectations to match. Agents, both men and women, were as likely to be larger-than-life characters as were conductors or, indeed, pianists. Such figures between 1920 and 1950 included the fierce South African-born Harold Holt, the Viennese-Jewish Lies Askonas, and Joan Ingpen, casting director at Covent Garden and New York's Metropolitan Opera, who founded Ingpen and Williams – the second name belonged to her dachshund.

Christopher Fifield, in his biography of the firm, described Ibbs and Tillett as 'to the British music industry what Marks and Spencer is to the world of department stores'. To them, though, Myra was not just another pianist, nor the relationship with her merely business-like. She seems to have regarded John Tillett as part of her surrogate family, writing to him by his first name after a sole 'My dear Mr Tillett' letter[1]. Rather than tracts demanding astronomical fees, introductions to the great and good, or other drawing downs of the moon, her letters are chatty, personal and concerned for his wellbeing. Still, she is never a pushover. Her style is not so much an iron fist in a velvet glove as a subtle-coloured titanium gauntlet that can be neither resisted nor removed.

Her career was transformed. After some 70 concerts in 1918 and around 82 in 1919, 1920 found her giving nearly 100. The following year brought three sold-out London performances in a matter of weeks, and her fees at last were professional, around 20 or 25 guineas, sometimes more. She returned to Holland with a six-week trip in spring 1919, culminating with Mozart at the Concertgebouw with Mengelberg.

The Gunn Sisters

The violinist Marjorie Gunn's name appeared in Myra's concert diary for the first time in spring 1918. Together they gave a Wigmore Hall recital on 13th March; Myra played in the sonatas and gave some piano solos, while an accompanist (the young conductor and early music researcher Anthony Bernard) took over in the shorter pieces. The programme included a Mozart Sonata in B flat, Szymanowski's Romance (its UK premiere), Franck's Prelude, Fugue and Variation arranged by Harold

Bauer, and Brahms's Violin Sonata No. 2 in A major. *The Globe*'s critic declared the occasion 'practically a joint recital with Miss Myra Hess, and it would be impossible to apportion to either a larger share of honour than to the other'.

Marj (Mary Marjorie Gordon) and her sister Anita, nickamed 'Saz' (Margaret Anita) were born in Strood, Kent – respectively in 1888 and 1900 – and grew up first at 17 South Avenue, Rochester St Margaret Intra, and later at Elm Lodge, 31 St Margaret's Street, Rochester. Their father, Barrett Gunn, was a Royal Navy surgeon. On 4th August 1913 the family moved to 56 Abbey Road, St John's Wood – round the corner from both Boundary Road and Carlton Hill. Here their mother, Florence Gunn (née Winckworth), got to know Lizzie Hess and the two families became friends.

Marjorie went to music school at Hindhead in Surrey and kept diaries full of the pleasures and pressures of practising and concert preparation, including plenty of humorous drawings; one depicts her on a bicycle, violin case strapped to her back and a particularly precious hat nestled against her front.

Before World War I 'Marj' travelled often to Germany, attending summer music courses in Dresden. Her trip in 1910 let her take in vast quantities of operas and concerts, especially Wagner, which she gobbled up; many weeks she would go to a performance at least every two or three days. Her diary entries are innocent and schoolgirlish even after she turned 20. In 1911 they chronicled her violin studies, how many hours she practised, what she played and how long she slept, plus affectionate descriptions of her little sister. Later she developed a close and lasting relationship with Ruth Howard, though of necessity they lived very separate lives; Ruth, an unmarried only daughter with three brothers, was expected to look after her parents as they aged. Marj appears to be Elizabeth Jane Howard's model for Sid, Rachel's female lover in *The Cazalet Chronicles*.[2]

Pictures from the early 1920s and 30s show two very contrasted sisters. Marj was tall and slender, with long face and big, bright eyes; she dressed in old-fashioned long skirts and full-sleeved blouses. Saz was shorter and stockier (though slightly taller than Myra), with fair hair cropped into a short bob. She is often shown wearing drop-waisted dresses, tidy white lace collars and strong walking boots. Marj was the more dynamic, forceful and intellectual, with a notably deep voice, and Saz the more stoical, pious and organised. Marj also adored animals, including cats, but chiefly dogs; in most photographs she has at least one four-pawed companion.

Marj made several Wigmore Hall appearances with Myra, who admired her playing so much that she sometimes wished the violinist were not such a good teacher. But Marj had a vocation for teaching: at Downe House School in Berkshire, she became head of music and stayed for decades. She conducted its orchestra and polished the girls' playing to the point that Myra could perform concertos with them. A recording remains from 1958 of their Bach D minor Concerto: Myra sparkles along to a diligent accompaniment. Later, Myra would send her students to Marj for accompaniment experience and coaching; they lavished praise on both her musicianship and her indomitable personality.

Marj and Saz inherited 56 Abbey Road and continued to live there together. In 1931 Saz became Myra's personal assistant, a role she never relinquished. The two were Myra's closest companions for the rest of her life.

Laying the Foundations

By 1920 Myra was giving about 100 concerts a year, split between recitals, charity performances, concertos and chamber music (including the brand-new Elgar Violin Sonata with Winifred Small in March that year, and trios with Jelly's sister, Adila). She was continuing to champion new works by friends, teachers and even Mackenzie, the Academy's principal. She played his Scottish Concerto with the Philharmonic Orchestra conducted by Albert Coates at the Queen's Hall, on 10th March 1921; a fellow Matthay pupil, Vivian Langrish, had hoped to play it and was not too happy when the task instead fell to Myra. She spent April and half of May 1919 in Holland, six weeks from Christmas to February in 1919-20, and had 16 concerts there across several weeks from new year 1921 – and in London she continued to teach. She made sure to spend time in the summers with Lizzie, who had relocated to Eastbourne; there, mother and daughter enjoyed watching the matches at the local tennis club.

In 1920, taking part in a three-day London Bach Festival, Myra heard for the first time since the Oxford performance Bach's Cantata No. 147, *Herz und Mut und That und Leben*, which Hugh Allen conducted. Struck afresh by the beauty of its closing chorale, *Jesu, Joy of Man's Desiring*, she hunted down the score on her shelves – she had a complete Bach edition – and took it to her piano to see if it could be played. It could, at least by her; and she began to sketch out a transcription. Within weeks she had finished it. Soon she was experimenting with playing it as an encore.

Perhaps the English words, by Robert Bridges, played a role in the piece's significance for Myra: she seems always to have been 'striving still to truth unknown'. She often said that her musical efforts were an attempt to get 'a little nearer the truth'[3].

Jesu, joy of man's desiring,
Holy wisdom, Love most bright,
Drawn by thee, our souls aspiring
Soar to uncreated light.
Word of God our flesh that fashioned
With the fire of life impassioned,
Striving still to truth unknown,
Soaring, dying round thy throne.
Through the way where hope is guiding,
Hark, what peaceful music rings,
Where the flock, in thee confiding,
Drink of joy from deathless springs.
Theirs is beauty's fairest pleasure,
Theirs is wisdom's holiest treasure.
Thou dost ever lead thine own
In the love of joys unknown.

The Friedbergs

Myra could have continued with her career as it was, but fate, in the shape of John Tillett, had other ideas. He was exploring contacts with artist managers in the USA, hoping to expand Myra's career across the Atlantic. After a year or so, he received a positive response.

The American music critic Cesar Saerchinger, reporting from London for *The Musical Courier*, had often heard and admired Myra at Wigmore Hall. He facilitated a connection with Annie Friedberg, who ran a small New York agency that represented her brother, the pianist Carl Friedberg, along with the Budapest String Quartet and the soprano Elisabeth Schumann. Saerchinger's advocacy must have been convincing: Annie, most unusually, agreed to book Myra sight unseen for an extensive US tour beginning in January 1922. This was the start of not one crucial relationship, but two.

The Friedberg siblings, born in Bingen, Germany, moved to the US partly by design and partly by chance. Annie, whose high energy and single-minded devotion to her musicians counterbalanced her volatile personality, started her company in 1912. Her brother, her chief client, happened to be touring the US two years later when war broke out; he was trapped there for four years. He then tried to return to Germany, but he had become well established in America and it wanted him back: he was recruited to the faculty of the Institute of Musical Art in New York City, which later merged with the Juilliard School.

Carl became a mentor and confidant to Myra, who on arriving in America would usually play him her programmes for his opinions and advice. His musical 'pedigree' gives this special significance: he had been a pupil of Clara Schumann, made his concerto debut in Vienna in 1892 with Gustav Mahler conducting, and the following year gave an all-Brahms recital in the composer's presence. Brahms then coached him on much of his piano music.

Myra was more associated in the popular imagination with Beethoven and Schubert; but she played more solo works by Schumann than by Schubert, and very substantial quantities of Brahms: solo pieces, chamber music and both piano concertos. Moreover, the Schumann Piano Concerto, which she recorded three times, was regarded by some fellow artists as 'hers'. If she was influenced by a disciple of Brahms and Clara, that would lend an extra ring of authenticity to her elemental performances of their music.

Coming to America

Myra thought long and hard before accepting the trip. Touring the US was a major undertaking and required months of planning. She sought Vera and Judy's opinions, but Uncle Tobs's most of all. Still, she was at the perfect stage for such a venture. At 32, she was well known, yet had nothing to lose; and to find an agent willing to book her – a supposedly unsaleable female pianist – on a coast-to-coast tour on recommendation alone, without having heard her play, was an extraordinary opportunity. The tour, from January to April 1922, was announced more than a year in advance, with American journals trailing it in 1920.

America would change not just Myra's life, but her musicianship too, through myriad impacts ranging from the contact with Carl Friedberg to the American Steinway pianos that she adored. She found the US's energy, freshness and extroversion a shot in the arm; and it was there that she found her most extensive and enthusiastic audience and reached a level of stardom that remained elusive in Britain, where she often seemed to have been taken for granted.

She could easily have decided to move to the States; several of her friends and colleagues made the leap, including Rebecca Clarke and Harold Bauer. But although Myra sometimes felt a wrench upon leaving America for home, she does not seem to have considered emigration. Instead, she chose both countries. She would spend around a third of every year, sometimes more, in the US, but never had to cut ties on either side of the ocean. Myra, who considered herself 'strong as a horse'[4] and had a healthy appetite for good company, good living and great music-making, effectively embraced two lives rather than just one.

A further advantage would have been the orchestras with which she worked in the major US centres. In Britain, orchestral playing was at a low ebb in the early 1920s. Ensembles such as the London Symphony Orchestra and the Hallé had been decimated by the Great War, and rebuilding was difficult since the country lacked the tradition and training available to musicians on 'the continent', besides its better-remunerated jobs. The US had the winning combination of higher pay, fewer World War I losses and the ability to attract the finest in emigré talent from Revolution-blighted Russia and war-torn Europe alike.

The atmosphere of the States not only affected *what* Myra played, but *how*. At first, she was apprehensive: would her type of pianism be appreciated there? Interviewed by Saerchinger for *The Musical Courier*, she later reflected:

> America has two reputations abroad. The one is that you have no judgment about matters of high art, and that nothing can succeed here except the sensational. I thought many times of coming here – and people used to ask me why I did not come. Some urged me to come; others warned me not to. And I made up my mind I was not the sort of artist to succeed here – not sensational enough.
>
> Other artists kept telling me that I had an entirely incorrect idea about America....that there was no place in the world where real art must stand so absolutely on its own feet....each member of the audience would judge the artist by his own individual reaction – people, you see, accustomed to think for themselves.[5]

Her view echoed that of Harold Bauer, who had begun touring the US at the start of the century and travelled amply to small towns and universities. 'In the beginning,' he recalled, 'I was often asked to play simple music by popular composers, "because," it was said, "our public will not understand the kind of music that is played in New York."' He notes a major change a few years later: 'People in small towns who had previously begged for a "light" program were positively insulted if there was the least evidence … that a New York program had been toned down to meet the supposed taste of a less sophisticated audience.'[6]

In the event, the States brought out the very best in Myra. Live recordings from her US performances in the late 1940s-1950s, for instance, capture her fieriest musical drama, with a colourful flair that belies her austere image at home. It seems that America released qualities in her that the comparatively repressive Britain preferred to keep under the piano lid.

Myra in her thirties

Travelling to the States was such a major undertaking that before she left, Myra gave a 'farewell' recital at the Queen's Hall, on 17th December 1921. John Tillett cabled Annie Friedberg to report an ovation: 'Eighteen recalls. Six encores. Extraordinary enthusiasm.'

The Times review two days later was full of praise:

> A large audience came both to enjoy her playing of Schumann and Chopin, and to wish her well in the undertaking which lies before her. She played Schumann's 'Etudes Symphoniques' and the 'Papillons,' Chopin's Funeral March Sonata, a Nocturne, and a Polonaise. The large hall suited her. Everything came out with a remarkably clear definition of its outline, notwithstanding a tendency to fast tempi. There was little of that suggestion of effort in the forte passages, particularly the climax of the finale to the 'Etudes Symphoniques,' and the first movement of the Sonata, which has sometimes been noticeable in Miss Hess's playing, and the wonderfully tight hold which she keeps on the rhythm of everything she plays had its full effect both in Schumann and in the Funeral March itself. Of the three larger works we enjoyed the 'Papillons' the most, for it gave us the full benefit of that indefinable and subtle quality called 'touch' which distinguishes the fine artist from the skilful executant.

New York, New York

Myra set sail alone on the RMS Baltic in January 1922, into a stormy Atlantic winter. The Baltic was one of the largest ships in the world, 729 feet long, designed to provide its passengers with state-of-the-art luxury, at least in first class; built in 1903, it was one of the 'big four' the White Star line constructed in the 20th century's first decade. But 'largest' is a sobering thought when you remember that the Titanic was 883 feet and today's Queen Mary II is 1,132. In short, the ship was not so big, the weather was foul and Myra was seasick.

Annie Friedberg met the frazzled pianist at the docks in New York – and now Myra had her first sight of the city that was to become her home from home. New York City's earliest skyscrapers were about the same age as Myra herself. The Flatiron Building had opened in 1902, the Chrysler Building was now in its planning stages and the Empire State was not even a twinkle in its architect's eye; its site housed the giant Waldorf-Astoria Hotel. The Twenties were not yet roaring. They were just getting started.

Myra was staying at the Hotel Wellington on Seventh Avenue. Here, as she unpacked, she watched the snowflakes continuing to fall over the busy streets and building sites of Manhattan. It was a tough winter on the US east coast: on 28th January, 28 inches of snow landed on Washington DC, crushing in the roof of the city's Knickerbocker Theatre.

As a dress rehearsal, Myra gave an 'intimate recital' at Steinway Hall on 12th January, which introduced her to an invited audience of press and promoters. Five days later she made her official New York debut at the Aeolian Hall. It was at 3pm and she would have to vacate the hall at pace afterwards, as that evening the Flonzalay Quartet and Osip Gabrilowitsch were performing. Over at Carnegie Hall they had competition from a recital by Kreisler.

Upstairs in the 42nd Street home of the Aeolian Company, the hall seated 1,100. It was very different from the company's compact London venue: a 'shoebox' with a 5,079-pipe organ and a generous stage with proscenium arch, its grandeur was a notch up even on the Queen's Hall. At its 1912 opening *The New York Times* described its 'chastened Louis XVI' style; the foyer boasted a 'double-flair marble staircase resembling somewhat the famous horseshoe stairs at Fontainebleau'. It was the kind of venue that induces a performer to rise to its challenges.

That icy Tuesday afternoon, Myra did so, performing Schumann's *Papillons*, four Scarlatti sonatas, a Bach Prelude and Fugue, Chopin's A flat major Polonaise and some Debussy preludes. As programmes went, it was intimate rather than ostentatious. And in the auditorium sat the grand total of 66 people.

It was not the quantity of audience that counted. It was the reviews. They could make or break an artist. Myra was made. The *New York Tribune* stated:

> She is every inch an artist; every fibre in her comely and well poised body is musical. Her knowledge, instincts, technical skill are of the highest order. She possesses not only fancy but the higher gift which is imagination. Her expositions are not merely intellectual, they are poetical also. The book of music is open to her… in Schumann's Papillons we heard the poet-musician singing with exquisite voice and comforting symmetry of phrase – perfect beauty of thought paired with perfect beauty of expression.

The New York World's Deems Taylor wrote:

> After Myra Hess had finished the printed programme … we caught

> five licenced music critics standing in the rear of the Aeolian Hall waiting to hear her first encore. … we have an idea they had forgotten to be critics and wanted to hear some more music … she plays like a musician and artist; and that means … that her technical equipment is perfect enough to be taken for granted … anything she does has intelligence, sincerity and understanding behind it. And so it is better than correct, it is beautiful.

Richard Aldrich in *The New York Times* was also enthusiastic:

> There was a constant invitation to delight in the music itself, to listen to it, to find in it the sole and sufficient purpose and end of the evening … There are not many such evenings to be passed at Aeolian … and it might be argued that there are not many artistic achievements of the same sort, so complete, so finished in their way.

Anita Gunn later remembered: 'Annie was up at cockcrow to see the reviews, and when, in person, she woke Myra from a sound sleep some hours later, she was heavily veiled to hide the fact that she had been crying with sheer excitement.'[7]

New Works, Old Tastes

Annie hurried to arrange a second Aeolian Hall recital on the afternoon of 6th February; this time Myra brought a heavyweight programme, giving New York a taste of everything she could do. She began with Mozart's Sonata in G major, then went on to the Chopin B flat minor Sonata, the Brahms Waltzes, O'Donnell's *Before the Dawn*, Bax's *The Maiden with the Daffodil* and *Gopak*, and Ravel's *Pavane pour une Infante défunte* and 'Alborada del Gracioso' from *Miroirs*, a dazzling virtuoso tour-de-force written in 1905, involving double glissandi, stamping flamenco rhythms and guitar-like effects of rapid-fire repeated notes.

This was probably the New York premiere of the Bax pieces. Even the Ravel was a rarity; his *Jeux d'eau* was becoming a popular recital item in the Big Apple, but 'Alborada' less so. Bax's orchestral works *In the Faery Hills* and *The Garden of Fand* had both had New York premieres at Carnegie Hall in 1921, so he was not unknown. But Myra's role as pioneer went unremarked. *The Herald*'s review commented only upon her 'smooth and musical' Mozart and 'cool and well poised' Chopin, referring to the rest as 'some shorter pieces'.

In the interview for *The Musical Courier*, Myra is quoted as if refuting her taste for bravura Ravel and slippery Bax. Even Brahms seems to risk excessive modernity; he had died barely 30 years earlier:

> Even in small cities out West where, I suppose, you would expect people to be less cultured than in the East where the civilization is older, there was the same love for the classics. And, more impressive still, there is an evident desire everywhere to know about new things. The people here want to understand.
>
> My programmes never include the ultra modern – or futuristic music. I am afraid I do not know what 'modern music' means – if it means anything. I just play the classics, of course including Brahms.

'Ultra modern' in 1922 tended to mean Schoenberg, who over a decade earlier had launched his radical expressionism in works such as *Erwartung* and *Pierrot Lunaire*, and Stravinsky, who in 1913 had unleashed the violent rhythms and polytonality of *Le sacre du printemps* into an unsuspecting Paris theatre. Beside them, Ravel and Bax, despite heightened personal languages, seemed comparatively safe.

'Does Not Play Like a Man'

Travelling by train, Myra visited Philadelphia (playing the Schumann Concerto), Toronto, Kingston, Cambridge (the Mozart D minor Concerto with the Boston Symphony Orchestra under Pierre Monteux), Galveston, San Francisco, Winnipeg and Minneapolis (Rachmaninoff's Piano Concerto No. 2) before returning to New York. Word spread and audiences flocked in.

By 5th March the New York Philharmonic had added her name to a list of artists appearing in its forthcoming performances. On 26th March she made her Carnegie Hall debut, playing the Schumann with Mengelberg (who on 9th February had conducted the US premiere of Ravel's *La Valse* there). 'I was nearly overwhelmed,' Myra told John Tillett, 'with Carnegie Hall packed, no standing room left even.'[8]

Two weekends later, on 9th April, they performed the Grieg Piano Concerto at the Metropolitan Opera House. The critical reception this time was more measured, though the *Tribune*'s reviewer noted that her first US season had 'made a very favorable impression'. He found her performance less suited to the size of the hall: 'The Metropolitan auditorium was not proportioned to her tonal powers. Therefore at times her interpretation sounded weak, whereas it was excellent both in conception and execution...'

Myra had anticipated this, writing to John Tillett that the theatre was 'too large for a piano' and that even the orchestra did not come over effectively when on stage as opposed to the orchestra pit. She was well placed to know, for when she was not playing she was often in the audience. 'This has been an exciting week,' she wrote to Tillett, 'have heard Rachmaninoff play his 2 concertos and have heard Harold Bauer for the first time since about 1913! Rachmaninoff is terrific. I also heard Lhévinne a little while ago. The "techniques" over here are enough to make you give up playing!'[9]

The pianists might have represented a new world, but the critics had the same old expectations. *The Herald* review ran: 'Miss Hess is one woman who does not play like a man. It is not essential to the health of art that every woman should play like a man ... Men should wish to hear the song of the eternal feminine and it certainly was heard in the playing of Miss Hess.'

In short, Myra was continually judged not as a pianist, but as a *female* pianist. Reviewers made complimentary comments about her 'comely' figure and good looks under flattering lights, but ignored the fact that 'femininity' was irrelevant to the music she played, or that there was such a thing as nuance. Do all men crash and thump at the piano? Do all women aim for excessive power by trying to emulate the men? The assumptions are meaningless in the face of the ultra-sensitive, poetic interpretations of Alfred Cortot, or the charismatic glitter of Irene Scharrer. Yet Myra continued to face this type of clumsy, brickbat preconception throughout her career.

Myra was making new friends rapidly in the US, however, and the Steinway family were paramount among them, in particular Frederick Steinway, third president of the US branch of the German-American piano firm, and his wife, Julia. Steinway's was a powerhouse in the American music business, and a history of the firm noted that 'not only did they provide [Myra] with superb instruments ... but she enjoyed a wide range of related services that smoothed the path of her progress from one city to another'[10]. Myra was especially close to Julia, whose social flair and star-studded dinner parties were renowned throughout New York's musical world.

For the moment, she depended on local Steinway pianos, rather than travelling with one; but she did have the services of a tuner, William

Hupfer, who toured with her until 1927. He was fond of card games and it could have been around now that Myra began to take to them herself. More crucially, he had a note of the better pianos' serial numbers and would repair and tune them according to Myra's requirements. Many were in a dubious state after being used in cinemas and music halls, or damaged during transportation. But by 1933 Myra, like Paderewski, had been given exclusive use of two pianos for her tours.

'I really am feeling enormously encouraged,' Myra told Tillett. 'I didn't for a moment anticipate having such a success, and shall soon have to buy some new hats!!!' She added, 'I have just about cleared expenses, but things are already shaping for next season when I shall hope to start a banking account!!!'[11]

When Myra left the Hotel Wellington on 15th April after several hectic months, she was looking forward to a well-earned rest on a slow boat home. Now she knew that she would be back in the US for new year, 1923. Nevertheless, in San Francisco, 6,000 miles from Hampstead, she had felt so alone that she had already begun to think about, in future, bringing a travelling companion.

Purring Over Pianos

In her second US tour, Myra found consolidation, acclaim and some unforgettable musical encounters. This time she travelled from Liverpool on the SS Adriatic, where her cabin had its own bathroom. In New York, instead of the Wellington, she stayed at the Hotel Laurelton on West 55th Street, two blocks from Carnegie Hall and of similar vintage. At a mere 12 storeys, it was smaller and homelier than some others, but convenient, quiet and well kept. From then on it would always be her base in the city.

The first thing she did was change her travel plans. The voyage had been so stormy that she could not face the idea of another so soon; she had been due home in the spring, then was back for American engagements in September. She put off the first return until June, and told John Tillett at once, since it would mean cancellations in Britain. Compensations seemed plentiful in the Big Apple: 'I have just been down [to Steinway's] to choose a piano for Friday,' she wrote. 'What instruments! I could have "purred" like a cat!'[12]

Engagements were soon flooding in for the following season: Chicago, Cleveland, Minneapolis. The music director of NBC, Walter Damrosch, called her 'darling', which she hoped would produce a re-engagement.

Annie mooted the idea of a round-the-world tour. More immediately, ups and downs followed in rapid succession. She wrote to Tillett:

> Personally, I don't think I was in good form until nearly the end [of the first recital] ... but everybody seemed to think I had 'grown' since last year (I am dieting strictly!!!).
>
> I played 6 encores and the critics weren't too bored, so altogether it was considered a success. I played far better at the Philharmonic last week ...
>
> I have just done 6 concerts in 8 days with some awful cross-country journeys. I am now in the train for 2 days and 3 nights. I have succeeded in making them turn the heating off, but it is appallingly stuffy and I wish the men wouldn't snore and spit. Am sorry to be so graphic! I must say that Englishmen are more pleasant to travel with ...[13]

The trip became more bearable when a friend named Mrs Newhouse joined Myra; she had come to America partly to keep Myra company, but also to explore employment prospects in California and British Columbia for her husband, an engineer in Egypt. With her, Myra planned an actual holiday in the west.

Beyond one unfortunate conductor in New York, to whom she had to teach the Beethoven Fourth Piano Concerto 'bar by bar'[14], inspiring musical encounters came thick and fast. She met and heard 'my beloved [Harold] Bauer' and went to a concert at the Beethoven Association that he had founded; he performed trios with Casals and the French violinist Jacques Thibaud, 'a revelation,' Myra wrote, 'of what can be done by three artists playing the same work quite differently at the same time!'[15] Bauer asked her to join him and Ernö von Dohnányi in a concerto for three pianos in the same series.

Bauer, the emigré Londoner, had started out as a violinist, only turning to the piano in his late teens. Paderewski – not his teacher, but a friend and major influence – used to tease him, saying that he should be a pianist because he had 'such beautiful hair'. Bauer had to his name, besides the Ravel 'Ondine' dedication, the US premiere of Brahms's Piano Concerto No. 1 and, in 1908, the world premiere of Debussy's *Children's Corner*. He had left England for Paris before World War I, then moved to the US; after becoming a US citizen in 1924, he went on to be head of the piano faculty at the Manhattan School of Music.

Myra clearly admired his playing, which had absorbed something of the all-embracing warm sound and grand-manner intensity that she adored in Paderewski himself; 'beloved' was not a word she bandied about for nothing. Nor was Bauer indifferent to her. Making a speech at a dinner in London, accepting the 1912 Gold Medal of the Royal Philharmonic Society, he was plagued by nerves. He wrote: 'I think the one thing that kept me from collapse was the smiling, affectionate faces of two dear young girls, Irene Scharrer and Myra Hess, who seemed a thousand miles away at the end of the long guest table.'[16] (The 'girls' were in their early twenties.)

Avoiding clashes with other artists was not easy, since a such staggering wealth of talent would be descending on New York at any one time. Myra's next Aeolian Hall concert, in March, was on the same afternoon Benno Moiseiwitsch was playing at Carnegie Hall, 'but the only alternative,' said Myra, 'was to give one the same day as Rachmaninoff!'[17]

On 14th April, she played through Rachmaninoff's Piano Concerto No. 2 with the composer accompanying her at a second piano: it was 'very thrilling,' she told Tillett, 'and he was so nice. He spoke very affectionately of you.'[18]

Rachmaninoff had settled in New York in 1918, having escaped the Russian Revolution. Previously he had forged a career as the compositional heir to Tchaikovsky, with that composer's blessing. In the west, having lost everything and made some perhaps disadvantageous choices – he turned down, more than once, the chief conductorship of the Boston Symphony Orchestra – he reinvented himself, of necessity, as a touring pianist.

Years later, Myra told Stephen Kovacevich more about her encounter with Rachmaninoff. The night before she was to play to him, she remembered that there was a traditional cut in the second movement of the concerto. 'Everybody used to do it,' Kovacevich says. 'It's minor, but it was there. She realised that she didn't know those extra two pages of music and she was worried that he would be offended. So she learned it. She spent all night practising.'

Rachmaninoff had not said much to her about her playing, but she could tell he was pleased. 'That was typical of Rachmaninoff – he did the same thing to Horowitz and only praised him a few days later,' Kovacevich relates. 'Then Myra went to hear him play [Schumann's] *Carnaval*, which is one of the greatest things he ever did. He had misread something, however, and as she knew him, she went backstage and could march up to him and say, "This is out of this world, but did you realise you've misread a chord?" He said nothing. But the next day at her hotel, she said, he sent her the biggest bouquet of flowers she had ever received.'[19]

A Berkshire September

Having postponed her return voyage, Myra was at large in New York without scheduled work, her expenses mounting up. Rather than worrying, she decided to enjoy it. 'It has made a big hole in my finances, added to the loss of the 7 concerts [in Britain],' she told Tillett, 'that is why I have decided to be consistently (?) reckless and "blow" another few hundred dollars on a holiday (but what a holiday!!!)':

> One doesn't do anything one expects to do in California! It is the most marvellous country, and I have quite decided to spend the summer of 1925 there!!?? ... We have bathed in the Pacific (d-----y cold!!), climbed 4,000 feet (party on mules and partly in snow nearly to our waists) and seen the coast from San Diego to Seattle.[20]

By the time she arrived home on 2nd June, Myra had planned further trips well into 1925. Autumn found her and Tillett juggling potential engagements – a month in Germany, more dates in Holland – but America was claiming Myra's heart.

She had a special role to fulfil there in September. The half-American Rebecca Clarke had moved to the States in 1916 and in 1919 had been runner-up in an anonymous composition competition run by the philanthropist Elizabeth Sprague Coolidge. The work in question, her Viola Sonata, astonished everyone when it turned out to have been written by a woman. People were convinced that it had to be by Ernest Bloch (who had won first prize), writing under a pseudonym – though as Rebecca noted wryly, it was a 'funny idea' that 'when he writes his very much lesser works he should take a pseudonym of a girl!'.[21]

Coolidge, who ran the Berkshire Festival, then commissioned a new work for it from Rebecca: a Rhapsody for cello and piano. For the premiere on 29th September Rebecca persuaded Coolidge to employ her great friend, the dynamic and powerful British cellist May Mukle, with Myra as the pianist.

The Rhapsody was Rebecca's most substantial work yet, in four movements and lasting 25 minutes. Its polytonal harmonies create a rapt yet often oppressive atmosphere, while the technical writing is unfettered since Rebecca knew that her performers could meet any challenge she threw at them. The festival kept Myra busy in her own right: the day before the Rhapsody premiere, she performed the Brahms F minor Viola Sonata with Lionel Tertis. Myra relished her time there, enjoying the company – not least, Harold Bauer, who played and told stories over dinner in fine style. Myra told Tillett: 'The country is glorious and it was quite a new experience to drive through the woods to the concert hall!'[22]

Unfortunately, the public and critics were baffled by the Rhapsody. One review grumbled that it was too gloomy. Perhaps he expected womanly charm rather than something so serious from a female composer; when Rebecca wrote two shorter, simpler pieces for violin and piano, they were praised for their 'real feminine personality'. Myra tried to bolster the disappointed composer, who came to stay with her in New York after the premiere, and to help her plan her next moves.[23]

By 12th October she was writing to her agent from Boston, where she and Tertis were again performing together. 'Tertis made a great impression and he has been tremendously enjoyable to work with, and altogether has only shown his most charming side,' Myra reported. 'I always hear he can be otherwise, but have never seen it.'[24] The pair were becoming frequent chamber music partners, a working relationship that proved long-lasting. As for her solo work, less than two weeks later she told Tillett that the Steinways were going to finance a New York recital for her on 17th November and that she would 'probably cancel my tour in England! !!!'[25]

Back in London, *The Morning Post*'s rapturous write-up of her January recital at Wigmore Hall suggests that Myra's American successes were increasing her value at home:

> Piano playing more finely balanced, filled with a diviner fire, a more exquisite grace, we have never heard. It is, indeed, difficult to sit down with her interpretation of Bax's magniloquent Sonata in F sharp minor still ringing in one's ears and write with the detachment an appreciation of such art demands. … the superlatives heaped upon her by the musical critics in America are not less than justified. We have watched Miss Myra Hess's artistic growth for many years, and London can be proud of the fact that it has produced one of the world's great pianists.

Her next triumph was Berlin. The *Courier Musical,* quoting an American critic who was in Berlin at the time, declared that 'in years no such success had been achieved by a new-comer', and that Berlin was 'at the feet of Miss Hess from henceforth. To have captured two continents in a year is indeed a matter to be proud of for a young English pianist!'

The boost to her career was clear by the time the Proms of 1924 arrived. *The Musical Times*'s review of her performances of the Schumann Concerto and Bach's Brandenburg Concerto No. 5 declared:

> ...last Tuesday ... (September 16) brought enough people to pack the hall ... partly because Miss Myra Hess was playing. The artist still 'draws' more than the work. But if that is to be deplored as a rule, admiration of Miss Hess, carried to any length this side of idolatry, is not only excusable but commendable.

Despite all, Myra was still up against the same overtly misogynistic prejudices Rebecca had faced in the US. A September concert at the Queen's Hall produced a sour and patronising response in *The Scotsman*:

> ...a huge audience, mainly composed of her own sex, was charmed with her playing. Miss Hess is essentially a woman's pianist, for a pearly touch, smooth scales and crisp little rhythms have always been women's delight, and Miss Hess with her neat technique can accomplish all this with consummate ease.[26]

The critic continued by finding that Beethoven's 'great Apassionata [sic] Sonata' was 'beyond her interpretive powers' (besides those of his own spelling) and that the best of the afternoon was music by De Falla and Granados, 'played with smoothness, neatness and delicacy'. More reviews of that type existed, even for a pianist who had just conquered two continents.

That same year in New York had begun with a landmark event of a very different kind: a new work that could not have been a greater contrast from Rebecca's dark, haunted Rhapsody, although it shared its title. On 12th February George Gershwin stepped out onto the stage of the Aeolian Hall to give the world premiere of his *Rhapsody in Blue*.

1 MH to John Tillett, 2 April 1922, see C. Fifield, *Ibbs and Tillett*, p544
2 Muriel Lhamé letter in *The Clock Tower*, No. 61, February 2021, The Friends of Medway Archives
3 Mackail, op. cit., p11
4 H. Ferguson, 'The National Gallery Concerts and After' in *Myra Hess by her Friends*, p101
5 C. Saerchinger, interview with MH in *The Musical Courier*, 20 April 1922
6 H. Bauer, *Harold Bauer: His Book*, p167
7 A. Gunn, 'American Pilgrimage' in *Myra Hess by her Friends*, p27
8 MH letter to JT, see Fifield, op. cit., p544
9 Ibid., p544
10 T. E. Steinway, *People and Pianos*, p86
11 MH letter to JT, 2 April 1922, see Fifield, op. cit., p544
12 MH letter to JT, 3 Jan 1923, Ibid., p546
13 MH letter to JT, 18 Jan 1923, Ibid., p546
14 A. Goldberg, *Los Angeles Times*
15 MH letter to JT, 18 Jan 1923, see Fifield, op. cit., p546
16 H. Bauer, op. cit., p225
17 MH letter to JT, 19 Feb 1923, op. cit., p547
18 MH letter to JT, 15 Apr 1923, Ibid., p550
19 Author interview with Stephen Kovacevich
20 MH letter to JT, 28 Mar 1923, see Fifield, op. cit., p549
21 R. Sherman interview with Rebecca Clarke, *A Rebecca Clarke Reader*, p171
22 MH letter to JT, 12 Oct 1923, see Fifield, op. cit., p552
23 J. York, 'Into the Light', *The Strad*, December 2019
24 MH letter to JT, 12 Oct 1923, see Fifield, op. cit., p552
25 MH letter to JT, postmark 29 Oct 1923, Ibid., p552
26 *The Scotsman*, 22 September 1924

'With the fire of life impassioned'
(1923–1933)

Myra off duty

The Duo-Art Recordings

Myra now found herself in the forefront of a generation ready to consign the Great War to the past: creative, visionary people who could grasp the reins of rapidly changing technologies all around. The first of these involved recording piano rolls.

The *Evening Public Ledger* in Philadelphia (23rd Jan 1922), where she played the Schumann concerto, carried a starry advert: 'Myra Hess, the celebrated English pianist, the soloist last Friday and Saturday with the Philadelphia Orchestra, makes records exclusively for the Duo-Art Reproducing Piano Company. Through this marvelous musical instrument you may hear Myra Hess in your home at any time.'

The Aeolian Company had started to make 'reproducing pianos' in 1914, after Welte-Mignon had been producing similar instruments for about nine years. Hole-punched rolls, fitted inside a piano powered by suction pumps, could create the illusion that keys were being controlled by the artist in question.

A real-time perforator would produce an original roll as the pianist played, punching around 3,600 rows per minute; the company claimed that this gave an accuracy on the first roll of 1/60th of a second. The producers added the performer's dynamics by hand, aided by the artists; this enabled Percy Grainger to say that the Duo-Art roll represented him not as he played, but as he would like to have played.[1] Over the years, Busoni, Paderewski, Josef Hofmann, Teresa Carreño and many more all recorded for the device.

Bauer was one of the most prolific, notching up around 200. Yet he often found the result discouraging because, he wrote, 'the dynamics, set to produce certain effects on the piano which was being used for such editorial purposes, varied when the record was played on another piano.'[2] He felt that tiny differences in tone quality and in the action's resistance made these problems insurmountable.

Myra's recordings for Duo-Art through the 1920s, in New York and London, ranged from Busoni's Bach Chorale Preludes transcriptions and Beethoven's Sonata Op. 79 to several Debussy preludes, her habitual Szymanowski etude and Rachmaninoff's Prelude in C sharp minor. Whatever the drawbacks, they were well received: a review in *The Musical Times* of January 1926 welcomed her Brahms C major Intermezzo, Op. 119 No. 3, as 'a precious little gem, giving one a special thrill of pleasure at the arpeggiated wafts of tone towards the end'.

Some audio recordings from them survive, including a Toccata by Maria Theresia von Paradis and Debussy's 'La cathédrale engloutie' (both listed in the 1924 catalogue). One cannot be sure how accurately they represent her, but even if lacking in subtle detail, they seem to capture some of her judicious balance of voicing and no-nonsense expressiveness. In 1926 she also recorded some duets with Bauer – with whom she had performed a Bach Concerto for Two Keyboards in New York at the start of the previous year ('very thrilling,' she told John Tillett[3]).

With a reproducing piano, Myra presented an unusual concert in December 1924. *The Observer* reported:

> Myra Hess, at the Aeolian Hall, has played a two-piano duet with her own ghost. Having recorded the solo part of the Grieg Concerto for Duo-Art Pianola, and arranged the orchestral parts for a second

> piano, she gave us the two together, the one played mechanically, the other in person ... Subtlety of nuance came just as finely from one instrument as from another, except that the range from pp to ff in the pianola treatment seemed to be rather smaller, and there was, perhaps necessarily, a trifle of dullness in the tone (the hand-played instrument was, however, of the better quality ...). ... and, of course, the remarkable Hessian variety of 'colour' was not all there. ... frankly, the playing of that pianola was a great deal better than the normal hand-playing of a good many pianists of renown....[4]

The Grieg rolls were presented with live orchestra around the country from Dundee to Bournemouth, under conductors including Sargent Wood, Cameron and Harty; they were even sent – and played in concert – as far afield as New Zealand. In London, in September 1926 Myra accompanied herself at a second piano at a celebratory dinner at the Prince's Galleries for the launching of the AudioGraphic project. Finally, the Grieg first movement was played three times a day for a week in autumn 1928 at the Plaza Theatre with what must have been a long-suffering orchestra, conducted by Frank E. Tours.

It was a startling manifestation of a system that enjoyed a brief but fascinating bloom.

Devilish Developments

On 18th October 1922, a group of wireless manufacturers in London formed an entity that they named the British Broadcasting Corporation. From Guglielmo Marconi's studio, 2LO, behind the Strand on Savoy Hill, it began daily broadcasts to the nation on 14th November. Music, drama and lectures ran side by side in the programming; and soon musicians could perform live on air from the premises, donning full evening dress for the occasion.

The music industry at first greeted this development with suspicion, which worsened when the BBC started to relay performances direct from concert halls. A broadcast from the Central Hall, Westminster, given by the BBC's own Augmented Wireless Orchestra, sparked a horrified response. William Boosey, head of Chappell's, which ran the Proms, refused to allow the necessary cabling to be laid at the Queen's Hall. Beecham, too, feared this 'devilish' invention would destroy the market for live performances. 'In ten years' time, the concert halls will be deserted,' he predicted. Quite the opposite happened: the wide availability of music in the home, plus the increased familiarity of musicians' names from the ubiquitous *Radio Times*, instead provided excellent free publicity.

Myra did not broadcast until 1927; but that year on 22nd July at 10.30pm, she could be heard in a half hour of short pieces. The *Radio Times* carried a striking photograph of her, with her strong, level brows, direct gaze and serious demeanour: the face of a woman whose life is dominated by devotion to her work. Her programme was a Scarlatti Sonata in C, the Gigue from Bach's G major French Suite, six of the Brahms Waltzes, the Intermezzo from Schumann's *Faschingsschwank aus Wien*, the ballet music from Schubert's *Rosamunde* (transcribed by Ganz), the first movement of the Chopin B flat minor Sonata and her own *Jesu, Joy* arrangement – to which was appended 'By request'.

Her American career, in the meantime, was soaring. In 1925 she was introduced after a concert to the conductor Wilhelm Furtwängler, who at once talked about having her play with him in Berlin, and a few weeks later Pablo Casals, who was similarly friendly and asked her to contact him if she was coming to Spain. Her Boston recital proved so popular that people were turned away. Rumour spread, much to her amusement, that she was about to go into the movies. By 12th March 1926 she was writing to John Tillett: 'Everybody thinks I play about 1,000,000 times better than I do. Gawd 'elp and bless 'em!'

Jesu, Joy Takes Wing

Myra's transcription of the Bach cantata movement, drafted by night in a moment of enchanted enthusiasm, was growing in popularity. The New York critic Richard Aldrich had encouraged her to begin performing it in public, and he was not wrong. *The Musical Times* spotted it in February 1926, reviewing a Glasgow concert by Myra, Jelly and Elisabeth Schumann; Myra's encore of *Jesu, Joy* was 'sufficient in itself to make of the concert an enduring memory'.

The flowing triplets and luminous chorale offered a contrast from the popular transcriptions that many Golden Age pianists had produced. Those were often designed to display virtuosity while reimagining pieces the audience would already know and love. Rachmaninoff tackled items including the Scherzo from Mendelssohn's *A Midsummer Night's Dream* and some of his own songs; Busoni scored enduring success with his version of the Bach D minor Chaconne; Leopold Godowsky produced a huge volume of pieces based on Chopin's études, which one might have thought were quite difficult enough already; and Cortot made solo piano arrangements of everything from Bach's Toccata and Fugue in D minor to Franck's Violin Sonata. Matthay had always encouraged his students to follow suit.

Myra's *Jesu, Joy* is much more difficult to play than its austere beauty suggests. The score is full of detail. She indicates different voices by the placement or direction of note stems, or by writing smaller notes for quieter lines. She instructs that the first time the chorale sounds, the tenor should sing out, and the second time the soprano. The phrase marks are placed subtly; nothing is foursquare. Moreover, the attention to voicing and the layering of the texture is fascinatingly consistent with how Myra approached most of the music she performed, to judge from her recordings.

Jesu, Joy was becoming so popular in Myra's concerts that Hubert Foss, head of the music department at Oxford University Press, persuaded her to let the company publish it. The sheet music was issued in 1926 and soon other performers were taking it up. Copies walked off the shelves and Myra received healthy royalties: a sixth of the published price per copy in the British Empire, one eighth beyond, with an advance of ten guineas.

This turned out to be the beginning of quite an adventure. OUP followed it up with arrangements for piano duet and for two pianos, as well as other Bach transcriptions that Myra made – *Sleepers, Wake* and the Adagio from the Toccata in C major for organ. Yet there was something extra in *Jesu, Joy*: a private, ineffable beauty and a sense of devotion that seems, with hindsight, to embody a sliver of Myra's soul in a way that the others, despite their beauty and expertise, never matched. Five decades later, the printers were still running off copies in batches of 20,000.

If Myra's recordings of it were famous, the Romanian pianist Dinu Lipatti's became perhaps even more so. In 1935, aged 18 and studying in Paris, he made his recital debut; his teacher, Paul Dukas, had died three days earlier, and in tribute, Lipatti opened with *Jesu, Joy*. Soon his sensitive, sparkling and impassioned playing captured a devoted public; he was hailed as Romania's greatest musician since George Enescu. At the height of his powers, Lipatti was struck down by leukaemia. Aged 33, desperately ill, he gave his last performance, culminating in Chopin's 14 Waltzes; but after No. 13 he lacked the strength for the last one. Instead, he played three Bach encores, with *Jesu, Joy*, the only one to survive in the recording that was later issued of the event.[5] Thus he seemed to close his career with the same work that had begun it. He died a few months later.

In 1932, OUP published a book of transcriptions entitled *A Bach Book for Harriet Cohen*. Harriet asked 12 composers each to contribute one, though George Bernard Shaw, a friend of Cohen's, termed the publication 'Five-finger Exercises for Harriet by Infatuated Celebrities'[6]. They included, among others, Vaughan Williams, Granville Bantock, William Walton, Frank Bridge and, of course, Bax. Most chose chorale settings from the cantatas (except for Eugene Goossens, who transcribed the Andante from the Brandenburg Concerto No. 2). Perhaps Harriet was hoping in some way to out-Myra Myra with this book. Yet none of the transcriptions ever attracted the popularity of *Jesu, Joy*.

Myra's views on Harriet's *Bach Book* have not emerged. But the story goes that once, calling on Myra in Carlton Hill, Harriet, unlike other visitors, was somehow not warned about the awkward flight of stairs down into the studio and came a cropper on the way in.[7]

There came, too, a strange decision from Harold Bauer to make his own transcription of *Jesu, Joy*. He recorded it in 1928 and Schirmer published it in the US in 1932. More technically complex than Myra's, it used double notes for the right-hand triplets, a chunkier bass with ample split chords, more inner voices and some changes in register.

This move, by someone she liked, admired and worked with, seems to have been fairly upsetting for Myra. Together they had recorded some duets for Duo-Art in 1926 – Burgmein's *The Story of Pierrot and Pierette* and Pierné's *The March of the Little Toy Soldiers* – and planned concerts together in the Netherlands in the mid 1920s, though that appears to have foundered after a misunderstanding over which agent was to organise the events. Now a letter in OUP's files regarding the issue of copyright in Bridges' words as used in Bauer's title suggested that Myra and Bauer were 'intimate friends' [sic] and that his transcription had been made with her knowledge.[8]

Whatever Myra thought, OUP was not happy. By February 1933 they were trying to prevent Bauer's version from being sold in Britain. Schirmer's Carl Engel protested that the issue was slight; surely Bauer would not wish to do anything to damage Myra, his friend and colleague, while she might concede that he had never intended to injure her.[9] Foss reckoned that the issue was not slight, and that injury would have occurred whether Bauer had intended it or not.[10] Myra rather confirmed a fallout when she wrote from New York to John Tillett several years later, saying that Bauer could not attend her concert, but had 'actually sent' her a nice telegram: 'Perhaps the stupid hatchet will be buried,' she remarked. 'There is enough misery in the world without quarrelling with one's friends???'[11]

In the end, Bauer's version was withdrawn from sale in the UK. In his 1948 autobiography he writes not one word about it.

Bauer was not the only problem. Myra had made the piece so well known that soon a plethora of other musicians wanted to transcribe and publish their own versions, besides recording hers. On Irene Scharrer's record, credit to Myra was omitted and OUP protested. By February 1934 the company was having to make it glaringly obvious to various American publishers that they regarded any other transcriptions as an attempt to 'cash in'[12] on Myra's success.

Myra herself protested about a recording in which the tenor John McCormack sang the chorale line over her transcription. She told OUP on 12th July 1941 that she was 'shocked by what I consider a most inappropriate representation of this chorale'; her arrangement was intended as a piano solo, not as an accompaniment. She also disliked Eugene Ormandy's orchestral version, objected to 'the inartistic record by the Philadelphia Orchestra' and asked OUP not to allow further exploitation of the arrangement without her written consent.[13]

The greatest headache was the title. There is no copyright in titles, but there is in poetry; and the line 'Jesu, Joy of Man's Desiring' is not a direct translation of the original German, but the first line of the poem by Bridges, the poet laureate. He had made a present of it to Hugh Allen for use in the cantata; Allen then gave the copyright to the Church Music Society to manage.[14]

The line's ambiguous status caused innumerable misunderstandings. People who considered they had carte blanche to use the title had to be informed (mostly by OUP) that they were in breach of copyright – and this continued until the work of Bridges, who died in 1930, reached the public domain.

Meanwhile, OUP was listing in a brochure its own publications of the piece: nine versions for combinations of voices or choirs, several more with orchestral accompaniment, four instrumental arrangements, one purely orchestral version and six for keyboard, including a solo by Leonard Borwick, one by Mark Hambourg for one piano, three hands, an arrangement for organ by Harvey Grace, and Myra's three – solo, two pianos and duet, though the duet version was actually prepared by someone else, based on Myra's transcription.

Oddly, it appears that at first no objections were raised to Bridges' line being used as Myra's title. It was not until 1941 that H.C. Colles of the Church Music Society wrote to Foss, explaining that their committee had discussed the issue at a recent meeting. One member had wished to proceed against Myra for copyright infringement. Colles had opposed this: he felt it would be 'indecent' for a Church society to make a claim against a secular musician, who moreover was Jewish. He could imagine the situation leading to adverse publicity in some 'anti-Christian' newspaper.[15] The matter was quietly dropped.

Quite how Myra had got away with it in the first place is far from clear. But she loved to tell the story of the off-duty soldier during World War II who was whistling the piece on a train. Asked by a journalist if he was interested in Bach, the youth responded: 'That's not Bach. That's Myra Hess.'[16]

Something Rich and Strange

Besides continuing to champion Bax, for whatever reason, Myra was finding other new music to explore. She gave the world premiere of the Piano Sonata by Frank Bridge at the Wigmore Hall on 15th October 1925. It was dedicated to the memory of Ernest Bristow Farrer, a young composer who had been killed in the last year of the War; the music seems angry, grim and grief-stricken. *The Telegraph* noted the composer's rising reputation: 'As conductor, as executant, and as creative artist he is held in high regard by English musicians; in each sphere his work is known by its deep sincerity ....' He nevertheless noted that the sonata, in which Bridge had dispensed with traditional tonality, inclined 'to dourness throughout'.[17]

The Times praised Myra, who had also played her Bach chorale preludes, some late Brahms intermezzi and Schumann's G minor Sonata: 'Miss Hess's playing showed extraordinary grip of the musical implications of every detail and convinced us of the rightness of much which looked inexplicable to the eye beforehand.'[18]

Myra's ability to adapt to the character of each composer and each piece she performed was well displayed in her kaleidoscopic mix of repertoire. At Wigmore Hall on 18th October 1926, she presented a huge programme including the Brahms Sonata No. 3 in F minor, Schumann's *Kinderszenen*, the Mozart Rondo in A minor, some Bach preludes and fugues – her favourite way to open a recital – and some challenging pieces from Albéniz's *Ibéria*.

A perspicacious review appeared in *The Observer* the next day, praising her 'exquisite' technique and the vitality of her interpretations:

> There is a freshness about her method of presentation that can only come from the fact that she is always accessible to new ideas … Miss Hess can, like a really fine actor, change her style with the changes in the programme. If her Mozart and Schumann were rightly differentiated, as they were, her Albéniz was perfectly modern in feeling, a totally other aspect of the art of pianoforte writing.

That December she was in Dublin, where Walter Starkie, translator, author and academic, reviewed her concert in *The Irish Statesman*, saying that she had won everyone's hearts:

> We have not heard her in Dublin for some years and in the interval she has broadened and deepened her musical style… Her rendering of the Brahms Sonata in F minor, op. 5…a great feat of technique and memory, but it made us see as in a vision the complete personality of young Brahms. …there is, in addition, a massive virility about her interpretations of Brahms that suggest the Amazon.[19]

The Columbia Recordings

Myra's first venture into the recording studio beyond the pianolas was with Jelly and the cellist Felix Salmond, who had premiered Elgar's Cello Concerto. In a set of 78rpm shellac discs, four minutes per side, they set down Schubert's Piano Trio No. 1 in B flat major; the centenary of Schubert's death provided a fine excuse, if one was needed. The recording, for Columbia, took place in New York on 28th-30th December 1927.

Jelly was experienced in the studio, having recorded short pieces with the pianist Ethel Hobday and duos with her sister Adila Fachiri; by 1930 she would be the most recorded female artist on the Vocalion label. For Myra, though, the process was a tad daunting. Besides pre-concert anxiety, she was prone to microphone shyness; and as a performer she was far from alone in feeding on the energy of an excited audience. The clinical ambience of a studio was a different prospect.

Asked in a 1962 interview if she liked recording, Myra responded: 'Hate it! I hate all machines. I hate this microphone! … I always feel it's a compromise. And I try never to judge a performance finally, even when it's broadcast – there's always between the listener and performer some mechanical device.'[20]

Not that one would guess this from the Schubert Trio recording. The three artists share an irresistible intensity, but their distinctive personalities balance one another. Myra's silky legato matches the expansive string players. Jelly's purity of sound eliminates all harshness; she had a trademark downward portamento, but it is not overdone, and her intonation has an instinctive exactitude. Salmond is an earthy, forthright counterbalance to the airy violinist, while Myra's firm yet flexible sense of rhythm and her deep-rooted bass tone cushions the textures and grounds the flow. There is plenty of room to breathe, making the impression collegial, witty and noble, without sentimentality or melodrama. One can sense them listening and responding to one another, with that magical Myraesque quality of empathy. It is almost a masterclass in chamber music playing.

Myra reflected on recording in an interview with *The Musical Leader* (a US periodical) soon afterwards, in an exacting tone:

> One finds out curious things about one's playing in making records, but from the standpoint of self-criticism it is invaluable. It is a cruel sort of mirror suddenly to have your rhythm handed you in a parcel. Wrong notes may be easily corrected: they are of superficial consideration in the making of a record. Rhythm and dynamics are the bedrock, and perfection of rhythm is of fundamental value. When the playing is exposed by taking away the personality and the impression created by the vision of a person, one discovers what is vital, interesting and legitimate. It shows how completely dynamics and rhythm are bound together in effect. You can see this very distinctly when you hear an uncorrected record....often you are fooled by an exaggerated dynamic which will make a passage sound distorted rhythmically when it really is perfectly regular.[21]

Myra's first solo recording sessions, also for Columbia in New York, quickly followed. She was in the studio on 17th January 1928 to record the Gigue from Bach's French Suite No.5 in G major and *Jesu, Joy*, then two days later the Ravel Pavane. She returned on 16th and 17th February for the Schubert 'Little' A major Sonata and ballet music from *Rosamunde*, plus three Debussy pieces: 'Poissons d'or' from *Images II* and the Preludes 'La fille aux cheveux de lin' and 'Minstrels'. In mid March she set down the Scarlatti sonatas in C major K159 and C minor, K11, Beethoven's Bagatelle in B flat, No. 11 from the Op. 119 set, and the Brahms Intermezzo in C major, Op. 119 No. 3.

The results are exquisite musical snapshots of the pianist with whom America had fallen so much in love. In 'Poissons d'or' – a piece inspired by golden fish on a Japanese lacquer cabinet – she matches refulgent tone and liquid textures with light touch, free-flowing phrasing and inner voices that rise up from the depths. She orients the listener with the sense of a focused ongoing thread through the thematic material, so the glistening textural effects never dominate or become an end in themselves.

'La fille aux cheveux de lin' is poised and rhetorical, with subtle, spacious phrasing. The Bach Gigue combines deft contrapuntal voicing with irrepressible high spirits. As for *Jesu, Joy*, its many voices mingle, through peerless control of touch and pedalling, into an ideal equilibrium of ebb and flow. That shining, halo-like tone has endured intact for almost a hundred years.

A Duo at Their Best

Jelly d'Arányi and Myra Hess enjoy some down-time at a tennis party

One night in 1922, after a private concert in a Charing Cross hotel, Ravel had asked Jelly to play him some Gypsy music from Hungary. The pianist Gaby Casadesus, who was there, recalled that the violinist played for two hours nonstop and that Ravel was 'mad with joy'.[22] He wove into a new work for her the essence of what she had shown him: the hypnotic power of the sound, the rhapsodic, improvisatory brilliance, the ecstatic dance that whirls to its close. Its title was *Tzigane*. Ravel sent Jelly the music only three and a half days before she was due to give its world premiere.[23]

The piano part is fiendish; Ravel himself demurred from tackling it and it seems that Myra too relinquished the task to a secondary 'accompanist'. But from 1927 onwards, she joined Jelly in embracing the composer's new Violin Sonata, with its bluesy slow movement; a review of a Westminster performance noted that they exchanged smiles and almost danced to the music. Discussing a forthcoming duo concert in New York, Myra asked Jelly whether they should programme the work or whether Ravel intended to give its first performance in America himself.

Jelly arrived in New York with the pianist Ethel Hobday, having sailed on the luxurious SS Berengaria on 19th November, to find herself overwhelmed with engagements. (Once someone asked Jelly why she travelled with elderly women. She riposted that it was less trouble than travelling with young men.) Szigeti asked her to replace him in a Bartók performance with the composer himself at the piano. Her debut at New York Town Hall, with Hobday, went swimmingly; and at the Beethoven Association Concert just after Christmas – where Myra was playing alongside the Harolds Bauer and Samuel – she and Myra gave the Ravel Sonata's US premiere. Szigeti and the composer did not perform it there until the following January. Then, sailing from Key West, Jelly and Myra headed for Havana.

They were bowled over by the beauty of the Cuban port. But it was a different kind of port – and other drinks – that dominated the place, which was not subject to US prohibition. The city was overrun with Americans who flocked in to indulge. Worse, Myra suffered a mosquito bite on her left eye. Jelly assured her the public would not notice, as in the concert the pianist's right profile alone would be visible.[24]

The event turned positively surreal, as Myra related in an interview:

> I was scheduled to appear at the Grand Theatro Payret, when I encountered a very new sort of experience. This theater is the only one available for concerts and shows, and when I came for rehearsal, I was confronted by a cage of lions – who had performed in a circus the night before and were awaiting removal. They were evidently anything but pleased with my music, if I was to judge by their continuous roaring, which was answered by other lions housed in the basement of the theater. I have never played for such an ungrateful audience.[25]

Nevertheless, she had her first (and maybe last) experience of enjoying jazz, a genre she regarded as 'Just a lot of noise generally … Only once did I hear a jazz orchestra which I could listen to with some interest, and that was in Havana.'

Myra and Jelly's American performances were so successful that they returned the following year with a recital in New York of Brahms, Mozart, Beethoven and Franck, and in Washington for an audience of ambassadors and retinues. They did not go back to Cuba. And in Britain, *The Daily Telegraph's* critic wrote that there had been no duo so fine since Ysaÿe and Busoni[26].

The Great Steinway Seduction

While Jelly struggled with the overheated, dry air of US hotels, which was doing her Bergonzi violin no good, Myra was travelling with a Steinway (though no longer with Hupfer; he had been reassigned to Rachmaninoff, whom he nicknamed 'Rocky'[27]).

Steinway's had been wooing her like the most passionate of pianistic bridegrooms. In 1925 they gifted her a new grand piano in London. After it arrived at Carlton Hill, Myra hurried to the company's offices at 1 George Street to hug the managers. She wrote to Frederick Steinway in New York: 'I still feel directly or indirectly that you are the Patron Saint. You can easily imagine the joy with which I am working, and I hope that you will hear very decided results when I come to New York.'[28]

Soon she began to find the company's generosity rather overwhelming, especially given her previous preference for Bechstein. Waiting for Benno to arrive to take her out to lunch on 12th February 1926, she wrote to John Tillett:

> Steinways are being so marvellously hospitable and attentive, that I am finding it very difficult to 'keep my head'. I wish I knew what to do. I think I shall try and see W. B. [probably the pianist Wilhelm Backhaus, who loved Bechsteins], if he comes over, and talk the whole thing out and risk the consequences. If you happen to know when he is coming, could you let me know, and if necessary, and possible, I would make a point of being here. It really is a problem. It is so wonderful to have superlative pianos to play on again, and if they (Steinways) will do for me in England what they do for me here, what in the ---- would you do in my place???[29]

Backhaus proved elusive, however; the hoped-for conversation probably did not take place. And the Steinways won.

The American-made Steinway pianos, manufactured in New York, have always been significantly different from their European counterparts from Hamburg. They tended to have a deeper, chunkier touch, with stronger projection in the bass, and a richer if heavier overall tone: something Myra could get her pianistic teeth into in a way she adored. Keys that present significant resistance are more controllable and can present an expert pianist with the chance to create a multifaceted range of colour. These instruments appealed to her more than those with a lighter touch designed for rapid-fire brilliance. Ironically, under the circumstances, that made them slightly more like Bechsteins, which tend to have a woody richness of sound with ample character and satisfying depth to the keyboard.

For their part, the Steinways were impressed with Myra's willingness to socialise with her audiences and patrons. Among them, she was making friends, some of whom proved loyal, lifelong supporters, virtually her American 'family'. One such was a philanthropist, Marie Brockway Pond, nicknamed 'Pondie': an older lady of vivacious character and upright bearing who became almost a mother figure to Myra until her death in 1957. She was about 60 when they first met in 1922; photos of her taken by Myra show her in a garden, clad in tweed suit, hat and tie. Among the first things Myra would do on arrival in New York was to call her or go straight round to visit, and they would often enjoy sandwich lunches together.

'Pondie' was the daughter of Colonel Nathan Patchen Pond, co-publisher of the *Democrat & Chronicle* newspaper in Rochester, New York. Back in 1883, she had co-founded a gymnasium for women and children in the town; during World War I she worked for the American Red Cross in France, chiefly in a canteen for US soldiers. When Myra first met her, she had been living for a long time as virtually a member of the well-to-do Sibley family, as companion to Margaret Harper Sibley (whose grandfather, Fletcher Harper, founded the Harper Brothers Publishing Company).[30] After Margaret's death in 1939 Pondie remained close to Margaret's daughter, Margaret Urling Iselin, whose illness and death in 1951 caused her much anguish, through which Myra supported her. She once told Myra – who was very surprised – that she would have liked to have been a biochemist.[31]

Next, there were Eugene and Rose Parsonnet, respectively a music-loving surgeon and a Matthay ex-pupil. After some years of fandom, they went backstage at one of Myra's concerts and simply scooped her up. Not only did they become her lifelong friends, but also their medic son, Victor, was her chief US page-turner after World War II. Later, as a heart surgeon he helped to develop the pacemaker and as a musical patron served as chairman of the New Jersey Symphony Orchestra.

Alongside new friends, there were old ones: Bruce and Rosalind Simonds remained central to Myra's American inner circle. She usually stayed with them when she was performing at Yale, where Bruce was dean of the School of Music, and they witnessed the slow practice by which she swore. Bruce once went out while she was beginning slow practice on the Brahms Variations on a Theme of Handel, which lasts about half an hour. When he returned two hours later, she had only just reached the closing fugue.[32]

Notes on Horowitz

In 1928 a young emigré pianist from Kyiv, represented by Annie Friedberg, made his New York debut. At Carnegie Hall he performed the Tchaikovsky Piano Concerto No. 1 with Beecham. Like Myra at her 1907 London debut with the conductor, he was not over-enamoured of the experience. Beecham, he said later, conducted from memory yet did not know the work properly; and their ideas on tempi were incompatible. But never mind; Vladimir Horowitz subsequently revolutionised everything that piano performance was, is and could be.

Blessed with transcendental virtuosity, the sonic imagination of a composer (a more lucrative performing career was his second choice) and the fire in the belly that comes from a background of insecurity and deprivation, Horowitz produced vast-concept interpretations of such works as Liszt's Sonata in B minor, Mussorgsky's *Pictures at an Exhibition* and the Rachmaninoff *Etudes-Tableaux*, to take a few examples. Many listeners considered him rivalled only by Rachmaninoff himself.

Horowitz had some tastes in common with Myra: he loved to work with Bruno Walter and also recorded with Toscanini, whose daughter, Wanda, he married. Otherwise, however, his approach could seem the polar opposite of Myra's. Sometimes he was her nemesis. Stephen Kovacevich commented: 'She adored Horowitz, but she was also disturbed by him. She couldn't help but be thunderstruck, but she had serious misgivings.'[33]

Those concerned the impact of his unbridled virtuosity on the public's tastes. After the Second World War, she returned to America to find, she wrote, that Horowitz had had a 'most pernicious influence'[34]. Those under his spell might fail to appreciate Myra's more leisurely and spiritually attentive interpretations; and certain critics, mesmerised by him, were a particular cause for concern.

The world proved big enough for both the pianists, and everything in between – but it may not have felt that way to Myra at the time.

'Popular' Music

Myra, like Bauer before her, was reluctant to raise her fees to levels that would price her out of small towns and universities. Annie feared she would become known as a low-cost artist, which might put off snazzier venues in the big metropolitan centres, and that Myra's uncompromising repertoire, to which she refused to add 'popular' pieces, would antagonise them. Both assumptions proved false.

Myra often began her recitals with three Bach Preludes and Fugues – and her audiences in Lincoln, Nebraska (in 1923), and New York (1925), to her astonishment, began shouting at encore time for 'More Bach!' Calling this 'without precedent', the critic Olin Downes wrote that Myra had already played an encore 'when someone in the hall called out "BACH". The name was taken up by many others in different parts of the auditorium until "BACH" could be heard from every part of the house'.[35]

Annie wanted 'popular' repertoire. The public wanted Bach. What about Myra? With her 40th birthday approaching, her world was expanding, but her repertoire was becoming more focused. She told the writer Roland Gelatt why she was turning away from French music: 'Their works are the shrimp cocktails of music. Every now and then I, too, like shrimp cocktails, but for a steady diet I prefer roast beef.'[36]

This high-protein music tended to be German and Viennese. There was more Bach: the Partita No. 4 in D major, with its generous, floridly ornamented Allemande. She embraced the unity of romantic sensibility and baroque inspiration in Brahms's Variations on a Theme of Handel; Mozart piano concertos were ever more crucial; and along with some select pieces of Schubert, Beethoven was at the top of her repertoire tree – as, really, he had always been.

At the start of 1929 it seemed that Myra's US life was on an unstoppable roll and the UK one not far behind. On 19th February she played a recent concerto by Ernest Bloch with Wood and his Queen's Hall Orchestra.

Then in April and May in New York she made more recordings for Columbia – mostly short pieces, but not exclusively.

Two Mendelssohn Songs Without Words – the 'Duet' and 'Spinning Song' – become, in her hands, miniature short stories: in the first, she strikes a fine balance between the two-voiced melody and its swirling background, with phrasing simultaneously logical and poetic; to the second, her sparkling touch brings microscopic clarity and gentle wit.

Palmgren's *Kehtolaulu* (Cradle Song) shows Myra infusing the melody with emotional shadings within the sound, a singerly technique that not all actual singers master. She then made a relatively rare excursion into Manuel de Falla's 'Ritual Fire Dance', a transcription from *El amor brujo* popularised by Rubinstein. She seems less comfortable with this flamenco-influenced idiom. It had given Rubinstein the chance to flex his showmanship muscles, but that quality came less easily to Myra, especially in an audience-free studio amid dreaded machines.

She was, however, in her element with Schubert's 'little' A major Sonata, D664. Throughout, she wears lightly her intelligent articulation of structure and line. Her shining legato both sings and speaks, the sound sustaining implausibly yet definitely during a very leisurely account of the second movement. The impression is less that Myra is constrained by the studio, more that it sometimes gives her the chance to slide into a world of her own.

On 11th June, she and Harold Samuel gave a duo recital at Wigmore Hall, making a powerful impression with the hefty collective tone of two grand pianos in the Bach Concerto in C minor arranged by Bauer, Samuel's own transcriptions of Bach chorale preludes, Mozart's Air and Variations in G, Schubert's F minor Fantasie and the Brahms Haydn Variations. *The Sunday Times* reported that they possessed 'four hands whose cunning it would be difficult to match in all England'.[37]

Myra was back there a couple of weeks later with Jelly, performing Mozart, Brahms, Schubert's Duo in A and Beethoven's Sonata in G Op. 96. And on 4th November the pair had another Wigmore concert – a farewell before they departed for the States – which included Bach, Beethoven, Mozart and the Schumann Sonata No. 1 in A minor. *The Morning Post*'s critic admitted 'I do not think I have ever heard it better, and perhaps never so well played'[38], while *The Daily Telegraph* termed it 'a masterpiece of interpretation, with never a doubtful touch… we were left at its close with the feeling that we had been listening to the authentic voice of a composer who is often played but seldom understood. This is high praise, but Myra Hess and Jelly d'Arányi deserve it. Not that they are not human and feminine and liable to err…'[39]

But while such recognition was bolstering Myra's confidence, a personal blow was about to hit her hard.

The Death of Lizzie Hess

In the summer of 1929, Myra wrote to Jelly from Cowden Hall in East Sussex, where she was at a house party and playing tennis.

Myra with her mother, Lizzie Hess

> I have been very worried, all the summer, about Mother. She has either been feeling perfectly well, or quite ill, and even she began to be alarmed. Now, poor darling, she is in the hands of the dentist…… and I hope that is the root of all the trouble… The Doctors can't find anything else, and apparently the dentist thinks her teeth could easily have been the cause of her feeling so ill. She is so marvellously plucky. The dentist is amazed at her spirit….. She is staying in London, with my sister.[40]

Lizzie's teeth were not the cause. That winter, she was diagnosed with incurable liver cancer. Dr Yarrow Eccles told Myra that she had only around six months left to live. Myra cancelled her American tour, citing 'personal reasons', and moved Lizzie into 8 Carlton Hill, where she cared for her with the help of her friends.

Of the four Hess siblings, Myra had the strangest home and the busiest schedule; but perhaps she also felt guilty at having distanced herself so much from family life. Her two brothers were further away geographically: John was an accountant in Birmingham; Herbert, who had married Celia Barder in 1916 and had two sons, Peter and John, lived in Weston-super-Mare; he, the other musical Hess, played the piano for silent cinema and also founded and conducted the Girls' Regency Choir. Their sister Irene, her stockbroker husband Bernard Davis and their three almost grown-up children had until then offered Lizzie a more conventional environment that was also a good deal plusher.

Saz Gunn often came over from Abbey Road to help with her care; Lizzie remarked on what an excellent companion she was[41]. Jelly (whose own mother had died of cancer in 1923) sent Lizzie a beautiful rambler rose in a pot, which Myra adorned for her with little toy dogs and cats before planting it in the garden[42]. Rebecca took Myra out for long and necessary walks on Hampstead Heath. Otherwise, Myra tried to entertain her mother with funny stories, flowers, card games and ceremonious teatimes, and to keep her comfortable with enough morphine to prevent her suffering pain. When she was away giving concerts, a night nurse would be on duty. Neither mother or daughter ever talked about death, an evasion that the Compton-Burnetts regarded as enervating[43]; but probably Myra was trying to conceal her own desolate emotions to avoid making Lizzie feel still worse.

Lizzie died on 15th July 1930, aged 67. She had told Ruth that the days in Carlton Hill, despite her illness, were the happiest of her life. She had seen at last that her youngest daughter loved her to the point that she was willing to sacrifice her career to care for her. Myra wrote to Jelly on 23rd July: 'The end was more mercifully simple & peaceful than I ever dared to hope for.'[44]

1 Pianola Institute website, https://www.pianola.org/reproducing/reproducing.cfm
2 Bauer, op. cit., p176
3 MH to JT, 6 Jan 1925, see Fifield op. cit., p554
4 *The Observer*, 9 December 1924
5 M. Ainley, https://ijm.education/piano/dinu-lipatti-the-myth-and-the-musician/
6 H. Cohen, *A Bundle of Time*,183-184.
7 NH interview with HF
8 C. Engel to H. Foss, 7 September 1932, OUP Archive
9 C Engel to H. Foss, 4 February 1933, OUP Archive
10 H Foss margin notes to the above
11 MH to JT, undated [1936-7], see Fifield op. cit., p559
12 Memo, 9 Feb 1934, OUP Archive
13 MH to H. Foss, 12 July 1941, OUP Archive
14 Note by H. Foss responding to letter of 23 Jan 1934 from T.C, Jarrett, OUP Archive
15 H.C. Colles to H. Foss, 24 April 1941, OUP Archive
16 McKenna, op. cit., p92
17 *The Daily Telegraph*, 16 October 1925
18 *The Times*, 16 October 1925
19 *The Irish Statesman*, 12 December 1926
20 MH BBC radio interview with Amis, 1962
21 *The Musical Leader*, 2 June 1927
22 R. Nichols, *Ravel*, p240
23 Macleod, op. cit., p146
24 Ibid., p180
25 *The Jewish Tribune*, 13 April 1928
26 *The Daily Telegraph*, 11 June 1928
27 Fiona Maddocks, *Goodbye Russia*, p120
28 MH to Frederick Steinway, 31 Aug 1925, see also McKenna, op. cit., p93
29 MH to JT, see Fifield, op. cit., p556
30 Marie Brockway Pond (1862-1957), Sibley Watson Digital Library, https://dslab.lib.rochesteredu/esw/mbpo
31 MH postwar American diary, unpaginated, Hess Family Collection
32 B. Simonds, 'Myra in America' in *Myra Hess by her Friends*, p47
33 Author interview with Stephen Kovacevich
34 MH postwar American diary
35 *Lincoln Star*, 20 Nov 1923; *Musical Courier*, 15 Nov 1923, *New York Times*, 1 April 1925
36 Gelatt, op. cit., p229
37 *The Sunday Times*, 16 June 1929
38 *The Morning Post*, 9 Nov 1929
39 *The Daily Telegraph*, 5 Nov 1929
40 MH to JdA, undated [summer 1929], private archive, d'Arányi family
41 Lizzie Hess to MH postcard, undated [1930], Hess Family Collection
42 MH to JdA, 'Sunday', summer 1930, private archive, d'Arányi family
43 McKenna, op. cit., p95
44 MH to JdA, 23 July 1930, private archive, d'Arányi family

Striving Still to Truth Unknown
(1931–1934)

Enter Saz

Myra's charmed existence through the Twenties had come to a devastating end. Now she was determined to find an equilibrium that would allow her to keep going. She was 40 and had begun to build a strong repertoire, besides her musical one, of strategies for survival.

As ever, she was plagued by nerves before concerts. She had taken to playing Patience alone in her dressing room in the agonising minutes before going on stage; it helped to induce calm and focus her mind. Travelling was another matter. Myra was a sociable person and disliked being alone – difficult when her vocation entailed so much of it. She had solved the question of living alone, for the duration of the Carlton Hill lease, and in the US she was surrounded by friends. But solitary existence on Atlantic liners and cross-continental trains could be soul-destroying. As Saz put it, 'It was an arduous business, travelling alone – and travelling was travelling in those days, when air-conditioning had not been invented and it took five days to get from New York to California.'[1]

After her holiday with Mrs Newhouse, Myra resolved that she could not continue life on the road alone. Back in London, she had sought, and found, a personal assistant: a Miss Hare, who looked after practical arrangements and served as her companion. Tragically, she fell victim to a brain tumour and died during surgery, a few months before Lizzie's death.

While Lizzie was ill, the Gunns had provided crucial support for Myra. Saz had proved her worth as a level-headed, patient, good-humoured carer. Marjorie had her teaching job at Downe House, but Saz was not employed and Myra asked if she would like to go with her to America for the 1931 tour. Saz stayed not for one trip, but for the rest of Myra's life, at home and abroad, becoming her indispensable amanuensis. Touring the US, they called themselves 'the Pilgrims'.

Saz soon found that part of her task was keeping the pianist's feet on the ground. '[Her name] was fast becoming a household word,' she commented, 'and in lifts and suchlike places I often had to hiss "Look out, you're becoming famous," as one saw recognition dawning in someone's eye…' Myra's 'vivid personality, her unaffected friendliness and sparkling sense of humour won her friends wherever she went'.[2]

A Protecting Veil

Myra once described herself and Saz as 'more like sisters than most sisters'[3]. Saz, who nicknamed Myra 'Missie', nevertheless played a circumscribed role in her life as secretary, old-fashioned companion and Woman Friday. In short, she did everything for her: packing, unpacking, correspondence, admin, phone calls, ironing, mending, poaching eggs (Myra generally fuelled up on eggs before concerts) and playing the card games which helped Myra to relax after days and nights of high adrenaline. When, on the way to perform Brahms's Piano Concerto No. 2 with Bruno Walter in 1951, Myra put her heel through the hem of her concert gown, it was Saz who had to leap into action with needle and thread.[4] Yet they had fun, too – according to Saz, 'high old times', roaring with laughter 'from morning til night'[5].

Saz also tried to protect Myra from too much attention. Some observers in Myra's later years suggest that she and Marjorie were almost oppressively proprietorial. Myra's pupil Yonty Solomon described Saz as 'very mannish, rather like a guard at Royal Holloway,' and reported that she used to wear a black and white polka-dotted dress and spoke in a staccato manner[6]. Stephen Kovacevich thought Myra 'could have had more fun,' citing that the Gunns would often keep fans away after a concert so that she could rest, rather than socialising.[7] That is not to say that she did not need to rest; in her last decade, her health was less than stable. Perhaps pragmatically she allowed herself to be shielded, to better concentrate on her work. If her close friends appear to be moths to her flame, she might have seen them more as a good, sturdy lampshade.

The administrator and broadcaster John Amis left a couple of throwaway sentences in a description (in his *Amiscellany*) of the National Gallery concerts, where he served as an assistant in his late teens. He described Myra as charming, gracious and conservative in her tastes, but with a surprisingly 'rumbustious' sense of humour. He added: 'Her entourage on the feminine side frightened me, but at that time I didn't know what lesbian society or behaviour could be like.'[8] He was referring to Myra's 'entourage', not necessarily Myra. But the comment seems to be the chief source of a widespread assumption about Myra's own inclinations.

How reliable is Amis? A cousin of the literary Amises, Kingsley and Martin, he became a popular figure in the music business, easy to spot across a crowded concert hall with his colourful bow ties and waistcoats. He certainly spent much time with Myra and the National Gallery concerts in his youth and undertook an enchanting broadcast interview with her in her last years. His book of memoirs is nevertheless peppered with semi-inaccuracies and no doubt inadvertently misogynistic sideswipes. For instance, he cruelly mocks some older women musicians' taste in lipstick, and even says he found Myra's playing 'too pretty'. Such comments make it rather difficult to trust his words.

Given Myra's mainly watertight guarding of her privacy, there are no simple answers. She generally surrounded herself, indeed shielded herself, with female friends whose personalities were as independent as her own. Theirs was the generation of 'surplus women', but also of the so-called 'new women', able to make the most of their single status and the increased opportunities in working life that had come with the 1920s.

Many of Myra's younger acquaintances later described the Gunns unequivocally as lesbians. Some considered that Myra herself looked 'masculine'. But those who were students in the 1950s-60s might have known little about the two million 'surplus women', and still less about Myra's disfiguring surgery in 1934.

On the one hand, even if lesbianism was not illegal, it usually had to be concealed from families for the sake of 'propriety' (and in Elizabeth Jane Howard's *Cazalet Chronicles*, Rachel must hide her love for Sid from her siblings). Some of Myra's friends loved other women rather than men, openly or otherwise, apparently including Ruth and Marj (the real Rachel and Sid), the Oxfordshire couple Tandy and Mary, and in the US probably Pondie, Willa Cather, and the actress Katherine Cornell, who was thought to have had a 'lavender' marriage. On the other hand, Myra's history included the affair with Antonietti and the Bax betrayal; and her post-war American diaries held occasional appreciative comments about the men she met, for instance noticing an attractive university president whom she lightly regretted was married. She termed Ronald Colman her 'pinup', was wowed by Laurence Olivier and unreservedly adored Toscanini. She nevertheless once told Maggie van Riemsdijk that sex did not interest her, and it looks as if the prospect of it, with the associated emotional turmoil, could have seemed more a threat than a temptation.

The only person with whom she demonstrably shared daily life was Saz, who was intelligent, sensible and witty, but also a doggedly devout

Christian in a way that suggests an inclination to traditional propriety, maybe even repression. The friendship was cosy, but the roles were distinct: Myra was the star, Saz the helpmeet, and it suited them both.

With Marj, they were a trio, and the Gunns' pets doubled their number. A drawing by Marj on the front of a Birthday Book for Myra shows the backs of the two sisters, two dogs and a cat sitting by a fire, arrows indicating that the greeting is from all five. In the rhymes, the Gunns' doggerel is laced with catty wit that would have had Myra laughing aloud – especially as they lose no opportunity to take a pot-shot at Harriet.

At Christmas 1933, they gave Myra an 'A-Z' of her life, the rhymes in Saz's tidy calligraphy on one side of a schoolish exercise book, with illustrations opposite by Marj. For Albéniz, she draws Myra at the piano, images of a bullfight billowing out from under its raised lid. For Crosswords, the three women are on the sofa, with Myra in the middle, concentrating on a page spread out on her lap. Other drawings show Myra surrounded by butterflies for Schumann's *Papillons*, or hunkered under a blanket with seasickness, or Jelly in the limelight. Here are some choice extracts:

A is for artiste, who plays the piano
And Albéniz too, who wrote the Triana
And the rounds of applause, with which both are greeted,
Lead to strings of encores which are always repeated.

B is for Bach, whose famous Chorale
Was set right by H. Bauer and sold überall.
There's a spurious edition by poor Myra Hess,
A failure, which ruined the Varsity Press.

C is the Crossword – oh come rack your brain,
It makes the time pass, when you go in a train.
The items of news are not noticed at all,
The dollar may drop or the Government fall
A murder committed, all white slaves set free –
'It's a word of twelve letters beginning with B.' …

I is for Ibbs and for Tillett as well
They will manage your concert and send in the bill,
For they know without them, not a penny you'd make,
With Barnstaple, Dorking and Sidmouth at stake –
The Leipzig Gewandhaus may ask you to play

But 'no, we are sorry, it comes on the day
When you're pencilled for Purley or else for Pauls Cray.' …

J is for Jelly. She's Joseph's great niece
She can play a sonata, or wild gypsy piece,
On the platform her garb catches everyone's eye
With her clothes and appearance, one really can't vie. …

L is for Lion and for Lioness as well
Of the Proms, she's the Queen, and the BBC 'Belle'.
The critics may carp and Newman may frown,
But she's the best pianist in all London Town. …

M is for M. M.! O mum is the word
Come beat up the Julep and warm up the curd
Put lids on your jerries and veils round your hat
And see her in Devon!! – we'll leave it at that.

N's for Next Season, ah now I can vow
She's thinking of programmes, note frown on her brow
There's masses of music, but nothing quite right
'The Chopin's too flowery, Scarlatti too light
Beethoven Sonatas are played night and day
Who having heard Schnabel would want me to play.'
We hope it's all settled, but something goes wrong
The keys are not suitable, contrast not strong
This Etude's too short and the other's too long –
It will none of it do; we must all start again,
Our reasons go snap, we can not stand the strain. …

V is the Virginal, played by Miss Cohen.
She says it's her instrument – but
there's
no
knowin …

Z is for zeal, which is far above praise
And firmness of purpose, by night & in days
We may laugh at our Missie, make free with her fame
If we sometimes seem beastly, it's only in game
For we truly admire her & thus do we say
'God bless her and keep her, today & alway.'[9]

Along with the sardonic snarl about Bauer's Bach transcription and the all-too-real angst over programme planning, there's a mystery. Who is the M. M. whom Myra is visiting, veiled up, in Devon? It might seem less suggestive if that verse's illustration were not a giant exclamation mark.

Myra had two friends whose initials fit the bill. The first is May Mukle, the cellist who had premiered Rebecca's Rhapsody with Myra. They were frequent chamber music partners in the early days. May was ten years older than Myra and had played in an all-female piano quartet, the English Ensemble, with Rebecca, Kathleen Long and Marjorie Hayward; she also worked with the d'Arányis.

Her Hungarian father was a well-known builder of organs, half the partnership Imhof & Mukle, and inventor of the 'orchestrion', an elaborate mechanical contraption that supposedly mimicked the sound of an orchestra. She gave the UK premieres of the duos for violin and cello by both Ravel and Kodály and was a keen champion of female composers, notably Rebecca, and of younger female artists trying to build careers.

In an Argyll Street basement behind Oxford Circus, May founded the M. M. Club, transforming her initials into Mainly Musicians: a few minutes from the Queen's and Wigmore Halls, it became a beloved venue for musical socialising and chamber music evenings. Its restaurant hosted performers, critics and music-lovers for lunch, tea, dinner and post-concert drinks. Vaughan Williams even turned down an offer of membership at the Athenaeum Club on Pall Mall because he was so fond of this modest but musical location. During World War II May transformed it into an air-raid shelter. Myra signed up to be a warden.

Still, there's no sign that May had any association with Devon, let alone mint julep, so the second candidate seems more likely: Mabel Reynolds, 'Mother Mab' – 'O mum is the word'. The Galsworthy family had a house at Wingstone, Manaton, in Devon, where Mabel's brother John and his wife Ada had spent much of World War I, and they were originally from that county. The history of Myra's friendship with Mabel, as related by McKenna, is full of what looks like eggshell-treading about the powerful personality that nearly 'overwhelmed' Myra. Harriet Cohen's lyrical description of her trip to Ireland with Mabel, whom she introduces as Myra's great friend, would in such a context acquire a very Harriet-esque bite – becoming, in her webbed hands, a double-edged sword against Myra that compounds the Bax debacle. But just one other mention pops up in one of Myra's postwar diaries, around seven years after Mabel's death: 'poor old M. M.'.

There the trail runs cold. Unfashionable though it may seem today, it looks very much as if Myra was simply married to her music, resolutely single and protecting herself from emotional and sexual involvements of any kind at all. As Saz and Marj said, 'we'll leave it at that'.

Depression and Growth

After the October 1929 stockmarket crash, a giant slump began that turned into the Great Depression. For Myra, concert bookings dropped, and fees too. Her demands regarding the latter had always been modest, so compared to certain others she had to make fewer adjustments. General quality of life was another matter.

Between 1929 and 1932 the worldwide GDP fell by 15 per cent. The reduced demand for European exports in the US was increasing unemployment across Europe and the UK; in the latter, it soared to 2.75m, hitting industrial areas hardest. A run on the pound in August 1931 proved devastating. Severe poverty took hold of a swathe of the population, not helped by Ramsay MacDonald's government, which decided to cut its deficit by reducing unemployment benefit by 20 per cent. Britain withdrew from the Gold Standard and devalued the pound. The Labour government was replaced by a National Government, also led by MacDonald. Meanwhile Oswald Mosley had resigned from Labour and founded the New Party, a far-right organisation ready to exploit the disaffection all around.

Ten minutes' walk from Carlton Hill, the new Abbey Road Studios was opened by Sir Edward Elgar on 12th November 1931. But Myra's recording career, having surged in 1928-29, now lay fallow. Between then and 1933 she seems only to have recorded one piece: Schumann's 'Vogel als Prophet' from *Waldszenen*, about three minutes long, in New York on 23rd March 1931.

At such a time, the arts might have seemed a luxury that few could afford. Yet Myra remained upbeat in public, telling a Pittsburgh interviewer: 'Depression? Music is a tonic for it. Audiences in such times are more discriminating. They like the classics and I'm glad they do. They are sincere about their interest.'[10]

In the same interview she extolled the marvels of Paderewski, an artist with 'something that can't be matched'. On 5th March their paths crossed in Indianapolis. He sent her a giant basket of roses, which arrived in her dressing room with a handwritten card. The overjoyed Myra carried his note around with her to concerts thereafter as a talisman.[11]

Irene Scharrer's career was in choppier waters – and not only because of the Depression. Having married Samuel Gurney Lubbock in 1915, she had two children and had done all she could to maintain her career alongside family life. She toured America in 1926, playing the Beethoven Piano Concerto No. 4 under Otto Klemperer. But then disaster struck: in the early 1930s, her husband became involved with a much younger woman, a married ex-pupil of Irene and Uncle Tobs. A scandal – hushed-up – ensued. He was dismissed from his post at Eton. He also abandoned Irene.[12]

The pianist lived alone in west London thereafter, devoted to the Christian Science faith. She kept going, up to a point. She gave recitals in Myra's National Gallery concerts during World War II and performed for the last time in a concert in memory of Matthay in 1958, playing Mozart's Sonata for Two Pianos with Myra. In 1933 she recorded Litolff's Scherzo; it was a bestseller. After that, she never recorded another note. Perhaps the blow to her personal life threw her professional life off course as well.

In an intriguing sequel, in 2016 three piano experts – Matthay's biographer Stephen Siek, the record company executive Mike Spring and the writer Jeremy Nicolas – visited Irene's granddaughter, hoping to gain insights into the pianist's life and work. They were surprised when she told them that Irene had not particularly liked Myra, but had built the friendship in deference to her mother. This story could not be confirmed first-hand by the present writer, but the three visitors separately described it in identical terms.

Myra's 1930 American tour sent audiences and critics into more than their usual ecstasies, despite all. Reviews suggest that her artistry was growing at pace – and she was carrying the American public with her.

An article in *The Sun*, New York, on 18th October 1930 credited her for awakening love for Bach's music all over the US. 'It soon dawned upon American audiences that here was a pianist who made Bach speak eloquently and immediately Bach became a vogue, so much so that if she offers a program that does not permit a Bach group, she has to respond to insistent calls with encores from the master's works... The names of Bach and Myra Hess are indissolubly associated.'

On 8th November 1930 she gave her first New York Town Hall concert since her mother's death. The programme included the Franck Prelude, Chorale and Fugue, Bach's Italian Concerto, Brahms's Handel Variations and a Chopin group including the C minor Nocturne and six Etudes – an afternoon of pianistic Alpine challenges. *The New York Times* reported that 'long after the hour when the recital would normally have been at an end … Miss Hess was returning to the stage and playing encores'.

As for the *Herald Tribune*:

> Her equipment has always been a splendid one; her technique is comprehensive, splendidly controlled and fluent; her tone is of extraordinary richness and her command of nuance and colour is unusually wide. There have been times in the past when one felt that Miss Hess, fine musician as she is, did not quite plumb the depths of some of the music she performed. Yesterday those moments were rare. The Andante of the Bach Concerto, exquisitely phrased as it was, seemed to tarry on the surface ... It was here and in one or two of the Brahms Variations that the ineluctable femininity of the playing style seemed inadequate to express the essential masculinity of the music. But such a regret is, of course, futile: when Miss Hess has gone through the metamorphoses of Virginia Wolf's "Orlando," it will be time enough to expect her art to be androgynous instead of feminine.[13]

'English Pianist Never played Better Than at Her Last Recital of Season,' declared *The New York Times* at the tour's conclusion in February, where Myra 'was greeted by an audience which occupied every seat and half the stage'. She played some Scarlatti, Mozart's Sonata in G K283, the Brahms Sonata No. 3, Schumann's *Papillons* and a selection of Ravel, Debussy and Albéniz: 'Rightly or wrongly, it has been said that few women can do justice to Brahms. Miss Hess … is one of the few. Brahms's gentleness, his bearish ruggedness and his "brown studies" were revealed in grateful measure. Throughout the recital there was a satisfying balance in the pianist's interpretations of the intellectual and the emotional, a balance which is rarely achieved on the concert platform.'[14]

She had played the Brahms sonata at the Queen's Hall, London, in October: 'Schumann spoke of these early sonatas as "veiled symphonies"; Miss Hess's interpretation was that of a great symphonic conductor,' *The Times* said[15]. Bach and Mozart were ever present; there was another Mozart concerto, K459 in F major, on 23rd October with the 'Philharmonic Orchestra' under Beecham; and with Jelly, duo programmes were as pure as could be. On 12th December 1931 they brought the Queen's Hall Bach, Mozart, Beethoven and Brahms.

But critics' continual ramblings about 'feminine charm' would have grated on Myra. In Britain, a review of her recital with Jelly on 14th October 1932 at the Queen's Hall bore the unfortunate headline 'Women's Sonata Recital', even though their programme of Bach's E major Sonata and two Brahms sonatas – including a violin version of Op. 120 No. 1 (originally for clarinet or viola) – gave 'the sensation of deep thought and intense feeling swaying every graceful phrase'.[16] Another review was headed, more suitably, 'A Perfect Ensemble'[17].

Far from worrying about superficial femininity, Myra was working away in private on the most serious music there was. She wrote to Jelly in 1931, in a flurry of programme-planning angst while on holiday in Suffolk, that she had spent the summer practising Beethoven's final sonata, Op. 111 – 'which I am not going to play, of course. … anyhow, not yet…'[18].

Her American season in 1932 began in January and encompassed 38 cities. Olin Downes, in *The New York Times*, welcomed her Schumann-focused recital:

> The performance of the Symphonic Studies [which followed the *Fantasiestücke* Op. 13] had a breadth and a sonority which have not always been associated with Miss Hess's style. Nevertheless she should be cautious of employing too much strength or losing the fine womanly qualities of her playing. Essentially this was noble interpretation, set forth in rich colors and with romantic feeling. … To her exceptional gifts she adds the constant growth of a real artist, one never satisfied with a given level of achievement, however high.[19]

More highlights that season included playing Beethoven's Piano Concerto No. 3 in New York on 5th April and in Cleveland, with Nikolai Sokoloff; and again in New York, the Brahms Piano Concerto No. 1 with the New York Philharmonic conducted by Bruno Walter, a conductor especially close to Myra's heart (she had previously played the Mozart D minor Concerto with him in London in 1926). Her outlook was greatly in sympathy with his humanistic and spiritual attitude towards music, besides the fact that he was a direct heir to the Austro-German tradition that was so important to her. Born in Berlin, Walter had in 1901 become Gustav Mahler's assistant conductor in Vienna, at the composer's invitation. He was Royal Bavarian Music Director and General Music Director of the Bavarian State Opera in Munich for ten years until 1923, and now, while holding the post of principal conductor of the Leipzig Gewandhaus Orchestra, he was in his first guest season with the New York Philharmonic. This placed him among very few conductors in the US who could 'claim succession to the royal line of Bülow, Nikisch and Mahler'.[20]

If the Brahms D minor Piano Concerto was a crucial heavyweight addition to Myra's repertoire, so was her programme for New York Town Hall in February 1933. The first half was all Beethoven: a selection of Bagatelles and the Piano Sonata Op. 110. After the interval came Brahms: the *Klavierstücke* Op. 119, followed by the Variations on a Theme of Handel.

Around this time, in addition, a new relationship was emerging in Myra's musical life: one that would pay dividends for the better part of three decades.

A Quartet in the Depression

The Griller String Quartet – violinists Sidney Griller and Jack O'Brien, violist Philip Burton and cellist Colin Hampton – began their career living together in a former railway carriage by Pagham Beach, West Sussex. It was the only way that the young men – or boys, as they were still in their teens – could make ends meet. From 1929 they shared a house. When Griller married Honor Linton in 1932, she became housekeeper to all four and remained so for 11 years.

'The BOYS', as Myra often called them, were protégés of Lionel Tertis, who had brought them together at the Academy. From him, they absorbed a ferocious work ethic. Determined to devote themselves to their quartet, they were the first such ensemble that the Academy had produced. Among those supporting and encouraging them was Harold Bauer's sister, Gertrude Hopkins, whom they nicknamed 'Hoppy'; she ran a concert series in St John's Wood. Early on they performed with Bauer himself and Felix Weingartner as well.

In 1932, four years after they had graduated, but when Griller was still only 21, there came the first reports of the quartet working with Myra: at the Three Choirs Festival in Worcester, they performed the Elgar Piano Quintet on 9th September in the College Hall. Myra also played some solos, including Szymanowski and Albéniz, following her triumph earlier in the festival in the Brahms D minor Concerto. Elgar himself, aged 75, was in town too, conducting some of his own works.

Myra, who had always admired Tertis's visionary musicianship and dedication, found soulmates in this young quartet, and Griller in particular. An East End lad born in 1911, he was brought up on Cannon Street Road in a poverty-stricken Polish Jewish immigrant family that was not remotely musical. His father had a 'provisions' store. 'It was the most depressing part of the world,' Griller remembered, 'surrounded by factories and docks. It was the most miserable, degrading upbringing … [but] everybody was simply striving to make a living.'[21] Griller was a workaholic even by Myra's standards, with a commensurately tough personality; his son, Arnold, recalled noticing that at rehearsals, Sidney would be firmly in charge. (Arnold was named after Bax, who was nominally his godfather.)[22] Even in his elderly years, the stocky violinist had a striking presence with a 'bounding, bouncing energy just waiting to be unleashed.'[23]

Jack O'Brien, the second violinist, was from South Africa; Philip Burton, the violist, was fanatical about Shakespeare and, as a more than nominal godfather to young Arnold, used to take him to Stratford-on-Avon annually for a week of immersion in the Bard; and Colin Hampton, the cellist, spent what spare time he had composing. Myra soon made them into her honorary nephews.

Writing to Griller from The Hague shortly after their first collaboration, she was eager to ensure that they were not upset by a poor review. 'Dear "Griller" – "Sidney" – "nephew" – what do you like to be called?' she wrote.

> We all know that there must be criticisms to make about any performance we give – but this is not a <u>true</u> criticism. Whatever the shortcomings were – here & there – it was obviously an enjoyable, & much-enjoyed concert! & even you, young as you all are – know when you are all doing anything worth while musically!
>
> To my mind, the development in your playing & interpretations in the last 2 years is extraordinary, & such real musical qualities are bound to be appreciated, & do please remember that no artist has ever escaped discouragement from critics – & it is a sickening fact that the more young people develop the more they begin to criticise! I can remember having marvellous notices when I played & as a tentative student - & when I knew I was beginning to 'grow up' there were lists of complaints!!

> The only thing to remember is that a poor criticism … is only temporary, & that it is your own sincere musical endeavour which is enduring, & bound to find its place with the public.

She then alludes to 'the little "material" matter', saying: 'please do not thank me. I am very grateful if you will all allow me to do this small thing for you.' Making a living as a quartet was difficult, since the ensemble had to share one concert fee between four, a fact little appreciated by promoters. Myra, having had her own financial headaches in the past, elected to help the Grillers whenever she could. She signed off as 'Auntie Myra' – before adding, as a P. S., a little advice:

> The only thing that worries me about you all – is that you are having to overwork just now? Do rest when you can. I am sure you could all do some quiet work by yourselves sometimes & save yourselves physically? I know how difficult it is – but spare yourselves when you can!
>
> P.S
> One little thing may I say – while I think of it? I am not sure about the 'harmonic' opening in the slow movement of the Franck – I don't think it has quite enough life in it - & as you can play pianissimo – it is hardly necessary? Do you agree?[24]

Myra, in her early forties, knew too much about the physical strain of overwork. Her schedule would take a toll on even the toughest constitution. A case of mumps laid her low for several weeks in Chicago – recuperating, she made good use of her time by starting to learn the Brahms Piano Concerto No. 2 – but that was only the start of the trouble.

She maintained the public image that all was well, and on 17th October 1933 made at Abbey Road her first London recording for Columbia. It was a group of short pieces, none of which made excessive physical demands: the Slavonic Dance No. 1 by Dvořák in piano duet with the conductor and composer Hamilton Harty, then three solo pieces – Chopin's Nocturne in F sharp Op. 15 No. 2, John Field's Nocturne No. 4 in A and the third of Edward MacDowell's *Sea Pieces*.

The recordings capture Myra in both grand and intimate modes. The nocturnes shine with eloquent legato, while the rubato has a winning combination of poise, control and what those critics would have called 'charm'. The MacDowell, a stentorian, processional piece, exploits her rich sound in a succession of finely balanced chords. As for the Dvořák, the two pianists bound joyously through it.

In private, though, Myra felt close to collapse. Her concert notebooks, now kept by Saz – who would have known exactly what was going on, even if nobody else did – gave the impression that everything was spiralling down towards imminent cataclysm: 1934.

1 A. Gunn, 'American Pilgrimage', *Myra Hess by her Friends*, p28
2 Ibid., p30
3 D. White, interview with MH, *Milwaukee Journal*, 24 November 1950
4 MH postwar US diary
5 McKenna, op. cit., p98
6 J. Meewezen, interview with Yonty Solomon
7 Author interview with SK
8 J. Amis, *Amiscellany*, p79-80
9 Hess Family Archive
10 *The Pittsburgh Press*, 4 March 1933
11 McKenna, op. cit., p100
12 J. Nicholas, 'The Lady Vanishes' in *International Piano*, Jul/Aug 2016, p67
13 *New York Herald Tribune*, 9 November 1930
14 *The New York Times*, 16 February 1931
15 *The Times*, 14 October 1930
16 Unidentified cutting in Edwin Evans's scrapbook
17 *The Daily Telegraph*, 17 October 1932
18 MH to JDA, [summer] 1931
19 *The New York Times*, 10 January 1932
20 Gelatt, op. cit., p89
21 T. Potter, interview with Sidney Griller, *The Strad*, January 1986, p681
22 Author interview with Arnold Griller
23 Potter, op. cit.
24 MH to SG, undated, likely c1932, courtesy of Arnold Griller

The World Turns on its Dark Side

(1934–1939)

THERE WAS ICE ON THE international wind in 1934: a brief civil war in Austria and an attempted far-right coup in France. A turning point came in British musical life when three of its most prominent composers all passed away, Elgar on 23rd February, Holst on 25th May and Delius on 10th June. Later, in Germany, Adolf Hitler would help himself to the title of Führer.

In America in January, the critic Lawrence Gilman showered Myra with praise in the *Herald Tribune*:

> One would like to speak at length of Miss Hess's consummate playing of the music of Bach ... especially the way she delivered the wonderful slow movement of the Italian Concerto, with its rich and delicate unfolding of rhapsodic melody, and of the superb exhilaration with which she made the Finale exciting. But it might suffice to say merely that performances such as these are above praise...

He took exception to the fact that Myra was only giving one New York recital that season. 'It seems needlessly draconian,' he wrote. 'Doubtless she knows her own business; but...'[1]

Myra did. In Boston, she checked into hospital for tests. She stayed with her friend Margot Rueter at 326 Dartmouth Street. 'Between ourselves,' she wrote to Bruce Simonds, 'I was "down and out" when I got here, and Margot Rueter's doctor took me in hand very sternly. I am grateful to her, as I suppose we never know ourselves when we are "sailing too near the wind"?? but I have literally been shut up and away from everything.'[2]

Determined to stay positive, Myra added that she was looking forward to her return voyage to Britain on the Ile de France – 'with Herriot, Paderewski (I believe) and Toscanini!' On the ship, as she later told Sascha Greiner, manager of the concert and artist department at Steinway & Sons, it was 'delightful and inspiring' to encounter the great Polish pianist. She played his Steinway while he was playing bridge.[3]

Her health issues were nevertheless of grave concern. She was afraid that she might have breast cancer.

A Little Treatment

Myra revealed the truth about her tests, ailment and treatment only to a few close friends. She knew how fast rumour in the music business could snowball. To the Simondses she wrote: 'the slightest indisposition is soon interpreted as the loss of a forearm or permanent paralysis of the wrists!!!!'[4] Inevitably, though, the worry ran much deeper.

The good news was that Myra did not have cancer, but a condition then known as Schimmelbusch's Disease. Technically it is not a disease at all. Often termed chronic cystic mastitis or adenosis, it involves a proliferation of cysts which make the breasts feel lumpy. It is not malignant and is brought on by hormonal changes, chiefly in perimenopausal women. In the 21st century it is known to clear up by itself. In the early 1930s, however, it was thought to carry a risk of being pre-cancerous. It was therefore treated with extreme surgery.

In April 1934, Myra went into the New England Hospital for Women and Children (now the Dimock Center) where she underwent two separate radical mastectomies. Her surgeon, Grace Rochford – a rare woman in the profession of that time – was a graduate of Tufts Medical School and had worked in consultation with Myra's doctors in England, presumably Dr Yarrow Eccles, before suggesting this solution.[5]

It is not clear whether any of Myra's lymph nodes were taken out, or if so, how many. Probably they would have been, as radical treatment was standard at the time. She appears not to have suffered oedema (the swelling of the arm that can result from lymph node removal); perhaps this was sheer good fortune.

Just two months later, the June 1934 Bulletin of the Institute of the History of Medicine (via Johns Hopkins University Press) published a paper by Charles F. Geschickter entitled *The Early Literature on Chronic Cystic Mastitis*. He wrote that Joseph Colt Bloodgood, a Baltimore scientist who had studied the condition in 1921, had concluded it was not precancerous, but he quoted Bloodgood's text: 'in the isolated and diffuse non-encapsulated cystic adenoma it may be safer completely to remove the breast or to perform the complete operation for cancer because of the incidence of cancer in 2 out of 31 cases'.

In the appendix, Bloodgood issued an update. He feared that 25 years earlier, he and his colleagues had been mistaken. 'We failed to confirm our diagnosis of malignancy by a follow-up of the ultimate results,' he wrote. 'None of the examples of Schimmelbusch's disease reported by me in 1906 died of cancer, and I am quite confident that these contributions of Schimmelbusch and myself added to the fear of cancer in the minds of many surgeons and pathologists.' He also refers to papers published in 1928 and 1931 by other researchers who he thought had made the same error.

For Myra, this rethink came too late. Methods of breast reconstruction scarcely existed; the surgeon Sir Harold Gilles devised a 'tubed abdominal flap' method in 1919, but did not carry out the first reconstruction using it until 1942[6]. The one sign of what Myra may have done about it is some references in her post-war American diaries to 'corset fittings' in New York. Those who met her later and considered her appearance rather 'masculine' may not have known that her 'feminine' curves had been surgically excised.

Exactly what Myra went through with such disfigurement, physically and emotionally, can only be assessed by the extent of her stiff upper lip. Often, the less she said about something, the worse it was. She told the Simondses only that she was having 'a little treatment'. [7]

She spent several weeks recovering in hospital, then convalesced in Boston's Hotel Vendôme. In June she and Saz sailed home, a trip disrupted not by Myra's health, but by poor Saz being stricken with appendicitis in mid-Atlantic. Back in England, once both women had recuperated, Dr Yarrow Eccles and his family hosted Myra, with Denise, for a holiday in Falmouth. The homeopath, Myra's housemates and her housekeeper all thought Myra had been put through hell for no good reason. It looks as if they were right. Friends later speculated that the operation marked the end of any intimate personal life she would have contemplated.[8]

Interviewed in St Louis four years later, Myra was asked if she had ever been married. 'Well, I have never been married, divorced, burnt or burgled – but I take that last back,' she said. 'I have been burgled. Quite a lot has been taken from me at one time or another.'[9]

For the moment, she could concentrate on recovery and the gradual resumption of practising and performance. She did so to extraordinary effect. Radical mastectomies can affect the back and shoulder muscles, reducing mobility. Yet after 18 months, on 2nd October 1935, Myra was on stage at the Proms with Wood, playing nothing less than the Brahms Piano Concerto No. 2 in B flat major. The longest concerto in her repertoire, it requires unflagging power and stamina. Even if the D minor concerto arguably needs more weight, the B flat is not a piece that anyone suffering lack of motion in the shoulders or injury to the back muscles would be likely to choose. Playing it may have been an act of decidedly Myra-esque defiance. She also joined forces with Jelly and the cellist Gaspar Cassadó to record Brahms's Piano Trio No. 2 in C major, Op. 87, at Abbey Road on 25th and 27th October 1935. Her declamatory phrasing and full sound are alternately meaty and melting; fresh from the B flat Concerto, her river of power almost bursts its banks in the first movement's coda. Rather muddy recorded sound is inevitable (it is long overdue for remastering), but as an example of three musicians putting their entire souls into a studio performance – rare for Myra – it is a gem.

Julia Myra Hess, CBE

Myra downplayed her surgery. If she mentioned it, she made light of it; otherwise she tried to put it behind her. Around the same time as her operations, Uncle Tobs, now 76, had had two of his own; Myra wanted to be there for him, and back in England she headed for High Marley, where Jessie found her 'more sweetly human & strongly modest than ever'[10]. She gave a lecture in her Carlton Hill studio for the students of the TMPS's Summer Festival. She was now the school's president and at its closing concert at the Queen's Hall she presented its annual awards.

As early as winter 1934, she sailed west again. That New Year's Eve she wrote the first of what would be, over the decades, many dozens of letters to a young composer from Belfast named Howard Ferguson. He lived with her friend and colleague Harold Samuel, a warm, jolly-natured pianist of great sensitivity, acclaimed for his Bach interpretations. Myra and Samuel had often given two-piano concerts together on both sides of the Atlantic, and it was on Samuel that she had played the practical joke of turning up in disguise at a competition. In another party trick, she and Samuel once stretched out flat on top of a piano to see if they could play a duet upside down.

Back in 1922, adjudicating a competition in Belfast at which the teenage Howard had impressed him, Samuel had invited him and his nanny, May Cunningham, nicknamed 'Pu', to move in with him in London. 'I can never get over the fact that my mother and father immediately agreed to this startling proposition,' Howard reflected later.[11]

Howard, now 26, had therefore lived ever since as companion, pupil and honorary nephew-and-heir to Samuel, who was 55. The nature of the relationship is not entirely clear – Howard was homosexual, but he always called Samuel 'Nunky', short for 'uncle' (and if there was more to it, they would have had to keep it under wraps). In New York Myra met Samuel for dinner. She wrote to Howard that he was lonely: '...that is inevitable and he realises that it is his own nature which is "at fault"... This travelling, performing existence is a hard - + lonely one - but we have our compensations & would be still more miserable if we weren't allowed to do it.'[12] On 14th January, she wrote again to tell him that in concert Samuel had 'absolutely surpassed himself': 'I have never heard him play so magnificently or so beautifully. It has been one of the greatest revelations of pure music that I have hoped to hear!'

In Chicago shortly before Christmas, Myra was staying next door to the concert hall, at the Congress Hotel, with her piano. The actress Charlotte Greenwood, appearing in a 21-week run of her comedy hit *Leaning on Letty*, occupied the suite above, with her husband Martin Broones. On the day of Myra's recital, which was at 8.30pm, the practising began first thing in the morning. The couple stayed in to listen to her, enthralled. But as day turned to evening and Myra still showed no sign of stopping even at 8.20pm, Greenwood wondered if she should phone down and remind her she was due on stage. At 8.27pm, there was a sudden silence. 'Three minutes later,' Greenwood wrote, 'Miss Hess was bowing to her audience that filled the spacious auditorium to the rafters and was embarking on a two-hour recital, fresh as a daisy.'[13] In her anxiety about Myra's performance, Greenwood was nearly late for her own.

Just as Myra was back in London and at full strength, she was struck down again, this time with appendicitis. She went straight from a Queen's Hall recital into a nursing home, having given the concert despite the pain and against her doctors' advice. While she was in hospital, she received a letter that informed her she was being awarded the CBE in the King's New Year Honours List 1936. She was one of only two women to receive it on this occasion, alongside 33 men. Reading the letter, as one article later reported, 'she burst into "floods of tears", thoroughly alarming her nurse, who rushed to the bedside, thinking something must be seriously wrong.'[14]

Recuperating after Christmas, Myra wrote to thank John Tillett for the gifts of a book and an azalea, the latter 'a joy to look at while I am hobbling about'. She added: 'My chief pastime at the moment is Jigsaw puzzles. How the <u>un</u>mighty fall!'[15] She knew she had to start planning her schedule in a more sensible way. Although she had postponed her embarkation for the US, rescheduling some January appearances for

February, it was soon evident that she had overcommitted by attempting the tour so soon after surgery. 'It was pretty mad', she wrote to Tillett on 29th February 1936, from the Laurelton.) It was not the first time Myra had overestimated her own toughness, nor would it be the last.

She was already booked for two concertos in Washington DC on 3rd and 5th January 1937. Working backwards, this would mean sailing before Christmas, which meant being prepared for the tour before that, which in turn required restricting her engagements in the UK. 'Do promise me not to book more than one (at the most?!!!) between my October London recitals,' she wrote.[16]

A trip to Scandinavia – her first visit – was a good excuse to cut back the UK schedule, though she was relieved not to be touring with a conductor whom she found dull. 'I suppose I ought to feel a pig for doing him out of it, but I presume he will be given another chance (with any other pianist??? H.C.).'[17]

The Scandinavian tour took place under the auspices of the recently formed British Council, as it became. It had been founded two years earlier as the British Committee for Relations with Other Countries, in response to growing global instability and extremism: communism in Russia, fascism in Germany, Italy and Spain. In 1940, during World War II, it gained a royal charter and its ideals were strengthened: 'to create in a country overseas a basis of friendly knowledge and understanding of the people of this country, of their philosophy and way of life, which will lead to a sympathetic appreciation of British foreign policy, whatever for the moment that policy may be and from whatever political conviction it may spring.'

Myra, already a national treasure, was among the first musicians it sent on tour, the composer Arthur Bliss having suggested her at its Music Committee's first-ever meeting in 1935. The 1936 trip took her to the major cities of Denmark, Norway and Sweden. It was neither her favourite experience, nor the most successful, but this did not seem to have much to do with her playing, or the reviews, which were generally positive. Rather, the organisation was so young that it appears not yet to have known the ropes. It had failed to create adequate publicity, let alone hospitality for the star pianist.

The CBE, in contrast, was a distinct upturn. She told Bruce Simonds: 'I went to the Palace to visit the King [Edward VIII, in his few months as monarch] – and it was a very picturesque and dignified proceeding – a somewhat motley procession of 250 receiving decorations. The King looked extremely handsome in a scarlet coat (the Irish Guards were "on duty") and he was touchingly solemn and earnest! These incessant wars are terrifying – and one is afraid that people will get used to them – and then it will be a case of "who next?"'.[18]

Old Prejudices, New Friends

'Hurrah for the Blackshirts' read a headline in *the Daily Mail.*[19] The article beneath it, by the paper's proprietor, Lord Rothermere, ended by exhorting young men to join Oswald Mosley's British Union of Fascists and National Socialists. Under this latest name, the organisation was garnering support in its fourth year of existence. It counted among its admirers not only Rothermere, but Italy's Benito Mussolini.

On 4th October 1936, called to protect a march through the East End by the BUFNS, police forces clashed with anti-fascist protestors in Stepney, an area home to a large community of Jewish immigrants who had fled the previous generation's explosion of anti-Semitism in eastern Europe. In Britain, as elsewhere, certain people, notably Mosley, were seeking to scapegoat the Jewish population for the economic hardship that dominated this grim decade.

Such were the crowds of protestors that Mosley, unable to lead his gathering towards Whitechapel, changed the route to the narrow thoroughfare of Cable Street. The resistance, made up of communists, Jews, Irish dockers, trade unionists and locals, united with the chant 'They Shall Not Pass!' They erected barriers, pulled up paving stones and pelted police with rotting fruit and boiling water, until at last the authorities ordered the march to turn back. It marked a downturn of fortune for Mosley's party, and not a moment too soon. Two days later, he married Diana Guinness (née Mitford) in Germany at Joseph Goebbels' home, with Hitler present. Yet it was not until Kristallnacht, in November 1938, that the British press opened its eyes and universally condemned the ongoing racist horrors in Germany and Austria.

Musicians were not untouched by British anti-Semitism. When cinema orchestras closed in the late Twenties, after 'talkies' became prevalent, the players lost their jobs – just as the Proms were beginning to welcome foreign orchestras, enabling the sleek machines of the Berlin Philharmonic and the Amsterdam Concertgebouw to show up the shreds and patches of the British ensembles. Annual UK tours by the Berlin Philharmonic and its conductor Wilhelm Furtwängler, beginning in 1928, made a particularly powerful impact.

The Incorporated Society of Musicians in 1931 issued a manifesto demanding that numbers of foreign musicians should be restricted, a move supported by, among others, Arnold Bax. Then after Hitler took power in 1933, German Jewish refugees began to seek safety elsewhere, including Britain. The ISM's house journal carried an article by Professor W. Gillies Whittaker which used inflammatory language alongside disingenuous declarations of support:

> The music profession is at the present time faced with a very serious situation on account of political and racial expulsions from Germany. Numbers of refugees are seeking a means of earning a livelihood in Britain. A turn of the wheel in Austria may produce a similar upheaval there, and there will be another invasion of our coasts. Be it said from the outset that our sympathies are entirely with these unfortunate beings… Our nation has always been in the forefront of helping distressed peoples. But we must face facts. Can we absorb these musicians without dislocating our profession?[20]

When the ISM began to impose limits on immigrant musicians, with pointed mention of Jews among them, referring to the 'enervating influence such foreigners would have exerted upon native musical art'[21], Myra resigned her membership.

In 1936, with British appeasement of Hitler in full swing, an exchange took place, instigated by Joachim von Ribbentrop, the German ambassador to Britain, in which the London Philharmonic and Beecham went to tour Germany, while the Dresden Opera came to London lock, stock and productions, to perform at Covent Garden. The latter engendered long-lasting ovations as audiences responded to their impressive artistic standards. The LPO trip found the orchestra and its sharp-tongued, blustery conductor becoming pawns for political propaganda on both sides; the British government hoped it would prove to the world that the UK was not '*das Land ohne Musik*', while Hitler could well have been using the tour to curry favour with the Prince of Wales, who was known to be sympathetic to the Nazis and was about to become King Edward VIII.[22] That idea went up in smoke when the new King abdicated shortly afterwards to abscond with the American divorcée Wallis Simpson. Yet it was all too clear that music was no longer merely music, but a force that could make a real impact in shaping world events.

Myra, as a Jewish British public figure, was sometimes successful in challenging the chunter of low-level anti-Semitic prejudice at home.

One example involved someone who became a close friend and a crucial member of the National Gallery concerts staff.

Myra often performed at the Three Choirs Festival, the oldest such event in the UK, if not the world: a celebration of British music held in rotation in Gloucester, Hereford and Worcester, it dated as far back as 1715. At a house party of performers and festival-goers at the 1937 festival in Gloucester, she sat down at the piano and began to play the Bach G major Gigue with such irresistible bounce that Sir Walford Davies whisked a radio critic named Joyce Grenfell off her feet and began to dance. Moments later all the guests had joined in and were conga-ing around the house. Joyce remarked that it was one of the most enjoyable moments of spontaneous exuberance she had ever experienced.[23]

It was through Myra's girlhood friends, the Farjeons, that Joyce made her theatrical breakthrough. Herbert ('Bertie') Farjeon – who had once snatched the Lafcadio Hearn book from Myra's hand – was now a critic for *The Tatler* and a fine writer of theatrical satire; his songs included, in 1920, *I've Danced with a Man who Danced with a Girl who Danced with the Prince of Wales*. He also staged revues in the West End. At a dinner party, hearing Joyce present a sketch of her own that had the guests in stitches, he invited her to write for his show. Soon, though, he recognised that only she herself could present her comedic monologues. Joyce, who lived quietly in the countryside with her husband, was somewhat astounded; but she made her professional debut on 21st April 1939, to rave reviews. She went on to become a national celebrity, especially for her sketches about a beleaguered kindergarten teacher, *George, Don't Do That.*

Joyce was a Christian Scientist, a religion she shared with Irene Scharrer, with whom she was also friendly. There had been evidence that earlier in life, Joyce probably held some of this era's habitual prejudices about Jews – but her deepening friendship with Myra transformed her attitude[24]. In 1938 she encouraged her mother to go and hear Myra play, praising the pianist for her objectivity and wisdom and terming her 'beyond words wonderful'. Soon she would not hear a word against her and indeed was wondering whatever made anybody anti-Semitic in the first place[25]. She and Myra enjoyed shopping trips and lunches together; later, at the National Gallery concerts Joyce became a stalwart sandwich-maker. In 1955, they travelled aboard the same transatlantic liner, the Mauretania, where they passed a happy evening trying out Joyce's new songs with Myra accompanying her at the piano.[26]

At another Three Choirs Festival, Myra bumped into Vaughan Williams in the interval of a concert that neither was enjoying. He asked if she really wanted to stay for the rest. She didn't. They sloped off together to the cinema, emerging ready to join, all innocence, the post-concert crowd at the end.[27]

To Wildwood Road

The lease on 8 Carlton Hill had run its 20 years, and Myra and the Compton-Burnetts were going their separate ways. Myra was by then able to finance a mortgage; she could command a fee of 75 guineas for a BBC broadcast (though equal pay for female artists was on nobody's radar: Artur Schnabel was paid 200 guineas for the same, and Pablo Casals 300).[28]

Myra Hess at her desk

She wrote to Bruce that after several months of house-hunting with Saz, 'I am borrowing the wherewithal to buy a delightful little house on Hampstead Heath. It appeared from Heaven apparently just as we were beginning to despair of finding anything ... It has a delightful music room looking on to an adorable little garden, with a golf course and woods beyond. It is only about 10 minutes further from town than Carlton Hill

– by car – so will be just as accessible and slightly inaccessible as I would wish for!'

No. 48 Wildwood Road, London NW11, in the Hampstead Garden Suburb, was a modern, detached house in imitation Queen Anne style: red-brick, flat-fronted, it stood foursquare opposite the Heath Extension. At the back, tall French windows opened onto the garden. Myra, bidding farewell to her studio, was nervous about practising: 'I still have the anxiety of acoustics – as there is no piano in "my" house and the room seems dangerously resonant – however there is a new process of putting seaweed on the walls, I believe!' [29]

The Mauls, who would occupy a flat within the house, moved in first; they dealt with the worst of the practicalities while Myra was away. For her birthday, 25th February, they sent her a typed poem illustrated with Marjorie's cartoons, headed *This Is the House That Miss Bought* and modelled on *The House that Jack Built*. It chronicles a chaotic chapter of accidents, but looks ahead to the creation of a beautiful garden and the polishing of wooden floors. When 'Miss' returned from the US, she could move straight in. The telephone exchange was called Speedwell and Myra might answer the phone to family members with a gleeful 'Speedweed!'

The interior, according to Sir Kenneth Clark, who was there many times during World War II, looked rather like the home of George Bernard Shaw or the headmistress of Cheltenham Ladies College, sporting assorted patterns of chintz, a plethora of photographs, imitation-Indian brass fittings, and a parade of white-tusked wooden elephants. Here, sipping milk or lemonade, he and Myra's other guests, including Sir Stafford Cripps, would often listen to her playing while the night deepened around them.

A Hero's Life

The cellist Emanuel Feuermann, 12 years Myra's junior, was from a musical family in Galicia and had studied in Vienna and Leipzig, where he – like Gregor Piatigorsky, Wilhelmina Suggia and William Pleeth – was a pupil of Julius Klengel (the long-serving principal cellist of the Gewandhausorchester from 1881). Klengel wrote that he had never before trained such a great talent and called him 'our divinely favoured artist and lovable young man.'[30] Feuermann had been thrown out of his teaching post at Berlin's Musikhochschule due to the Nazis' race laws. He escaped to London and here in 1935 married Eva Reifenberg. Here too, he and Myra recorded the Beethoven Cello Sonata in A major, Op. 69, on

23rd June 1936. The sympathy between cellist and pianist is evident from the start, in their shared realisations of the themes' contrasting characters, their intense rhythmic vitality and an unfailing sense of give and take. Perhaps in chamber music, Myra's horror of the studio was lessened; she and her partners were, in a sense, performing not only with but to one another.

Their duo could have had a fine future, had Feuermann stayed in London. Fate determined otherwise. He was in Vienna when Hitler annexed Austria in March 1938. Trapped and in mortal danger together with his wife and small daughter, he was helped by the violinist Bronislaw Huberman to flee to Palestine. The family moved from there to America; Feuermann established a top-level US performing and teaching career, recording with Jascha Heifetz and becoming a professor at the Curtis Institute in Philadelphia. Tragically, in 1942 all this was cut short by his death aged 39, due to complications in surgery.

Myra joined a very different musician on the platform of the Queen's Hall on 4th November: her old friend Mengelberg. He was conducting the BBC Symphony Orchestra in an eclectic programme that began with a Vivaldi Concerto Grosso (long before the 'early music movement', this was perfectly acceptable on a symphony orchestra) and ended with Strauss's *Ein Heldenleben*, which the composer had dedicated to him. As centrepiece, Myra played the Brahms Piano Concerto No. 2.

The violist Bernard Shore, who was in the orchestra, recalled that Mengelberg stretched the hours 'like elastic, which nearly breaks by the end of the last rehearsal'[31]; the idiosyncratic conductor took 25 minutes for the orchestra to tune up, then devoted the entire first rehearsal to the start of *Ein Heldenleben* up to the solo violin entry, which is about eight minutes of music. Strauss himself was at the concert and took a bow; he was in London for the Dresden Opera's residency at Covent Garden, where his *Der Rosenkavalier* was winning tremendous acclaim.

The significance of the occasion, with the tone-poem's composer and dedicatee conductor, somewhat overshadowed Myra, but *The Times* reported: 'Miss Hess gave an admirably clear performance, which emphasized the lyrical side of the music and was … memorable for the beauty of the slow movement.'[32]

Myra had performed with Mengelberg in Holland earlier that summer and played the Schumann Concerto with him in New York.

Rehearsing for the latter, he upbraided her for her wayward rhythm in the second movement, saying it made it impossible for him to accompany her. Myra, furious, plonked metronomically through the rest, while Mengelberg stewed and the orchestral musicians shook with suppressed laughter. Later she thought of dropping out of the concert – until the contrite conductor appeared at her dressing room door with a bouquet, promising: 'I follow you anywhere.'[33]

There was more to the Queen's Hall concert, however, than Myra appearing alongside the conductor who had propelled her to fame, plus one of the day's greatest composers. At this point, the politicisation of music was intensifying in Germany under the Nazis and in Russia under Stalin; as the effects rippled out, nowhere could be immune.

Three years earlier, Strauss had become chief conductor at Bayreuth's Wagner Festival after Arturo Toscanini resigned in protest at Germany's new Nazi administration. The regime had founded the Reichsmusikkammer – an official governmental department charged with bringing the country's musical life into line with its political and racial ideology – and Strauss accepted the post as its president. He was in his seventies and seems to have thought he could do some good from the inside. But in 1935 a letter he had written to his Jewish librettist Stefan Zweig was intercepted. It read:

> Do you believe I am ever, in any of my actions, guided by the thought that I am 'German'? Do you suppose Mozart was consciously 'Aryan' when he composed? I recognise only two types of people: those who have talent and those who have none.[34]

This was not so much critical of the regime as of the whole notion that music could be restricted by ideology. Strauss was no Nazi, but he made the common mistake of thinking artistic issues could rise above it all. After a dressing-down from Goebbels – who allegedly shouted at him that Lehár was the better composer – he was ignominiously fired.

The ideal that music and politics should not be mixed was well and good, but far from the reality of the extremist regimes that were now seeking to turn art into propaganda. After World War II, Mengelberg himself turned out to have been sympathetic to the Nazis, even though Myra's Jewish origins (and Mahler's) can have made little difference to him in the beginning. Just how uncomfortable the situation must later have become for Myra is something we can only imagine.

'Hyphenated Heifetz'

Myra had a run-in in 1937 with one of the most eminent musicians then resident in America, the violinist Jascha Heifetz. With the baritone Lawrence Tibbett, Heifetz was organising an American Musicians' Guild, supported by numerous colleagues. Myra had only just arrived in the US in January 1937 when he visited her, hoping to recruit her too. Probing the issue beyond its supposed work 'for the freedom of artists all over the world', Myra told Tillett that in fact the 'Dickstein Bill' for the Senate, which Heifetz's guild wished to support, would tighten restrictions on visiting artists, which of course included her. Concert managers were responding by forming another association, intending to prevent the bill from being passed.

As *Time* Magazine had reported the previous summer, the bill was a response to restrictive policies in other countries. Italy had banned foreign performers except those with residency, while Poland, Germany and Russia would not let touring musicians take their earnings out of the country. Britain was permitting them to come and perform only when they were proven to be beyond competition with native artists. The French rule was almost as stringent.

> To rectify this unfavorable trade balance against U. S. talent, the Immigration Committee was considering a bill which would require all foreign actors, singers, and orchestra conductors except those of 'distinguished merit,' to secure special permission from the Department of Labor before being allowed to work in the U. S. The merit qualification was what brought the Guild to Washington. Also no mention had been made of solo instrumentalists and dancers. The Guild wanted to put all foreign artists through the Department of Labor's strainer.[35]

The 115 charter members included Mischa Elman, George Gershwin, Rosa Ponselle and Fritz Reiner. Heifetz himself was an immigrant, of Lithuanian Jewish background; Reiner was from Hungary and Elman from Russia. It seems strange, however, that Heifetz should seek to add Myra, a non-immigrant foreign musician, to the list. 'I told him my reason for resigning from the ISM and that I had intended never to belong again to any such Association,' she wrote.

Heifetz 'also rather held a pistol to my head by saying that later on it might become compulsory for all artists to join (it smacks somewhat of the Soviet ?????).' She adds, wickedly: 'It would be terrible if H.C. were forced to play the virginals to the Immigration Officers, to pay or pave her way into the United States?'[36]

Eventually Myra wrote to Tillett: 'I have still refused to join, in spite of more entreaties from the "hyphenated Heifetz" (thank you for the marvellous title) … as far as England is concerned, the statistics are going to make those look very foolish, who are saying that we are so nasty about letting foreigners in!!! …I have told Heifetz … that I cannot join their Guild unless I rejoin the Society in England, which I don't want to do, and that until the general issue becomes more urgent (I was rather pleased with that), I cannot make a decision. If we all HAVE to join, it will be time enough, but many people think this Dickstein Bill will not be passed. So that's enough of that.'[37]

Balkan Adventure

In autumn 1937, Myra undertook a rare tour to eastern Europe and the Balkans. It was arranged by the British Council, hot on the heels of her Scandinavian trip. Once again, it could have gone better.

There were arguments over her programme; at first the committee wished her to play more English music. She responded that she was willing to replace Brahms or Schumann 'with any British work of equal calibre', but doubted any such thing existed. She pointed out too that the English repertoire she had played abroad had had some poor reviews; it would do more harm than good if she were to play British music and it was not well received.[38]

Finally she resorted to ancient rather than modern: music by Purcell, Arne, Farnaby and Peerson, alongside Bach's Fantasia in C minor, *Jesu, Joy* and the Organ Fugue No. 7 arranged by De Kresz; then the Beethoven Sonata Op. 110, five late Brahms piano pieces and the Schumann *Etudes symphoniques*. A number of the 16th and 17th century English works appeared in a book of selections from her repertoire published by Winthrop Rogers Edition in 1938; however, she rarely performed them thereafter.

Her itinerary took her through Prague (Smetana Hall, 23rd Nov-ember), Budapest (Great Hall of the Academy of Music, 25th November), Bucharest (Dalles Hall, 30th November), Sofia (Bulgarian Hall, 2nd December), Belgrade (Hall of Kolarcheva Zaduzbina, 4th December) and Zagreb (Hall of the Conservatorium, 8th December). For six concerts she was paid £300, inclusive of all expenses (about £17,000 in the 2020s).

Myra was, essentially, being used as a propaganda tool. Her playing was supposed to demonstrate that the British were not such an unmusical nation after all – against a background in which Germany, generally considered the most musical and cultured nation in Europe, had been taken over by a fascist regime. But after this tour, in a letter of 17th February 1938, E.C. Rapp of the British Consulate in Zagreb told the British Council that Myra's propaganda value was somewhat reduced due to 'the general feeling that she is not of British origin'. In the biography they circulated to the local promoters, the first paragraph included the information that Myra was 'of British parentage', but clearly that was not enough to combat those old, ingrained prejudices.

Behind the scenes, the preparations were fraught. The British Council was anxious in case Myra was not well known enough to attract an audience. They approached the various British Societies and clubs in the relevant cities – but all they were interested in, it seemed, was reduced price, or preferably free tickets. The Bucharest organisation demanded 100 complimentary seats, which, the Council replied politely, 'puts us in rather a difficult position'[39]. Opportunities were missed to provide decent publicity, despite exhortations from the Belgrade British Legation, which pointed out that the matter had been so badly managed when Keith Falkner toured there that, not knowing the singer, few people turned up, unwilling 'to buy a pig in a poke'[40]. The council also made a special plea to the local legations and chanceries to make Myra welcome, mentioning that she had felt hurt by the lack of hospitality on her former tour.

The council's measures sometimes backfired. A begging letter to eight local journalists, seeking coverage, produced no response – except in Romania, where its recipient, Miron Grindea, a young writer from Bucharest's *Adeverul*, interpreted it as carte blanche for him to take control of all Myra's local publicity. The council, while acknowledging that he had been asked to help, had to respond to communications from startled Chancery staff suggesting that he was overstepping the mark.

That in turn produced a backhanded response from the honorary secretary of the Anglo-Rumanian Society in Bucharest. He stated that Grindea's involvement made one wonder whether the artist was well known, 'or a young man [sic] whose name has not reached beyond England'[41], and proceeded to apply an arm-twist regarding a quid-pro-quo London engagement for the local Royal Symphony Orchestra's conductor, George Georgescu, should he offer Myra an advantageous Bucharest concerto.

Georgescu was duly approached for an engagement for Myra; she did her best to comply, offering a choice of three concertos and even agreeing to forego a fee so as not to put the Council to further expense. Georgescu in any case proved unavailable.

Myra performs in Budapest during her British Council Balkan tour, 1937

Myra travelled out on 17th November via Harwich and went by train through Groningen and Arnhem overnight to Leipzig and Dresden. She arrived in Prague on 21st November. After the final concert in Zagreb, she travelled via a three-day stop in Vienna, an overnight train to Calais and then home to the white cliffs of Dover.

Despite all, the concerts were enormously successful. The British Legation in Budapest reported (in a wonderful case of Prague-related nominative determinism) to Lt-Colonel Charles Bridge of the British Council that 'The hall was well filled despite the fact that there were two other concerts on the same evening. The audience were enthusiastic and Miss Hess, who appeared to be pleased by her reception, was induced to give a number of encores. The Minister gave a luncheon for her and, after the concert, the Vice-Consul, whose wife is a keen musician, gave a reception.'[42]

The Bulgarian-British Association in Sofia wrote: 'All day the phone has been ringing and people congratulating us on that 'wonderful' concert last night. Several asked if it would not be possible for Miss Hess to remain over and give another concert on Sunday – they assure me she will have a packed house.'[43]

Ticket sales in Belgrade started slowly, but picked up after she was persuaded to broadcast on local radio for half an hour from Bucharest. The organisers were eager to have her back the following winter. And in Zagreb one review read: 'To-day the whole of Zagreb already knows that Myra Hess is the most sensational artiste who has visited our city for centuries ... One cannot write about Myra Hess. One has to listen to her.' The critic continued that the audience listened 'with almost religious concentration. Tears fell from many eyes. Everyone in the hall felt that he was experiencing a very rare and great artistic sensation.'[44]

Another Zagreb review commented: 'English reproductive art has unfortunately been entirely unknown in our country until lately. This is due to the often wrong and superficial judgement, casually given, that England, an ancient land and one with a great musical tradition, has nothing much to show in that sphere to-day...'[45]

Myra herself described the audiences as 'most cordial', Prague as the most beautiful of the cities and Budapest 'marvellously situated'[46]. In the latter she lunched with the composer Ernö von Dohnányi, and wrote to Jelly, a Budapest native, 'It seems quite wrong to be here without you! & am having a heavenly time'[47]. During her Dresden stopover, she had heard Cassadó performing with the pianist Friedrich Wührer, but she said nothing of the atmosphere in Germany, preferring to report that the next day she met the guitarist Segovia on the train.

Organisational glitches, however, were plentiful. Myra's correspondence with Tillett depicts a roller-coaster winter trip: appalling weather, even more appalling roads and, worst, a lack of punctuality that infuriated the scrupulous pianist.

To her sardonic wit, nothing was sacred. She wrote from the British Legion in Sofia in a letter dated 'December 3rd (probably) 1937':

> Time means nothing at all to Roumanians and Bulgarians, and I never know which day of the week it is. I wish you could have seen and heard our arrival this morning. We were met by one Bert Andrews! a touching old chap, who spends his life persuading the Bulgars that they love music, and especially British?! Mr Kramona, who speaks German, Christo Petkoff!! gabbling in French, all this at 7.30 A.M.

> with snow on the ground and fog in the air!! I had a charming letter from the Minister, Maurice Peterson, inviting us to stay here, and it is a delightful change after the very interesting, but screeching Roumanivlatperkaliescus?? and their overpowering aroma of garlic. My hand will be too stiff to play tonight if I begin to tell you everything, or a quarter of the amazing things of the last week.[48]

In Bucharest, she was invited at short notice to dinner at the Legation ('they forgot to invite us until nearly 7, the dinner at 8.30!'). She played to Romania's Queen Marie, who was ill in bed; Myra performed in an antechamber and the Queen ('absolutely charming') received her before and after. Her public concert was 'a scream', due to begin at 9pm, but with the audience only just seated half an hour later. 'By the end of the evening they became wildly excited and crowded round the platform, yelling and screeching until it sounded like feeding time in the monkey house…' [49]

This rather squashes the oft-repeated argument that European audiences did not appreciate Myra's artistry. These ones certainly did. It was chiefly history – the Second World War followed by the Soviet era – that kept her away thereafter. Germany under the Nazis was impossible, but she remained a star in the Netherlands. Indeed, in western Europe, it was chiefly Paris that did not especially warm to her, although she continued to perform there (at the Salle Gaveau in June 1935, for instance). But the difference in tastes between French and British piano audiences has often resulted in a substantial mismatch between the pianists that each most appreciates.

If Myra was becoming jaded with touring, it was no wonder. Heading for a boat across the Danube, she reported:

> We swerved through an unending procession of double or treble horse vehicles driven by innumerable fur-hatted ruffians. The surface of the road would have been quite good, if there had been less mud, and when there wasn't enough, they were throwing it all over the place from the ditches! It was appallingly cold waiting for the ferry and we were thankful to get into the Wagon-lit after an endless, and again smelly business of passports and luggage. I wish the British Council would give their artists a diplomatic pass…
>
> I would like to talk to the British Council (if they care to listen?!!). I have the same impression as in Scandinavia, that there should be much more organisation.[50]

That was putting it mildly.

Myra's American trip shortly afterwards provided quite a contrast. On 7th March a radio broadcast on the Ford Sunday Evening Hour in Detroit found her performing the first movement of the Grieg Piano Concerto with Victor Kolar and the Detroit Symphony Orchestra, two Chopin Etudes, and a Bach Gigue. She was offered a fee of $3,000. Convinced that this was far too high, she riposted: 'Why, that's ridiculous!' This was misinterpreted and the amount was raised to $4,000.

The live broadcast proved a little too eventful. First Myra's hotel room door refused to budge; she only just got out and away to the hall on time. There, she sat at the side of the stage while the orchestra began the programme, but when it was time for the Grieg, the conductor unaccountably failed to wait for her to reach the piano before launching the initial timpani roll. She had to make a running dive for the keyboard in time to play her opening cascade. No wonder the performance sounded so spontaneous.

Although Myra often played the Grieg Concerto, she never made a commercial recording of it (other than her Duo-Art piano roll); this single movement is all we have. She brings a giant, craggy tone to the ubiquitous Nordic masterpiece, with a deep-dug richness to the sound even at high volume. The Chopin études with which she followed it are also absent from her studio discography, but she performs Op. 25 No. 1 and No. 3 with lightness, lyricism and unfailing flair, wrapping up the second with an ecstatic, melting trill and a final chord like a satin bow. Last, the Bach G major Gigue, that favourite party piece, is full of Myra's sparkle. During its brief two minutes, it seems to incarnate her whole irrepressible personality.

Myra did not mince her words about her frustrations with the touring life. Interviewed in St Louis that year, she remarked succinctly: 'There are not more female pianists because most women are too sensible to wish to spend their lives on trains.'[51]

A holiday on Lake Como with Uncle Tobs and Denise did all of them much good. Myra needed a good break; and Matthay was mourning Jessie, who had died after many years confined to a wheelchair by rheumatoid arthritis. The pianists enjoyed the fresh air, rowing on the lake amid glorious mountain scenery.

Refreshed, Myra was ready for more recording in the autumn: this time the Schumann Piano Concerto, conducted by Walter Goehr, with a smallish orchestra assembled for the occasion and identified only as

'Studio Orchestra'. The sessions took place on 5th October and 5th November; the result became a bestseller. She recorded the concerto a second time in 1952, with the Philharmonia under Rudolf Schwarz; the first version is freer in atmosphere and more intimate (even if some of its modern transfers are better than others), while the orchestra in the second is sleek and fuller-toned. Each is a snapshot of Myra at very different times of her life. Her experiences in the interim had changed her not only into a different kind of person, but also into a different kind of pianist.

The Strange Case of Willa Cather and the Queen

Myra's strengthening status and confidence could have been making her increasingly merciless. Humour was often her strategy of choice for survival, but it seems to extend to practical jokes even on those she liked and respected. One case in point may have been the American novelist Willa Cather, whose book *The Song of the Lark* (1915) is a touching portrait of a gifted young singer's rise to operatic success.

Cather admired and liked Myra and did not only attend her concerts, but sometimes met her and Saz for lunch or tea. On 21st September 1940 the writer sent an enthusiastic letter to her sister, Elsie, about the latest developments in the British royal family. After the abdication crisis, King George VI and Queen Elizabeth had been crowned at Westminster Abbey in 1937. Cather enclosed a newspaper clipping, remarking that the new queen was a friend of Myra Hess and had been a childhood companion of Anita Gunn. She relates that Anita had grown up on a farm bordering the child Elizabeth's home estate. Saz and Myra had showered her with outrageous stories about the exploits of the young Elizabeth.

Saz and Marjorie were, however, born and raised in a middle-class family in the Rochester area of Kent, and later in Abbey Road. In neither is there any trace of royalty. Although Queen Elizabeth the Queen Mother's birthplace is disputed, one theory is that if it was not London, then it was St Paul's Walden Bury, Hertfordshire; she spent much of her childhood there and at Glamis Castle in Scotland. The Gunns had no obvious link with either place. Moreover, the Queen's attendances at some of Myra's National Gallery concerts, and her enthusiasm and moral support for Myra, had no discernible connection to Saz, who was on war duties at the time. In short, Cather's account seems rather odd.

Perhaps she was misremembering; after all, by autumn 1940 Myra was being kept away from the US by the war. But still – even though

Myra was a staunch royalist, was it nevertheless possible that she and Saz had noticed how excessively fixated some Americans could be with the British royal family? Had they decided to have a private laugh at their distinguished friend's expense?

Myra and Schumann

Although Myra had in her repertoire more works by that arch-romantic Robert Schumann than almost any other composer, she did not record as many as she might have. In a 1962 interview, pressed to identify recordings she was proud of, Myra complied only with reluctance, but *Carnaval* was the first she mentioned. Made in 1938, it has become a classic that shows both the work and its performer at their finest.

Myra's student Richard Contiguglia relates the story, gleaned from Saz, of its genesis:

> Recording in those days was a 'do or die' proposition. Anita Gunn told us that she had just finished playing 'Paganini' in *Carnaval*, which skips all over the piano, and Anita said it was just perfection. But the engineers said, 'We've got to do that again...' They were recording directly onto LP, not on tape. She had played it to perfection, but had to repeat it maybe more than once to be able to get something that was transferable directly to an LP. Saz said that the recording experience must have been anathema to Myra: she needed a live audience to give her best.[52]

The recording took four challenging sessions to complete, but one might never guess that from the result, a true carnival of character and colour. Myra's tonal opulence is evident from first to last, while her clear textures make the most of Schumann's inspired interweaving of voices. In 'Eusebius', touches of subtle yet delicious lingering at the top of phrases adds to their sighing effect, yet without overstatement. 'Florestan' is whimsical, urgent, haunted by the ghost of *Papillons*. Anyone looking for charm would find it in the stylish unfurling and wrapping up of her phrasing; and the cavalcade of characters comes bounding out of the piano as if each is taking their turn for a monologue on a theatrical stage. The whole culminates in the grand march of the Davidsbündler against the Philistines, leaving us in no doubt that the enemy is routed, with unbridled celebration to follow. Well into the 21st century, the *Gramophone* critic Bryce Morrison was terming this *Carnaval* 'one of the finest ever recorded ... everything is a distillation of years of the most single-minded skill and affection'.[53] He is not wrong.

Jelly and Schumann

At home, Jelly d'Arányi was in the midst of a bizarre chain of events.[54] Her sister Adila was friends with the Swedish minister in London, Baron Erik Palmstierna, a keen member of the Society for Psychical Research. He had identified Adila as a psychic 'sensitive'. Jelly was not interested at first, but sometimes attended séances at which 'the glass game' – a Ouija board – spelled out messages ostensibly from the beyond. In 1933, a 'message' arrived purporting to be from the spirit of Robert Schumann, asking Jelly to find and perform his long-suppressed violin concerto.

Jelly's great-uncle, the legendary violinist Joseph Joachim, had been a friend of Robert Schumann's and remained close to Clara for the rest of her life. This concerto had been written for Joachim in 1853; only a few months afterwards, Schumann, who had long been unwell, suffered the final breakdown that propelled him, in spring 1854, into a mental hospital, where he died about two and a quarter years later. Fearing the work betrayed his failing state of mind, Joachim, Clara and their close friend Brahms elected to leave it unpublished. Joachim played it once, but never again. He had kept the manuscript. After his death, it passed to his son Johannes, who deposited it in the Prussian State Library in Berlin. Here Palmstierna, on a diplomatic visit to the German capital, found one of its manuscripts lurking in the wrong file.

When word got out, everything spiralled out of Jelly's control. The Nazis' Ministry of Propaganda conscripted the 'lost' work and planned to launch it as the new Great German Violin Concerto, hoping it would replace the Mendelssohn, the country's most popular, which had been banned due to its composer's race. Complicating matters further, the American violin prodigy Yehudi Menuhin was alerted and wished to play it too.

Jelly was trapped between, on one side, a younger, newer talent; on the other side, Joseph Goebbels, who tasked the violinist Georg Kulenkampff with the first performance; and everywhere, the scepticism of all to whom she asserted a right to premiere it herself. She and Adila believed wholeheartedly that they were in touch with the spirit of Schumann; they even argued over the details of the bowing he had advised via the moving glass. Against Goebbels, however, little could be done; Kulenkampff gave the modern premiere in Charlottenburg, with the Berlin Philharmonic conducted by Karl Böhm, on 26th November 1937.

It proved a public relations disaster. The concerto was very far from the heroic work that the Ministry of Propaganda had envisaged. Even a reworking – by Hindemith, uncredited since he was persona non grata with the regime – did not solve the issue. Complex and fragile, this concerto was quite unsuited to the Nazis' purpose.

Jelly finally performed it in London on 16th February 1938, with the BBC Symphony Orchestra under Boult. It was not a roaring success. Howard Ferguson, who was there, found it dull, despite pleasant moments; he had hoped for at least some sign of wildness. Worse, public controversy had blown up around the issue of the spirit messages, following an interview with Jelly in *The Listener* and a new book by Palmstierna, *Horizons of Immortality*. Jelly sent Myra a copy of the book. The pianist promised to read it, commiserated with her about the fuss over the premiere, but kept a safe distance.

The incident acquired a powerful symbolic force: the conscription of an artwork for propaganda purposes that ultimately backfired on its perpetrators. Perhaps it represented a cultural tipping point towards the war: a confirmation that music could not be purely music any more.

The journalist Reed Hynds, interviewing Myra in distant St Louis in December 1938, reported that she was deeply disturbed by the economic and political chaos all around. At one of her concerts at Queen's Hall during the Czech crisis, her audience was allowed to listen to a radio message from Neville Chamberlain before the performance began:

> Since I have been in this country I have heard that some Americans think all that was a 'putup' job, a synthetic 'war scare'. Believe me, anyone who was in London at the time knows better. We were perilously teetering between war and peace, sanity and insanity.

What kept her going, she added, was her sense of humour:

> It may be conceited to say so, but I think I have one. Why conceited? Because a sense of humor is the most valuable thing in the world, except possibly health. A sense of humor keeps one from taking oneself too seriously. It keeps a person like me going. That and being told that one's music counts. Nowadays, with the world so full of unrest and turmoil, the artist is apt to feel himself pretty insignificant.[55]

Kristallnacht – the 'night of broken glass', a pogrom against Jewish businesses and communities in Germany and Austria – had taken place on 9th November 1938, only a few weeks earlier.

Kindred Spirits

Among Myra's friends, a new figure was gaining prominence: Howard Ferguson became her neighbour, moving into 106 Wildwood Road early in 1939. After Harold Samuel's untimely death in 1937, Howard lived temporarily in the gardener's cottage on the Hampshire estate where his friends Gerald and Joy Finzi were building a house; but when a lease came up in Wildwood Road, it proved the perfect solution. He lived there for the next 24 years. The prospect of Myra as neighbour must have been an encouragement.

Soon Myra was fulfilling a similar role in Howard's life to that of Samuel – honorary aunt in place of honorary uncle – and he nicknamed her Auntie. She became deeply attached to him, emotionally dependent on his support and good opinion; and she championed his music whenever she could. If she was, for him, his new version of his uncle and mentor, to her he might have represented a safer version of Bax: a creative kindred spirit whose music she could encourage, but without any element of sexual threat. Howard became Myra's regular correspondent and confidant – she often addressed him as 'Darling Howardie' in letters – and they remained close for the rest of her life.

Photos of Howard in the 1930s show an alert, bright-eyed young man, prematurely egg-headed, his long oval face tipped with a determined chin. If his gaze is focused and lively, so is his music; a tonal composer in an age of burgeoning modernism, he carved a distinctive musical niche with traditional means, which probably hindered his progress in the avant-garde-hungry post-war years. He was born in Belfast on 21st October 1908, had studied at the Royal College of Music with R. O. Morris and Vaughan Williams, and, trained by Samuel, was a fine pianist.

His works from the 1930s included a superb violin sonata, a Partita for two pianos or orchestra, and his Octet, which blended Schubert-inspired instrumentation with the cool-tempered incisiveness of Ravel. His stormy Piano Sonata, composed in 1938-40, is thought to reflect both the onset of World War II and the death of Samuel, to whose memory it is dedicated. Myra played and recorded it to inimitable effect.

Howard was a genial soul, well informed and cultured, and an excellent cook whose repertoire apparently extended to a superb French onion soup. Like Myra, he enjoyed card games and he shared with her, as well as with Finzi, a sharp-edged sense of humour. He and Finzi had bonded at a concert of Richard Strauss's Alpine Symphony, conducted by the composer, during which the thunder machine fell over into the middle of the orchestra. Meeting at the end, each found the other helpless with laughter.[56]

By summer 1939, when Howard had settled in the Garden Suburb, the prospect of war was all around. Hitler had already annexed Austria; in March 1939 he defied the Munich Pact, which had ceded the Czech Sudentenland to Germany, and invaded Bohemia and Moravia. In August, the Molotov-Ribbentrop Pact for non-aggression between Nazi Germany and the Soviet Union was formed, which to others only threatened what peace remained.

Myra went on holiday with Saz and Marj that summer. While they were in Brighton, a fortune-teller told her she would soon have 'an unusual opportunity to lead'.[57] She pooh-poohed that. Watching world developments, it was no wonder if she was filled with fear and despair.

On Friday 1st September, Germany invaded Poland. Britain and France were pledged to defend it. It was clear that the war had arrived. That night, the Prom was curtailed. Harriet was playing the Beethoven Piano Concerto No. 2, which should have been followed by the 'Pastoral' Symphony. Instead of the second half, Sir Henry Wood – who had never before addressed an audience – had to make an announcement:

> Owing to the special arrangements for broadcasting which are now in force, the BBC very much regrets that the Symphony Orchestra will no longer be available for these concerts in London. I am therefore very sorry to say that from tonight the Promenade Concerts will close down until further notice. I must thank you again, my dear friends, for your loyal support, and I hope we shall soon meet again.[58]

His wife, Jessie Wood, wrote that the two of them drove home, deeply depressed, in the first blackout (which, along with evacuation, began immediately, even before the war was fully declared). After this he never again saw a fully lit street.[59] He died in 1944.

At the next day's Prom, Myra was scheduled to play both the Beethoven Piano Concerto No. 4 and the Franck Symphonic Variations. She had travelled straight back from a recital in Harrogate on the Thursday night, arriving at 5am, anticipating rehearsals. The concert did not happen. At home, she closed her piano.

1 *New York Herald Tribune*, 20 January 1934
2 MH to Bruce Simonds, 6 March 1934
3 McKenna, op. cit., p100
4 MH to Bruce Simonds, 6 March 1934
5 McKenna, op. cit., p101
6 T.W. Uhlen and L.B.Colen, 'History of Breast Reconstruction', *Seminars in Plastic Surgery*, 2004
7 MH to Bruce Simonds, 6 March 1934
8 Author interviews, various
9 *St Louis Star-Times*, 22 December 1938
10 J. Matthay to B. and R. Simonds, 29 May 1934, see Siek, op. cit., p589
11 Howard Ferguson, *Music, Friends and Places: A Memoir*, p9
12 MH to HF, 31 December 1934
13 G. Hayter-Menzies, *Charlotte Greenwood: The Life and Career of the Comic Star of Vaudeville, Radio and Film*, p145
14 E. Burgoyne, interview with MH, *The Queen*, 18 June 1941
15 MH to JT, 27 December 1935, see Fifield, op. cit., p559
16 MH to JT, 29 February 1936, Ibid.
17 Ibid.
18 MH to BS, 6 August 1936, see McKenna, op. cit., pp109-110
19 *Daily Mail*, 15 January 1934
20 Professor W. Gillies Whittaker, 'The Foreign Artist Problem', *A Music Journal, The Official Journal of the Incorporated Society of Musicians*, November 1934, p9, see M. Haas, 'Exiled Austrian and German Musicians in Great Britain', Orel Foundation, 26 October 2014
21 Ibid., 'The Incorporated Society of Musicians. What it has done and is doing for the Music Profession', *A Music Journal, The Official Journal of the Incorporated Society of Musicians*, November 1935 , p. 11-12, Ibid. Haas
22 E. Levi, 'How the London Philharmonic became a Pawn in a Nazi Propaganda Scheme', *BBC Music Magazine*, accessed online 19 October 2021
23 J. Hampton, *Joyce Grenfell*, p103
24 Ibid.
25 Ibid.
26 J. Hampton, op. cit., *Joyce Grenfell*, p203
27 U. Vaughan Williams, *R.V.W.*, p239
28 McKenna, op. cit., p104
29 MH to BS, 6 August 1936
30 http://www.cello.org/cnc/feuerman.htm
31 B. Shore, *The Orchestra Speaks*, p114
32 *The Times*, 5 November 1936
33 Sir P. Mason, 'Anglo-Dutch Autumn' in *Myra Hess by her Friends*, pp79-80
34 Richard Strauss, letter to Stefan Zweig, 17 June 1935
35 *Time Magazine*, 'Music: For Major Leaguers', 8 June 1936
36 MH to JT, 7 January 1937, see Fifield, op. cit., p559
37 Ibid.
38 Pamela Collins to Ernest Mackower, 5 October 1937, British Council/National Archives
39 British Council to Chancery of British Legation Bucharest, 15 Nov 1937, BC/NA
40 R.H. Hoare to British Council, 20 October 1937, BC/NA
41 D.G. Mateescu to Mr Farquhar, 28 September 1937, BC/NA
42 British Legation Budapest to Charles Bridge, BC, 16 Nov 1937, BC/NA
43 Bulgarian-British Association to Pamela Henn-Collins, 6 December 1937, BC/NA
44 *Večer*, Zagreb, 9 December 1937
45 *Novosti*, 9 December 1937
46 MH to JT, 3 December 1937, see Fifield, op. cit., p562
47 MH to JdA, 27 November 1937
48 MH to JT, 3 December 1937, see Fifield, op. cit., p562
49 Ibid.
50 Ibid.
51 *St Louis Star-Times*, 22 December 1938

52 Author interview with John Contiguglia
53 B.Morrison, Myra Hess-1938-1942 Recordings, *Gramophone,* accessed online https://www.gramophone.co.uk/review/myra-hess-1938-1942-recordings
54 This episode outlined in Macleod, op. cit., pp186-203 and further explored by the author in her book *Ghost Variations*
55 *St Louis Star-Times*, 22 December 1938
56 *Letters of Gerald Finzi and Howard Ferguson*, see also Byron Adams review in Notes, Vol 59 No 1, September 2002, p87-88
57 McKenna, op. cit., p116
58 A. Jacobs, *Henry J. Wood*, p342
59 Ibid.

'Admission: One Shilling': the National Gallery Concerts Begin

(1939 – 1940)

The announcement came on 3rd September, from the Prime Minister Neville Chamberlain:

> This morning the British Ambassador in Berlin handed the German Government a final Note stating that unless we heard from them by 11 o'clock that they were prepared at once to withdraw their troops from Poland a state of war would exist between us. I have to tell you now that no such undertaking has been received, and that consequently this country is at war with Germany.

Myra was surrounded by such a complete and instant shut-down of cultural life that at first she shut herself down too. Amid the emergency orders – blackouts, mobilisation of forces and the closing of all cultural venues – she decided to stop playing and devote her energy to war efforts instead.

She put her name down for the Women's Voluntary Service, which was organising the evacuation of London children. Howard remembered that she used to drive youngsters to the country; she enjoyed driving, he reported, was good at it, and during the war downsized her car to an Austin Seven to save petrol (which was rationed before food was)[1]. She also intended to be an air-raid warden. Saz and Marj decided to become drivers for the London Auxiliary Ambulance Service – with the unintended consequence later that they sometimes gave Myra a lift to a concert in the vehicle.

Most entertainment venues were closed at once, with no indication of how long this situation might persist. Sir Kenneth Clark, director of the National Gallery, sent his priceless collection of paintings away to hoped-for safety around rural Britain. He reflected that the closing of cultural life resembled a penitential ritual over the prospect of another war.

Yet people needed mental and spiritual stimulus nearly as much as food: 'No one felt this more strongly than Myra, who became increasingly convinced, as those strange, unreal September days of the "phoney war" passed by, that countless people were being starved of music and that she must try to do something about it,'[2] Howard wrote.

The pianist vented her frustration in a furious letter to F.W. Ogilvie, director general of the BBC, and copied to Boult, its head of music, complaining about the dreary emergency programmes that were being broadcast. She considered there was a critical lack of 'good music befitting the dignity and seriousness of the present situation' and that the BBC was ignoring 'the persistent and earnest desire for the spiritual help and encouragement which is being voiced by people of all classes everywhere'.[3]

In short, there was a vacuum in place of good music. Myra was the person to fill it.

A leading article appeared in *The Times* on 23rd September, headed MUSIC IN WAR: NEEDS AND MEANS.

> The sooner something is done to restart the musical life of this country ... the better. It is not simply a question of the provision of music, for which there is a more urgent demand in times of stress, as experience of the last War showed. It is that without some sort of functioning of the whole apparatus of music, life in the organism will be extinguished.

The article pointed out that no amount of gramophone records and broadcasts could replace the vitality of live music, let alone the UK's intricate ecosystem of professionals and amateurs, teachers and pupils, critics and listeners. Musicians, it continued, were now in a perilous financial position, with all engagements cancelled virtually overnight. Music itself, it further proclaimed, was likely to perish if it were not continually recreated by living artists:

> ... it is psychologically certain that the desire to assemble and meet together in the search for inspiration from contact with great minds in the beauties of sound will the more strongly assert itself the longer this time of stress continues. Musicians would be wise to prepare for the moment when that demand becomes insistent ...

If the West End were a prohibited area at night, concerts could take place at lunchtime ('as they have been for years in Manchester and other towns'); orchestral concerts might function occasionally in the afternoons; and chamber music concerts could rise in prominence:

> Smaller concerts and recitals are possible with even less change from the old conditions, and it is heartening to note that the veteran pianist, Mr. Frederick Lamond, is to open the autumn season on a Saturday afternoon in October at Wigmore Hall just as though Adolf Hitler had never been born.

Several different anecdotes exist regarding how the idea for Myra's National Gallery concerts began to take shape. First, the *Times* article proves that the need for music was recognised at a national level and the concept of lunchtime concerts was already in circulation.

One version of the story relates that a young couple from Romania, Miron and Carola Grindea, helped to crystalise for Myra the value of music in troubled times. Miron was the critic who had responded so heartily to the British Council's hope for publicity around Myra's 1937 concert in Bucharest. His wife, Carola, was a pianist. They had moved from Bucharest to Vienna and according to their daughter, Nadia Lasserson, they had come to London ostensibly for a two-week holiday on the day of the war's declaration, with nothing but a five-pound note.[4]

The Grindeas walked from Brompton to the Hampstead Garden Suburb to see Myra, and there found her piano closed and covered in a cloth. Carola asked why; Myra said that until the war was over there were more important things to do. Carola, disappointed, begged her to play them one piece – she responded with a Brahms intermezzo – and then remarked that Myra's role in the war should be to play to people to raise their spirits.

This tale has been repeated often, but rather over-interpreted as the source of the Gallery concerts. It helped to prove that music was still needed – but not more than that. One interview with Myra from 1941 mentions simply that she had played for some young friends to cheer them up 'and found, to her joy, that music had, at any rate, some small part in a world at war'.[5]

Howard credits the substance of the idea instead to a High Marley weekend with Uncle Tobs plus friends and disciples including Denise Lassimonne, Hilda Dederich, also a Matthay student and teacher, and Ronald Jones, who worked in advertising. There, Myra had asked the other members of the party whether they thought it might be possible to arrange some concerts – and if so, where? Denise Lassimonne replied: 'Why not in the National Gallery?' The sceptical Myra at first responded, 'Or perhaps in Buckingham Palace!'

With nothing to lose, however, Myra and Denise paid a visit to Sir Kenneth Clark and asked if Myra might be permitted to give a concert in the emptied gallery once a week. Depressed by his denuded building and the atmosphere of malaise, he leapt at the chance.

'I greatly admired her playing, but I had never met her and was immediately captivated by her enthusiasm and complete absence of affectation,' he wrote. 'I said she must not give a single concert in the Gallery. She must give one every day. She recovered rapidly from the shock and said it could be done. She knew most of the leading performers and would have no difficulty in persuading them to appear for trifling fees.'[6] Sir Kenneth spent much of his time dealing with how to balance the books. On one occasion he had funded out of his own pocket the transport to safety of one of the Gallery's Titians.

Britannia Waives the Rules

At the Gallery, everything moved fast. Clark obtained the Trustees of the Gallery's approval for the concerts within 48 hours. He then set about navigating the obstacle course of a Home Office diktat that no more than 200 people should gather in one place; the Office of Works, which had been eyeing the gallery premises for government use; and the entertainment tax of H.M. Customs and Excise.

The first National Gallery Concert, 10 October 1939

All these issues were waived, in due course. Clark voiced persuasive arguments regarding good provision of air raid shelter beneath the gallery, the likelihood that volunteers would staff the concerts rather than paid employees, and the lack of anything valuable left inside that anyone might steal. Still, he insisted these were routine concerns, while Myra was the real heroine: 'She must have been worn out; but it never showed; she was sustained by the romantic ardour of someone who sees a dream coming true.'[7]

With Saz busy driving an ambulance, Myra asked her niece Beryl Davis, Irene and Bernard Davis's second daughter, to become her administrator. Beryl, who was 28, was devoted to her aunt and only too happy to agree. She moved into 48 Wildwood Road with Myra and documented the entire concert series day by day. Barely five foot tall, self-effacing in business-like suits and horn-rimmed spectacles (she was extremely short-sighted), she had a fine sense of humour which helped her through the many challenges of the war years. Assisting Myra became the centre of her world.

The next person Myra recruited was Howard, who was away in Belfast, working on his Piano Sonata. After her urgent summons, he came back to London on 11th October, ready to provide the help she needed. By then, two official committees had formed. The Executive Committee included the Musicians' Benevolent Fund's director Frank Howes, the National Gallery's Keeper William Gibson and Ronald Jones as secretary-treasurer. On the General Committee were Vaughan Williams and Sir Walford Davies. Myra and Sir Kenneth were on both panels. The membership varied as the years went by. Howard joined the Executive group; later, so did Emmie Tillett (John's wife, formerly his employee Emmie Bass, who was Myra's agent for the rest of her career). Sir Henry Piggott later joined the General Committee, whose role was symbolic: a rubber-stamping of the events via distinguished names.

And so, on 4th October, Myra, having worked at the piano all her life, found herself chairing a committee meeting for the first time, aged 49. 'What do we all do? Move round one, like the Mad Hatter's tea-party in *Alice in Wonderland*?' she quipped.[8]

The discussion set the pattern for which the concerts became fabled. They would start at 1pm each weekday, with a repeat performance later on Tuesdays and Thursdays. Admission was one shilling at lunchtime, two at teatime. The ethos would be informal: people could stroll in and out between movements. The artists were to be paid a flat fee of 5 guineas, no matter, as Myra said, whether it was Moiseiwitsch or a young beginner: not a princely sum, but welcome at a time when most engagements had evaporated overnight. Profits would go to the Musicians' Benevolent Fund, which gave grants to those in the profession suffering financial hardship. (Ultimately, the Gallery concerts raised about £16,000 for them, equivalent to about £550,000 in 2024.)

Vaughan Williams was an active contributor and began by exhorting Myra not to call him 'Dr Vaughan Williams'. He told her that most of the young women of his acquaintance (here he was being a charmer) called him 'Uncle Ralph' when they wished to be respectful, or 'V.W.' if not: 'Won't you do one or the other according as you consider me a man or a mouse.'[9] He suggested, too, that profits from the concerts should be divided between the artists rather than given to the MBF – the musicians could then make donations themselves, if they desired – but this idea did not prevail.

Myra lost no time in beginning to invite prospective performers. On the day of the committee meeting, 4th October, she wrote to Jelly. Adila, devastated by her husband's death earlier that year, had sold the Chelsea house and moved with Jelly to Ewelme in Oxfordshire:

> My Sai,
>
> Can you, would you, WILL you come to London? In the midst of this nightmare we are living in, a dream of mine is about to come true.... I am to be allowed to give concerts in the National Gallery, and we are only waiting for the final word from the Home Office.
>
> I spent two hours with Sir Kenneth Clark, yesterday (he asked me to give you his love....) and I could have hugged him for his enthusiasm..... Our idea is to have seven concerts a week!!!.. Mid-day (shilling admission) from Monday to Friday, and additional concerts twice a week at 4.30 (2/6 admission....) We shall have to ask the artists to accept a nominal 'expense' fee to begin with, until we see how the public responds, and the concerts will be in aid of the utterly!!!.unemployed musicians. Frank Howes will look after the fund, as chairman of the Mus. Benevolent....
>
> Where do you come in?????? OVER and OVER again, if you will???? Gaspar [Cassadó] is here, and is terribly thrilled and anxious to 'make music', and here is our opportunity to play all the trios we have longed

to do. Also our opportunity to play all the Beethoven, Mozart, Bach Sonatas...etc???. For the first two weeks of this ghastly catastrophe I couldn't even open the piano, but so many people have begged me for music, and two concerts this weekend were such touching experiences that I have 'come to my senses', and realise that music is of the utmost importance, to help people to keep their sanity and belief in truth and beauty, which a large part of the human element is trying to destroy? So......it is our duty, however small our gifts may be, to contribute all we can to the spiritual stability of a better world.....

It is going to be a tremendous thing to organise, and although Ibbs and T. will help, it will be my work to make the programmes, or rather choose the 'performers'.....

I do hope Adila will take part too? It will help us all, perhaps, to keep our sanity, and ideals???

If the word comes from the Home Office in time, we want to begin next week, so will you be a darling and answer by return, or send me a wire saying YES.YES...... I shall be at Bournemouth tomorrow, but hope to get back in the evening. We are going to have a 'dress rehearsal' at the Nat. Gal. on Friday afternoon, with the piano.... acoustics....etc...

I will let you know the moment everything is really settled, and of course I would love to have you in the first concerts. If you can't arrange to be in London so soon, then we must wait until you can be here.

God bless you & all my love to you & Adila

Your

Pishkosz[10]

The first concert took place before any agreement from the Home Office had been received. The setting had to be identified and adapted, fast: the best place appeared to be under the glass dome on the second floor, Room 37. The space is octagonal and the audience could be arrayed through its three deep transepts. A rudimentary wooden platform was installed to raise the players by a couple of feet; Myra sourced the boards herself from

Ruth Howard's brother, David, who ran the family's timber business. Steinways provided a piano, free of charge but for its transport.

The acoustic seems far from ideal, given the dome and the multidirectional audience; there can be excess resonance and sound quality varies depending on where one sits. Still, in October 1939 other circumstances were not exactly ideal either. Myra and her colleagues made the most of what they had. Putting up a curtain helped to dampen the sound, as did the sizeable audiences. Everyone seemed pleasantly surprised that it was not worse – and delighted at the prospect of concerts in a hall in which, as Myra was well aware, no note of music had been heard before.

Sir Kenneth's tasks ranged from sourcing 500 chairs to giving a press conference on the Friday before the first concert. But with little publicity beyond word of mouth, an announcement on the radio and a small notice in a newspaper, a lunchtime concert as soon as Tuesday 10th October looked like a gamble rather than a guaranteed success. Myra decided to give it herself, 'in case the whole thing is a flop'.[11]

She chose a full-blooded programme: two Scarlatti sonatas – in B minor, L33, and G major, L387 – then the Preludes and Fugues in B flat minor and C sharp major from Book 1 of Bach's *Well-Tempered Clavier*, Beethoven's Sonata Op. 57, the 'Appassionata', Schubert's Dances (not credited as 'German' this time), Chopin's D flat major Nocturne and E flat major Waltz, and the first three Intermezzi of Brahms's Op. 119, with Bach's G major Gigue and *Jesu, Joy* as encores. She played it all again at 4.30pm. (After two and a half months, the teatime concerts were dropped as the income did not seem to justify the extra strain.)

The concert queue outside the National Gallery

On the appointed day, the gallery doors were due to open at 12.30pm. At 12.20pm, the committee looked out of the window, expecting to see a couple of hundred people waiting outside. Instead, a gigantic queue was running all along the north side of Trafalgar Square. Soon around a thousand people were cramming into the concert space. Some had to be turned away. When the chairs had been filled, later arrivals sat on the floor. More than half had to stand. So unprepared were the team that when the first person in line presented half a crown for his one shilling admission fee, Beryl, who was on the door, had no change. A gallery attendant had to be dispatched pronto to the bank.

Sir Kenneth listened, from behind the curtain, to Myra playing *Jesu, Joy*, surrounded by her audience of 'tired and anxious' people craving the spiritual sustenance of music. 'I confess that, in common with half the audience, I was in tears,' he wrote. 'This was what we had all been waiting for – an assertion of eternal values.'[12]

The Times carried a cool yet astonished-sounding review:

> The idea of luncheon-hour concerts has caught on immediately. The National Gallery ... was packed out at the first of the new series of concerts which began yesterday. All seats were filled at once, several hundred people stood even as far back as the third gallery away and many failed to gain admission. Miss Myra Hess, who has been the prime mover in the scheme, led off very appropriately with a piano recital. ... The attentiveness of the audience in the quiet building was especially noticeable in view of the number of those who were standing, and the acoustics, which may need to be tested from various angles for different types of programme, were at any rate sufficiently good to enable all the passage-work in the slow movement of the Appassionata to be clearly heard at a distance. ... Plainly the National Gallery, deserted by one Art, has found a new function in the service of another.[13]

The Manchester Guardian was more effusive:

> There were soldiers, sailors, men of the A.F.S., and women of the A.T.S. among the audience. They cheered Miss Hess when she appeared, and as they listened to her (surely no woman plays Beethoven's 'Appassionata' so well) many did not hide their emotion in the concert-goer's usual tight-lipped way. This indeed, was no ordinary concert but a generous civilised gesture in the face of music's great obstacles. War has all but robbed Londoners of music.

> It seemed a proper and a dramatic thing that this 'musical gesture' should have been made in this temple of another art from which art has fled. [14]

With proof of success, the organisers pressed on. The first week of the concerts continued with a violin and piano recital by Eda Kersey and Kathleen Long, songs from the baritone Roy Henderson and pianist Gerald Moore, and on Friday 13th, piano trios with Myra, Jelly (who must have responded with alacrity) and Gaspar Cassadó. They performed for a second time in mid December. On 31st October, Myra gave a recital with Jelly's sister, Adila Fachiri.

The d'Arányi Fallout

After that, something appears to have gone tragically wrong between Jelly and Myra. The numerous letters that Myra had written to her duo partner since 1918 cease beyond her first, open-hearted summons to the Gallery.

There is only one, possibly inconclusive account of what happened. Jelly's biographer, Joseph MacLeod, writes that in 1940 the violinist found herself receiving an hour-long lecture from Myra asserting that 'she was crippled and could no longer play'. Afterwards Jelly had written to her assistant that she felt she was 'a corpse – musically'. When MacLeod asked Jelly outright what had happened between her and Myra, Jelly told him firmly but simply: 'The war'.[15] He could only speculate on whether the argument was political (though Jelly was not political in the slightest) or musical.

Myra, as Stephen Kovacevich comments, 'was not the girl next door'[16]. Her 'dark side', however, was part and parcel of her inner strength. Besides, having conquered her own health issues and acquired an extra indomitability in the process, she probably had scant patience for others who might be unable, for whatever reason, to follow suit.

There is ample evidence that Jelly was suffering a conglomeration of physical problems. Her various reported but inconclusive symptoms suggest RSI at best or rheumatoid arthritis at worst; and in 1934 an accident in Amsterdam had thrown her from a vehicle head first into the road. It left her with lingering effects that may have included dizziness, headaches and extra sensitivity to light and sound. As always with musicians – witness Myra's surgery that same year – everything was hushed up.

Jelly's account tallies with others who attest to Myra's astronomically high standards, and her sometimes brusque manner of expressing them. The iron fist would have emerged where musical matters were concerned – and Jelly would have known Myra well enough to see through any vestige of velvet glove. Whatever happened, it seems to have been irreparable. There is no trace of Jelly's letters to Myra; and in her book, McKenna wrote not a word about this extensive, 21-year partnership.

In the early 1940s, a group of Jelly's supporters – including Vaughan Williams (who had written a concerto for her) and Lady Violet Bonham-Carter – tried to find out why she was so rarely being engaged for performances at the BBC, planning to intercede on her behalf. Unfortunately, rumour had laid blame upon Myra and her influence in the music world following the quarrel.

Jelly's popularity and renown, however, made it unlikely that one person's opinion, even Myra's, would have had such an impact on decision-makers who were themselves experienced, knowledgeable musicians (notably Boult). By 1941 adverse comments about Jelly's fading technical abilities had intensified. After a six-strong listening panel from the BBC submitted a negative report, Boult was charged with telling Jelly apologetically that her broadcasting career was effectively being brought to an end. It was a tragic situation for someone who had been one of the most mesmerising, colourful and inspiring violinists of her day. She would still have had much to offer, even if it was no longer quite perfect. But in music, that is not enough.

It seems most likely that Jelly's worsening problems were the cause of the fallout with Myra, and not vice-versa. Such was the strength of Myra's words, however, that – as with Harriet years before – it was perhaps easier for some people to blame her and 'shoot the messenger', rather than face the message itself. Still, it must have been deeply upsetting for Jelly when her partner and friend reacted in such a way.

There is only an occasional passing mention of Jelly after that in Myra's surviving correspondence and diaries. It is almost as if her duo partner had ceased to exist. Something almost Soviet-like attended Myra's rare but devastating fallouts: she seems to have un-personed these unfortunate souls. Another, possibly, was Sir Kenneth Clark; he was a close friend during the National Gallery years, but wrote that after the war Myra spent most of her time in America: 'Alas, we never met again'[17]. Yet Myra was plentifully in Britain and gave concerts galore, including annual recitals to open the Royal Festival Hall season. The sorry end of the Gallery series may be more responsible for that situation than the institution's former director wished to acknowledge. Nor is there any sign of Myra having much contact with Arnold Bax, or indeed Aldo Antonietti, who was teaching at the Academy.

The exception is Harriet. Despite Myra's digs at her, their paths crossed too often for such ostracism to be feasible. She was the only enemy with whom Myra dealt by keeping her relatively close.

Myra did urgently have to prevent another potentially serious fallout. Annie Friedberg had booked her an extensive season, beginning in November, that would have taken her as far afield as Australia via Honolulu. Myra now had no intention of going, and Annie was incandescent with fury.

Myra sent a telegram:

> Realise seriousness of breaking contract but regret must cancel November December STOP National Gallery Daily Concerts commencing immediately and imperative I remain here STOP Cannot refuse national service STOP Beg everyone appreciate my obligation in unprecedented circumstances STOP Deeply regret my work will keep me in England for the duration of the war. Hess[18]

After the iron fist by cable, the velvet glove went by post:

> A cable has gone to you today, and it is going to cause much sorrow and tribulation to us both. Knowing this, I appeal to the faithfulness and courage I have known in you all these years, to accept it as a minor disaster in a world where so many worse things are happening. I need hardly tell you how seriously I have considered making this sacrifice for my country. I have discussed the question with the wisest people I know, and all have insisted that these National Gallery Concerts cannot be continued successfully without my leadership. I choose every programme and every artist, and I hardly have time to eat or sleep.
>
> I beg you to consider the significance of this war. We are facing the annihilation of everything we hold important, and this wonderful opportunity to provide some spiritual solace seems, in some mysterious way, to have been given into my hands.[19]

Annie, however, refused to accept this. Myra compensated her to the tune of $500, but Annie continued to battle with her over her breach of contract for about a year.

The Return of Music

Four days after the National Gallery concerts began, the Queen's Hall hosted a full-scale orchestral performance. The London Symphony Orchestra was conducted by Wood and Moiseiwitsch was the soloist in the Beethoven 'Emperor' Concerto; the programme also included Elgar's Symphonic Prelude *Polonia*, Dohnányi's Suite in F sharp minor and Beethoven's Symphony No. 5. Neville Cardus, for the *Manchester Guardian*, described it:

> Crowds are swarming to concerts in London, hungry for music. This week-end Queen's Hall has been packed from floor to ceiling for the London Symphony Orchestra [...]
>
> To hear again at Saturday's concert the 'Emperor' Concerto was like coming out of the grave. As Moiseiwitsch played the solo part with a ravishing touch the vast audience sat transfixed ... Faces momentarily lost the ache and strain of the world, lost also the need of the mask or façade. The grave beauty of the slow movement rocked and stilled thousands of hurts and anxieties. ... For in these days music is for those of us who know it not just an escape; on the contrary, it is the only reality, not only as an aesthetic experience but as a philosophical fact. ... I have heard profounder performances of the 'Emperor' Concerto than this one ... but I have seldom known a more moved and uplifted audience. ...[20]

After the initial lockdown, London was by no means a city devoid of music. Only at certain times during the Blitz in 1940-41 did Myra's Gallery concerts soldier on more or less alone. Yet they had acquired a special status and became the only series whose programmes were listed in detail in *The Times*'s weekly updates.

Soon musical organisations around the city and across the country began to respond to the National Gallery concerts with daytime events of their own. By mid November, lunchtime concerts had been started at St Margaret's Westminster. The conductor Harry Blech launched some on Sunday afternoons in Swiss Cottage. A series of lunchtime concerts at the Royal Exchange, which was started in 1943 and organised by Hilda Bor, continued running at the Bishopsgate Institute later and evolved into the City Music Society.

The Royal Philharmonic Society was staging concerts at the Queen's Hall on Thursday afternoons and the London Symphony Orchestra and

London Philharmonic Orchestra performed on weekend afternoons. At Sadler's Wells, opera fans could attend *Rigoletto* or *Il trovatore*. The Manchester Mid-Day Concerts Society, which had been founded in 1915, continued to run and carries on in the 21st century. In Birmingham, the Barber Institute's newly opened concert hall began to hold lunchtime concerts, extending to evening concerts when the war ended.

The Gallery concerts' example was also travelling well beyond Britain. Myra's friends the van Riemsdijks in Amsterdam started a series in the Rijksmuseum. In New York's Metropolitan Museum a group of musicians led by Ernest Hutchinson launched weekly concerts. In Canada, at the Toronto Conservatory of Music, a copycat series attracted enthusiastic audiences and raised several thousand dollars to send to London in support of the National Gallery events.

Myra had demonstrated beyond doubt the value of live music in boosting morale; this continuing impact helped to lay the foundations for musical life in postwar Britain. A Committee for the Encouragement of Music and the Arts (CEMA) was formed to put on concerts for people in air-raid shelters, hospitals and factories; later, chaired by Maynard Keynes, it evolved into the Arts Council of Great Britain.

Myra agreed to be on CEMA's first panel. No doubt she could have devoted herself entirely to musical organising, advocacy and planning, if she wished. Yet she had no plan to abandon the piano. She sought, with unflappable energy, to do both.

Sandwiches, Royalty and Chamber Music

Lady Irene Gater, attending a Gallery lunchtime concert, had noticed that it was indeed lunchtime and she was hungry. She took to Clark the idea of a canteen for audience members who were as hungry for a meal as they were for good music, but had little spare time for either.

Audiences until then had been encouraged to bring sandwiches to eat while they listened, but Howard found the rustling paper wrappings intrusive, and he cannot have been the only one. Lady Gater therefore organised a sandwich bar in the Gallery's Tuscan Room, which opened on 2nd November. Listeners could stand here to eat and listen. Income from the canteen provided a major boost to the concerts' finances and the amount of money they could donate to the MBF.

Joyce Grenfell joined the team of volunteers who staffed the bar and spread the fillings, juggling that service with her theatrical appearances. She invented some fine uses of rationed ingredients. Among the favourites were honey and raisin in brown bread; cream cheese and date; ham and chutney; and 'generous slices of good damp station cake'[21], plus coffee that was soon termed the best in London.

Myra backstage with Howard Ferguson and Joyce Grenfell

So successful was the canteen that in July 1940 Lady Gater opened another in the gallery basement, this time for war workers; it served light lunches between 12 noon and 3pm for members of the fighting services, A.R.P. workers, nurses, and government employees from nearby ministries. The profits went to war charities.

On 26th October a VIP guest arrived for the concert. *The Times* reported:

> The Queen paid an informal visit yesterday to the lunch hour concert at the National Gallery. She arrived at the Gallery just before the artists - the Spanish 'cellist Gaspar Cassadó and the English pianist George [actually Gerald] Moore - stepped on to the platform, and took her seat in the body of the hall with Sir Kenneth Clark, Director of the National Gallery, and Mr. Ronald Jones, secretary of the National Gallery Concerts. The Queen expressed her admiration ... and enjoyed the concert so much that she intends to pay further visits.[22]

She was as good as her word. Perhaps it is no coincidence that when in 1942 the concerts committee were desperate for more audience seating, they were able to borrow 50 chairs from Buckingham Palace. Myra was among musicians invited to play there to entertain the Queen while Augustus John was painting her portrait in 1940. One day she took Saz along and presented her to Her Majesty (again the peculiar tale of a childhood friendship is unmentioned). McKenna tells the story that the Queen remarked to Saz that it must be dull at the ambulance station without air raids. Saz agreed, but said she would rather have it that way.

It might seem strange that not more of these concerts organised by a pianist were piano recitals. In the first couple of years, little more than one a month took place. Moiseiwitsch appeared a week after Myra's inaugural concert; he was a close friend whom she could easily recruit. The popular Solomon (known only by his first name since his child prodigy days – his surname was Cutner), Nicolas Orloff, Mark Hambourg and Denis Matthews all gave recitals in those early months and Irene Scharrer performed an all-Chopin programme. But Vivian Langrish, a former Matthay student who had known Myra for about 40 years, was reportedly hurt that he was never invited.

Instead, a majority of the concerts were by chamber ensembles; and by the end of the war, it was clear that chamber music was by far the most popular fare on offer, especially string quartets. This took many by surprise.

The Menges, Kutcher, Stratton and Blech string quartets were important contributors, and the Griller Quartet often performed with Myra herself. She was dismayed when her honorary nephews feared being called up. She had written to them en masse just after the outbreak of war:

> You are a very important 'institution' in England, and at the moment I think you should be allowed to carry on with your work. Whether

> the authorities can appreciate the fact that a quartet is unique from the point of view of integrity remains to be seen – BUT in any case nothing must be done before you are actually called up (presuming you have not been already?)....
>
> People will soon be begging and clamouring for music and there should be work for you as soon as it can be organised. I do appreciate your wanting your devoted 'Auntie's' opinion and you have my whole-hearted blessing to carry on with your music. If you are urgently needed in other capacities later on – and may heaven prevent it – I know that none of you would hesitate to 'play the game' – whatever that might be?!
>
> In the meantime....if music be the food of sanity – play on. This has been written in instalments punctuated by sirens and whistles. At the moment I have put my name down for A.R.P. [Air Raid Precautions] and we can only live from day to day – wondering what next?[23]

Sir Walford Davies, Master of the Kings Musick, suggested that during the hostilities, 'musicians might contribute more to a war effort as musicians rather than as inefficient aircraftsmen' – and fortunately, the air ministry agreed[24]. Howard, the Griller Quartet and many more were therefore drafted into the RAF Band at Uxbridge, where they were only required for 'duty', ie rehearsals, in the mornings and could then go home. The Grillers became the RAF's official string quartet for the duration, and, like their colleagues, gave frequent concerts for the forces. Howard effectively commuted between his duties there and with Myra, until the Gallery concerts were recognised as essential war work, when he was released from the band. He once recounted that Myra's earthy sense of humour was rumoured to be the source of all the jokes in the RAF: 'You can imagine they were fairly fruity!'[25]

Harriet appeared at the concerts for the first time on 1st November, also with the Griller Quartet; indeed, the war was bringing a select few signs of a rapprochement between the old adversaries, who now had more to unite rather than divide them. She was back in December in a recital with the baritone Arthur Reckless, and subsequently performed the Franck Piano Quintet with the Stratton Quartet in May 1942 and solo recitals in December 1941 and August 1943.

But in whatever form it took – string quartet, piano quintet, singer and pianist with another instrumentalist, a chamber choir, an ensemble from the London Philharmonic Orchestra or instrumental sonatas – chamber music flourished. It seemed born of a collegiality that served the unspoken congregational aspect of the concerts' founding ideals.

Interviewed by *The Times* on 11th October, just after the concerts' first anniversary, Myra commented: 'On the musical side, I think the great thing is that we have killed the absurd belief that there is no public in this country for chamber music. We have offered nothing but chamber music and we have never lacked a deeply attentive and appreciative audience.' Besides, as she later noted in a post-war interview in Canada, 'Everybody was very busy during the war and there was nobody to tell the people that this sort of music was over their heads. So they came and liked it.'[26]

Team Spirit

Howard had quickly become Myra's right-hand man in the planning process. They would map out the programmes about a month in advance, after which much of the contacting and cajoling of musicians was down to him; Emmie Tillett would finalise the contracts, with invaluable support from her employee Sadie Lereculey. It was, Howard told Finzi, a joy to help.

He also recruited an eager 17-year-old lad to 'nanny' the concerts: this was the young John Amis. He had to oil the invisible but essential side of the proceedings, making sure everything was prepared, keeping the musicians happy and doing the book-keeping afterwards. Sometimes he would turn the pages; occasionally he even had to push a nervous musician out onto the platform.

After the performances he might have lunch with Myra, Howard, Beryl and other friends at the Garrick Hotel, behind the National Portrait Gallery. Myra called him 'Robert' because she thought he rather resembled Schumann. When suffering an attack of nerves, she might say to him (he reported): 'Why do I ever say I will give a concert? I'm never going to appear in public again. Robert, remind me about this when I come off, will you?' [27]

Myra and Howard assumed at first that an orchestra could not fit into the gallery. Then it became clear that a small one could, an ideal size for Bach or Mozart concertos. On 16th November they invited the Tudor Strings, of which Vaughan Williams was president, with a harpsichordist, Lucille Wallace. Its conductor, Cuthbert Bates, became the first person to raise a baton at the gallery.

On 23rd November they went further: the Boyd Neel String Orchestra was conducted by none other than Sir Henry Wood, on Myra's insistence. She, violinist Frederick Grinke and flautist Gordon Walker were the concerto soloists. She often called upon Neel himself to conduct a Bach or Mozart concerto thereafter, though he remembered 'one day doing the Bach F minor with Myra and bomb obbligato!'[28] In due course, Myra achieved a long-held dream of performing all the Mozart piano concertos, in chronological order (they did 21; there are now known to be 27). She had misgivings, but went ahead anyway, and triumphed.

Myra and Howard were inundated with proposals from artists, especially young performers, who wished to take part and listed their potential programmes. The planning process therefore had to assure a good balance and minimise clashes. Myra was eager to support young talent, but she was careful not to admit repetitions of a work that might have been recently performed by someone else.

Too many young pianists would offer the Beethoven 'Appassionata' or 'Waldstein' sonatas; what, she wondered, about all the others? This sparked the idea that in due course, the Gallery would host every one of the complete 32. Another complete cycle, the Beethoven string quartets and chamber music for piano and strings, became a further long-term project.

Among the younger pianists in the line-up was Denis Matthews, who had been recommended to Myra by his teacher, Harold Craxton. He had long been mesmerised by what he termed Myra's 'magic properties, the spiritual quality in her playing, call it the gift of making the piano sing with a human voice, call it more simply "personality" or "soul"'. Although he did not study with her formally – she had little time for teaching then – he became something of a protégé and would consult her for advice, or sometimes play the orchestral part of a concerto on a second piano for her to rehearse. He also enjoyed writing cadenzas for her Mozart concerto performances, as she had long abandoned attempts to create her own. He found her 'always experimenting and seeking to improve what had seemed to us perfect. "I do hate fools!" was a favourite expression of self-reproach.'[29]

Given the frenetic anti-German atmosphere that had prevailed in the previous war, Myra was pleased to find that her Gallery audience was perfectly able to distinguish between German culture and the corruption of it by fascism. Nobody now blamed long-dead composers for where they were born. She watched with relief as they lapped up Bach,

Beethoven, Brahms and Schumann. The BBC refused to broadcast the German language for the duration. But at the Gallery, songs in German were accepted without question.

The mezzo-soprano Elena Gerhardt had left Nazi Germany for Britain in 1935. Myra accompanied her in Lieder recitals from time to time and admired her tremendously. 'Her deeply moving interpretations have the element of eternity,' she wrote in her preface to Gerhardt's autobiography, 'and leave us with a positive memory such as we retain of great paintings, sculpture and architecture.'[30]

A photograph of Elena Gerhardt, inscribed to Myra

She visited Gerhardt and her husband to ask her to participate – but at first the surprised singer protested that she could not sing Lieder in translation and that she was, in any case, still a German. Myra insisted that she must sing in German and that she was so loved by the British public that her nationality would not matter. Gerhardt had considered herself retired, 'but I really could not resist the temptation to sing to the public again,' she wrote. 'Thank you, dearest Myra, for bringing all this happiness into my life again!'[31]

The recital took place on 1st December 1939. On the way there in a taxi, the pianist Gerald Moore recounted, Myra had mapped out how she would respond should there be objections to the German language, though she said not a word to Gerhardt about it. Walking on to begin, Myra was tenser than she let anybody know. Such a roar of applause greeted Gerhardt, however, that in her relief she sang better than ever.

When news came that Hitler had invaded the Netherlands in May 1940, Myra, who held a deep affection for the country, was profoundly upset. The attacks were at their worst when she and Gerhardt were due to give their next joint concert. The distressed singer rang her that morning. She was convinced she could not possibly sing in German at such a moment. Despite her own inner turmoil, Myra again assured her it would make no difference, and talked her into going ahead. In the event, they were greeted by such an ovation that it was quite a few minutes before Gerhardt could begin singing. Myra recounted later: 'In the First World War, we weren't allowed to mention a German word. Songs had to be sung in English and Schumann's "Warum?" was called "Pourquoi?" … It was a nice proof that in this war, music and the words written for the music were more important.'

In all, Gerhardt performed in 22 of the concerts, sometimes with Myra, other times with Gerald Moore. Once Lionel Tertis joined them in Brahms's songs for mezzo-soprano and viola. On another occasion, the usher asked Gerhardt how many pupils she had. He had tried to explain to the crowd massing outside that the concert was full, but dozens of people were declaring themselves her students in the hope of being admitted.

Going Cuckoo

For New Year's Day 1940, Myra put on a concert that became a legend in its own right. The next day *The Times*, perhaps delivering the understatement of the musical year, reported that 'a certain levity was discernible in its treatment'. One highlight was Schumann's *Carnaval* – a set of 21 short pieces depicting masked revellers, full of musical ciphers and witty portraits of the composer's friends. Normally it is for solo piano; this time it was played by ten artists taking turns on two pianos. Myra and Benno opened the proceedings, followed by Cyril Smith and Kathleen Long, William Murdoch and Eileen Joyce, Lance Dossor and Irene Scharrer, and finally Clifford Curzon and John Simons, before Myra and Benno returned for the final rousing and topical 'March of the Davidsbündler against the Philistines'.

New Year's Day 1940 – 'a certain levity'

The concert also included a Mozart duo for cello and bassoon, and Myra and Benno bouncing through the Brahms Waltzes in duet, but it culminated with the Toy Symphony – a piece then thought to be by Joseph Haydn, later attributed to Leopold Mozart, but subsequently found to have been copied but not composed by him. We may never know who wrote this outrageous 18th-century 'cassation', or divertimento, in three movements for two oboes, two horns, strings and a gaggle of toy instruments, but whoever it may be is missing out on posthumous accolades; and whether it was Myra, Howard or someone else who first thought of putting it on with an all-star line-up on the toys, it was a stroke of inspiration. Myra, Irene and Benno – plus Elgar on the cymbals – had all appeared in a charity performance for the Red Cross of another Toy Symphony, by Richard Blagrove, back in 1918. Perhaps that explained it.

All that day's performers took part, plus the concerts committee and some of their friends. Clark conducted, despite never having tried such a thing before. In preparation, he lunched with Sir Thomas Beecham, who went through the score with him in detail; and Clark took his task so seriously that he castigated Myra and Elena Gerhardt for mucking about at the back. 'I banged away on the cymbal,' Gerhardt remembered, 'always coming in at the wrong time; but we achieved what Myra wanted – gaiety.'[32]

The Times critic continued:

> Sir Kenneth Clark ... added yet another art to his many accomplishments and conducted a spirited performance. The strings were provided by the Menges Quartet, but on this kind of occasion it is the wind and percussion which provide the airs and graces. Miss Irene Scharrer and Miss Myra Hess played the cuckoos with a marked difference of phrasing, Miss Scharrer favouring the legato style, Miss Hess the catch-in-the-throat between Cuck and oo. Mr. Moiseiwitsch had an airy way with the quail and a firmer touch with the triangle. Those aqueous instruments, the nightingales, poured smooth trills from the lips of Miss Joyce Grenfell and Mr. John Simons. The indefatigable secretary of the concerts, Mr. Ronald Jones, croaked richly on the rattle, while the drums employed a whole galaxy of talent – Mme. Gerhardt, Miss Denise Lassimonne, and Mr. Murdoch. A member of the peevish tribe of critics, even, was allowed to add his querulous note to the battery and had his chance, like the rest, of coming in in the wrong

> place. The audience came early and in large numbers to take part in an auspicious jollification.

Benno hit the triangle so hard that he dropped the stick. Myra and Irene were overcome with laughter and had to stop playing. Joyce remarked that while the audience of 1,280 seemed to have enjoyed themselves, nobody could have had as much fun as the orchestra did. It was a much-needed moment of levity for all.

The Times had carried an article on 30th December headed 'A Stock-Taking: National Gallery Concerts'. It noted that even though most West End theatres had reopened, along with the crucial transport hub of Oxford Circus tube station, London had had only two orchestral evening concerts during the autumn. But the Gallery concerts were a conspicuous gain, highlighting the ideals, shared with the Proms, of high quality and easy access:

> Herein something new has been achieved in London's music … The type of short chamber concert in which the smaller forms of music could be enjoyed with the informality for which they were designed has been publicly unobtainable hitherto. … The fact that the concerts are daily events, at which one can always be sure of hearing something good, has brought to them the eager audiences and the keen attention that similar conditions have evoked at the Proms. … on the economic side the provision of a building and service by the Trustees is a factor of importance, which might be examined at some future time when the question of a subsidy to the art of music is under consideration. … The shock of war has not been all loss if it produces something new and valuable like this series of concerts, which is already developing into an institution.

When the concerts reached their 100th event on 28th February 1940, Myra performed the Mozart G minor Piano Quartet with Isolde Menges and her quartet, which also played Schubert and Mendelssohn. This was the first Gallery concert to be broadcast by the BBC. So far about 65,000 people had attended, 260 artists had appeared, £1,500 had been paid in fees and £1,000 donated to the MBF. 'Miss Hess has every reason to be proud of the venture, which she launched in the disturbed and perplexing conditions of last autumn,' *The Times* wrote, 'and it will be surprising if some permanent mark is not left upon London's musical life by the success of her experiment.'

As for the canteen staff, they were working 'like beavers' – especially when Myra herself played, when an outsized queue was assured. One April Friday in 1940 they made and sold 1,700 sandwiches. Joyce reckoned they would have sold still more, if they had had the bread. By the time the concert started, she and her co-workers felt 'whacked'. 'But it was the [Brahms] Horn Trio… and it did the trick. Heavenly music it is.'[33]

1 N. Hess interview with HF
2 H. Ferguson, 'The National Gallery Concerts and After', *Myra Hess by her Friends*, p90
3 MH to F.W. Ogilvie, 15 September 1939, BBC Written Archives
4 Author interview with Nadia Lasserson
5 E. Burgoyne, interview with MH, *The Queen*, 18 June 1941
6 K. Clark, *The Other Half*, pp27-28
7 Ibid.
8 H. Ferguson, op. cit., p94
9 https://vaughanwilliamsfoundation.org/
10 MH to JDA, 4 October 1939
11 H. Ferguson, op. cit., p91
12 K. Clark, op. cit., p28
13 *The Times*, 11 October 1939
14 *The Manchester Guardian*, 11 October 1939
15 J. Macleod, *The Sisters d'Arányi*, p272
16 Author interview with SK
17 K. Clark, op. cit., p30
18 MH to Annie Friedberg, 9 October 1939
19 MH to AF, 4 December 1939
20 *The Manchester Guardian*, 16 October 1939
21 J. Grenfell, 'Julia M.' in *Myra Hess and Her Friends*, p61
22 *The Times*, 27 October 1939
23 MH to SG, 5 Sept 1939, courtesy of Arnold Griller
24 Ferguson, *Music, Friends and Places*, p52-54
25 NH interview with HF
26 MH interview, *Winnipeg Free Press*, 8 March 1954
27 J. Amis, *Amiscellany*, p85
28 B. Neel, *Orchestras and Other Adventures*, p106
29 D. Matthews, *In Pursuit of Music*, p88-89
30 MH in E. Gerhardt, *Recital*, pvii
31 E. Gerhardt, op. cit., p126
32 E. Gerhardt, op. cit., p128
33 J. Grenfell to her mother, *Darling Ma*, p189

Against All Odds

(1940–1945)

Ringing the Changes

BEHIND THE SCENES, the Gallery concerts' practical problems were endless. One of the first Clark had to tackle was the bells of St Martin-in-the-Fields, which rang for five minutes every day at 1.25pm. Clark used his diplomatic skills to persuade the vicar to shorten the peals to three minutes from 1.27pm and requested a pause in the concert in progress at that time. Most performers, though, would not simply stop a piece of music in mid flow. The letters continued until the Gallery team finally managed to prevail and obtain silence.

In the summer, military brass bands would play in Trafalgar Square, right outside the Gallery. This was more difficult to challenge, because the London County Council sourly insisted that they gave benefit to a far greater public than that served by the National Gallery Concerts. Myra herself finally won this battle, but not until 1943. She agreed to a photo opportunity beside a bomber plane in the square, making an appeal for War Savings; in return the bands were stopped. It was a measure, perhaps, of just how significant a public figure she had become.

Meanwhile, Clark had to fend off worthy applications for use of the Gallery for other purposes: an office for various arts organisations displaced from their own by bomb damage, or a ballroom for national workers. The Warden, William Gibson, wrote polite but firm replies. Along the way, Myra found herself being consulted on how to fund the stewards who staffed the ladies' toilets.

The concerts were just short of their first anniversary when, following the fall of France in June, the Battle of Britain began and, on 7th September 1940, the Blitz. Bombing raids became daily occurrences. The National Gallery was blessed with a strong basement and their weekly programme began to state: IN CASE OF AIR RAID WARNING THE AUDIENCE WILL PROCEED DOWNSTAIRS WHERE ADEQUATE PROTECTION IS AVAILABLE. The concertgoers appeared undaunted. During air raid warnings, nobody could be admitted to a government building; rather than cancelling, however, most artists postponed start time until the danger had passed.

The concerts soon had to shunt in their entirety to the downstairs shelter, which accommodated only a few hundred people. This situation continued until June 1941. The roof leaked and the water had to be collected in a series of buckets; the piano was protected by a waterproof cover.

Myra performs at the National Gallery

On 15th October, Myra was told that a time-bomb had fallen on the gallery. Within half an hour she had managed to relocate that day's concert to South Africa House, nearby on Trafalgar Square. It was the only time the concerts moved out. But another time-bomb turned up straight afterwards, due to which they transferred to a distant corner of the building. It exploded two days later, in the middle of a Beethoven string quartet.

The Stratton Quartet was playing. Its violist, Watson Forbes, had arrived to find a bomb disposal squad on the premises; the group was then given the all-clear to begin the Op. 59 No. 1 'Razumovsky' Quartet. 'It was during the very tricky second movement – Beethoven's little game of using one note rhythmically repeated – that the explosion occurred,' Forbes related. 'Consternation! Some people immediately rose to get out to safety, others cowered beneath their seats – we just played on. Personally I was counting the beats like the blazes, since it is an easy movement in which to get lost.'[1] Myra later said of the incident: 'I think this is an historical example of British tenacity and presence of mind.'[2]

There were no injuries, but the bomb shattered the windows of the downstairs concert room. With nothing to intervene between her hands and the icy winter air, Myra played in a fur coat. 'Performers battled with blue fingers, helped only by a couple of oil-stoves on the platform, while the audience wrapped themselves in rugs and top coats,' Howard wrote. [3]

Myra had in her personal ammunition several invaluable qualities. One was her sense of humour; there is precious little sign that it ever let her down. Next, she was extremely bright, able to build on her existing skills in whole new ways. She could extend her expertise at performing to public speaking, the principles of which she had probably learned from Jessie Matthay. This enabled her to become a powerful, eloquent advocate for music and musicians. She had one more vital attribute: that untranslatable daring known as *chutzpah*. As Howard put it, 'she knew exactly what she wanted; she did not mind how much trouble she took to achieve it; and she was able, with an irresistible combination of humour and urgency, to charm almost anything out of anybody.'[4]

Mending the gallery roof required extensive lobbying of the Ministry of Works by Clark, Lady Gater and Myra. Once, repairs were underway when another attack undid the lot. After the war, Myra told the interviewer

Jim Fassett a delightful story (although it may be apocryphal – nobody seems sure how she got hold of the oranges):

> I knew a very nice young man at the Office of Works, and at that time we had forgotten about oranges. We never saw any, but somebody had sent me some from Tasmania or Australia or somewhere – so I rushed down to Trafalgar Square with the oranges and met this young man and I said if you have that ceiling mended this afternoon I'll give you the oranges. So he had the oranges and the ceiling was mended. Those oranges proved very valuable. If I had gone through the usual channels of government offices, it probably would have taken three weeks to get the roof mended.[5]

In private, she was trying to keep her personal compass steady. In December 1940 she wrote to Bruce Simonds in America:

> We never have a shade of doubt about the ultimate triumph of Light over Darkness. I only hope we shall keep our sanity when we turn on all the lights and open the curtains wide. Although there have been various vicissitudes....we have not missed a day's concert at the National Gallery. These last weeks have been particularly strenuous, and my programs so varied that I sometimes feel like the chameleon who burst when placed upon a piece of Scotch plaid. You ask if I practise? Precious little...at least the kind of practicing [sic] I like to do, but the Lord seems to be with me and when music is needed as never before, the imagination seems to be forthcoming when one actually gets to the concert. It is incredible how we can adapt ourselves to a state of existence beyond the direst imagination, but the steady belief that 'all will be well' keeps us sane and full of determination.[6]

After the raids decreased in June 1941, the concerts ventured back upstairs. They continued there for the rest of the war, but for three months in summer 1944 when attacks by 'doodle-bugs' – flying bombs – proliferated, sending the musicians and their listeners back to the basement.

Months of reduced audience numbers in the shelter had played havoc with the concerts' financial model, and it was largely thanks to Myra's American fans that they were able to continue. Professor Arthur Mendel, who was editor of the American Musicological Society's journal, organised an appeal. It raised more than £4,000 as 'a token of appreciation' (Howard wrote) 'for all that she had done and was doing for music and her country'.

It was not only philanthropists who contributed, but musicians such as Toscanini, Rachmaninoff and Heifetz, music lovers and even members of concert hall staff. The previous summer, Tanglewood had hosted 'A Festival of Britain' with the Boston Symphony Orchestra under Serge Koussevitzky, proceeds of which were intended for the National Gallery Concerts via the Allied Relief Fund.

Myra wrote to Julia Steinway, thanking her for the company's support:

> I feel a little shy about a Myra Hess Fund for British musicians but if you think my name will gather my friends around the cause, then this is no time for modesty! I can't tell you what it would mean to have any financial help. Not only are we faced with a hard winter and the plight of so many musicians is appalling, but as I told our audience the other day – I want to keep this little oasis of peace going in the heart of London, and although we may be a small community, the principle of not being deterred by these evil forces is important.[7]

The amount of money left Myra feeling quite overwhelmed:

> I cannot tell you how deeply I have been touched by the response from all my friends. Perhaps you can imagine what this means to me. It has lifted me out of the inevitable cloud of sorrow that surrounds us, and I am so thrilled to know that I need not worry about the future of our concerts. It would have broken my heart if we had had to give them up, and it would have been a disaster financially and spiritually to all our musicians, and the many hundreds of regular members of our audience would have been deprived of this respite from the grim happenings in our world.

She voiced her thanks publicly in a transatlantic broadcast in June 1942, in a speech that sounds even more statesmanlike than the statesmen of the day:

> The last time I spoke to you, my friends in the United States and Canada, I spoke, like tonight, from the heart of London. Since then, Nazi bombs have again wounded this great city, and many other cities and villages throughout the country. As you know, my work takes me through the length and breadth of this green island. And now that spring is here, Nature has spread her cloak over the hideous scars of war. Lilac, laburnum, flowering thorn and apple blossom cover ruin and desolation with a living tapestry. This camouflage of Nature

> has its counterpart in the people of this country. Their spirit at this moment is protected by a shield every bit as magnificent.
>
> My concerts take me to small towns, badly blitzed, where what was once a concert hall is either a burnt-out ruin or a large and exceedingly ugly crater. But people are quick to find a substitute, and I find myself playing in a school hall, a cinema, a dance hall, or an ancient Elizabethan barn. In the old days one had to advertise a concert extensively. Now, the news immediately gets around by word of mouth that on 'such and such a date' so and so is giving a concert. And on 'such and such a date' there is not even standing room. I have discovered a new audience that wears dungarees and overalls – people from the factories who, Heaven knows, have little enough time for themselves, giving their days and nights as they are, to the defence of our country – men and women who have stood for hours by their machinery, willingly giving up their whole lunch hour to hear us play Bach or Schumann. Once a person really decides to listen to it, music is the most immediate communication there is. For anybody who wants to think, music gives them all they need; for anybody who wants to forget, it will give them that too.
>
> I wish there were some way in which my fellow musicians and I could show you our deep and heartfelt gratitude. Your great understanding of our need for music in these dark days is a symbol of the spiritual bond between our two countries – a bond which will be a great factor in the future of the world. Perhaps in imagination you will come with me to the National Gallery after one of our bad night-time raids, the audience a little pale from lack of sleep, listening to our playing, serenity returning to their minds and their faces, convincing us all again of the healing power of music.[8]

She concluded by playing to her broadcast audience one of her best-loved 'signature' pieces: the Brahms Waltz in A flat major.

When the series reached its 500th concert on 14th August 1941, Myra made another heartfelt speech. She acknowledged that reaching this landmark had exceeded her highest hopes, related the story of how the concerts began and described the many difficulties, both explosive and financial, that had threatened them. But above all, she pointed up the full significance of music as a human and social need, especially in times of trouble:

> Although we are extremely happy to be up here, and to be able to admit large audiences again, those somewhat uncomfortable months downstairs were extraordinarily moving....and proved once and for all that music is not only a pleasant diversion... as some would have us believe....but to many thousands of people it is a necessity - for the preservation of those spiritual forces for which we, as a Nation, are ready to give our lives.
>
> Since Elizabethan days....there has probably never been such a demand for music as there is today...throughout this country....and it is not only the musically educated who come to concerts....many come because of the instinctive feeling of SECURITY which great music can give....to all who have an ear to listen.

She went on to thank her colleagues, performers and assistants, as well as the lavish financial help they had received from the US and Canada, before concluding:

> I have the feeling that these and countless other proofs of interest are significant of a spirit of unity in this Nation for the preservation and strengthening of spiritual values - expressed in this case by music - This unity has been created by the dangers and high courage of the war; but if it could be carried on into the Peace which will follow - if we could prevent ourselves from slipping back into the moral laziness of easier days - THEN perhaps this dark agony will not have been in vain, and we may be ready to bear our part in building a new world out of the wreckage of the old.

Myra put her fund to good use, not solely within the concert series. In September 1943 she wrote to Sidney Griller, whose quartet was struggling financially:

> Dearest Sidney,
>
> Howardie has assured you that I have a very private Fund with which I can do what I D – B – like! In politer terms, those are the conditions made by the various donors.
>
> Please always let me know if there is a pending 'morendo' in your bank account. Who else would I prefer to benefit by this useful little fund?[9]

Home and Away

Myra had much to contend with beyond the gallery. The Heath Extension, opposite her house, was now home to six anti-aircraft guns, which were being fired all night. They were, moreover, targets for the Nazi bombs. Myra's house survived by sheer good fortune; the actor Alistair Sim's neighbouring house was destroyed by a direct hit that miraculously left hers intact. She loathed the air-raid shelters; she and Beryl, rather than remove themselves to one nearby, would hide under the piano, where they continued their paperwork for the concerts, did crosswords or played card games. Like many others, they learned to turn their slippers upside down before going to bed lest shattered glass should find its way into them.

By November 1940, Myra had found a solution to this local 'inferno' (as John Maul, who was serving as a volunteer policeman, termed it). While other people were leaving London, she moved further in. 'It seemed like the hand of the Lord when the lady next door [at 54 Abbey Road] to Anita and her sister fled from London and wanted to let her house,' she wrote to Bruce Simonds. 'I have taken it by the month (for a mere song…or perhaps a cadenza…).'[10] Marjorie and Anita were busy with their ambulance work, but now in their studio Myra and Marj could spend spare evenings playing violin sonatas together. It did not escape Myra's friends' notice that she had exchanged the guns of Hampstead Heath for the Gunns of St John's Wood.

Not all her friends and colleagues were so fortunate. The pianist Kathleen Long's home had been destroyed; she retrieved a concert dress from the wreckage and gave a performance the same day, which Myra said was the finest she had heard her play. Sir Kenneth Clark and his wife were asleep in their flat at 5 Gray's Inn Square on 7th September 1940 when a blast blew them out of bed: a bomb had destroyed the two first floors of the block, leaving their apartment 'hanging rather precariously over the void'[11]. On the night of 10th-11th May 1941 – the worst night of the Blitz – Clare Mackail was at a prayer meeting of her Group at 43 York Terrace when a 500lb bomb struck a house two doors away. The blast shattered the glass roof directly above the women. As it fell in, Clare suffered a broken back and leg; many of her companions were killed.

Harriet Cohen's St John's Wood cottage in Abercorn Place, which Bax had funded for her, was destroyed by an incendiary bomb that burned to a cinder her precious collection of music manuscripts as well as her piano. She promptly moved into the Dorchester Hotel, persuading them to let her sleep, as she put it, in a camp bed on the kitchen stairs, where (to Bax's consternation) she stayed for about a year. Myra, though commiserating with Harriet's plight, joked among friends that people would say she, Myra, had arranged for the Nazis to drop that bomb. And it was Myra, not Harriet, who gave a gala recital at the Dorchester that November in the presence of the King and Queen.

Before the war Harriet had toured widely, including a 1934 trip to Russia, where she was enraptured by the music of Shostakovich. She became the first British pianist to perform his 24 Preludes and Fugues. Myra gave her a Gallery concert in December 1941 which Harriet devoted to Russian repertoire – Shostakovich, Kabalevsky, Polovinkin and Mepurnov (a programme she had previously performed for the BBC in 1935). She had also visited Palestine, where she met Chaim Weitzmann, had dinner with the British High Commissioner and Golda Meir and narrowly escaped from a gun battle near Nablus. The experience made her into a vociferous Zionist activist as the situation of the European Jewish population became increasingly perilous. In Britain she began to give lectures on the subject. Mentioning the National Gallery concerts in her autobiography, only in passing, Harriet did not comment on them being Myra's initiative.

Unlike Myra, she did not cancel her American tour in the winter of 1939. On heading home in April 1940, she lobbied British officialdom with the idea of establishing an international Jewish Army; this, however, was given short shrift. In the background, her affair with Bax was rumbling on, seemingly undimmed by each enjoying myriad others. Bax had been knighted in 1937; in 1941 he was appointed Master of the King's Musick.

Some musicians removed themselves from the war altogether. Benjamin Britten and his partner Peter Pears, who were pacifists, spent the first part of the war in the US, before returning in 1942 on a Swedish cargo ship that took about a month to make the perilous crossing to Liverpool. Beecham had also departed for America, not through pacifism but for his own safety, leaving the London Philharmonic Orchestra, which he had founded, without a conductor and without money. Its continued existence depended on a giant fundraising effort.

It was lucky to survive something still worse. On that terrible Blitz night of 10th-11th May 1941, hours after the Royal Choral Society and the LPO, conducted by Sir Malcolm Sargent, had performed Elgar's *The Dream of Gerontius*, an incendiary bomb struck the Queen's Hall. By dawn, that beloved venue was gutted beyond repair. The orchestra's instruments, left there after the concert, had gone up in smoke. Moura Lympany arrived expecting to rehearse the Franck Symphonic Variations, having spent the night under her piano. She could only stare helplessly, alongside heartbroken orchestra members, at the only thing left: a music-stand bearing sheet music for *Loveliest of Trees* by Muriel Herbert. Myra had given her last concert at the hall on 27th April, performing the Schumann Concerto with Boult.

That was the end of the British capital's only hall genuinely well suited in capacity, acoustics and location to large-scale orchestral music. Wood's Promenade Concerts moved to the Royal Albert Hall, where he conducted the opening night on 12th July, ending by 9pm so that everyone could get home in time for the blackout. By 1943 the Proms were well embedded in this new, much larger venue; that year the series sold around a quarter of a million tickets. A bronze bust of Sir Henry Wood, salvaged from the Queen's Hall ashes, is still displayed annually at the Proms and crowned with a laurel wreath on the Last Night.

Myra by no means confined her performances to the Gallery. She was busy with charity concerts: a recital at the Palladium for the National Sunday League in March 1940, for instance, or performing around the country for the war wounded. In one home for victims in Blackpool, she was asked to autograph the piano after her concert; this cannot have been a solitary request. In November 1941, she took part alongside Irene, Ernest Read and Uncle Tobs in a half-hour dramatization on the Home Service of *The Life and Work of Tobias Matthay*; all of them played themselves.

She was in Scotland when Hitler's deputy, Rudolf Hess, arrived there too, by parachute, in a startling attempt to create a rapprochement between Britain and Germany. Myra's surname inevitably caused some hilarity; by now, those not in the know occasionally assumed she was Mrs R. Hess, despite her touring Britain unchecked. Benno (a rejected suitor) sent her a teasing telegram: 'How devoted your husband must be to fly all the way to Scotland to meet you!'[12] Moreover, Myra tripped on an Aberdeen curb and was then astounded to see a headline: 'HESS HURTS ANKLE'. Later that month, she could have enjoyed headlines in *The Times* such as 'Hess's Knowledge of Nazi Plans', 'Hess as Hitler's Astrologer' and 'Mr Bevin on Hess's Record: "A Murderer"'.

That June in Wolverhampton Town Hall she made with the City of Birmingham Orchestra a rare studio recording of a concerto: Franck's Symphonic Variations. She had hoped to work with her friend Leslie Heward, the CBO's principal conductor, but he was unwell; Basil Cameron took his place. Myra's playing of this introspective music is focused and soul-searching; perhaps she inadvertently captures some of the emotions that she and her colleagues had been experiencing in those dark times. It was the first time the CBO had recorded a concerto and they respond mellifluously in conversational exchanges with Myra's eloquent phrasing. The total effect seems full of longing, shadows and hope.

The following March in Manchester she recorded with the Hallé Orchestra under Heward: Mozart's Piano Concerto in C major K467, with cadenzas provided by Denis Matthews. The result, however, was not released in Myra's lifetime. The sessions' problems were blamed on 'wartime exigencies', including sporadic disruptions to the power supply, which caused serious fluctuations in the pitch. The master tapes, regarded as unusable, were not retained. The performance was eventually reconstructed from test pressings in 1990 and is included in APR's admirable set of Myra's complete studio recordings, thanks to digital enhancements.

Myra, by insisting on maintaining her patriotic duties at home, had chosen what the poet Robert Frost termed 'the road less travelled by'. She was missing her American tours, but had no thought of changing direction. She wrote to her friend Lady Margaret Campbell at the British Embassy in Washington DC, outlining her feelings:

> My work is so formidable these days, that the rest of my life seems to have been a holiday... I am so homesick sometimes for America that I can hardly bear to think about it, and I would give a great deal to be visiting you now, in Washington.
>
> There were rumours that I was to come over on a 'goodwill' tour, but I could not possibly leave England until this terrible nightmare is over. Although the musical community may be small, in this chaotic world, many thousands continue to come to our daily concerts at the National Gallery, and nothing has deterred us since October 10th 1939.....Nearly two thousand people came during this last week of such grim ordeals.
>
> The task of making twenty programmes every month falls mainly on my shoulders, and besides playing most weeks myself I have also been touring all over the country with the London Symphony Orchestra. The audiences have been marvellous, and I feel that the only way I can contribute to the great effort our country is making is to provide

> a few peaceful hours in the midst of the turmoil. The concerts have provided over £11,000 which is spent in the small fees and by giving donations to the Mus. Benevolent Fund, and during the last few months I have had the most touching and generous donations from America. Some friends started a Fund in my name, and the cheques continue to pour in.... Without this help we could not have carried on in our temporary concert-room, which is very small. I am hoping that we can go back to the larger one again, which will enable us to make a profit instead of a weekly deficit. Amongst many other things, I am learning the delights of committee meetings!!.... [13]

During 1941 Myra penned some thoughts on her continued efforts and their value for a magazine in the US.

> I'll never forget, after one of the worst London air raids through which nobody slept at all, I drove to the Gallery down streets filled with debris of all kinds. Houses were demolished everywhere. 'There'll be a small audience today,' I thought, but we had an overflow house of 500 people - a little pale from lack of sleep, but listening to our music, serenity returning to their minds and their faces. They had come, through streets littered with broken glass and reeking with dust and smoke, to get the spiritual strength more vital to them than physical rest - the healing power of music.[14]

The Unsung Activist

Less publicly, Myra was becoming a lobbyist on behalf of the Jewish refugees who were fleeing Nazi-occupied lands in fear of their lives. While Harriet was giving public lectures with grand visions, Myra was working behind the scenes, together with Vaughan Williams, to bring aid to as many individuals as she could. She had been putting her efforts, and her money, behind her convictions for a good while.

In 1938, after much lobbying, the British government agreed to a scheme by which unaccompanied Jewish children aged approximately between 11 and 17 could be brought to Britain to lodge with foster families. For the 'Kindertransport', each child needed a guarantor – a private citizen or organisation – to make a deposit of £50 (equivalent to about £2800 in the 2020s) for child care, education and, supposedly, eventual repatriation, because the government did not wish to commit public funds to this. The rescue trains were mostly arranged by organisations such as the Central British Fund for German Jewry and Youth Aliyah, or groups like the Society of Friends (Quakers). A British banker, Nicholas Winton, quietly instigated the Kindertransport from Prague, rescuing 669 children without even telling his wife. His motto was: 'If something is not impossible, then there must be a way to do it.'

Myra at the piano

Many of the youngsters never saw their families again; most of those left behind were slaughtered in ghettos and death camps. The separations were traumatic, and some of the children later spent years searching for the truth about what had happened to their families. But before war broke out the scheme was able to save the lives of around 10,000 young people.

On the list of Winton's Prague Kindertransport on 29th June 1939 are the names of two sisters, Ella and Josephine Eberstark, who left together with a third sister, Alis. Their parents and grandmother were murdered in Majdanek in 1942. Although they had an uncle in London, they were put up with other Kindertransport youngsters in Wyberlye, formerly a convalescent home, near Burgess Hill. A personal guarantee for Ella and a bank guarantee for Josephine were made by Miss Myra Hess of 48 Wildwood Road, London NW11.

The supporters of the Kindertransport were desperate to recruit sponsors. Ella, Josephine and Alis's uncle and aunt in London, Heino and Lotte Dorner, had encouraged Heino's sister and brother-in-law to send their three girls. The Dorners knew a pianist couple, Franz and Tamara Osborn, who may have been a contact point with Myra. Franz, a former student of Artur Schnabel from Berlin, had escaped to London in 1933; he played at the Gallery concerts, with the violinist Max Rostal. Otherwise, she may simply have heard about it on the grapevine. Myra had no personal contact with the girls, but the Eberstarks' relations have commented that they were not the only Kindertransport children she helped.

Ruth's niece Elizabeth Jane Howard as a teenager used to frequent the National Gallery Concerts, mesmerised by the playing of Denis Matthews (with whose teacher, Harold Craxton, she had piano lessons), Nina Milkina and of course Myra. She remembered Myra, who was fond of the whole family, playing duets with her mother and calling her father to source wood for the Gallery platform. Years later, as a celebrated novelist, she received a fan letter from a reader, an elderly lady in Hastings. The letter told her that Myra had got her and her sister out of Germany, saving their lives.

In 1940, Churchill presented the refugees with a new horror. At first only 'enemy aliens' thought to pose a direct threat to national security had been interned, but now, fearing a 'fifth column' of insurgents posing as Jewish refugees, Churchill began to have them interned in camps on the Isle of Man, as well as various racecourses and incomplete housing estates. This policy often resulted in the incarceration of fascist sympathisers from Germany, Austria and Italy alongside Jewish people in desperate circumstances, innocent second or third generation members of families of those backgrounds, and numerous political refugees. After the Battle of Dunkirk in June 1940, 27,700 refugees were arrested. Eight thousand were deported to camps in Canada and Australia. It was later admitted that in this process there had been blunders.

In the Hutchinson Camp on the Isle of Man, some of the Austrian and German intelligentsia famously created a newspaper, lectures, a camp university and art classes; and they put on concerts of their own. Three members of the Amadeus Quartet first met at an internment camp at Prees Heath in Shropshire, still in their teens, then built their friendship on the island. Yet the popular, rather rose-tinted view of all this cultural activity is far indeed from the whole picture.

First, there was the shock: the internees had chiefly believed in the liberal, relatively welcoming attitude of the British. Worse, given the potential for an imminent Nazi invasion with uncertain outcome, the underlying terror was that if Britain did not prevail, then the Jewish immigrants, having been rounded up and detained together, would be easy to hand over for extermination.

The composer Hans Gál, director of the Mainz Conservatory before 1933, had fled Germany with his family. His diary from the Isle of Man reveals a litany of bullying, despair and suicides; his youngest son took his own life there. Egon Wellesz, a successful composer of symphonies, suffered a complete mental collapse in internment after attending a performance of Schubert's *Die schöne Müllerin*. Cultural pursuits depended on the good will of the commanding officers, many of whom were out of their depth or clueless. Family separation, cold, overcrowding, illness and the fact that nobody knew how long this heinous situation would carry on exerted ongoing strains both psychological and physical. Some of the younger inmates took an available route to freedom by joining the British Army[15]. Others died for lack of medical treatment.

When it turned out that only about 4,000 among the tens of thousands of internees might be potential security threats, arguments began over who should be eligible for release. Spotting writers and academics on the agreed list, Clark lobbied for visual artists, arguing that art depended on freedom of expression, which had been denied to them under the Nazi regime. If scholars and writers were released, why not artists?

As for artists, so for musicians. Myra joined forces with Vaughan Williams to advocate for them, including Wellesz and the pianist Ferdinand Rauter, engaging in lengthy battles with the authorities to have them released. Norbert Brainin, Sigmund Nissel and Hans Schidlof – the three-quarters of the Amadeus Quartet to be – were also among those they assisted.

Vaughan Williams had been a co-signatory in a diplomatically worded letter to *The Times* – with his Dorking neighbour and fellow campaigner E.M. Forster (author), H.H. Gordon Clark (high sheriff of Surrey), and Wilfrid Greene (Master of the Rolls) – seeking to ameliorate a situation in which Jewish and other refugees were being interned with Nazi sympathisers; in which even elderly refugee husbands and wives were being cruelly separated; and in which tribunals being mooted to decide on those suitable for release needed to include decision-makers with 'wide Continental experience'.[16] The implication was that many people had no comprehension of the cataclysm unfolding in mainland Europe. In October, following a White Paper, Vaughan Williams was asked to chair the Home Office Committee for the Release of Interned Alien Musicians and to recommend those of 'undoubted distinction'.

Rauter, a non-Jewish Viennese immigrant, was among the first internees released in December 1940; he had spent 23 weeks in four camps in succession, ending with Mooragh on the Isle of Man. He now set up a Refugee Musicians Committee, with the folk music specialist Cecil Sharp's former assistant, Maud Karpeles. The board included Hugh Allen, Vaughan Williams, George Dyson and Stanley Marchant, and, side by side, Harriet and Myra. Besides trying to arrange musicians' release, they intended to help them by making connections with teachers and music colleges; they also wished them to be spared from compulsory employment in, for example, munitions factories, which could damage their hands. Nissel, when released, had to work in a metal factory in the East End.

Dyson, as head of the ISM, had formerly played a role in bringing in protectionist measures aiming to prevent refugees supposedly taking work from British musicians. Myra, who had resigned from the ISM over this, simply overrode that at the Gallery. So, too, did Richard Tauber, the popular Viennese Jewish tenor, who toured Britain unencumbered. It looks as if the ISM's regulations were fortunately a type of 'gentlemen's agreement' – kept by general consent, but if flouted, lacking any solid mechanism for enforcement.

Rauter was beginning a life-changing partnership with the Icelandic singer Engel Lund. Together they performed folk songs of myriad origins which Rauter arranged for voice and piano, including several dozen in Yiddish. Through touring these programmes, circumventing divisions via music, they fostered connections between different communities, putting traditional songs from assorted countries, societies and political stances side by side. At the Gallery, Myra had Lund and Rauter perform their 'Folk Songs from Many Lands' 26 times. On 1st May 1941 it included songs that were German, French, English, Yiddish, Swedish and Danish, which Lund liltingly introduced in turn. In a tally of works performed in the concerts' first five years, 32 Yiddish folksongs are listed. So are 26 from 'Germany, including Austria'.

In that same time span, according to the concerts' fifth anniversary book, around two dozen of the musicians were refugees from the Nazis, from France, Germany, Austria, Hungary, Poland and Latvia. They would benefit not only from the fee, but also from a chance to perform, which could restore a crucial part of their sense of identity, besides winning reviews, recognition, contacts and sometimes BBC radio broadcasts.

Rauter was instrumental in creating, in 1942, the Austrian Musicians Group and later the Anglo-Austrian Music Society (which evolved into the Austrian Cultural Forum). Myra played in one of its early concerts at Wigmore Hall, on 27th October 1943, performing the Brahms B major Trio with members of the Rosé Quartet.

Rauter's plan for this organisation prompted Vaughan Williams to write him a lengthy letter. Here he exhorted him and his fellow Austrian musicians to assimilate into English culture, rather than occupying a culturally superior separate cell which might potentially threaten the less expert 'tender little flower'[17] of English culture. Indeed it was awareness of the immigrants' perceived superior musical training that had previously made the ISM so nervous. This theme recurred time and again in Vaughan Williams's letters, whether on the supposedly shoddy level of opera performance at Sadler's Wells or considering if the Berlin Philharmonic Orchestra should be permitted to emigrate as one body to New Zealand (he thought it should not: it would be too dominant and non-assimilated. Later, he reflected that he had been wrong.)

Far from trampling on anyone, the immigrant musicians enriched musical life in Britain, not only through performances, but also by nurturing, through their influence and teaching, a new generation of artists. Myra's Gallery concerts were often their launch pad. Among them was Peter Gellhorn, the pianist and conductor who became chorus master at Glyndebourne, the private opera house in the South Downs; it was soon virtually an outpost of the old Charlottenburg Opera in Berlin, with Rudolf Bing as general manager, Carl Ebert as artistic director and producer and Fritz Busch as music director. Gellhorn, who lived to be 91, lived in East Sheen, south-west London, and went on to serve as director of the BBC Singers and Choral Society (now Symphony Chorus). He was the first composition teacher of George Benjamin, became chorus master at the Royal Opera House, and well into his eighties conducted the Barnes Choir, terrifying the amateur singers of the neighbourhood by demanding standards that pushed them far beyond their modest expectations.

There was Maria Donska, a pianist from Poland who had studied with Schnabel; the exposure she gained at the Gallery helped her to build her career in Britain, although she suffered a nervous collapse through anxiety about her family's fate in Poland (they were indeed murdered by the Nazis). The pianist Julius Isserlis, who had escaped Soviet Russia for Vienna, then had to escape once more; in London he settled in Roehampton. His three children all became prominent musicians, his son Steven a world-renowned cellist. Peter Stadlen, another magnificent pianist, was among those on whose behalf Vaughan Williams personally lobbied; he went on to become music critic of *The Daily Telegraph*.

From Hungary, the pianist Louis Kentner distinguished himself as a magisterial Liszt player, his interpretations marked by impeccable poise, poetry and grand romantic sweep. He had come to London with his first wife, Ilona Kabos, in 1935; it was at the National Gallery, however, that he gained crucial recognition in Britain. During the war he was the piano soloist, uncredited (at his own request), in the soundtrack for the film *Dangerous Moonlight*, for which Richard Addinsell wrote his *Warsaw Concerto*. He became a naturalised British citizen in 1946 and worked for many years with Yehudi Menuhin, whose sister-in-law Griselda Gould became Kentner's second wife.

The elderly violinist Arnold Rosé played at the Gallery with his string quartet in December 1939, including the cellist Friedrich Buxbaum from Vienna alongside two English colleagues. Rosé was Mahler's brother-in-law and had worked with Brahms. He had escaped Vienna, but his daughter Alma Rosé met her death in Auschwitz in April 1944, apparently by poisoning. She had survived until then by organising and conducting the concentration camp's Women's Orchestra. Her violin was mysteriously retrieved and brought to her grieving father in London.

Max Rostal, a former violin student of Carl Flesch, had taught at the Berlin Hochschüle until the Nazis took power. He came to Britain in 1934, bringing some students with him, including Maria Lidka, who also performed at the Gallery. Rostal himself played there a number of times, including with Franz Osborn on 24th August 1942. When Brainin, Nissel and Schidlof were freed, Rostal agreed to teach them free of charge, then introduced them to the cellist Martin Lovett, with whom they formed the Amadeus Quartet (Schidlof moved to the viola and changed his first name to Peter). The Polish-Jewish child prodigy violinist Ida Haendel, another student of Flesch, had stunned audiences with her performances at the Queen's Hall in 1936-37; she, too, performed several times at the Gallery.

One of the most unusual figures was Karl Haas, who had fled Germany for Britain in 1939: he was a musicologist, conductor, player of the viol and viola d'amore and specialist in early music. He lived for some years in Abbey Road, a few doors up from the Gunns. Later he became music director of the Bristol Old Vic. He and his London Baroque Ensemble were regular Gallery performers, making their public debut there in 1943. With impish humour, he noted that 'baroque' could also mean 'bizarre'; thus their eclectic repertoire extended back to the 16th century, but also forward to the 19th. Their concerts often included, besides Bach cantatas and Handel concertos, first performances – for instance, unknown works by Haydn (trios for two flutes and cello) and Dvořák (two waltzes for string quartet) – and were some of the few complemented by programme notes. They gave the series an influence in the first stirrings of what later became the early music movement. Still, in pieces requiring an organ they could only use a portable instrument; and so, in the programme alongside the regular, prominent credit 'Steinway Piano', there would appear a second line: 'Hammond Organ'.

The situation for refugee composers was rather different. The Gallery concerts did not generally prioritise new music. Myra sensed, accurately enough, that her listeners wanted the musical equivalent of the institution's paintings: reassuring classics that they knew and loved and that would boost their spirits. The contemporary music included was the least frightening sort: typically, works by Howard, Moeran, Vaughan Williams and Britten, some light Stravinsky, a taste of Rawsthorne, Roussel and Respighi, plus the delectable Rachmaninoff and his friend and contemporary Medtner. Harriet introduced some little-known Russian repertoire, headed up by Shostakovich. But only one piece of Schoenberg was played in the first five years: his lavishly romantic string sextet *Verklärte Nacht*.

The music of refugees did occasionally feature: three sonatas and a string trio by Hindemith (who was politically persona non grata in Germany), some pieces by Franz Reizenstein, who played them himself, and the Hungarian Matyás Seiber, whose daring individuality startled some of the audience, but who was one of very few refugees able to build a successful career as a composer in Britain. Most had to find other ways to survive. Gál was brought to Edinburgh by Donald Francis Tovey, the Reid Professor of Music, to catalogue the faculty library; after Tovey's death, he held the professorship himself. Wellesz became an academic at Lincoln College, Oxford. Berthold Goldschmidt worked behind the scenes at the BBC. Walter Bergmann was recruited to teach at Morley College, where Michael Tippett ran a groundbreaking, egalitarian music department.

Tippett himself, a conscientious objector, went to prison in Wormwood Scrubs for three months, rather than compromise by taking on non-musical work in substitute for national service. Myra, whatever her views on conscientious objectors, gave a recital at his invitation at Morley College. She was also a co-signatory to a letter to *The Daily Telegraph* arguing in favour of musicians being allowed to continue practising, so to speak, purely as musicians:

> … There is clearly a great body of opinion which believes that artists, whether they be painters, musicians, dancers, actors, writers or composers, are of more value to their country in their trained capacity, often in key positions, than serving generally with the fighting forces. In the immediate war circumstances they render service of a national character in the maintenance of morale, and their art serves well as a balance to the inhuman tendencies which are the inevitable accompaniments of war. Our art is a measure of our civilisation, and our artists its guardians; it would indeed be a grim irony if, by neglect, we lost the means of its preservation in a struggle for its protection.
>
> The urgency, then, for the preservation of our art, for the protection, even against their will, of its practitioners, and the need in war for all talent to be used to its best advantage, prompts us to suggest that a council should at once be set up to advise The Ministry of Labour to reserve some measure of our talent and devise the best means of its employment in this emergency.
>
> … there is no time to be lost if irreparable damage to our cultural life is to be avoided.
>
> We are, Sir, yours etc
>
> Berners, Paul Nash, JBS Haldane, Hermon Ould, Myra Hess, Osbert Sitwell, Stanley Marchant, R Vaughan Williams, Edward Marsh, Hugh Walpole.
>
> Art and Entertainment Emergency Council, London, W1, March 4.[18]

Myra's support for refugee musicians has rarely been granted enough credit. Howard's brief memoir of the National Gallery concerts barely mentions it. Why? Perhaps one explanation is that it went with the attitude of the day. Many refugees remained reluctant to speak about their backgrounds, or about their immigrant status, in the following years – whether because they wished to put the trauma behind them, or because they sought to assimilate and were wary of a society that held a good deal of ambient anti-Semitism, or to avoid misunderstandings with those who had simply not the first clue about the magnitude of their experiences.

The Fifth Lion

A teenage girl from Surrey used to come up to London for the Gallery concerts as often as she could; later, she – Diana McVeagh – became a musicologist, her work including a complete edition of the correspondence between Howard Ferguson and Gerald Finzi. 'I don't know why my mother allowed me to go, as there were V1 and V2 bombers overhead,' McVeagh remembers, 'but the concerts were an absolute lifeline.' She remembers that there was one picture on display in the Gallery, which was changed once a month, and that all the women in the audience wore hats. It was chilly – 'it was cold *everywhere*' – but the canteen had 'the best coffee in London.' As for Myra, 'she was adored, almost like a goddess. She was like Churchill: we will never surrender!' No other musician had such a status in Britain, 'either then or probably now. You couldn't compare her to anybody else.'[19]

As a child, Fiona Fraser, née Douglas-Home (niece of the later prime minister Sir Alec Douglas-Home) was brought to hear Myra play at the Gallery. Her mother worked in the institution's publications department and knew Myra well. The concert made an indelible impression, as Fraser recalls:

> Even to this day, whenever I hear *Jesu, Joy*, tears come to my eyes because it invokes that remarkable performance of hers. I was a very naive little girl from the country and the extraordinary atmosphere was such a contrast from anything I'd experienced before. There was apprehension, but also a sense of joy in the gallery, from people being able to be there, even with bombers flying over. It was the most exceptional experience musically that I've ever had, and a turning point for me, because depth of listening came into my consciousness, with an awareness of the power of music and the power of the personality propagating it.[20]

To pick some landmark moments of the concerts means leaving out others, so numerous were they. But one such was undoubtedly Kathleen Ferrier's first London recital, on 28th December 1942. The Lancastrian contralto was just beginning her career. Audiences were falling in love with her indigo-velvet contralto voice and her warm, open, down-to-earth personality – she was a former telephone operator and was nicknamed 'our Kaff'. Her breakthrough came towards the end of the war: Benjamin Britten was bowled over by her singing in Handel's *Messiah* at Westminster Abbey and chose her to sing the lead in his new opera, *The Rape of Lucretia*, at Glyndebourne in 1945; it was her stage debut. According to Gerald Moore, Myra loved to accompany 'Kath' in private and lent her a piano indefinitely. At the Gallery she sang Brahms and Schubert.

Britten and Pears performed there soon after their return from the US: their recital on 22nd October 1942 included Schumann's *Dichterliebe* and Britten's *Seven Sonnets of Michelangelo*, written two years earlier. Tippett also came in to conduct the Morley College Choir in a programme of 16th-century madrigals, Debussy and Purcell on 18th March 1943.

Dennis Brain, the greatest horn player of his day, appeared 26 times. He was in the (belated) world premiere of Howard's Octet in February 1943, which *The Times* critic enjoyed:

> The scoring is exceedingly effective; the ideas are serious and diversely disposed if not entirely free of reminiscence, but why should not music occasionally remind one of former pleasures? Ferguson does not rely on precedents; his thought is his own, his aim is beauty, and his pursuit of it is spontaneous.[21]

Moiseiwitsch could oblige Myra by producing virtuoso marvels at a moment's notice. Robert Ponsonby, the future director of the Edinburgh Festival and the Proms, recalled that when Rachmaninoff died in 1943, Moiseiwitsch – who had been a good friend of the composer – gave the tribute concert at the Gallery. Myra announced that after a difficult journey, the pianist had only just arrived, but had agreed to 'muck about'[22] with some of the late composer's Preludes, which he did to brilliant effect.

The tenor Roland Hayes was one of the few African-Americans to perform at the Gallery concerts. Born in 1887 in Georgia, where his mother had formerly been a slave, he was inspired by hearing recordings of Caruso, and in time rose to become a legendary interpreter of art song who broke down racial barriers alongside such singers as Paul Robeson and Marian Anderson. He was cited at one point as the highest-paid tenor in the world. His repertoire was all-encompassing, ranging from Dowland to Debussy. During his first visit to Britain in 1920 he was much helped by the actor and academic Dusé Mohammed Ali and, in the music world, by Roger Quilter; he lodged in St John's Wood, found representation with Ibbs & Tillett and got to know Myra, spending a day with her and her mother in the country. On the night of his Wigmore Hall debut he had severe pneumonia, but refused to cancel; to his astonishment, he received rave reviews and was invited to perform at Buckingham Palace for King George V and Queen Mary.

American tenor Roland Hayes in recital at the Gallery with Myra at the piano

Hayes visited Britain many times in the 1920s, but his international career was curtailed in Europe after the Nazis took power. In 1943 he was touring Britain to perform for the troops; he also gave a concert in Plymouth with an all-Black US Army choir at the invitation of Lord and Lady Astor and sang at the Royal Albert Hall. He gave a Gallery recital on 15th October, with Myra at the piano, in a programme including six 'American Negro' spirituals, among them 'He never said a mumblin' word', which (he noted in a memoir) was composed by his great-grandfather. He and Myra also gave several private recitals together. In

Hayes's biography, a caption on a photograph of them relaxing together describes Myra as a 'British accompanist'.

Gerald Moore appeared more often at the Gallery than anybody except Myra herself. After his 75th performance there, with the cellist Eileen Croxford in the air-raid room, Myra sprang a surprise, presenting him with an engraved Georgian silver cup for the occasion. At her suggestion, on 31st January 1945 he gave a lecture-recital on the art of accompanying; Myra had been impressed by his sense of humour in a series of BBC broadcast talks he had given and thought it would make a refreshing change. Speaking after the war at the annual St Cecilia's Day Festival Dinner in aid of the MBF, Moore paid tribute. Referring to the four Landseer lions at the foot of Nelson's Column, he said: 'There are five lions in Trafalgar Square. Myra is the fifth.'[23]

The violist Watson Forbes was the third most frequent performer, whether playing solo, working with his quartet (first the Stratton, later the Aeolian), or participating in other ensembles. An RAF band member, he always wore uniform. 'If our Commanding Officer was in a good mood,' he reminisced, 'we would be let off in time to catch the 11.45 train from Uxbridge, which got us to the National Gallery in reasonable time for the 1 o'clock concert. If he was feeling mean, it would be the 12 o'clock train, which got us there just in time to rosin the bow, grab the music and mount the platform.'[24]

The sight of musicians performing in uniform proved meaningful for the beleaguered audience. Members of the RAF's orchestra were recruited to accompany Myra's Mozart concertos, and the Griller Quartet, similarly attired, appeared around 60 times. They played Ernest Bloch's gigantic Quartet, which took up an entire concert, on several occasions, and they often performed with Myra. They travelled, frequently with Denis Matthews, to play to the armed forces; mostly they were well received, but one RAF officer asked them to play more quietly, while another, when they wanted to rehearse beforehand, responded: 'Good God! You've come all the way down here and you don't even know your stuff?' [25]

Myra's premiere of Howard's Piano Sonata on 23rd April 1940 was a noteworthy event – or rather two events, as she played it again at 5.30pm, having revived repeat concerts at tea-time on Tuesdays. On either side, the Menges String Quartet, who had known the sonata's dedicatee Harold Samuel well, performed Haydn and Hugo Wolf. Joyce Grenfell, who heard the sonata 12 times across three months or so, was bowled over by it: 'It had me in pieces,' she said[26]. 'The value of this sonata, however, does not rest on a personal sentiment,' *The Times* critic wrote. 'It is a work outstanding for its real and direct expression of musical ideas and the ability to support the ideas in terms of modern pianistic technique.' Myra played it 'with skill and sympathy' and it was deemed 'a work of genuine power'.[27]

It induced the newspaper to devote a leading article to a consideration of the piano sonata as a genre a few days later (27th April), concluding: 'It [the Ferguson Sonata] is music which one can see into at once ... But, if we cannot play it, let us be thankful we can hear it. Let us be specially thankful that we have Miss Myra Hess, who makes us live in it with her, because she plays it to herself. That, at any rate, we may say, is how we should play it if we might borrow her hands.'[28]

Myra herself gave 146 Gallery concerts across those six and a half years, which averages out as one roughly every two and a half weeks. She played everything from Bach's Brandenburg Concerto No. 5 to the entire Mozart piano concertos cycle, from duets with Howard to the premiere of his Five Bagatelles (28th September 1944), from the Brahms Horn Trio to Debussy Preludes – and innumerable performances of *Jesu, Joy*.

Sometimes when an artist was ill and could not appear, she would jump in to save the day; other times she would twist a fellow artist's arm into joining her, notably Irene Scharrer. 'Once,' the latter remembered, 'when the casualty happened to be a man, Myra made a little speech to the audience when we went on the platform, and I suddenly heard her thanking me for coming at such short notice, and for so kindly stepping into Mr So-and-so's breeches. Realising what she had said, she doubled up with laughter and the whole audience was in uproar.'[29]

Beethoven for a World at War

In 1942 Humphrey Jennings and the Crown Film Unit made an extraordinary documentary – propaganda without being overtly propagandistic – called *Listen to Britain*. In 20 minutes, he captures images of Britain at war, without narration, the images amplified only through their sounds. The National Gallery concerts are very much a part of the story. Jennings films Myra in full flow in Mozart's sunny-spirited G major Piano Concerto, K453: a tantalising glimpse of her sparkling gaze, her interaction with her colleagues in the orchestra and the way her light, deft touch would bounce about the keyboard. Howard, in uniform, is turning the pages; the Orchestra of the Central Band of the RAF are likewise attired and are conducted by Wing Commander R. P. O'Donnell,

When all the seating was taken ...

... audience members at the concerts stood or sat on the floor

brother of Myra's first cellist partner. Myra – her piano positioned behind and to one side of the orchestra, rather than in front – is wearing a white cardigan. The Queen is in the audience.

The film also captures the gallery and its visitors. Two ladies sit on the stairs munching sandwiches, untroubled by all the activity around them; the audience sit quietly, some tired but smiling, an injured soldier in his bandages, others solemn and thinking of faraway events, and some visibly enchanted by what they are hearing. Myra's music becomes as much part of the soundtrack of Britain at war as the clank of farm machinery, the shunting and pounding of factories, the singing of children skipping around their school playground, the young people dancing to a big band in a Blackpool ballroom, the whisper of the wind through fields of barley and the oak leaves on summer branches. Over Charing Cross station there looms a giant Zeppelin.

Joe Mendoza, Jennings's assistant director, was looking for suitable music when, hearing a recording by chance, he fell in love with the Mozart G major Concerto. 'Myra Hess said K453 wasn't in her current repertoire, but if we gave her three weeks' notice of the recording sessions she would have it ready for us,' he wrote. She had added that he should 'see Mr Ames [sic] about the platform'[30], so Mendoza found himself on a runaround to have a special platform made – after which, Myra asked him what colour the carpet would be (though this was for a black and white film). He sourced a light blue one from Harrods. The filming went well. A little while afterwards, Myra rang to say that the Queen would be coming to a concert and that she would play the same Mozart concerto for Her Majesty: might Mr Jennings be interested? The crew went along; HM agreed to take part and once the concert was over they were able to film her, with Myra at the piano to hold HM's attention.

This was not the end of Myra's film career with Jennings. In 1945 he made a documentary twice the length of the earlier one, entitled *A Diary for Timothy*. Framed by the first six months in the life of a baby named Tim, and boasting a score by Addinsell and a script by E.M Forster spoken by Michael Redgrave, it traces the progress of the war during that time. The upbeat energy of the 1942 film has gone; this delves beyond the stiff upper lip into the darkest days of the war.

Jennings films injured pilots immobile in hospital listening to planes passing overhead; minesweepers working with caution on the beach; the start of an air raid with sirens, a blackout and a doodle-bug exploding; and John Gielgud performing in *Hamlet*, contemplating Yorick's skull.

He also returns to the Gallery and presents Myra performing the first movement of the Beethoven F minor Sonata Op. 57, the 'Appassionata'. 'Some of us think it is the greatest music in the world,' says the narration over it. 'Yet it's German music and we are fighting the Germans. This is something we will have to think over later on.' Ultimately Jennings and Forster argue for a fairer type of peace, which Tim and his generation must someday build. (The real Tim grew up to be a teacher in Brighton.)

The documentary used only brief extracts of the Beethoven, but the footage of the whole first movement survives as a separate entity. Jennings captures Myra at her most indomitable: a firebrand whose pianistic power mingles with far-sighted wisdom, and whose infinite compassion incorporates the fury of an avenging angel. It is also the only film from the war years that shows extended close-ups of her as she plays. Piano students can examine her choices of fingering, but her facial expressions are no less telling; she never emotes and she shows little other than pure concentration. Yet a plethora of feelings, including apparent hurt, anger and determination, seems coiled within her.

Few broadcast performances have survived from the Gallery, probably because there were fierce arguments with the BBC over the fee to be paid to the musicians, the radio station being reluctant to provide their usual level. A famous live recording, however, captured Myra and the Griller Quartet playing the Brahms Piano Quintet on 25th August 1942. With their taut ensemble, the lean yet expressive strings and Myra's pianism both supportive and shining, their account flames with furious energy, precisely directed. This and Myra's 'Appassionata' seem to share a sense of purpose: great seriousness plus an all-giving commitment.

Yet it is impossible to tell, listening with decades of distance, how far that impression arises genuinely from the performance and how much, conversely, we might be 'projecting'. Are we hearing the musical reality of these wartime performances, or experiencing, subjectively, what we want or expect from them? Perhaps it is a bit of both…

Dame Myra

In the King's Birthday Honours in June 1941, Myra was created Dame Commander of the British Empire 'for her lasting services to British music, and to world musical achievement' – the only person to receive this honour on that occasion. The announcement appeared in the newspapers on 12th June 1941; and it was the next day that the Queen came to hear her Mozart K453.

Myra could invite two guests to her formal investiture at Buckingham Palace – and she took Saz and her housekeeper, Ethel Maul. They witnessed her receiving her damehood from King George VI; the monarch had a quiet word in the process, telling Myra how much the Queen was enjoying the Gallery concerts. Those who speculated that the Queen herself might have put Myra forward for the honour could well be right. On 10th October 1942, a letter from the Queen's Private Secretary informed Myra that the Queen had learned it was the third anniversary of the concerts, which 'owe their existence to your inspiration and much of their success to your musicianship', and praising the way her audiences 'daily gather to hear the succession of programmes which in many cases provide their only opportunity of enjoying this kind of recreation'. He sent from Her Majesty every good wish for the continued success of a wartime work of real value, and ended: 'Believe me.'

The day before the royal honours were announced, *The Times* carried news of another accolade: Myra was being awarded the 1942 Gold Medal of the Royal Philharmonic Society. It is the highest mark of esteem in the British music business, from the organisation that commissioned Beethoven's Ninth Symphony. Myra was only the second female instrumentalist ever to receive it (the first was the pianist Arabella Goddard in 1871), and the first pianist since Rachmaninoff ten years earlier. This time, on 17th January 1942, the medal was presented by Vaughan Williams, whose speech referred to her as 'our greatly loved and deeply revered Myra'. The presentation took place in a packed but freezing Royal Albert Hall, after she had played Beethoven's Piano Concerto No. 4, wrapped in a white fur coat.

She wrote to thank 'Uncle Ralph' two days later:

> I am still aglow from Saturday & I can never, never thank you enough for your sweetness to me.
>
> As a Dutch friend of mine would say 'it was a great emotion' & knowing that you do not love such functions my appreciation of your goodness in coming is deeper than I can ever express. It is very lovely & gratifying to have the medal but the way you presented it to me will be one of my most heart-warming memories – Bless you 1942 times![31]

There was renewed appreciation, too, from the Queen, who attended the 1000th concert. It was on 23rd July 1943 and marked the third in

Myra's Mozart concertos series, including the D minor K466, which was broadcast. Myra received a note from HM's secretary: '...The Queen desires me to tell you how much enjoyment she has derived from your delightful playing in the two Mozart concertos, and to record anew Her Majesty's recognition of the great debt owed by a grateful host of London music lovers to a development which will always be associated with your name.'

The year 1944 brought Britain three months of terror under a barrage of V-1 rockets – the notorious 'doodle-bug' flying bombs. Imminent strikes were signalled when their droning sound stopped dead. Once Myra was performing the Schubert Impromptu in B flat major when the unmistakable sound materialised above. After the war, she recounted:

> Just as I was beginning the lovely minor variation I heard a flying bomb approaching. I made a tremendous crescendo to cover the noise of the bomb as it flew over the gallery, and as it passed over, an equally unauthentic diminuendo. The amusing thing was that the crescendo synchronised so completely with the horrible noise overhead that no one was conscious of what I had done. No one, that is, except some friends who were sitting trembling in the artists' room. If anyone had walked in during the middle of it they'd have thought it was the Brahms B Flat Concerto![32]

The American writer Mary Lee Settle (who went on to found the PEN/Faulkner Award for Fiction) was working for the American Office of War Information in Britain at the time. She was attending a Prom, high up in the Albert Hall's gallery, when a doodle-bug flew overhead while Myra, a tiny, distant figure, was playing Mozart:

> We could see its faint shadow through the dirty glass [roof]. The pure, small sound of Mozart was the focus of a dead silence. Her fingers never faltered. We were hypnotized by her concentration, and the bomb exploded a hundred yards away across Kensington High Street in Kensington Gardens. She had kept us from a panic that could have killed many people.[33]

Worse still was the V2 rocket, which made no warning sound at all before exploding upon its target with devastating force. When the first V2 hit Chiswick, the news was suppressed; people were told that a gas main had exploded. Therefore, for a while, the V2s were called Flying Gas Mains. Joyce Grenfell remembered hearing Myra play Beethoven's Third

Concerto at the Albert Hall when a V2 bomb exploded within earshot: 'Startled, Myra's hands rose from the keys and came down again an octave higher than Beethoven had suggested.'[34] It took ingenuity for her to put this right – but right it she did. The mishap was Myra's sole, accidental concession to Hitler.

Looking Ahead

The liberation of France in August 1944 signalled the onset of new hope. It also opened up, in due course, the chance for visiting French musicians to perform at the Gallery. Myra played Beethoven and Brahms on 9th March 1945 with the elegant and poetic French violinist Jacques Thibaud; and in January the baritone Pierre Bernac had appeared, with the composer Francis Poulenc at the piano. They had performed shortly before at Wigmore Hall. This, wrote one critic, 'afforded Londoners opportunity for hearing French songs, new and old, authentically and exquisitely performed … M. Poulenc's old wit is still ready to come to the surface at a touch as in the song "Paganini," which M. Bernac flicked off his tongue in flashing strokes of mockery.'[35]

Myra chats to a serviceman at the Gallery

At last the country could begin to consider how it would rebuild after the horrors it had experienced – which, even if less devastating than those of many other countries, had left some 384,000 soldiers killed in combat, about 70,000 civilians dead, swathes of London and other cities destroyed and countless people injured and traumatised.

A major question hung over the future of London's musical venues after the destruction of the Queen's Hall. On 5th March 1945 a concert in memory of Sir Henry Wood at the Royal Albert Hall aimed to raise money for a new hall for the capital. It was a suitably huge event, combining the London Symphony Orchestra, London Philharmonic Orchestra and BBC Orchestra, with three conductors: Sir Adrian Boult, Basil Cameron and John Barbirolli. The teenaged Ida Haendel played the Mendelssohn Violin Concerto and the programme included Vaughan Williams's *Serenade to Music* and a new fanfare by William Walton, among much else.

Yet instead of rebuilding the beloved Queen's Hall, plans were afoot to construct a venue in the gloomy industrial wasteland of the South Bank. Music was about to become a tool of social engineering.

A leading article in *The Times* on 27th April posited:

> Of all the difficulties with which music in London has had to contend since the outbreak of war that of its housing has been the most persistent. It has now reached such a pitch of desperation that immediate palliatives must be sought. We cannot afford to wait for the maturing of any of the various plans that have been put forward for a Music Centre, for an Arts Centre on the South Bank, or for the great public hall which his Majesty's Government must provide for the capital of the Empire or the L.C.C. for the needs of the citizens of no mean city.

The Royal Albert Hall was unsuitable, it pointed out, for anything but big choral works.

> The National Gallery, though not ideal for music, has proved a godsend, and has shown, incidentally, that the mere provision of house-room by the State has made cheap music financially possible by removing overhead charges that have proved too onerous for many a similar enterprise in the past to bear. The future of the National Gallery concerts is now under discussion.

Finally there came 8th May 1945: VE Day. London burst into life. People jumped into the fountains in Trafalgar Square outside the Gallery and crammed into trucks to race through the city. Crowds danced and sang in the streets. The division of Germany and eastern Europe between the USSR and the Americans was far away; here, all that mattered was that the war was over.

For Myra and her teammates, the future was not looking quite so bright. Their efforts were about to come to an end more ignominious than anybody had anticipated.

1 T. Potter, Interview with Watson Forbes, *The Strad*, July 1991
2 *London Evening News*, 10 October 1941
3 H. Ferguson, 'The National Gallery Concerts and After' in *Myra Hess by her Friends*, p95
4 Ibid., p94
5 Jim Fassett, CBC interview with MH, 1952
6 MH to BS, 2 December 1940
7 MH to JS, reprinted on Myra Hess Fund flier
8 MH script for BBC broadcast to USA, 28 May 1942
9 MH to SG, 1 September 1943
10 MH to BS, 2 December 1940
11 K. Clark, op. cit., p33-34
12 McKenna, op. cit., p155
13 MH to Margaret Campbell, 20 April 1941
14 Hess Scrapbook II, cutting with unidentified source, see McKenna, op. cit., p152-3
15 The author's father-in-law, Herbert Eisner, left internment in the Isle of Man by joining the Pioneer Corps
16 *The Times*, 23 July 1940
17 R. Vaughan Williams to F. Rauter, 16 August 1942, VWL1680, Vaughan Williams Foundation
18 *The Daily Telegraph*, 9 March 1940
19 Author interview with Diana McVeagh
20 Author interview with Fiona Fraser
21 *The Times*, 18 February 1943
22 R. Ponsonby, *Musical Heroes*, p1
23 G. Moore, *Farewell Recital*, in Collected Memoirs, p312
24 T. Potter, op. cit.
25 D. Matthews, op. cit., p81
26 J. Hampton, *Joyce Grenfell*, p104
27 *The Times*, 24 April 1940
28 *The Times*, 27 April 1940
29 I. Scharrer, 'A Unique Friendship' in *Myra Hess by her Friends*, p4
30 J. Mendoza, 'How Humphrey Jennings Saved My Life', *The Veteran* no. 94, 2001, pp.18–27. 'Ames' no doubt meant 'Amis'
31 MH to RVW, 19 January 1942
32 MH interview in *Winnipeg Free Press*, 8 March 1954
33 M. Lee Settle, 'London – 1944', *The Virginia Quarterly Review*, Vol. 63, No. 4 (Autumn 1987), pp565-586
34 J. Grenfell, 'Julia M.' in *Myra Hess by her Friends*, p69
35 *The Times*, 10 January 1945

The Battle of Trafalgar Square
(1945–1946)

It was the actress Dame Sybil Thorndike who voiced the issue that was on everyone's minds. On *The Times* letters page on 12th April, she wrote: 'Are the concerts at the National Gallery to continue in post-war London? What these concerts have meant and will mean to many thousands of people is constantly being brought home to me, and all sorts and conditions of men and women want an assurance that this music shall continue to be available in their post-war lives.'

With hindsight, the outcome looks inevitable. The National Gallery was bound to return to its original purpose. Its crowds of visitors had to be able to circulate; the presence of a platform, a Steinway, hundreds of chairs and people in them would always be incompatible with that. But Myra had seen the faces of her troubled listeners transfigured by the solace of music; she would never have relinquished the future of such a transformative experience without putting up a powerful fight. She responded in the Letters page of *The Times*:

> My committee and I have been extremely touched by Dame Sybil Thorndike's appreciative letter ... The present position is that the trustees of the National Gallery have generously given their permission for the concerts to continue in the meantime. Precisely how long 'the meantime' will extend must depend upon eventualities: personally, I would like chamber music to go on for ever in the National Gallery. At the moment we are considering practical ways and means, and to this end it is more than encouraging to be assured of a wide public desire for the continuation of the concerts.

The public divided into those who supported the concerts versus those who wanted the paintings back. 'It would be a sad prospect indeed if, in happier days, those whose daily toil only permitted a lunch-time view of pictures were to find the rooms containing their favourite Holbein or Vermeer given up to a performance of Bach, or, at best, were merely permitted to tip-toe round the walls, pursued by the angry looks and "sh's" of an enraptured audience,' read one objection.[1]

Another – from inside County Hall, the seat of London's local government – suggested that 'Lovers of painting (many of whom are music lovers) have during the war been reduced to starvation. And when the glorious procession of great masters re-enters London from the obscurity of the Welsh hills, I hope they will not find the dome of their gallery occupied by guests to whom they have already extended so generous a hospitality. Music and painting may be sister arts, but they cannot live together. Like so many families it is better for them not to try.'[2]

A third letter suggested the building of a separate room in the gallery for concerts and lectures: 'The nation provides museums and buildings for the exhibition of paintings and sculpture, might we not therefore ask for one room for the enjoyment of music?'[3]

While the arguments raged, Myra missed VE Day. She had left Britain for the first time since 1939 and gone to Holland on her first aeroplane (a de Havilland Harrow with two engines, one of which fell off several weeks later). The flight was delayed by bad weather and she arrived in Eindhoven one hour before her recital. It proved, she said, 'one of the most moving concerts of my whole life'[4] – and as an encore she played the Dutch National Anthem.

Not all of the Netherlands had yet been liberated. For months, as she wrote to Maggie van Riemsdijk (whom she was not able to see on this visit, to the sorrow of both), she had refused to go until the whole of Holland was free. But then: 'I realised I had no right to be so cowardly when you, here, were showing the whole world what heroism means'[5]. Over six days, she had a taste of the devastation that Hitler had wrought across Europe. Sir Paul Mason, who knew Myra in the 1950s when he became British Ambassador at The Hague, wrote that during this tour Myra 'travelled throughout the country playing to the people in towns and villages, in city halls and village rooms, on every sort and quality of piano, good, indifferent and downright bad. Neither she nor anyone else could speak of this experience without emotion: the thronged audiences so long deprived of an outlet for their feelings: the national anthems sung with everyone in tears.'[6]

Richard Dimbleby was the first journalist to broadcast from the British Second Army's liberation of the concentration camp Bergen-Belsen. His report on 19th April was delayed for several days because the editors in London could not believe the apocalyptic scenes he described.

He recounted that amid a mass of bodies, often he could not tell who was living and who was dead. He spoke of an oven in which 10,000 inmates had been concussed then burned alive, three at a time, in retaliation for the murder of two guards. He reported a pit the size of a tennis court, 15 feet deep, at one end 'piled with naked bodies that have been tumbled in one on top of the other'. He compared it to the plague pits of Europe 300 years earlier.

Arguments would rage for decades, and may continue for centuries, about how much was really known of the concentration camps during the war. Some was undoubtedly suppressed. A documentary overseen by Alfred Hitchcock was made about the liberation of the camps. It stayed unshown for 40 years.

When the pictures began to come in, Mary Lee Settle was enlisted to help her employers decide how much graphic detail the American public could take. She was shown the photographs. If she had no violent reaction, they could be published. If she retched, they were censored. She recalled that a delegation of MPs insisted on inspecting the report to see if it was true. One of them, 'a nice Conservative lady MP, Mrs Smith'[7], subsequently took her own life.

Myra and her colleagues had fought to save what individuals they could, in the face of the xenophobic press that insisted the UK was taking in too many refugees.

The bottom line was that, had Hitler defeated Britain, this would have also been the fate of innumerable British Jews, Roma, homosexuals, those with physical or mental disabilities, political dissidents and more. Despite Churchill declaring 'We shall never surrender', nobody could be certain exactly what the outcome would be until it was all over.

Then came 6th and 9th August 1945: the United States Army Air Forces dropped atomic bombs on Hiroshima and Nagasaki.

What can music do to help? What could anything do to help, faced with the ultimate destruction of humans by fellow humans: the concentration camps and the atomic bombs? Perhaps the profound underlying fear and uncertainty is why Myra's concerts mattered so much. Music did not only bring escape. It made palpable, subconsciously, not just the opposite of war, but the *inverse* of it.

Instead of conflict, people actively experienced togetherness. Instead of physical destruction, music brought them the creative building of sound that contains revelations of the soul. While war threatened death under the bombs, chamber music showed people working together towards an affirmation of the spirit, shared by all, in a language that transcends words.

Myra was not the only person to provide that symbol. She was nevertheless the one who best demonstrated its absolute necessity. She did not try to make music rise above politics. Instead, she weaponised the experience of music-making and attendance, turning it into an act of resistance.

She had put it succinctly in a broadcast to America in 1944 about her National Gallery audience:

> The longing for good music had been no craving for a drug to blunt the senses and bring forgetfulness. It had become for many a means of expressing the ideas and beliefs for which we are fighting and of keeping them alive and burning in the hearts of people who might otherwise lose the sense of high endeavour in the cramping monotony of their lives.
>
> I hope and believe that from this ever-increasing knowledge and love of music among the people, will spring a renaissance which will go far in shaping the postwar world, whose future lies so much in the hands of our two nations. It is our heritage of tolerance and freedom which is the antithesis of all Hitler has striven for. Knowing our two countries as I do, I look into this future unafraid, for I believe that we can create a state of existence where standards of culture and beauty can take their place.

On 29th May, Sir Kenneth Clark convened a meeting. It concluded that the Gallery concerts could continue for another year, since there was nowhere else for them to go. Clark was about to retire, however, and the curator and art historian Philip Hendy – tall, charming, charismatic, smooth-talking – was appointed in his place, assuming the role in January 1946. His previous posts had included being director of the Leeds City Art Gallery and Slade Professor of Fine Arts at Oxford University. The departure of Clark, who had been so instrumental in bringing about the concerts, signalled a downturn in their fortunes.

A blow to Myra arrived in the form of a bitterly worded letter from the gallery's Keeper, William Gibson (who had a family connection to Hendy via their respective wives, both of the Ogilvy family). Despite having been the concerts' secretary-treasurer for two years, he was opposed to their continuation. He now resigned from the committee, telling Myra that while it would be ridiculous to expect her to see anything but good in continuing the concerts, to him the decision was 'shocking and heartbreaking'. He saw it as confirmation that in Britain the fate of the visual arts was invariably sacrificed to 'other interests'.[8]

Queuing outside the National Gallery

Myra had anticipated this and answered diplomatically, arguing that her concerts only occupied a small portion of the Gallery and attracted people who might not otherwise have ventured in. But it failed to change his antagonism.

Elsewhere, Myra was being deluged with honours. First, she was awarded an honorary doctorate at the University of Manchester. Next, the MBF held a gala dinner for her at the Savoy Hotel. The charity had received such lavish sums of money from the concerts that they were determined to thank her in style, after many years in which such occasions had been impossible.

For the 'Tribute of Gratitude to Dame Myra Hess in recognition of her wartime services to music', 320 guests put on their mothballed evening clothes and feasted upon a menu that was affected by wartime privations, but sounded very much better in French: La Ravigote du Pêcheur Britanique (British fish with onion and herb sauce), followed by Le Vol-au-Vent Savoy with Petits Pois Frais au Beurre and Pommes Persillées (filled pastry with parsley potatoes and peas), and for desert

Le Biscuit Glacé Succès (a coiled almond biscuit) and Gaufrettes (crispy wafers).

Attendees ranged from the Viscountess Cholmondeley to Mr and Mrs Maul. Musicians present included Lionel Tertis, Denis Matthews, Isolde Menges, Sidney Griller, Eileen Joyce, Roger Quilter, Eric Coates, Gerald Moore and Kendall Taylor. Myra would have seen the beloved faces of her friends cheering her on: Howard, Irene, Denise, Joyce, Beryl, Marj and Saz. Sir Arnold Bax was there, as was Miss Harriet Cohen. They had both been among the donors to the presentation, the list of whom also included Sir Thomas Beecham, Adila Fachiri and Jelly d'Arányi.

The MBF had commissioned a bronze bust of Myra from the sculptor Jacob Epstein and at the dinner it was presented to the National Gallery, accepted by Sir Kenneth (though Myra must have been its official owner, because she bequeathed it to the Royal Academy of Music). To Myra herself they presented the gifts of a gramophone and records by her faithful musicians – alongside speeches, toasts and a poem by John Masefield, poet laureate, which Joyce Grenfell read to the assembly. A commemorative pamphlet was headed DAME MYRA HESS: HER BOOK, with gothic lettering in her favourite powder-blue.

Trumpeters from the Royal Military School of Music played fanfares composed for the occasion by Bax, Bliss and Walford Davies; Baroness Ravensdale and Lady Gater both spoke; and finally Myra, in her new doctoral robes, conducted the Griller and Menges Quartets in the Toy Symphony, with an assemblage of celebrity guests. On the cuckoos she had Irene and the BBC's Director of Music, Victor Hely-Hutchinson; on the toy trumpets, Denis Matthews and the principal of the Guildhall School, Edric Cundell.

Responding to the toast, Myra said that she had always wanted to make music a part of everyday life. It must, she said, be free from the restrictions set by a 10s 6d seat and one's best clothes: 'I have always been sure that there was a vast potential audience who had been debarred from music by existing conditions.' She added that she had been surrounded and helped by wonderful friends, and thanked each in turn. And she stressed: 'Why is it that music has received official backing during the war? We were told it was to keep up the morale of our people and to be a comfort and inspiration. If this is so, do we not need that inspiration as much as ever?'

The message was not misplaced. Sir Kenneth was able to announce during his own speech that the Trustees had agreed to keep the concerts going. (At least, for the moment.)

The Queen sent a message via her private secretary to Frank Howes, the MBF chair, speaking of how gladly she associated herself with those paying tribute to Dame Myra that night. 'The Queen looks back to her visits to the National Gallery Concerts as some of the happiest hours of the dark times through which we have passed,' it read. 'Her Majesty feels sure that many of those who have, for five years, trooped daily to Trafalgar Square must have thought, with The Queen, as they listened to your guest entrancing her hearers as she played Mozart or Bach, that indeed in her "sweet music was the art which killeth care and grief of heart," and what gift, in days of war, could be more timely?'[9] Alongside The Queen's signature in the list of Patrons was that of Winston Churchill.

It was a veritable night to remember. Just five days later, Myra was back on stage at the Albert Hall, playing not one but two concertos: the Grieg and Beethoven's No. 3, with Alec Sherman and the New London Orchestra, in aid of the Help Holland fund. The music must go on.

Despite the celebrations, by November Myra was in full combat mode. At the Gallery, the paintings were back and the seating area had been much reduced to allow for visitor circulation. The concerts doubled the admission price to two shillings to compensate; audience numbers held up nonetheless. Myra was already envisaging that she and Howard must soon return, respectively, to performing and composing and that the concerts should be managed by a new, paid administrative team. She urged the committee to take a decision as soon as possible, so that incoming administrators could have time and 'the knowledge of some degree of permanence'.[10]

Her own conflict was that Holland wanted her. She was invited to perform at the season's opening concerts of both the Concertgebouw in Amsterdam and the Residentie Orchestra in The Hague. But the dates there would clash with the anniversary of the Gallery concerts on 10th October. 'I shall probably give up everything here in October,' she wrote to Maggie van Rijmsdiek. 'Although it will be almost too moving, I cannot refuse the honour your country has shown me in wanting me to play at your first concerts. My heart is too full even thinking of it … Even the thought of walking down those steps at the Concertgebouw is overwhelming and I shall need all my courage. How strange and moving it will be to play in all those beloved old places.'[11]

One person she would not be reunited with in Holland was her former manager there, Johan Koning. He was thought to be a Nazi collaborator and had now vanished. Another was Willem Mengelberg. A passionate advocate of German music and culture, he at first appeared to fall into a common enough trap, insisting, like many naïve idealists, that politics and music must never mix. When the war began, he had viewed the invasion of the Netherlands as not such a bad thing, because he thought German control might be a positive influence on cultural life. A story circulated that he had toasted the Nazi invasion in 1940. Mengelberg said he had been misquoted.

He failed to anticipate the end results of the anti-Semitic race laws. Although he tried to intercede on behalf of Jewish musicians from his orchestra, he managed only to see them deported to labour camps rather than concentration camps. He did not leave a single statement against the Nazis. After the war, the Dutch government deposed him from the Concertgebouw, banned him from working in Holland and removed his passport. Tainted and disgraced, he never conducted again. He spent his last years in isolated exile in the Swiss mountains. Finally his biographer, exploring his papers many years later, discovered notes suggesting that his admiration for Hitler and his own anti-Semitism were all too real.

Myra performed instead with the conductor Eduard van Beinum, who had been Mengelberg's assistant; and she was overjoyed, above all, to be reunited with Maggie van Riemsdijk, who had travelled through Holland with her in what now must have felt like another world. Lost for words at her old friend's home, Myra went to the piano and played her *Jesu, Joy*.

The Death of Uncle Tobs

On Tuesday 11th December at High Marley, where Denise was caring for him, the 87-year-old Uncle Tobs suffered a mild heart attack. He rallied briefly. Myra drove down two days later – though all she could do was watch him sleeping, afraid that he would awaken and worry about what had brought her there. The distant slumbering form was her last glimpse of her beloved teacher. On Saturday morning, Denise called to tell her that it was all over.

After the cremation and a sparsely attended funeral service in Woking, Myra took Denise back to Wildwood Road, where the honorary sisters mourned together. After another few days, they held a private ceremony to scatter the ashes near High Marley, mingling those of Uncle Tobs with those of Jessie. 'He is always beside me when I play,' Myra later said.

Paying a moving tribute to him in a broadcast, she recounted:

> A lesson from Tobias Matthay was far beyond a dissertation on technical problems. Although every scientific explanation was at his fingertips, he always insisted that every difficulty overcome was but a step towards the ultimate goal of musical expression. Beauty in music was his religion and the whole of his life and work were devoted to its service … My own affection and gratitude to him are beyond all expression; but the debt of an individual is of small account compared with the far-reaching importance of his work … I count myself as profoundly blessed to have been, since childhood, under the care of a man so great in character and achievement.[12]

The most pressing matter now was the future of the Tobias Matthay Pianoforte School. Myra had been on the school's board of governors and became its President. The TMPS had struggled through the war, but after inevitable financial setbacks it was on the point of bankruptcy.

The four Trustees were the executors of Matthay's will, in which a clause said that Myra should succeed him as principal of TMPS, or Denise if Myra could not accept. Myra did; but less than three weeks after his death, on New Year's Day of 1946, she took responsibility for closing it down.

She wrote to all the TMPS's teachers on 28th December:

> With the passing of our beloved Uncle Tobs, the continuance of the School presents innumerable problems.
>
> We, the four appointed Trustees – Denise Lassimonne, Hilda Dederich, Vivian Langrish and myself, have view [sic] the situation with the closest consideration and have reluctantly come to the conclusion that the many difficulties are insuperable.
>
> After six years of war, and the inevitable dispersal of professors and students, the School would require to be entirely reconstituted if it were to continue. This would involve the finding of a new home, the necessity of which has already been felt with the many new students who have joined us since the end of the war. For this, and the many other expenses, a large capital sum would be needed.

> Only a few weeks ago, Uncle Tobs spoke to Denise Lassimonne of the many problems concerning the future and expressed his opinion that these difficulties might prove to be insurmountable, in which case, he was fully aware that the School as such, might have to come to an end.
>
> It was our desire to call a general meeting to inform all the professors of this decision, but as we consider it advisable to close the School before beginning a new year – the time is too short to gather everyone together. As two of the Trustees are out of town, I have communicated with them by telephone and they have approved of my signing this letter in the name of us all.
>
> We presume and hope that all your School pupils will continue to study with you privately. We shall endeavour to notify all the students by the beginning of the year; in the meantime no doubt, you, yourself, will be communicating with some of them.
>
> Although we do not feel it is possible to carry on the School itself, there can be no end to Uncle Tobs' work, and we, his disciples, will have the great privilege of continuing to spread his teaching and of perpetuating his spirit, which has been the guiding force in our lives since the foundation of the School in 1905.[13]

The decision may have looked abrupt, even harsh, and came as a shock to some of the teachers. It was probably sensible, however. Keeping the TMPS going would have required a giant commitment of funding; after the privations of the war, few people could contemplate such input. Myra herself had had no fee for any of her Gallery work. To make matters worse, Denise was not well. Besides the blow of losing her honorary father, she would also lose her home; she would have to sell High Marley, where she had lived for more than 25 years. Over the first months of 1946, she fell into a deep depression and was advised by the doctor to take complete rest.

A complex legal situation and much damage limitation followed. A clause in Matthay's will had stipulated that eventually any remaining assets in his estate, after the deaths of Denise and his sister Dora, should go to the Royal Academy of Music. His lawyers feared that trouble could lie ahead if Myra's decision had disrupted any beneficial prospect for the Academy – assuming the school could have remained viable in the long term – and advised her to make peace with the institution.

Myra's olive branch resulted in the start of a Tobias Matthay Memorial Trust to support young pianists. Fundraising concerts in 1946 and 1947 included one by Myra at the Royal Albert Hall, and the American Matthay Association made a donation. Her charm offensive involved presenting the Academy's annual awards in July. But the TMPS was not saved. Denise chaired the last meeting of its council exactly a year after Uncle Tobs's funeral. Myra was away on tour and missed it.

Frank Mannheimer came to Denise's rescue. While she was still in a slough of despond, he took her out to tea and, on a paper napkin, began to map out the summer courses that he suggested she could offer. This had never occurred to her. He had thought of everything: appropriate fees, the structure of the classes, how to house the students – virtually all that she needed to know. Denise took up the idea and for 35 years maintained successful summer sessions that gave her a whole new lease of life.

For the Moment…

While Myra was dealing with the end of the TMPS, the National Gallery situation was imploding, in a way that she was never able to forgive.

She pushed the issue herself; she had to, because she had tours to plan and there seemed to have been no significant movement since November on what 'for the moment' really meant. In early February 1946 she wrote to the chairman of the Gallery's board, Vincent Massey, the High Commissioner of Canada:

> I understand there is every probability that our fate may be decided at the General Meeting on February 14th and there are two points I would like to stress finally. Firstly, that I would willingly continue the partial sacrifice of my own career if the Trustees decided that music should become a permanent institution in the National Gallery; but secondly, that the practical difficulties have now reached a point that make it impossible for me to continue the organisation of the concerts under temporary conditions.
>
> I need hardly tell you with what suspense we await the final verdict.[14]

Afterwards, Myra believed that Massey had neither passed this letter on, nor discussed it with the other trustees. They would not have known that she was offering to make that sacrifice; only that she was eager to get back to business as usual alongside a new, paid team. She may have been right.

Still, to be both a touring concert pianist and the permanent director of the Gallery concerts looks either implausible or impossible. Myra was accustomed to making sacrifices, but how far would that go? Was she really ready to give up so much of her performing? The fact that she was in Oxford giving a recital when the 14th February meeting was held seems, if not to prove the point, then at least to illustrate it. She asked Philip Hendy to telephone her at her hotel that night to tell her what had happened.

The call never came. Instead, a letter from him was waiting for her at home the next day. He apologised for not having been in touch by phone, having been at a dinner party; and the line to The Mitre in Oxford was engaged, twice. He enclosed a report that the trustees had agreed to circulate to the newspapers. Myra read it in horror.

In her absence and without consulting her, the trustees had made an executive decision to close down the concerts. They had also sent out a press release:

> The Trustees of the National Gallery have decided that the date of the last midday concert there should be April 9th. Dame Myra Hess, who is retiring from the direction of these concerts in April, has asked the Board for a decision as to whether the concerts should end then or should be continued indefinitely under new management…[15]

The excuse given was that concerts would disrupt the Ministry of Works' plans for the Gallery's repair and restoration, following the wartime bomb damage. That was fair enough. But the notion that Myra was 'retiring' from their direction was, first, untrue; secondly, it made the whole thing sound like her doing.

Myra, supported by Howard, reacted with fury. 'I have never had such a blow,' she said in one interview. 'If the decision had been made by a large group of people I would have respected their opinion. But I gather it comes from a small group … who do not wish the music to continue.' Howard wrote to Massey demanding an amendment in the Gallery's records. *The Daily Mail* printed a correction, blaming a 'misunderstanding'. Yet to Myra the Gallery's actions probably looked like actual dishonesty.

Everything could have been handled very differently. Hendy later told McKenna that the misunderstandings arose from emendations to the press release dictated to him by Massey, the word 'retirement' among them. He gave Myra emollient words about the outcome being far indeed from what he himself would have wished. This did not stop her from feeling that the institution was effectively stabbing her in the back.

The Petition

The press took strong notice, since the Gallery concerts were so influential. A report from *The Times*, on 22nd February, made it clear that the multidisciplinary idea of concerts in an art gallery had affected the forming of the brand-new Arts Council. It noted: 'In this country institutions have a way of growing out of small experimental seeds sown ad hoc' and suggested that the concerts had been exactly such an instance, sparked by a need to restore London's musical life, but subsequently gaining much more significance:

> The association of the arts … is an idea that is gaining ground. The very existence of the Arts Council with its three sections, theatre, music, and visual arts, makes concrete the underlying unity of the arts as sensory, emotional, and imaginative experience. In the wake of its work in its previous incarnation as Cema, Three Arts Clubs have sprung up all over the country … and the appropriateness of picture galleries as places for music when physical circumstances allow has become increasingly recognized. The Barber Institute at Birmingham embodies the idea in a form that makes Londoners envious. Music has a long-standing alliance with architecture, dancing, drama, and poetry. Cannot music and painting reach some mutually advantageous accommodation, since they have both learned recently what it is to be homeless?

Then on 14th March an announcement appeared saying that the concerts would not end on 9th April …but on 10th. 'Dame Myra Hess said that she hoped most earnestly that others would find ways and means of perpetuating these concerts elsewhere, so that the ground won for chamber music during the last six and a half years should not be lost.' There were discussions about moving them elsewhere, even about building a new hall for chamber music, named in Myra's honour, on a site at the bottom of Haymarket, moments from the Gallery. But Myra would have none of it: it was the Gallery or nowhere. All or nothing.

The decision was scarcely less painful for the musicians. Eight string quartets co-signed a letter of protest to *The Times*, declaring: 'What the promenade concerts have done for orchestral music in this country, the National Gallery concerts are now doing for chamber music'. As for the devoted public, Myra's team could take one more step: Alec Sherman organised a public petition.

The leaflet was strongly worded and included a return address – 52 Kensington Church Street – with a place for a one penny stamp.

> Do YOU want the NATIONAL GALLERY CONCERTS to continue?
>
> In the past six-and-a-half years, these concerts have brought a wealth of the finest music to the people of England. The audiences have been gathered from all over the country and the concerts have become an integral part of the cultural life of the nation.
>
> NATIONAL GALLERY CONCERTS are to end on APRIL 10th.
>
> This would be a calamity. The only hope of the decision being reversed, is a Petition from all who want the concerts to go on. If you have enjoyed the NATIONAL GALLERY CONCERTS and do not want to lose them, please sign the following petition and post immediately (a penny stamp is sufficient). DO NOT DELAY. TIME IS SHORT.[16]

Responses flooded in. There are approximately 4,000 names and addresses on the surviving lists. Signatories included luminaries of the arts world, among them Augustus John, Arthur Bliss, Constant Lambert, Janet Craxton, Eric Shilling, William Glock and Clifford Curzon.

But the vast majority were the ordinary people, music-lovers old and new, who had flocked in from Dulwich, Oxford, Reading, Ewell, Chiswick, Ilford, Sweden, the Girl Guides Association, Hammersmith, Morden, Worthing, Sevenoaks, Cheam, Edinburgh, West Hampstead, Cambridge, Brighton, Chigwell, Amersham, Winchester, Barnet, the Ministry of Health, Darlington, Pinner, Staines, Bristol, Bath, Catford, Enfield, Devizes, Stanmore, Aldershot, Watford, Banbury, Sittingbourne, Croydon, Dorset, Aylesbury, Eton College, Romford, Richmond, Weybridge, Bedford, Southend, and very many more.

It was to no avail.

In the programme, announcing the date of the last concert as 10th April, there appeared this notice:

> In answer to innumerable requests to transfer the Concerts elsewhere, Dame Myra states that she and her Committee regret they cannot undertake this formidable task, as new surroundings would necessitate an entirely new organization. They had hoped to establish

music in the National Gallery as a permanent institution, from which Dame Myra would never have severed her connection. As this ideal cannot now be realized, they hope most earnestly that others may find ways and means of perpetuating such concerts elsewhere, so that the ground won for Chamber Music during the past six and a half years may never be lost.

'Farewell'

Musicians, no matter the surrounding sound and fury, must put everything aside and concentrate on the music they are performing. Myra was dealing with rebuttals to the press and the deep pain of betrayal by a national institution that had become the centre of her life. Amid all this, she had to perform Mozart's E flat major Piano Concerto K271 at the Royal Albert Hall with Sir Adrian Boult on 20th March. She had ignored the doodle-bugs; now she had to ignore her internal demons.

Her last recital in the National Gallery series was on 5th April; she chose the magisterial music of Beethoven's last two sonatas, Op. 110 and Op. 111. Greeted by standing ovations at both ends of the event, she told the audience that she felt unable to perform in the very last concert because the emotion would be too great.

The 10th April 1946 was exactly six and a half years since she had played the concerts' first note. The last concert was the 1,698th. Queuing started at 9am. Rather than a grand extravaganza, it was a chamber music programme of the type the audience had grown to love so much: the Griller Quartet performing Haydn's Op. 33 No. 2 and Beethoven's last 'Razumovsky' Quartet, Op. 59 No. 3. 'Rooms were brimming by the time Dame Myra Hess took her seat and the Griller Quartet the platform to fervid acclamation,' *The Guardian* reported. 'Enthusiasm was as warm and gratitude as deep as one expected for those who have given London its easing hours of music ...'

After the last note, there was a honeyed speech from Hendy, explaining why the concerts must end – repairs and cleaning – and holding out the hope of resuming once this was done. Whether anyone believed it, we will never know. Myra, inundated with flowers, stood up to speak for the last time at the Gallery. 'Even a glimmer of hope that we may have music here again relieves the gloom of this sad parting,' she said. 'These flowers should really go to the Griller Quartet who have travelled all night to play to us today.' She paid tribute to those who had helped her so much, ensuring the smooth running of the events despite all. Over the years there had been a total of 824,152 attendances and more than 700 musicians had performed to them.

> It is seldom that we do not wish to be someone else; but for once I would not have changed places with anyone in the world. The experience of those six and a half years has been the greatest privilege any musician could hope to have. If I had died the day peace was declared, I would have felt my life's work was complete.
>
> We are sad that the continuity of these concerts must be broken, not for the sake of music alone, but because we feel that the union of the Arts could stand for so much in this world of disunity. But with the announcement of the Trustees in mind, and Mr Hendy's comforting words, perhaps we may look forward to the day when the reconstruction of the Gallery will permit us to return and resume this perfect alliance of music and painting.

The Guardian's reporter noted:

> For six and a half years and five days a week ... the whole literature of chamber music had been accessible to everyone at these concerts. It was unprecedented in the world. So, surely, has been the bringing of music to a central place in the life of a bombed city. That was in the minds of all as they cheered Dame Myra and turned away from the close of a London chapter.

Myra added (her capitals): 'IT IS SAID SOMETIMES THAT MUSIC IS A FORM OF ESCAPE, but the experience of these years has made us understand that it is infinitely more IMPORTANT THAN THAT.'

She finally gave heartfelt thanks to Howard Ferguson – and concluded: 'With gratitude to so many indispensable people I say: farewell.'[17]

In the early 1960s, Fiona Fraser, by then a photographic archivist at the Gallery, met Myra at an informal recital by the latter's student Stephen Bishop in West Hampstead. She found Myra remarkable: 'She had extraordinary charisma when one is talking to her, and was full of warmth, humour and insight.' Fraser relates that when Myra discovered where she worked, she said: 'One thing I would really love to do before I die is to play once more at the National Gallery.'

'The following day,' Fraser says, 'I was passing Philip Hendy's office and his door was open. He called me in to look at two new pictures he'd fallen in love with. I told him that I had been talking to Myra Hess the night before, and that she would love the opportunity to play here once more. He said: "Oh, no, no, no – sorry, much too expensive for security. We can't embark on anything like that." And I, being a very junior member of staff, didn't continue trying to persuade him. That's one of my deep regrets. It would have just been wonderful.'[18]

1 Alan Lawrence, letter to *The Times*, 14 April 1945
2 J. P. Blake, letter to *The Times*, 7 May 1945
3 Elizabeth M. Baker, letter to *The Times*, 3 May 1945
4 MH diary, see also McKenna op. cit., p182
5 MH to MVR, 7 May 1945
6 Sir P. Mason, op. cit., p80-81
7 M. L. Settle, op. cit.
8 W. Gibson to MH, 6 June 1945
9 A. Penn, printed in *Myra Hess: Her Book*
10 MH to Trustees of National Gallery, undated, November 1945
11 MH to MVR, 29 August 1945, see McKenna op. cit., p196
12 *Musical Times*, January 1946
13 MH to professors of TMPS, 28 December 1946, with thanks to Stephen Siek
14 MH to Vincent Massey, 5 February 1946, see McKenna op. cit., p189
15 Press release, 14 February 1946
16 Petition text, National Gallery Archive
17 MH speech transcript
18 Author interview with Fiona Fraser

New Beginnings

(1946–1949)

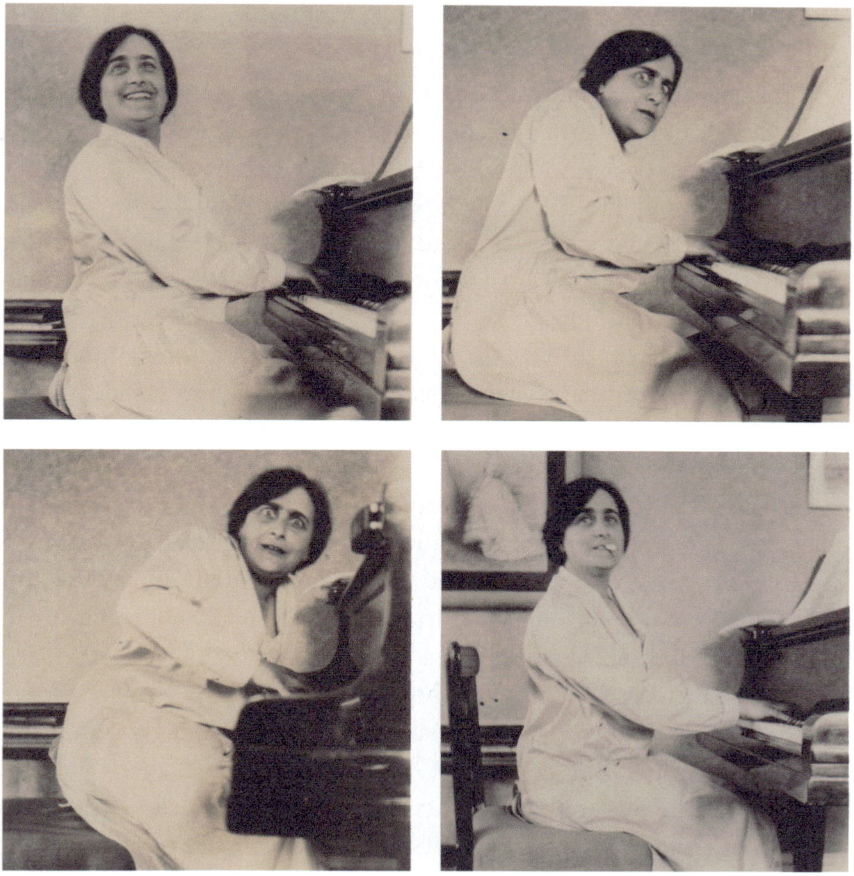

Myra in mimic mode at the piano

THE FIRST THING MYRA DID on 10th April at her desk was to thank her closest colleague.

My darlingest Howardie,

In 500 years I couldn't thank you enough for your colossal work. I consider that the tremendously high standard of the National Gallery Concerts is entirely due to you. For your forbearance and blessed kindness to me, perhaps I can thank you one day with 109, 110, & 111! And so, my darling, you are liberated at long last, and may we all benefit by your freedom.

Your completely devoted and for once inarticulate old

'sign please'

Myra[1]

She must have heard and uttered the words 'sign please' innumerable times during the concerts' administrative tasks. Now it was time to accept the situation and begin to move on. She had little choice.

A Dutch tour in May brought healing balm. She and Saz enjoyed encounters with old friends, packed halls and, in The Hague, a glimpse of Churchill. Crowds had amassed to welcome him, although he did not appear until nearly midnight.

The difficult conditions meant that compromises were inevitable. During her first entry in her Mozart concerto in The Hague, 'PING went a string!!! High E flat, which I knew I would need often…' At the Concertgebouw, despite a piano in a dubious state, the concert was unforgettable: a horse-drawn carriage brought her to the hall, where she played to 1,600 people. 'Terribly moving concert & played encores until ¼ to 11 (concert began at 8:00). Had to see a lot of people and by the time we had gathered up flowers and ourselves the horse had gone home!'

Another day, she arrived for a radio broadcast of Mozart's Piano Concerto in E flat, K271. Mozart, however, wrote several concertos in E flat and nobody had verified the Köchel number required. The conductor turned up with a different one. 'Complete drama and chaos.' After a fruitless search for orchestral parts, Myra offered Beethoven's Fourth instead, or the Mozart A major K488 if there was a score from which she could play. There was, but it was a photostat. 'The pages revolved like a windmill … & finally one page decided to sever itself permanently … I had to laugh - but I must say I was slightly "flustered" when I had to face the microphone with a concerto I hadn't played for ?? months.'

Her diary from this trip sparkles with delight at her warm welcome – and also the quality of the food, a notch up on the meagre fare available in Britain. There was even chocolate pudding. And she notes, when invited to a party with Mrs Churchill at the British Embassy, 'Magnificent lunch ending with superb Stilton cheese!!! LOVELY GRUB in fact.'[2]

She was often up until the small hours, playing either Picquet (with others) or Patience (alone). But when she did manage to sleep, she suffered recurring nightmares about a mysterious, non-existent pianist named 'Madame Pugnati', seemingly sparked by anxiety that someone else might have usurped her place in the affection of American audiences. Beryl speculated that she might have been thinking of Guiomar Novaes, but after the cumulative pressures that Myra had been undergoing for so many years, her subconscious scarcely needed a real figure to prompt fears that everything might perhaps be over.

Atlantic Dreams

The journalist Harriett Johnson interviewed Myra during her first postwar visit to the US and left a vivid description:

> Dame Myra's deep-set questioning eyes still retain the serious but mellow expression which music lovers through many years have deemed so characteristic of her face. Her eyes can laugh too – as spontaneously and infectiously as the words she speaks are strong. Her healthy vitality and spontaneous charm are as abundant as ever. The war has not diminished her zest for life. 'I'd like to get up on top of the Empire State Building and shout 'Thank You' for the financial help I got from the United States which made possible the continuance of our war time concerts' [she said].[3]

For Myra, returning to the US after seven years away was a shock to the system. Crossing the Atlantic in early August – for once, without Saz – Myra wrote to Beryl: 'I have never hated leaving England so much - & hate the lethargy of a sea journey.'

'The feeling of complete dead isolation when you get on board is horrible. You suddenly seem to belong nowhere at all,' she noted in her diary. She wondered if she would feel better on a simpler boat rather than a floating luxury hotel. A so-called 'austerity menu' serving up enough meat for a normal week's ration, delicate white rolls and fruit galore worsened her sense of guilt. 'It is going to be extremely difficult to accept the maddeningly unfair distribution of the world's "goods",' she reflected. 'Perhaps I shall be expelled from the USA for bad behaviour.'

She spent some of the voyage in her cabin, reading Evelyn Waugh's *Brideshead Revisited*. 'I feel completely "disorientated" & as if my ghost is coming back to America,' she told Howard. '... The more I think of our work together, the more I realise that it was one of those rare experiences that will increase in value till the end of one's life. I think you know what I mean but you can hardly know what a great person you are - Nunky [Samuel] knew it - & I am overwhelmed when I think of your complete devotion & absorption in a life which took you right away from your own work. I know of nobody else who could or would have done it. I am only cross when "I" am praised for the colossal achievement at the N.G.'

Photographic portrait of Myra by Florence Vandamm, late 1940s

New York swamped her with emotional reunions – and the chance for her first proper rest since the outbreak of war. The perspicacious Pondie had organised a holiday near Silver Lake, New England, with two friends named Helen and Eleanor. Here Myra could be incommunicado and practise to her heart's content. She re-memorised Howard's Piano Sonata and played it to her impressed companions; she also started practising the 'Emperor' Concerto since there was a chance, as yet uncomfirmed, that she might play it with Arturo Toscanini.

Their cottage was simple, but attractive. Myra reported that the water supply was unpredictable, but she adored her music room surrounded by pine trees, with a log fire that Pondie tended devotedly. A heavenly scent of pines arose when the sun deigned to come out; it was, she learned, the wettest August since 1885.

Pondie was now over 80, but would shrug off anyone else's concerns with 'Why worry?' Eleanor, who was always chattering or singing, accompanied Myra on rambles through the woods and hills and did the cooking. In the US, rationing had ended with the war, unlike in Britain; Myra nearly wept at the prospect of chicken cooked in wine. Nevertheless, butter remained pricey and meat almost non-existent. One day, after lunching at a nearby inn, Myra wrote: 'I nearly made a fool of myself with a tenderloin steak.'

Eventually, Myra had the strange feeling that England had vanished like Atlantis. She wrote: 'The peace and simple life here is perfection and I must try to rise to it … one can enjoy things to the full and yet have one's heartstrings stretched to breaking point.'[4]

She slept copiously – helped by her sleeping 'pillies' – and enjoyed reading Mozart's letters: 'Isn't it frightfully, appallingly, touching & infuriating to think of his begging for work – or rather a living – & what lovely silly letters he can write … It is like reading a miracle all the time – & hits one below the belt every single word one reads about him?'

One day, the group visited a well-known kennels that was home to numerous Huskies. There they rode on a cart pulled through the woods by a team of the creatures, led by a 'veteran' dog that had been on an expedition to the South Pole. Pondie had dressed as if for an elegant New York tea party of the 1890s, which amused Myra. But she was besotted. It is not easy for busy, travelling musicians to keep pets. She rarely wrote about her love for animals, but this was an exception: 'There were 6 puppies which I would rather not talk about. I WANT them all.'

Meanwhile, she was having a running argument with Arthur Mendel, the musicologist who had organised the American appeal that kept the Gallery concerts running after the Blitz. Now, in striking contrast, he was berating her for starting the trills and mordents in Bach on the lower note instead of the supposedly correct upper one. Myra disliked the dogmatism implied by insistence on this without fail, regardless of context. She gave a verbal shrug: 'Surely the fact that we can "sing" on the piano (in Sarabande of G min [English] Suite for instance) makes a considerable difference? It is "nice" to be consistent, but I wonder if Bach wouldn't have broken the rule with our instruments. I always feel that the ornaments and variation on the piano - what about it??'[5]

The holiday helped to recharge Myra's batteries, not a moment too soon; the onslaught of her New York comeback was a time of great intensity, not to say anxiety. Her first concern – her relations with Annie Friedberg – fortunately proved less of an ordeal than she had feared. Before heading for Silver Lake, she had arrived at the Laurelton to find Annie pacing about the foyer, waiting for her: 'Oh – my – my – she looks so terribly & pathetically ill that we shall never be able to be cross with her, even if she books 10 concerts in one day! She is being surprisingly un-troublesome so far - touching wood...' There was also a rapturous reunion with the Steinway family ('"Billy" Steinway and Mr Greiner suggested a "celebration" in the BAR next door...').

Beryl and Saz sailed out to join Myra in New York – and Beryl wrote to Howard, describing the extraordinary atmosphere at the 12th October recital at New York Town Hall. Annie would have preferred Carnegie and persuaded Myra to agree to a later concert there, although the pianist disliked it and was reluctant. Town Hall, by contrast, was a welcome return. Myra, Beryl reported, was nervous all week, but on the day not at all, while the hall had sold out as soon as the concert was announced; people were queuing for standing room, tipping the doorman to get in. John Steinway noted that the foyer was so crowded with disappointed would-be concert-goers that the Fire Department had to be called to monitor the health and safety situation. Beryl wrote:

> At 3, Myra swept on to the platform. There was a moment of tense silence. Then the audience stood. The applause was sustained & dignified (she had intended saying a few words before playing – but she felt & was right – that it was not the moment) so she went straight to the piano & was as cool as could be. The Bach [French Suite in G major] was most beautiful & she was sufficiently un-nervous to play the ornaments to her own liking & to Arthur Mendel's for a joke!! At the end of the Suite – the audience simply 'let go' & shouted & screamed. Then came the Beethoven ... with Myra right bang on top of her form..... she had the entire audience reduced to uncontrollable tears...[6]

Myra's solution to Mendel's Bachian demands was that in repeated sections, she played the first rendition in his preferred format, then the second in her own. Next came the Beethoven Variations in F minor and the Sonata Op. 110, the Brahms F minor Sonata Op. 5 – and numerous encores. Ruth Steinway, who had no idea of the ongoing British reliance on clothing coupons, was startled to see Myra sporting the same black dress and shoes that she had worn seven years earlier.

After the first half, Myra made the speech she had been contemplating. *The New York World Telegram* reported it:

> I have been praised far too much for the work I have done in England during the war. In 1939 it seemed incredible and fantastic that I could serve my country by the mere organizing of chamber concerts. When the National Gallery reopened its doors on October 10 1939, we began our great adventure of giving chamber music to the people. Six and one half years of concerts! In those dark times music found a response not only from musicians, but from among people who had never been to a concert. It was a token of spiritual renaissance. I am telling you all this because it was your help that enabled us to maintain this unbroken series of 1698 concerts. We were threatened with a serious financial problem. It was then that you came to our rescue. Generous contributions reached us from all over America, continuing even after you yourselves were faced with the enormous burdens of war. I wish I could make you see what these concerts meant to people. Then, perhaps, you would imagine the measure of my profound gratitude … This welcome you have given me is more than a personal tribute. It is a symbol of enduring unity between your people and mine.

Afterwards the Steinways held a reception for Myra at Steinway Hall, in tribute to all she had accomplished during their seven years apart.

The next day, Virgil Thomson, a razor-penned critic and composer, produced a sour write-up. Olin Downes, though, said in *The New York Times* that it was not possible in a review to give 'more than an indication of the effect, for example, of the mystical sonata, Op. 110, of Beethoven, as she played it yesterday, with all imaginable intimacy and inner feeling … Enough that the tone quality, as well as the inflection of phrase and coordination of thought conveyed the musical essence … This was not a virtuoso imposing a dominant personality upon an audience, but a true and modest musician who was saying, in her own way, 'These are some of the pages of Beethoven that I most deeply revere. I hope that I can persuade you to feel them with me.'[7]

This was the start of perhaps Myra's most triumphant tour – in which she performed on the Bell Telephone Hour on the radio (a 'circus,' she said), raised the roof with 'Kousse' (Serge Koussevitzky) and the Boston Symphony Orchestra, and played to President Truman in Washington DC.

From coast to coast, a new generation was hearing her for the first time. For the Juilliard School piano student Marshall Izen – later a puppeteer, ventriloquist and musical humourist – a first glimpse of Myra in Orchestra Hall, Chicago, in October 1946 proved revelatory. He and his friends had known about her only from reports of the National Gallery concerts and a recording of the Schumann Concerto. 'Thus we were unprepared for what happened that evening,' he recounted.

They were unsure what to make of the reception that greeted her. The conductor Desiré Defauw (whom Myra nicknamed 'Deskie') held her hand high as they walked onto the stage. The brass played a fanfare and the packed audience jumped to its feet, cheering. Soon her performance told them all they needed to know. 'Dame Myra's serene playing of the Beethoven Fourth Concerto's deceptively simple opening measures signalled that we were about to have a rare musical experience. It combined expressiveness and nobility with an other-worldly tone unique to the artist.'[8] These young musicians had formerly been in thrall to the razzle-dazzle of Horowitz and Rubinstein; Myra's musicianship completely changed the way they listened to piano playing thereafter.

Myra felt overwhelmed, but rose to the occasion. 'I don't know what has happened to me, but the more moving things are, the more calm I become,' she told Howard. 'I couldn't think how I would begin the [Beethoven] G. ma. after a fanfare....but suddenly there was complete quiet and calm.....It is very extraordinary how one seems to play better than one is accustomed to....in this country.....'

And the best was yet to come.

Myra and the 'Maestro'

Myra had never yet had the chance to perform with Arturo Toscanini. The Italian conductor's anti-fascist stance and advocacy for artistic freedom during the war had marked him out as an artist of unparalleled principle and determination. Now he wanted her to work with him and the NBC Symphony Orchestra. She was only the second female piano soloist he had ever invited (the first was Ania Dorfmann).

In mid October the offer came through: a radio broadcast of Beethoven's 'Emperor' Concerto on 24th November. From then on, the name 'Maestro' in Myra's correspondence and diaries only ever meant Toscanini – even though their musical relationship was far from easy. On this first occasion, they switched to a different concerto five days before the performance. Myra wired Howard: 'Delightful affectionate but fantastic afternoon with Maestro finally deciding Beethoven Third Sunday he unexpectedly and passionately prefers it to Emperor tell anyone interested special love.'

There was more to the switch than she let him know. She had already mentioned how difficult she was finding the preparation, writing on 3rd November: 'I am beginning to "get into" the Emperor again, but I wish I had played it more recently. I am amazed at the number of notes I have to leave out in the beginning of the last movement, and wonder how I ever get the rhythm right??... It is somewhat disturbing having to practise it "on the road" and at present I have an abortion of a Steinway piano called a Spinet....in my room. It has to be tuned every few hours!!!'

Toscanini was notorious for choosing what could politely be called very brisk tempi. At a meeting with Myra ahead of the rehearsals, he demonstrated his preferred speed for the first movement. It was so fast that Myra knew she would never be comfortable maintaining it. With a stroke of inspiration, she suggested that perhaps they could consider playing the Third Concerto instead of the Fifth, because (ostensibly) it was less often heard. To her relief, Maestro agreed.

It did not quite dispel the drama. Again Myra had to employ her well-honed diplomatic skills after Maestro, in rehearsal, brought the orchestra in early in the slow movement, which meant she missed four bars. She made a gentle joke and plea out of it at the end, which amused him, but afterwards he let off steam in despair at his own carelessness. Finding him 'utterly dejected', Myra had to talk him down, taking his hand and recounting Casals' comment: 'The moment we stop beginning, we stop altogether.'

Saz told Howard that the pair had reached a compromise: 'The first movement was faster than she usually plays it, but the slow and last were sheer perfection. To have his wonderful steadiness in the last movement, was beyond all price.' She was impressed by how much work Maestro had put in, rehearsing with orchestra alone on Thursday and with Myra on Friday and Saturday before the Sunday broadcast:

> She was as nervous as ten cats, of course, but profoundly happy, as he was so terribly nice about her playing. He listened in to her broadcast with Kousse, on the previous Tuesday and had heard her often before, without anyone knowing he had. He said he had never forgotten a performance she gave of the lovely Mozart F major, with Hans Lange and the N.Y. Phil. which must have been at least ten years ago. I felt sure that, in spite of all the stories we had heard of his dictatorial and arbitrary methods with soloists, that he would be ready to co-operate with a sincere and musical point of view, such as Myra's and that probably his other soloists got what they deserved! And so it proved to be.
>
> Myra played really magnificently and what made it one of her greatest achievements was, that she did meet him half way on some points and yet achieved an outstanding creation of the concerto ... We went back to dinner with him afterwards and one felt an overpowering sense of being in the presence of real greatness, although he is so sweet and gentle. He has complete unself-consciousness and simplicity. He loves Myra dearly and I very much doubt if this will be her last performance with him, God willing. His vitality is quite incredible for any age and when one realises he is just on 80, it leaves one gasping.[9]

Myra sent Howard a telegram on 27th Nov: ONLY JUST COMING DOWN TO EARTH AFTER SUNDAYS MARVELLOUS EXPERIENCE WORSHIP THE MAESTRO TELL ANYONE.

The broadcast was later issued as a record. The first movement is not only faster than Myra would have chosen, but also faster than most other pianists and conductors generally attempt. The *alla breve* rhythm makes it take wing; and Myra manages to relax the pace somewhat after the first entry. There is a slight tug-of-war, Myra gently trying to pull Maestro back while he attempts to push her on. Critics have quibbled over who was responsible for this. They complete the first movement in a jaw-dropping 14 minutes and six seconds, compared for instance to 18 minutes 52 seconds for Daniel Barenboim and Otto Klemperer, or 16 minutes 11 seconds for Martha Argerich with Claudio Abbado.

After the roller-coaster first movement, Myra brings rhapsodic poetry to the Largo's opening solo; Toscanini and the orchestra respond with warmth and affection, even if in the middle section the orchestral racehorse strains at the bit during Myra's surges of triplets. The finale is supremely fiery, Myra meeting the Maestro's challenges with determination. The whole performance exists in a state of danger, pushing everyone to the limits of the possible. Perhaps Myra enjoyed being out of her comfort zone.

Stephen Kovacevich recalled Myra describing a telling encounter with Toscanini. She had played a concerto with him, after which he conducted Beethoven's Fifth Symphony. In the latter he was unsatisfied with his own performance. Most musicians, feeling something had not gone well, would acknowledge it with regret, then move on. Toscanini was different. 'Myra went backstage to congratulate him and heard him screaming in his dressing room: "I sinned against the Holy Ghost!" He wasn't religious, but music was sacred to him.' That was Myra's outlook too.[10] She added Toscanini's baton for their Beethoven Third to her select collection of lucky souvenirs and kept his photograph on her piano, along with one of Uncle Tobs, for the rest of her life.

After the Toscanini turmoil, Myra succumbed to flu. Cancellations had to be made and her Carnegie Hall recital, scheduled for 14th December, was postponed; miraculously, the hall was free for her to play there on 21st instead. Saz explained to Howard that Myra was unable to give two recitals including his sonata in New Haven and Boston: 'The wear and tear of the last 7 ½ years, plus the incredibly moving experience of this tour, have not left her with 100% of resistance to cope quickly with such a thing as flu. Above all, after the tremendous impression she has made here, it would be madness to play unless she is absolutely on the top of the wave…'[11]

Myra wrote from the Laurelton on 14th December, when she should have been on stage. 'I can see the artists' entrance of Carnegie from my window,' she told him, in handwriting scrawlier than usual. 'I am putting my fingers on my nose at it today (& shall no doubt do the same this time next week!)' News of his finished violin sonata – for Yfrah Neaman, a gifted young violinist from Lebanon who was a close friend to both – had cheered her up. 'I have had a most wretched "siege" & have been utterly hors de combat for the last fortnight. Touching wood (with every part of my anatomy?) I feel alive again today & pray I may pursue the upward path for next Saturday. I have worked a little this past week – but only to keep my fingers & brain from turning into the best Scotch porridge.'

However much she thumbed her nose at Carnegie Hall, the auditorium was waiting for her. Her programme included two Scarlatti sonatas, Schubert's Sonata in A minor D537, Beethoven's 'Appassionata', Howard's Sonata and a group of Chopin works – the D flat major Nocturne Op. 27

No. 2, the Grand Valse brillante in E flat Op. 18 and the Scherzo No. 3 in C sharp minor. Overflow audience members were seated on the stage.

She had something else to look forward to: 'I am going to have lunch with the Maestro on New Year's Day & I had a heart-breakingly lovely letter from him,' she wrote on 30th December. 'How we will talk when you knock at the door at 48 [Wildwood Road]?! Unfortunately none of the important critics were at my recital on account of postponement & so near Xmas. Notices were merely perfunctory announcements.'

Soon she could set off for home, suitably lunched and fully recovered.

Home Turf

Britain was in a woeful condition, especially compared to the plenitude in the States. Rationing had worsened after the end of hostilities to include limits on bread; while the official diet was healthy, with no limits on fruit and vegetables, it could be dispiriting. With bomb-shattered cities from Coventry to Liverpool to Southampton needing vast amounts of reconstruction, the fate of classical music was not uppermost in anybody's mind; no decisions were being made about venues in the capital, which now lacked not only the Queen's Hall, but also the Aeolian Hall, which had been taken over by the BBC.

Radical shifts in approach were afoot. John Maynard Keynes had become head of CEMA in 1941; by 1945 it was providing funding for 46 arts organisations. Keynes died shortly before the Arts Council gained its royal charter, but he had left a successfully established 'arms-length' principle: the organisation would report directly to the Treasury, and was supposed to operate with autonomy, rather than being controlled by central government potentially with a political agenda. Using public money to support the arts, instead of leaving them reliant only on private philanthropy and box-office takings, effected a transformation in the UK's artistic environment, opening it up to a wider audience than ever before.

The new head of the Arts Council, J Steuart Wilson, invited Myra to join the committee. Her National Gallery concerts had mirrored the Proms' success with the principle of making high quality music available for all at a modest price. The Arts Council seemed to take its cue from this; its subsidies were intended to let ticket prices stay low, fulfilling the ideal that everybody, in every walk of life, had the right to access high-quality art, theatre and music. Myra's Gallery concerts had helped to demonstrate how necessary this was on an emotional, spiritual, social and human level.

Ambition was in the air despite the challenges, and new orchestras were coming into being alongside the LSO and Beecham's London Philharmonic. The record producer Walter Legge launched the Philharmonia Orchestra with a concert on 27th October 1945 conducted by Beecham. Then – in a familiar pattern – the irascible conductor fell out with Legge and created yet another new orchestra, the Royal Philharmonic. The BBC had five orchestras of its own, established well before the war. The organisation launched its Third Programme in 1946, a broadly cultural station that broadcast for six hours every evening.

In many wartime photographs of Myra, tension is palpable in her expression, while her eyes are filled with unfathomable depths of emotion. Those years had left everyone battered, including her, and now she sailed home from the US to a winter in which Londoners often lacked heat, light and adequate food. Her social world had changed, too, with the deaths of not only Matthay but also Mabel Reynolds, in 1942.

Myra's first concert back was on 22nd February 1947 at the Albert Hall: Mozart's C major Concerto K467 with the BBC Symphony Orchestra under Boult. She played, according to one review, 'with her customary sensitiveness and charm, making an especially beautiful impression in the slow movement … It may be that the first movement needs a more vigorous treatment and more splendid tone. But criticism must make due allowance for the handicap of the sub-arctic conditions which compel performers to wear fur coats and audiences to muffle themselves in blankets.'[12]

For Harriet, the world could have changed again with the death in 1947 of Elsita Bax, whom Arnold had never divorced. Harriet's affair with him had seemingly settled down into habit; he nicknamed her the affectionate 'Bunty' instead of the romantic 'Tania', and both were sometimes busy with other entanglements. Asked in an interview how intimate she was with Sibelius, Harriet replied 'As intimate as I was with Elgar', which probably caught the journalist rather off guard. Nevertheless, she had been waiting for many long years for Elsita to pass away, and had high hopes of becoming Lady Bax thereafter. But Arnold did not tell her.

If life was difficult for artists as well established as Myra, who was freezing, and Harriet, who was having serious problems with her sight (physically as well as metaphorically), it was still worse for young musicians trying to start their professional lives in a postwar wasteland.

Activism is a habit that dies hard and Myra turned her energies to the support of the next generation. First, she, Vaughan Williams, Albert Sammons and Lionel Tertis jointly signed a plea on *The Times* letters page on 22nd May 1947, urging the exemption of music students from compulsory conscription in peacetime. There is little sign that their words had much impact; conscription was not reassessed until 1957 and ended only in 1960.

The year before – indeed, the day before the last National Gallery concert – *The Times* had carried a letter signed by Myra, Vaughan Williams, Bax, Boult, Dyson, Stanley Merchant and Edward Dent, campaigning to save Paul Hirsch's music library, the world's most renowned in private hands, which had been evacuated from Frankfurt to Cambridge, but was in danger of being sold off. The owner was willing to forgo part of its worth if it could be kept intact and in Britain. This was more successful: the entire collection went to the British Library.

By summer, Myra was busy helping to set up a scholarship fund in memory of Matthay at the Academy. It aimed to support British students in the challenging period after graduation, so they could concentrate on career development without the urgent need to earn an income. *The Times* reported: 'It is hoped to raise £10,000 for the scholarship fund, towards which the American Matthay Association has already made a contribution.'[13]

Privately, however, Myra's spirits were not at their finest. In October, for Howard's birthday she sent him a fervent letter and a gift of cigars – 'a token of my deep love and thankfulness for your most wonderful & blessed friendship…

'If I have any reason left,' she added, 'you have helped to save it - & if you hadn't encouraged me to go on playing in public in September, I might have fallen by the way. I may wish sometimes that you had pushed me over the edge, but with every inch of "me better self" I bless & thank you.'

Stokowski, Olive Oil and Op. 111

Myra set off for the US in October on the Queen Mary. In her letters there is a sense of relief; and her biting wit is revitalised. From her letter to Howard of 26th October, she seems disenchanted with campaigning: 'Bless you for voicing or rather echoing my own feelings about these devastating "projects".' She was soon enjoying, instead, her American social life, thrilled to see Pondie 'in wonderful form', and then visiting the pianist and teacher Olga Samaroff, the ex-wife of the conductor Leopold Stokowski.

Olga, from Texas, was originally named Lucy Hickenlooper. She had, Myra wrote, 'a terrific sense of humour and was frightfully funny about her ex-husband. Apparently every time he marries he gives different statements about his ancestry. Consequently he is now too embarrassed to meet any of his ex-wives or various children. He speaks with a Polish accent now - so Olga says & excepting for a few warts looks like Liszt!!'

Stokowski, from Marylebone, was in fact the son of an Irish mother and a London-born father of Polish descent. His larger-than-life performances and orchestral transcriptions were often controversial for their extremity (not least in Disney's *Fantasia*), an approach somewhat at odds with Myra's own. Her tour now began with three concerts with him and the New York Philharmonic.

On 2nd November she gave what turned out to be the city's first-ever performance of Mozart's E flat Concerto K449, and subsequently Olin Downes welcomed her Schumann: 'It is hardly possible to praise her performance too warmly. She sang the lyrical music in the simplest, the most perfectly adjusted and most poetical manner...' He judged Stokowski's accompaniment as 'wonderful'.[14] Myra was less sure, writing to Denis Matthews: 'The performances with Stoko were very odd ... although he took so much trouble and enjoyed the performance himself, I didn't feel there was anyone there...if you can understand what I mean?'

She planned to dispatch parcels of food to her friends in Britain via Rose Parsonnet, 'and I will mention OLIVE OIL for you,' she assured Howard. '(By the way, Saz says that even John Barnes [a local department store on Finchley Road] has it now??).'

After six weeks, Myra had given 13 concerts. On a well-earned rest day, 11th December, she told him: 'It has been pretty terrific, but enormously gratifying. & I have come to the conclusion that one is no more terrified playing to 3,000 than to 300 - & it seems ineffably more worth while! Also, the acoustics of the larger hall are much better than the small ones. [Beethoven's Op.] 111 is growing I think & that makes up for a lot of clammy apprehension!'

From Washington DC, a letter to Howard (who now had a teaching post at the Academy) is scrawled on headed notepaper bearing the legend: 'Dame Myra Hess Suite, The Hotel Raleigh'. You can almost hear her chuckling as she writes: 'Well, well, well – you may be a professor, but have you a suite?' Her eponymous apartment had two bedrooms and a magnificent parlour: 'It is terribly touching and equally frightful.'

She added that there was a diary en route home, describing 'a rehearsal yesterday with H. B. [Harold Bauer] ... for duets at the Manhattan School tomorrow!!! It is incredible with his progressive mind that he should play like a wilted Aspidistra!' A harsh judgement, perhaps, upon someone she used to admire so much; maybe the *Jesu, Joy* issue still rankled. (At Myra's MBF dinner after the war, the commemorative book was headed *Dame Myra Hess: Her Book*. When Bauer published his autobiography in 1948, its title was *Harold Bauer: His Book*. This may be pure coincidence, but if so, a strange one.)

Myra's Carnegie Hall programme on 22nd November, which she also took to Boston's Symphony Hall, was a gargantuan prospect. Op. 111, Beethoven's final sonata, is one of the ultimate prizes in any pianist's repertoire and the last piece she had played at the Gallery. Now she performed it at Carnegie Hall for an audience of 2,700. She set it alongside Bach's Adagio in G major (his transcription of Albinoni), Schubert's Drei Klavierstücke D946, five of Schumann's *Albumblätter* Op. 99 and his *Carnaval*.

The New York Times reported that she held the audience spellbound:

> It is impressive just to see her at the piano. She seems so indomitable and yet so undefeated in maintaining the open sensitivity of her spirit. ... one gets the impression that the music which is so much a part of her, which was there all the time, is merely being made audible ... [In the Beethoven] It may have been mere fancy, but as she played the first movement she seemed to be reliving some of the bombings of London. There was terror in it, and fury and a sense of fate. [15]

Myra was being mythologised to a degree, but she suffered fools less gladly than ever. Challenged by an interviewer before the Boston date on her excessively meaty programme, she retorted: 'I'd rather bore my listeners with great music than play trash for immediate appeal.' Besides, her listeners were far from bored; she met with adulation wherever she went.

The tour was not without mishap. At the Chicago Symphony Orchestra she was caught up in a fracas. Its conductor, Artur Rodzinski, had a good name for building and improving orchestras, but a reputation for a certain capriciousness. He had left the New York Philharmonic the previous year, supposedly feeling hemmed in by the management; he had, however, dismissed 14 players. In Chicago, 24 hours before the concert, his wife called the orchestra to say he was ill. The assistant conductor, Tauno Hannikainen, had just one day to rehearse Myra's concerto and learn Shostakovich's Fifth Symphony from scratch. Then at the last minute Rodzinski returned, but to do only the Shostakovich. Halfway through the concert, the management called a press conference and announced that Rodzinski was fired. Myra told Howard:

> You may have heard that Roszinski has been "fried" in Chicago & the atmosphere was appalling – talk about sizzling steaks – every blooming city we touch seems to be sizzling with intrigue. It is sickening. I played Schumann with the assistant Conductor - a tense but musical Finn - a Beethoven 3 with R. The public were out to scream their approval of him & disapp. of the Board of Trustees, but thank heaven they did listen peaceably to the concerto. I played with them again in Milwaukee & wasn't sorry to leave all that behind me! … R will stay until the end of the season unless he messes up!! He is brilliant, but I have always missed any spiritual quality in his music.

The bigger picture was brighter:

> For the time being, I am terribly keen to play over here as much as possible. Apart from the enormous stimulation for oneself, I have been tremendously gratified by the response to my kind of playing… if you know what I mean? Marvellous though he may be, I still maintain that Horowitz has been the most pernicious influence over here, and the interest and touching appreciation of so many young people makes me feel I have a real job to do…..and the fact that I can fill the big halls with my kind of programmes refutes the blasted managers' theory that only fast and loud playing attracts the box office!!!!.

Shards of Glass

Other musicians were venturing back to the US, notably Moiseiwitsch, who, like Myra, had not left Britain since 1939. Now *The New York Times* welcomed him at his recital on 8th December as 'one of the best in the world' and noted that in the war he had given about 800 concerts in the UK, 'making music wherever people wished and needed it'[16]. Having heard Mrs Churchill broadcast an appeal for her Aid to Russia fund, he had offered to play a concert a week for her for the duration – ultimately a hundred of them.

Harriet also toured the US that winter and, like Myra, travelled out on the Queen Mary, but in late January and through a terrible storm. A warm welcome awaited her, the critics praising her 'keen intelligence' and 'cleanness, clarity and precision'. This had the unfortunate side-effect of highlighting her discontent with her career at home. Back in London, she grumbled to the BBC that it had only given her two recitals in seven years.

Fate had worse in store for her. In May 1948 the details of Elsita Bax's will were revealed. Her death was news to Harriet. How Bax had managed to keep it from reaching her is a mystery, but when she challenged her lover of 30 years about this monstrous secret, he told her another. For 20 of those 30 years, he had had another mistress. Her name was Mary Gleaves. When he spent time on the west coast of Scotland, at a little hotel in Morar which looked out across the Silver Sands towards the islands of Eigg, Rum and Muck, he took Mary with him. He did not intend to marry Mary. Neither did he intend to marry Harriet.

A terrible row ensued. A few days later, Harriet, at home, was carrying a tray of glasses. She tripped, fell and cut her right wrist so badly on the broken shards that she severed an artery and damaged her tendons.

Or so she said. Neither her biographer nor Bax's credits the story with much likelihood: her injuries were so severe that they had to have been deliberate. Poor Harriet, who had sometimes threatened suicide for effect, may finally have attempted it.

She recovered, but the damage left her unable to play the piano for three years. George Bernard Shaw exhorted her to try conducting. Bax, perhaps contrite, wrote her a Concertante for Left Hand, which she performed at the Proms in 1950. It was only in December that year that she could give concerts with two hands again. Bax still did not marry her.

Two Lovely Black Eyes

Myra experienced injury in summer 1948 too, but it was mild and accidental. A new International Summer School of Music was being founded at Bryanston, Dorset. The idea came from Artur Schnabel, who suggested that his former pupil, William Glock, should run it. Myra was among those taking part; others included the pianist Maria Donska and the Amadeus Quartet.

Driving to pick up Denise en route, Myra had a 'contretemps' with her new car. An inner tyre burst, whizzing her off the road. 'By the hands of all the merciful gods I escaped any major injury,' she told Howard on

13th August, '& apart from [here she draws music over the words] "2 lovely black eyes" Auntie's face is as usual!' After slipping a 'charming policeman' ten bob and her autograph not to report the accident, she spent the rest of the day in bed at the house of some friends nearby, 'with a plaster on me nose'.

A doctor advised her not to do her first Bryanston concert, but she soon found 'wonderfully responsive audiences' there. The only disappointment was the ration-era communal supper: 'one sausage & some stale lettuce'. And she had a surprise for Howard: 'I kissed Glock!!!!! I had nagged him so mercilessly that it suddenly seemed imperative to seal the joke – just before I was going to play. Johnnie [John Amis, now Bryanston's administrator] was "back stage" when it occurred & nearly lost his trousers & everything else in amazement!!!'

Home again, she worked on Beethoven with the tenor John McCormack, scheduled various social events and promised to go to 11 Downing Street to help Isobel Cripps with 'a pack of young people' (Sir Stafford was now Chancellor of the Exchequer). As for the summer school, it relocated in 1951 to Dartington in south Devon, where it became internationally renowned. It was partly the ideas and connections that Glock made there that shaped his approach when he became the BBC's controller of music a decade later.

A Moral Choice

Soon after Bryanston, a landmark in postwar cultural relations took place in which Myra played a crucial role. The Berlin Philharmonic Orchestra under Wilhelm Furtwängler was to tour Britain for the first time since the war. She agreed to be soloist for its London concert.

Furious arguments had raged over Furtwängler's position in Nazi Germany. Unlike Toscanini and others, the renowned conductor, at the height of his powers, had remained there throughout the hostilities. Suggestions as to why included his widow's account that Goebbels had threatened to send his orchestral musicians to the eastern front if he left[17]. But again, political naivety had something to answer for: the old-chestnut belief that artists had to occupy moral territory higher than mere politics. Music and politics supposedly could not mix. Yet history continually proves that they are inextricably entwined; time and again those attempting to ignore this fell over their feet as surely as Harriet had on Myra's studio stairs.

In 1933, soon after Hitler came to power, Furtwängler had invited Schnabel, Kreisler and Menuhin – all of whom were Jewish – to perform concertos with him. They all refused. The conductor was annoyed that they had hampered his attempts to prove that art was beyond politics. The veracity of their cause was proved soon enough. But during the war, Furtwängler did help to rescue some musicians; for instance, he assisted the violinist Carl Flesch in escaping occupied Holland.

The Berlin Philharmonic's 1948 British tour was the brainchild of John Collins, founder of the Christian Action movement, who that year was appointed Canon of St Paul's Cathedral. Visiting the ruins of Berlin, he found the mighty orchestra confined to playing light music in the city's American sector. Emmie Tillett – now Myra's British agent, following her husband John's death – helped him to organise it, and there was high-level support from Cripps, who was among the charity's patrons.

Christian Action took on the expense, which was not modest. The total cost of the tour was cited as about £18,000. Three York aircraft, chartered to bring the orchestra over, cost £2,400 and their return trip to Berlin was anticipated to be around the same again, unless the Russian blockade were to be lifted. The gigantic outlay suggests that the charity thought it a profoundly meaningful cause. Some local sponsorship helped; a Birmingham businessman, William Riley, contributed £5,000.[18]

The tour comprised 15 concerts around Britain, some under Furtwängler, others with the young Romanian conductor Sergiu Celibidache, who was now principal conductor (the Russians had appointed Leo Borchart at the end of the war, but he was shot dead by an American sentry after failing to stop upon instruction). Nearly 80 per cent of the 100-strong Berlin Philharmonic Orchestra had joined it before the war. Two-thirds of the orchestra lived in the US zone, one third in the British and only three members in the Russian zone, one of whom, a clarinettist, had been unable to travel. Arriving in Britain, *The Daily Herald* stated, the musicians could talk 'of nothing but "the joy of being in a normal city once again".'

Myra performed Beethoven's Piano Concerto No. 4 at the London concert on 3rd November. Objections were plentiful, not least from Beryl; she was afraid people might think Myra was condoning the Nazis' genocide against her own race. From a greater distance, Myra's American friends were even more baffled.

Ironically, however, the angriest response came from the Musicians' Union, for a completely different reason: the visitors were undercutting its members. The orchestra and both conductors had agreed to perform for expenses and 'pocket money' (five pounds a week each), while Myra gave her services free.

The concert took place in front of 6,000 people at the challenging venue of Empress Hall, Earl's Court – 'no fit place for music,' according to *The Times*. Collins had initially planned to welcome the orchestra to St Paul's, but that foundered when it turned out the cathedral was not permitted to charge for tickets. The audience dress code was informal, to avoid embarrassing the musicians, only one of whom possessed an evening shirt. They played instead in a mixture of morning and lounge suits. Furthermore, they had had to borrow the orchestral parts from the London Philharmonic Orchestra: their own library had been evacuated to Bavaria, but according to Furtwängler, its hiding place had been burnt out and 'only a little was saved'[19]. Film of the rehearsal with him on the day of the concert shows the musicians gaunt-faced, playing the finale of Brahms's Symphony No. 4 as if their lives depended on it. Behind Furtwängler, the piano stands ready for Myra.

The Observer grumbled about the venue's stadium-like ambience; nevertheless, 'Dame Myra's opening concerto chords came to us … on cushions of air, echoless and uncommonly sweet'[20]. *The Times*' critic said that Myra's performance had 'a touch of the crusader's fire', but the review got around the political awkwardness by focusing on the atrocious acoustic instead.[21]

For Myra, a Jewish musician – and the only one on stage that night, besides being the only female performer – to stand up hand in hand with Wilhelm Furtwängler in front of the Berlin Philharmonic could only be a statement: the war was over and the only way forward to a better world was through reconciliation and, if not forgiveness, then acceptance of the idea that musical genius could go – hand in hand – with human fallibility.

Was Myra's wartime stance at all comparable to Furtwängler's? Some commentators have claimed so: both artists had stayed in their own country, tapping into the power of music and keeping the art alive. There, though, any resemblance ends. Myra had faced no mortal dilemma, no personal threats from a rogue regime, no prospect of exile, and indeed no decisions more awkward than breaking a contract with her American manager and finding ways to ensure the continuation of her concerts while under bombardment.

Perhaps what made the concert possible was Myra's gift for empathy. She would try to imagine herself in Furtwängler's shoes, and those of other musicians faced with similar choices; she wondered what she would have done in their place; and she wondered even what she would have done had the German invasion been successful, but allowed the National Gallery concerts to continue. She concluded simply: 'Who am I to judge?'[22]

Furtwängler had already become the first non-exiled German conductor to return to Britain after the war; during 1948 he came to the UK four times, giving 21 concerts with four different orchestras. The bigger question should perhaps have been the Berlin Philharmonic itself.

As orchestral musicians rather than starry soloists, its members were scarcely recognised by the press of the time as individuals with their own histories; each, however, would have had a lengthy story to tell. After Hitler's rise to power and the imposition of race laws, four Jewish members of the orchestra had been forced to leave their jobs and the country. Four more whose wives were Jewish had to flee. The rest had to have 'Aryanisation' cards by the end of 1935. Some of them might once have been Nazi sympathisers. They had narrowly escaped being conscripted to the Eastern Front, then experienced the intense bombardment of Berlin. Nazi bombing had destroyed London's premier concert hall; the Allies' air raids had destroyed the Berlin Philharmonie. Then came the ruined city's division between the Americans, Soviets and British. Myra, beside Furtwängler, could attempt to rise above it all; but what silent courage it must have taken for her to do so in front of this orchestra is another matter altogether.

The controversy ran and ran. A couple of months later, Myra was in New York when the pianist Walter Gieseking, celebrated for his exquisite Debussy, but considered a Nazi sympathiser, was attempting to give a concert. 'It may have been in the English papers that they are trying to prevent his coming here,' Myra wrote home. 'It is all seriously narrow-minded. Apparently Gieseking hasn't been granted a Visa in spite of Carnegie Hall being sold out ? for next Monday evening. It is possible that he did play too much with the Nazis, but that doesn't apply to Furt…' One day she bumped into the violinist Mischa Elman in Central Park. 'We had a loud and heated argument in the street about Furtwängler and Gieseking, disagreed and got nowhere.' She had a similar phone conversation with Felix Salmond a few days later.

On the day of Gieseking's concert, Myra noted: 'We shall keep our eyes glued to Carnegie Hall this evening, as no one knows IF Gieseking is going to play, or what will happen if he does…… We have read that

Furtwängler has refused to come, and Jehudi [sic] [Menuhin] has written to the President about it.....'

Gieseking was arrested hours before he should have stepped on stage at Carnegie Hall. The *Tribune* reported on 24th January: 'The Justice Department announced that Gieseking, who arrived in this country Saturday, agreed to leave [the US] after it called a hearing to determine whether he should be excluded from the US. The hearing was called off, as was the concert.'

But the Furtwängler incident travelled with Myra. 'It comes up and I am questioned wherever we go.'

1 MH to HF, 10 August 1946. *Unless otherwise indicated, all letters from MH to HF in the following pages are in the British Library's Myra Hess Collection.*
2 This and previous quotes from MH's Netherlands diary, 1946, Hess Family Collection
3 H. Johnson, interview with MH, cutting from unidentified newspaper
4 This and following quotes from MH's postwar American diaries, Hess Family Collection
5 MH to HF, 10 September 1946
6 Beryl Davis to HF, 16 October 1946, British Library, Myra Hess Collection
7 *The New York Times*, 13 October 1946
8 M. Izen, booklet notes for *Myra Hess, Live Recordings from the University of Illinois, 1949*, APR 7308
9 Anita Gunn to HF, 25 November 1946
10 Author interview with SK
11 AG to HF, 4 December 1946
12 *The Times*, 24 February 1947
13 *The Times*, 18 June 1947
14 *The New York Times*, 3 November 1947
15 *The New York Times*, 23 November 1947
16 *The New York Times*, 9 December 1947
17 Recounted in Tony Palmer's documentary, *The Salzburg Festival: A Brief History*, Isolde Films, 2006
18 *Birmingham Gazette*, 3 November 1948
19 *Daily Herald*, 30 October 1948
20 *The Observer*, 4 November 1948
21 *The Times*, 4 November 1948
22 R. Gelatt, op. cit., p231

Auntie Myra's Diaries

Myra's American tour diaries, typed on copious sheets of light airletter paper, were designed to tell her friends about her 'doonings'. She would send them home for everyone to circulate, to save her writing individual letters to each person. They are a treasure-trove – and she continued the practice for most of the next decade. She designed them to entertain, and in spring 1948 chronicled her West Coast adventures with flair and humour.

In Pasadena she was waiting for a young man to arrive to turn her pages in her recital (of which more anon), but he was running late...

> Saz bravely took his place, minus her glasses... I started with Mozart Adagio and Gigue, by request, and then floundered into Italian Concerto [Bach]. I was distractedly anxious about the young man ... and pictured him in a pool of blood on the highway. I played a few of my special wrong notes, which nearly gave S. and me the giggles, but it wasn't apparent to the audience, fortunately. Thank goodness, young man arrived, having run out of gas... After interval came Schubert Dances and Schumann Etudes Symph. (without my notes...). All was going rather well until a dying fly fell with a flop onto the keyboard. I was in the middle of the unflagging Finale and couldn't make up my mind exactly what action to take. Certain passages in its proximity made it bounce backwards and forwards and it was quite obvious that the last page couldn't be faced in its presence. SO....with a dramatic comma, not imagined by Robert Schumann, I swept it off the keyboard with a wide back-hander.....and finished with unusual éclat.[1]

Myra and Saz had arrived in America on 10th January. Their ship had been delayed by fog, a concert in New Brunswick had to be cancelled and there were ructions with Annie, who seemed 'more scatterbrained than ever'. In an 'uphill' visit, Annie brought a list of locations for Myra's next tour; Myra protested that she had not even got her head around the current one yet. '[Annie] had cried all night because I had been angry with her re not cabling me on boat....oh dear....'

Maybe the American music business knew more about Annie's state of health than Myra did. The agent Arthur Judson, founder of Columbia Concerts Corporation (later Columbia Artists Management), whom Myra termed 'the IT of all the frightful managerial ITS', sent a 'genty from the Philharmonic Society' to try to persuade her to leave Annie. 'They were willing to let her work for me next season, but wished to sign a contract for 1951.....He didn't stay very long.... And I only pray that A. will not hear of his visit by any mischance.' Whatever Annie's difficulties, Myra was determined to stay loyal.

The 'genty' had also brought news that Bruno Walter wanted her to play Mozart concertos with him the following season in New York. This won a more friendly response.

On 22nd January 1949 Myra took New York Town Hall by storm. The day before such an event was generally a time when she did not know where to put herself. 'January 21st: Penult. day before N.Y. recital always a bit of a trial........ 10 a.m. a corset fitting.....worked, didn't work.....' But then came concert day:

> Worked all the morning, very softly.....ppp.....feeling more and more unmusical. Early lunch, donned red dress again and R. and G. [Rose and Gene Parsonnet] came at 2 o'clock. Annie furious that so many people turned away from Town H. and 'not amused' when I said that it was better than having no one there. It was a most wonderful audience and after playing nothing but Bach and Schubert for nearly two hours, I feel I can do anything I like in N. Y. I really was surprised and deeply gratified by the response to such a programme. I made my little speech....and V. [Victor Parsonnet, Rose and Gene's son] turned the pages perfectly again. I played Bach: Gigue G. maj. P and F. C sharp and the Adagio for encores, and then had the lights turned up..... There were a great many musicians there and apparently the 'Elite' of N.Y. I had to see an endless procession of people afterwards. They seemed to come from all over the world. Masses and masses of most overwhelmingly lovely flowers which R. brought back, in a taxi and got things ready for a small party ... [She lists the guests, who include 'Richter' – presumably Sviatoslav]. ... Saw Times and Tribune at midnight, both dyspeptic and disappointing, but as all the people I mind about thought it was the best playing I have done here, who cares?

While the diaries were for general consumption, Myra's letters to Howard – who was away teaching in South Africa (the home of his partner, the composer Arnold van Wyk or 'Nolsie') – sometimes show the real Myra behind the public exuberance. She wrote to him on 28th February:

> The N. Y. critics have suddenly taken a most violent dislike to me.... and Olin D. said it was a bore to hear ALL Schubert's dances..... I felt like sending him a picture of blood, sweat and tears spent in the compiling....of the group I played..... I have had to try and pacify my friends, who have been so upset and furious, but as everyone I respect and mind about thinks I am playing better the C's can drown in their baths (if they take any....) Everywhere else, so far, I have been approved of in papers, but in various ways ... The audiences have warmed the cockles of your aged Auntie's stalwart heart...[2]

In Washington DC, playing a concerto, she wore her red velvet – so much for the myth that she only wore black on stage – and 'nearly expired with heat'. Enjoying the cooling effect of her jade amulet down her back, she realised, a chord or two in, that she had not turned the necklace round to its rightful position. But where concert dress was concerned, Myra had a new devotee: the fashion designer Main Bocher.

For her first postwar American tour he wished, to her amazement, to give her a gown ('a tribute', according to Saz). Subsequently he became her couturier of choice. Born the same year as Myra, in Chicago, he was for a while an American in Paris, where he trained to be an opera singer – though his studies were interrupted by a spell as a US intelligence officer during the First World War. Having reputedly lost his voice on the day of his debut, he gave up music and turned instead to fashion journalism, working his way up to become editor in chief of French Vogue. At last, at 12 avenue Georges-Mandel, he opened his first *maison de couture*. After leaving war-torn France for New York in 1940, he set up a showroom on Madison Avenue; during the war he designed uniforms for American women's military corps such as the WAVES and the SPARS, the female coastguard unit.

His label, Mainbocher, was known for elegance, classic simplicity and practicality, qualities that would suit a discerning concert pianist literally down to the ground. Main and Myra developed a close friendship, lubricated by splendid dinners. His concert dresses for her would often feature black lace, a red or beige sash, or pleats, which (as she told a fashion interviewer) she particularly enjoyed.

Stokowski, Koussevitzky, Maestro

Myra was due to play the Brahms D minor Concerto with Stokowski. Eager to go through it with her in advance, he invited her to the house he shared with his wife, Gloria Vanderbilt. Myra described the encounter in colourful terms.

> January 28th. At 4 o'clock went to tea with ~~MAESTRO~~.......Stokowski, to discuss concerti..... Was shown into the most bizarre and golly-amazement sitting-cum-studio-cum-chromium room, by an officious man-servant, who failed to tell S. that I had arrived.... This gave me much more than enough time to peruse his wife's shrieking oil paintings, with doors to match canvases. Sickly green three-cornered chairs and sofas with hard little cushions like brightly coloured hot cross buns...

She found Stokowski 'utterly unaccountable and so completely easy and natural, in such surroundings. ... his young (exceedingly young) wife has a studio leading out of the bizarre room, and I noted that there was an exquisite bed as well as painting materials.'

The discussion was productive: 'He has amplified some of the scoring...but I pray it will not be in bad taste. At least, he bows the opening as I have always wanted it: Down-Down in 2nd bar......We went through it thoroughly, also Mozart C maj, and it was all most sympathetic and serious. We were only disturbed by the most wonderful sunset, with the sky-scrapers in relief against red and gold, with the river below.'

At the first Brahms rehearsal, Myra worried over their disagreements about the tempi: 'I could picture Johannes' beard dropping off hair by hair.' The next day, which was devoted mostly to preparing the Mozart, the orchestra told her that Stokowski had never worked so hard with any other soloist. 'It is certainly necessary,' Myra reported succinctly. In the concert, 'I wasn't displeased...but it is queer playing with S. In spite of his "notorious" personality and his real seriousness and actual enjoyment of the music, there is a complete void.... I don't feel that there is anyone real on the platform...'

A recording of the Mozart from 6th February makes interesting listening. Myra is sparkly and delivers her cadenzas with panache, but she is audibly not at her happiest; the coordination between piano and orchestra sometimes hangs by a thread.

In Toronto she was appalled to find that she was expected to play 'God Save the King'. 'Wondered how "it went" and practised it on a miniature Celeste "back stage"..... Nice lanky youth turned pages for me and supervised my practising the K. He didn't agree with my harmonies, but "they say" there never was such a performance and it ended exactly Jesu Joy...... As a great number of the audience stood when I appeared, it seemed the moment to dispose of the Anthem.....and we all settled down.'

Working with 'Maestro' Toscanini and the NBC Symphony Orchestra was utterly different. For the concert on 16th February, Saz, Myra and Victor Parsonnet, her page turner, set out 'in all states':

> [Beethoven's] Coriolanus and Eroica, absolutely stupendous. Every minute of a rehearsal is like a super-performance, the men giving more than all they have. It is a picked orchestra and the NBC know that most of them will leave when the Maestro is not there any more. All the players are aware that something extraordinary happens when the M. takes his baton in hand. Concerts cease to matter, as you feel that music is being indestructibly created and going out into the world. He had some wonderful tantrums banging the score on the desk like a baby with a spoon, in a high chair. Noone minds, as they realise that he is asking for the moon and the stars and the whole firmament...and they eventually give it to him. I went to see him and he was as adorable as ever... V. went off, as white as a sheet with exhausted excitement, and the Pilgrims [Myra and Saz] were so hungry that they went down the road for a large meal at 6 o'clock.

On 22nd February she was invited to a 'ghastly dinner given by a fabulous and notorious adventuress named ?????' to meet Fritz Kreisler. Other guests included Charles Boyer and Irving Berlin. She told Howard:

> It was worth it, as I sat next to him [Kreisler]. He talked in the most moving way about everything and was terribly, terribly touching. There was 'music' afterwards.... Copeland [Aaron Copland], a v. nice fellow, but looks like a stranded cod.... [Copland] Played Clair de Lune and some savage Spanish pieces without even flushing.... Maggie Teyte sang, and oughtn't to have... after a large dinner.... An Italian nearly burst his guts about nothing at all...and then [Nathan] Milstein played the violin much too well... Thank goodness nice Main Bocher suddenly appeared and brought me home.

Two days later she had a memorable encounter with Maestro, at a more intimate dinner given by 'his right-hand man at NBC':

> He (the M.) was adorable and told a touching story of having been put 'in prison' at school, at the age of ten, because he had been fascinated by his first sight of a piano. As he was supposed to be learning the cello only, it was considered an outrage that he dared to touch the piano….. He lived on bread and water for a week….in his little uniform….It was a free school and his Fatherrr had no money….. Sir O.[Osbert] Sitwell was there … A heated argument arose about Gieseking and Furtwängler and I said much too much for much too long. At the end, the Maestro said that everybody was bad and that sometimes he couldn't bear to see himself in the glass….. In spite of rumours that he was against F. he said that the cases between G. and F. were quite different, so who should count?????? Sir O. walked back with me. I think I like him ?????????

For her recital in New York on 26th February the hall was not full, but Myra pragmatically reflected that she had played in the city six times in five weeks. The day before, it was her birthday. Inundated by parcels, flowers, telegrams and cables, she 'crept hither and thither like poor old M. M. in slippers and my Tootsie WEE DRESSING GOWN. Playing the piano was out of the question, and why worry? Apparently the "Radio" kept announcing my centenary, which brought forth unexpected trophies.'

Recital day began with 'a hateful morning, loathing my "profession" with unusual depth'. Then she managed to put both legs through one side of her best concert knickers, entailing an awkward change during which her 'mile-long Mainbocher dress hit the ceiling'. But the concert went well: 'In spite of my ill-will towards my "calling", everyone seemed to think I played better than usual, and I played encores until the audience had to be removed for another concert.'

En route to Boston, and Saz had their own drawing room on the train; Myra noted that the trains were being speeded up to compete with air travel. With the Boston Symphony Orchestra, 'Kousse' was 'in terrific form, but oh, oh… Johannes [Brahms] would have been out of breath. I whispered to Vicky "this is going to kill Grandma…" The slow movement was very beautiful and the orchestra sounds as marvellous as ever, but I felt as if I had walked to Brighton at a speedy trot…'

The next day's rendition went less 'breathlessly fast': 'Although it isn't how I feel the concerto throughout, it is always terrifically stimulating with K. and this heavenly orchestra, and I have never heard the slow movement played more movingly … There was unusual excitement and even if it wasn't to Johannes' taste, it was stirring.' Afterwards, Koussevitzky and his wife, Olga, treated her to a sumptuous old-fashioned tea.

Finally there was an interesting encounter and an accident. The encounter was with the Reverend 'Ted' Ferris, an Episcopalian preacher who was brother-in-law to Myra's New York friend Dorothy Shepard. His father was dying; a few weeks later, from Chicago, Myra sent him her condolences. She had been reading his work since 1942, when Dorothy began to post her copies of his sermons, and first met him in 1946 when he came to see her backstage. He became an increasingly important correspondent and spiritual adviser to her as time went by.

Early in the Brahms at Symphony Hall, she broke a fingernail:

> As there are no long tuttis after the opening, I hadn't a chance to see how much damage had been done… there was a great flake sticking up….from my thumb….It CAME OFF…..in the last octave passages and thank goodness there was still something left underneath…. It was somewhat disturbing….but R. and S. said I didn't play badly, as I feared ….. The slow M. was wonderful again, and K. nearly in tears….. It was a sad evening, feeling that it MAY be the last time I shall have played with him and this orchestra. The concerts with him have been high-spots…and milestones for over 20 years.

In Minneapolis Myra found the hall much too large, with a capacity of around 4,500, an audience of 3,000, and 'a v. nice youth' turning pages. 'He was so moved by the music that I hardly dared to look at him…. his eyes constantly filled with tears.' But the concert on 14th March was 'SOLD OUT … ha… ha…. and an absolutely inspiring audience. I was almost afraid of how much I was enjoying it, comparatively speaking.'

The Illinois Concerts

A snapshot of Myra's playing in spring 1949, captured in two concerts at the University of Illinois, Urbana, on 17th and 18th March, speaks volumes about the growth of her artistry during the war years. These recordings[3] suggest, too, that her live performances could give a very different impression of her musicianship from those she made in the studio.

Each concert involved solo works followed by a Mozart concerto with the university orchestra. Alongside Mozart's K271 in E flat and K467 in C major, the repertoire included the Chopin F minor Fantasy, Schubert's B flat major Sonata D960, Bach's Partita No. 4, Beethoven's D minor Sonata

Op. 31 No. 2, and, for encores, several perennial favourites: her selection of Schubert German Dances, the Brahms C major Intermezzo Op. 119 No. 3, Scarlatti's G major Sonata Kk14 and Chopin's E flat major Waltz Op. 18.

Marshall Izen, in his notes for the APR release, remembered asking Myra why she made so few recordings. 'I hate them,' she told him. 'I feel like I'm going to my own funeral when I hear myself play.' But the Illinois concerts show a musician in her element, from her humorous spoken introduction to the irresistible flow of airborne rhythm in the Schubert Dances. She is at her most emotionally open and, indeed, charismatically electrifying.

After the 17th March concert, Myra noted that the University of Illinois Sinfonietta 'really played it [Mozart C major] beautifully and there was such enthusiasm that we decided to repeat the last movement (a little faster).' At the rehearsal the previous day, 'I hardly knew what I was at…. but the student orchestra was standing on its toes with enthusiasm and the conductor, a Dutchman [John M Kuypers], is a real musician and had trained them quite wonderfully. Various piano students had evidently been rehearsing with them for months.'

The Chopin Fantasy has her hallmarks of magical voicing, shining sound and eloquently turned phrases, but there is a fiery drama to it that is not often present in her studio recordings. At times she can almost make the sky fall in. The Schubert sonata, increasingly central to her repertoire, has both a clarinet-like mellifluousness and a profound instinct for the music's knife-edge balance between laughter and tears. She plays with incisive bounce and sparkle in the Bach, plus deep empathy for the mystical atmosphere of the Allemande. Beethoven's 'Tempest' Sonata – her only recording of it – is introspective, delivered with grandeur but particularly striking for its exquisitely gradated tone-colour in the first movement's moments of recitative. The Scarlatti is faster and more vigorous than her studio version, and the Mozart concertos bubble over with wit and good humour.

Perhaps the American Steinway she was playing had a role in her approach; the novelty and delight of this reunion, after touring on ramshackle instruments in postwar Britain and Holland, would hardly have worn off. 'It was so exciting to play on my superb NY piano, and all kinds of things that are extremely difficult on our poor old pianos at home became quite easy. (excepting my London piano, of course.)'

In Urbana, Myra and Saz stayed at the beautiful house of the university president, whom Myra deemed 'extremely attractive'. She was rewarded for her efforts at the closing party with 'the most unmentionably good piece of roast beef', while the piano students bombarded her with questions until she nearly lost her voice; she was rescued by 'our nice President's (beg pardon.) wife'. 'It was all very worthwhile,' she wrote, 'but I hope never to have quite such a week again. We all parted as old and bosom friends and of course I have promised to go back, next year, having decided I wouldn't...'

Three years later, she heard some of the recordings – and, for once, was not displeased. 'For the first time in my life I began to have a shadow of a conception why you all like my playing..... I heard the Bach D maj Toccata and am going to bring a copy home if poss. We also heard Mozart 271, which was quite good too.'

Conductors and Colman

In Chicago, Myra was looking forward to rehearsing with Adolf Busch. The violinist and conductor, not Jewish but passionately anti-Nazi, had fled Hitler's Germany, as had his brother, Fritz, who became the first music director of Glyndebourne. 'We embraced with intense nostalgia for the past,' Myra noted. At first he rehearsed their Mozart concerto rather little, which disappointed her, but the 22nd March concert was another matter: 'Busch said that he had gone through all the parts very carefully, marking phrasing etc. I couldn't believe my ears when they began the Tutti. It was so "delicatessen" and sensitive and B. kept turning to me, with a seraphic smile, which was duly reciprocated... and so we began and so we continued...in fact we were both so touched by the music itself that we were nearly dissolved in tears... It was one of the most lovely musical experiences I have ever had.'

For the Brahms D minor the next day, 'AT LAST Johannes was present.' It left Myra wondering if the concerto was 'too difficult a piece for my increasing years', but nobody else seemed concerned. Over dinner, she and Saz 'lost their hearts' to Busch and his wife, talking about 'almost every subject and every part of Europe and they were deeply touching in their love for and belief in England'. Finally on 25th March, 'I did get the better of the concerto... it has been one of the most wonderful weeks of "musizieren".....and nice to finish up with "the best and biggest" Brahms..... Quite sad it is over.'

The train through Nevada brought long stretches of mountainous country, with few signs of habitation: 'The colours are fabulous and some of the mountains snow-capped ... Had lunch at about 8,000 feet, deep pure snow and pine trees ... It was all rather confusing, as we were due to arrive in warm, sunny California within an hour or two, and by the time we got back to our "boudoirs" we were going down, down, down like Alice in W.[wonderland] and by 3.30 we were in the middle of a perfect summer's day, with all the orchards in blossom.'

The hall in Sacramento was 'a barn of a place and they were clearing it up after a Boxing Match', but again, the concert pleased Myra more than she had expected. And so to San Francisco: 'Heavenly day, orchards in full bloom and approach to S.F. quite wonderful with the two great bridges.'

Spring in California brought many delights, from reunions with old friends to the ample food ('a famous salad at this hotel, shrimps, lettuce, anchovy sauce and GARLIC...'), and from lavish suites that made Myra and Saz laugh at their splendour, to a tour of Beverley Hills in which famous actors' houses were marked on a map. Myra and Saz had their first experience of lunch at a drive-thru: 'We stopped at a terrible "road house" where you "drive right in Marj" and girls in trousers and pill-box hats come out with little trays which hook on to the open windows of the "automobiles"...'

Myra was overjoyed to work again with 'the boys': the Griller Quartet was now quartet in residence at Berkeley, where they were being paid a proper, professional salary for the first time (much to the disapprobation of certain British critics, who had responded to their departure as if to a national betrayal). They had had to overcome a glitch when the South African Jack O'Brien's US visa was not provided in time; the other three had to begin their tenure as a string trio before he could join them. Myra lamented to Sidney that she was not free to devote herself to playing piano quartets with them in the interim.

In San Francisco, she heard Isaac Stern play the Beethoven Violin Concerto, before giving a recital of her own at the Opera House. 'Bach Partita, Beethoven Op. 110 and Brahms Variations and I was moved beyond words by the completely absorbed listening... I played 6 encores (who should count??) and it was an unusually gratifying and thrilling experience.'

Myra had been warned, however, that Los Angeles audiences could be restive and she was perturbed that as the Baptists owned the concert hall, she could not practise there until almost 1pm for a recital beginning at 2.30pm. In the event such a crowd turned up that she had to start 20 minutes late. The close attention of the audience made it a moving occasion for her. It proved that 'people really want serious programmes, even in Los Angeles ... Masses of wonderful flowers, including an exquisite little basket from the Ronald Colmans.'

Myra's 'pinup', Ronald Colman: photograph inscribed to Myra

The elegant British actor and his wife invited Myra and Saz to a dinner party when they returned from a few days at Coronado Beach (where Myra sat by the sea reading Evelyn Waugh). It was 3rd May. Over to Myra:

> We donned our evening dresses and Swee [new nickname for Saz] wore my concert velvet cape and I my little black fur coat and we started out for Beverly Hills most fashionably late.....A fantastic view of Los A. on the way, with myriads of coloured lights. The Colmans' initial invitation, in the form of a typical Hollywood telegram, reached us in San F. ending with 'Do you remember us on the Queen Elizabeth last year'..... They promised only a small party and there were ten of us, including Brian Ahearne and the Douglas Fairbanks Junior. Another British actor Rex Evans and Ronald C's special Producer.
>
> He, Ronnie, is even more handsome in real life and above all is an aristocrat in the true sense of the word and a most perfect host. His wife is a cousin of our darling Colonel Britain and is ravishingly pretty. They have a small daughter they adore and so far she has not been allowed to see Daddy on the Films or realise how famous he is. ... Douglas F. sat between S. and me and I had R. C. on the other side and considering all that has happened to them they are amazingly natural and serious; in fact the Colmans are the only people in the Film world about whom there is never a breath of criticism or scandal. We are also amazed at what a real person young Douglas F. is too and they all have 'our' kind of humour..... The house is fabulous and we were almost overpowered by the scent of giant stocks as we drove up to the front door. Though fabulous it is all in the best of taste and the dinner table was exquisite....food likewise....and of course Champagne flowed. We sat by a log fire until I suddenly felt like playing to them. There hadn't been a hint that I should do so and they were touchingly excited. The piano HAD been a Blüthner, but was strangely disorganised... It didn't really matter, especially as I was completely out of practise [sic]...and it was a revelation to have them asking for Bach's P's and F's [Preludes and Fugues] ...Brahms etc.... Ronnie really knows about music, (she too) and when I played bits of the Brahms D. Min. Concerto he sang the orchestral parts. He was in the London Scottish in the first war and has the Mons Star and altogether we are bewitched by him. It seemed incredible to find ourselves in such a mis-en-scène, but it was a perfect end to our Californian visit.

The following day the 'Pilgrims' took a train called The Chief all the way back to New York, across two days: 'The distance will be 3134 miles….. further than from N. Y. to London.' And home again on the Mauretania: 'We transferred from QE on 28th with Heifetz, Benno, [William] Primrose & heaven knows who else on board.'

Sawdust and Scores

Myra, who was five foot three, had precise demands for the height, or lack of it, that she needed for her piano stool or chair. On more than one occasion she asked to have the legs of a chair sawn down to shorten it, creating a flurry of press interest. In San Francisco, April 1949, performing Beethoven's Piano Concerto No. 3 with Pierre Monteux, she was given a piano stool that would not lower. 'I was inches too high. Nothing makes me more nervous…..I would rather sit on the floor…..so another had to be brought on. The audience felt it highly amusing, but I didn't find it so funny…..However, Monteux was so nice and thoroughly understanding about my discomfort.'

Monteux himself she described as 'quite a "sweetie" with coal black hair and a brisk, twitching little grey moustache, an immensely long baton and shoulders rather like dear old Sir Henry's. Also, small French feet, which hurry him on and off the platform…'

On another occasion, she was rehearsing with the Chicago Symphony Orchestra and Rafael Kubelik when the swivelling piano stool proved recalcitrant. Kubelik came down from the podium to give her a hand. 'She turned to the orchestra with a sweet smile,' Howard related, 'and said "That's the first time I've been screwed up on the platform by a conductor!" She told me this when she came back to England and said, "Why did they laugh so much?"'[4]

More problematic was Myra's recently adopted preference not to play from memory. During the war, she had devoured a vast amount of repertoire, with scant practice time disrupted by administrative duties, air raids and in 1944 the need to listen out for doodle-bugs, so she often played from the score, with Howard or John Amis to turn the pages. Now she had decided to continue doing so; hence the need for Victor Parsonnet and other page turners.

The unspoken requirement for pianists to play by heart added extra pressure to the stresses of performing; to remove it would be a relief, provided audiences and reviewers accepted the situation. But in America they watched with surprise as she approached her piano with music and page-turner in tow.

In 1948 she was relieved, she told Howard, to find that in the US, 'playing with my music has been received more satisfactorily than I imagined possible. I now look upon it as a real and important "campaign", having discovered at Toronto Conservatory AND Yale that certain degrees are unobtainable unless the students play from memory. In both places I hear that some of the most musical students fail on account of it…'

Often she would make an explanatory speech. In Boston, January 1949, she found her 'little remarks about playing with music' so warmly applauded that the ushers thought she had finished her first two pieces and began to admit latecomers – 'and if N. Y. accepts my music as Boston did, it will be very nice indeed.' Her friends and her audience were encouraging: after the New York recital, she found that 'Pondie is quite reconciled to "my music".....and it is being taken more sensibly than I dared to hope, in this unaccountable country.....I have a feeling that I may get used to it myself!!!!' In Toronto in February, she commented: 'The fact that using music is such an innovation shows how appallingly artificial the whole musical outlook has become.'

Performing from memory went back to the time of Liszt and Clara Schumann. The latter, as a 13-year-old prodigy, had been adversely criticised, even called 'insufferable', for doing so. She lived to regret it when she was older and distrusted her powers of recall; but the damage was done and the resulting expectation gradually became a tyranny. Reviewers often responded to Myra's use of the music with horrified disapprobation. In a 1953 interview she remarked pointedly: 'We've trained the public to think we're infallible, when there are days when some of us can't remember our own telephone numbers.'[5]

The broadcaster Jim Fassett, interviewing Myra, asked whether Matthay had had views on using the music. She refuted that idea, inserting a slanted implication that it mattered not a jot: 'I never remember Mr. Matthay talking very much about it, because the thing he minded most about, always, was the integrity of performance … Whether you stood on your head or had your music or didn't have your music was irrelevant, as long as you got somewhere near the spirit of the music.'[6]

Other pianists were delighted: Clifford Curzon was among those who pointed out that Myra had freed them to follow suit. One of Myra's page-turners, in Stockton, California, was a music student who told Myra that he thought Illinois University in Urbana had changed its exam rules on the matter thanks to her example.

But in the end, Myra's music was only an aide-memoire. Bruce Simonds once noticed that she did not wear her glasses on stage, but always practised with them on. He asked her if she could *really* see the music without them. She responded, with habitual wit: 'I can *just* see it.'[7]

During her tours, Myra met a number of piano students who turned her pages and she took a keen interest in their progress. Some played to her; a few later came to London to study with her. They included the twins Richard and John Contiguglia, and Stephen Kovacevich (who was still Stephen Bishop then). She often wrote of characters like 'a very nice boy, budding pianist, to turn pages', and for the youngsters themselves, it was an honour – and sometimes a terror – to be on stage with Dame Myra Hess.

Victor Parsonnet wrote a vivid memoir about his experiences turning for Myra, from his schooldays through to his early medical career and first two years of marriage. He was proud that his long arms and his height – six foot two – gave him an advantage over even such redoubtable substitutes as Ralph Kirkpatrick, Paul Hindemith and Arthur Mendel, of whom he admitted to being jealous should one of them do 'his' job. Being a trainee doctor could be less helpful. Once he swallowed a tranquillizer offered by a pharmaceutical company representative, only to drowse off during a matinée in Carnegie Hall in front of some 3,000 people. 'The applause awakened me,' he remembered.

He built up an intimate picture of her personality and lifestyle on the road. In the dressing room after finishing a concert, she would be self-critical among her entourage, including his mother, Beryl and Saz, grumbling that she had played 'awfully', seeking reassurance that it was really not too bad. Only after that could she face the fans at the stage door.

Later, in the hotel room, Rose would kneel on the floor to warm Myra's soup on an electric heater, as the cord was too short to reach the table; Saz and Beryl would make tea and bring out biscuits. Winding down, they would talk – or rather, listen to Myra talking, sometimes telling 'risqué' stories, but occasionally turning gloomy and wondering why she put herself through it. Victor sensed that she disliked the adulation at such moments, and 'knew that it did not replace the things she never would have, like family and children'. The next day, the doubts were gone and the cycle began again.

His parents told him that in her youth Myra had been a beauty. Victor found her 'handsome' and noted that her long hair (which he was privileged to see loose once) and her legs were sources of pride to her; but it was her magnificent bearing on stage that made her beautiful. He noticed her 'flirt' with audiences while she played – 'as if to say, "just listen to this next passage"' – and was not surprised that she disliked recording, since her relationship with the crowd was so crucial to her results. He never found out why she had not married: 'My mother knew, but would never tell. There were rumors of an unrequited relationship with someone, perhaps Harold Samuels [sic]...' [8]

Harold Samuel, Howard's 'Nunky'? Surely not. Was it Bax? Another Harold? A smokescreen? We'll probably never know.

Doctor of Music

On 9th June 1949 Myra went up to Cambridge to be conferred with an honorary doctorate. It was the first year that women had been eligible for this; therefore the vice-chancellor, C.R. Raven, asked Myra to speak at the celebratory lunch. Oxford had been conferring degrees on women since 1920, yet at Cambridge for another 28 years female applicants, though able to study at the women's colleges, were still not awarded their rightful qualifications. Myra already held honorary doctorates from the universities of Manchester, Durham, London, St Andrew's and Reading (and Leeds would follow in 1951). Her response at Cambridge would speak volumes.

She took Howard with her to Cambridge's Senate House. The occasion was formal, with strict protocols to observe and speeches in Latin. Howard watched the grand procession from the gallery, while sunlight streamed through the central double doors upon tassled mortar-boards, the Chancellor's gold-embroidered gown and his train-bearer. The six honorary graduands each wore the gown designed for their respective degree: Myra, as Doctor of Music, had cream-coloured brocade with red facings, 'and a very fine sight she was, too,' Howard noted.[9]

When her turn came, applause held up the ceremony for several minutes. The Chancellor, Jan Smuts (following his defeat in the South African general election the previous year), teased her about it later, saying that he was sure she must have organised it specially. Howard found it heart-warming, proof of the love and esteem in which 'our Myra' was held. Afterwards, the entire company paraded through the town centre to Christ's College for the formal luncheon.

The introduction was warm indeed, though the original was in Latin. An English version was sent to Myra in advance:

> ...she who comes last on our list has by her art been able to give spiritual refreshment to a greater number of people, to convey more pleasure, more solace in the hardships and anxieties of present-day life, than most of those who have won a name in science or scholarship. By her magic touch she has charmed the ears and warmed the hearts of thousands ... without her faithfulness and loving labour the workers of London, when the perils of war pressed hard upon them, would have had practically no opportunity of relaxing in hard-won enjoyment... She preferred to share the dangers and inconvenience of their life, rather than desert her own people at a time when they were in especial need of the solace which she, above all others, knew how to provide. How much those midday concerts meant, the humblest shorthand typist who attended them could testify better than I. In short ... she is one completely unambitious for herself, who out of sheer love of music and warmth of human feeling exercises her art to the greater happiness of others.[10]

In her speech, responding to the toast of the new honorary degree holders, Myra drew on her ability to treat serious subjects with a touch of humour that drove home her message:

> Chancellor, Vice-Chancellor, my Lords, Ladies and Gentlemen,
>
> I always view the prospect of speaking in public with profound trepidation: indeed, had I known my fate a week ago, I would undoubtedly have spent the entire journey from America, pacing the decks of the Mauretania, rehearsing a speech, instead of spending a good many hours, as I did, playing innumerable games of ping-pong.
>
> However, my acceptance of the invitation to reply to the toast of the honorary graduates, made by the well-beloved Chancellor, was given without hesitation when I realised that in this year of all years, it was fitting that the response should be made by a woman. For I understand that it is only recently that we women have been admitted to full membership of the University.

Cambridge may be justly proud of having appointed a woman professor before Oxford took such a bold step: but there must have been a certain uneasiness in many minds about the equivocal position of this distinguished lady. Now that this has been rectified, I am sure it must be gratifying to Professor Garrod and to countless others to know that their University has at length – if I may so put it – made honest women of them.

This has been a seemingly light-hearted prelude, but I should like to say most seriously, how deeply honoured I feel to be among the first women to be made honorary graduates of Cambridge University, for which I have so great a reverence and affection. Keen though my own personal pleasure is, at receiving this honour, it is a still deeper gratification to think that the gesture has been made to the musical profession, or rather to music itself. For I believe that in recent years music has begun to take its place as a vitally important element in the life of the community. I say begun, because we have not yet found a wholly satisfactory way of presenting music so that it shall be available for all who may want to hear it. During the war, my experience at the National Gallery and elsewhere was a revelation. It proved, beyond doubt, how real was the need for music in the lives of people in almost every walk of life. Day after day, many hundreds would come to hear programmes of Beethoven Quartets, Bach Cantatas, and all that was best in Chamber music; and to many of them, the enjoyment of music opened up wholly unsuspected horizons.

Typical of all this, was a young sailor, who strolled into the National Gallery by chance one day. After the war, I happened to meet him, now a civilian, and he shyly told me his story. He said 'Me and a pal was walking round Trafalgar Square on our 'alf days leave. We saw there was a concert, and thought we would see what it was like. We went in, you was playing that day, Miss, and a damned good show it was.' He then told me that by the end of the war, six of them, Petty-Officers, whenever they had a day's leave, would never miss an opportunity of coming to the concerts.

This is only one instance of what must have happened thousands of times. The opportunity then existed for people to discover that something had been missing from their lives; nobody told them that a Beethoven or a Mozart Quartet was high-brow, or beyond their understanding; they just sat back, listened, and a new world opened to them.

Since Elizabethan days there has probably never been such a demand for serious music as there is today. Not only in England, but all over the world, it is evident that this demand cannot be satisfied by the conventional series of concerts, which financially are beyond the great majority of people. Yet how important it is that a way should be found to enlarge the scope of public music-making.

In times as unsettled as our own, music can have a profound influence for good. It is unfettered by the barrier of words, and needs no translation, and therefore it is one of the great forces that can bring people together in mind and spirit.

How is this consummation to be achieved? At the moment, it is difficult to give the answer. We must hope that the forces of habit and prejudice in the musical world will gradually give way to a more enlightened view of our present needs. This reformation may take time, but perhaps it will come about in the same happy way in which this University has found it possible to reconcile tradition with the claims of emancipated womanhood.

And now, not only for myself, but also on behalf of my distinguished colleagues, may I express my heartfelt appreciation to the Chancellor for his very kind words of welcome today, and to the University, for the great honour they have bestowed on us.[11]

Hippopotamus

Myra had planned a packed schedule for winter in America – but her 1949-50 tour ended in hospital. In January 1950, after just three concerts, she came down with an illness that Dr Grace Rochford, who had carried out her mastectomies, announced to the press as infectious hepatitis. Myra called it 'hippopotamus'. She had to cancel everything for February and spend March recuperating before travelling home. Ted Ferris subsequently noted, however, that it had dissipated very quickly for hepatitis, and Myra's doctors in London thought it had been a gall bladder attack – a condition that later caused her major problems.

Saz wrote to Howard on 8th February: 'She is really making wonderful progress, largely owing to her own inimitable handling of an almost intolerably maddening business. She has faced up to the bitter disappointment, with her own unique courage and sense of proportion, flavoured with humour.'

Myra had heard that the BBC wanted to make a feature of her 60th birthday on 25th February, and was hoping that Howard might give a talk about her. Saz joked with the ailing pianist that it might be a chance for Howard to get certain things off his chest.

He went ahead, to Myra's delight. She wrote to him from the Laurelton on 20th February: 'I must wish you "luck out of muck" as Beecham said at the end of a rehearsal of a work he didn't like!! If I wake at 6am on Sunday, I shall think of you having your fling about your diseased old Auntie – All joking apart, I do think you are a saint to do it & I wonder how many times you have wished you had said NO! I can't imagine that I could be of any interest for more than a minute and a half – perhaps that is all the time they'll give you? I do hope your recording machine won't turn into Donald Duck again.' She added that she was getting stronger and had learned to relax for the first time 'for ??? perhaps 20 years! … I have enjoyed the incredible luxury of no responsibilities – no obligations – sheer Heaven!'

Once she felt better, though, Myra made up for the American disaster by enjoying a visit to Holland in late spring, where she was soloist with the Concertgebouw Orchestra for the royal opening of the Holland Music Festival. She had been made a Commander in the Order of Oranje-Nassau in 1947 and Queen Juliana came backstage to meet her after she performed Mozart's E flat concerto K271.

Casals Returns

At her own request, Myra had given a recital with Pablo (Pau) Casals at the Cambridge Theatre, London, on 3rd November 1945, when he was performing in Britain for the first time after the war. All proceeds from the tour were donated to the RAF's Benevolent Fund. She had heard that he was appearing with another pianist, but quietly asked Emmie Tillett, who was agent to both, if she could play instead. She feared she might never have another chance to work with him.

It was an astute observation. The Catalonian cellist, who was nearly 70, had long been an impassioned campaigner against the fascist regime of General Franco. He had hoped to enlist British assistance in this situation and believed that his efforts might prove fruitful; but now he was beginning to recognise the duplicity that faced him. At encouraging meetings, cabinet ministers, journalists and royal officials were happy to discuss democracy in Spain; but he would then read fawning, pro-Franco reports in papers such as *The Daily Mail* and *The Daily Telegraph*, which left him feeling that, in the end, Spain was being abandoned.

Urged on by Myra herself, he had met King George VI's secretary and reminded him that UN members had a moral duty to see Spanish democracy restored. Despite the official's assurances, he realised the mission was hopeless. Myra intervened with Sir Stafford Cripps for him, but Casals felt that the politics and the principles were irreconcilable. He had planned to return to Britain the next spring, but cancelled everything until the position of England in respect to Spain would be changed.

Myra wrote to him after their concert, heart on sleeve:

> I cannot find words to express the joy and honour I have had in playing with you. It has been one of the deepest experiences of my life. If I can ever shape a phrase as you do, that would be my testimony of gratitude! For so many years I have carried the sound of your playing in my ears, and now you have reminded us again of the supreme power of Beauty and Truth. I thank you with all my heart and my prayers and wishes go with you. [12]

Along with Toscanini's baton and Paderewski's card, Myra kept in her collection of musical relics part of one of Casals' cigars. These souvenirs came from artists who approached music-making with humility and the highest of standards; but they were also people of unimpeachable moral principle and political integrity. Three were artists who stood up against fascism. The other, Paderewski, had become president of Poland.

Portrait of a Pianist

'I'll not be photographed, thank you.' Myra was talking to a reporter from *The Milwaukee Journal* in November 1950 – more about clothes than music. She gave a rare but substantial interview, which proved rather more illuminating than the countless reviews expecting womanly charm from her playing. 'I don't mind so much not being a raving beauty,' she explained, 'but I don't have to look hideous all over the newspapers.'

The reporter, Dorothy Witte, remarked that Myra could say no and stick to it. The voice, she wrote, was 'deep and rich and a little amused'.

Myra, smoking a long English 'cigaret', told her that as a child she had never wanted to be a professional pianist and would have preferred to be a dancer. Saz explained to Witte the proper positioning of the title 'Dame' beside 'Myra', rather than 'Hess'.

The conversation turned to concert dress and Myra's preference for black: 'I sound better than I look and I like to match my piano,' she said. '...And as a matter of fact, I want people to listen to me and not to notice me.' When Witte asked what Myra would wear for her Milwaukee concert, Saz wondered what the platform floor would be like; rough boards could cause havoc with a train. Myra responded that she would try her new Mainbocher gown: 'People who come to a concert should listen with their eyes closed, anyway.' Her sentence ended 'with a chuckle'.[13]

Myra's American season had got off to a fine start in October and Annie suggested that she give an all-Beethoven recital at Carnegie Hall in January. Her 'own lovely piano' was ready for her concerts and she planned to take the Beethoven programme ('109, 57, 110......my, my.....') around the country.

New York seemed crowded and crazy, the effects of the newly threatening Cold War becoming evident. Myra wrote home:

> The reports of hoarding and resulting shortages have been grossly exaggerated and everything is obtainable in the shops. Meat is frightfully expensive, but the ordinary necessities of food much about the same. The fear of Russian aggression seems more economic than military and that Russia is out to break this country financially by forcing it into inflation. So many think that is our situation also? So far, we have come across more feeling of fatalism than ordinary war hysteria, although the Radio does its best to create the latter. ... I have never been more aware of an almost terrifying opulence, here in New York, as if all the Limousines are rushing towards a precipice, and everyone living at a pace that can leave them no time for thinking ... A walk down Regent Street would be a comparative rest cure.

She tried out the Beethoven programme at Ann Arbor on 14th November, despite being 'crippled with pre-Beethoven-triple-Sonata-programme panic' – playing to a spellbound audience 4,000 strong. 'I felt as if I had had twilight sleep or giants' nightmares and could hardly believe I had done such a thing ... It was a great experience in every way and proves once again that the best music reaches most people. In 70 odd years, no one had given a Beethoven recital at the University, Schnabel and I have now played 109 and no one but me…has played 110.'

In Minneapolis the orchestra had not played Beethoven's Piano Concerto No. 3 for years, 'and it sounded like it…..[Antal] Dorati (conductor) became quite uncomfortable, knowing that he ought to have prepared it. I kep' me temper (just….says Swee…) … Thank goodness, the rehearsal had shaken both orchestra and conductor and they were on their tip-toes to redeem themselves. D. poured with perspiration and his hair turned into seaweed….the nett result was quite a spirited performance and not without a musical quality.'

By the time she reached Chicago, she was tired of interviews and met '…a most objectionable reporter from one of the Chicago horrors …' Asked for her views on the world situation, 'I told him that I thought one of the worst and most menacing evils was NEWSPAPERS…… Strange to relate, no article appeared in his paper.'

Her Beethoven recital brought her 'one of the most moving audiences I have ever had' and she was thrilled by Rafael Kubelik's response: 'He had rehearsed all day and said he was completely refreshed by listening to 3 Beethoven Sonatas. We discussed 6 Mozart concertos for my next visit here.' The next morning Saz had to clean her concert dress, which was 'absolutely FILTHY … my feet were jet black from the dirt on the stage'.

Somehow the trains worked despite snow and strikes. Back in New York, Myra attended a play, *Call Me Madam*, where the Duke and Duchess of Windsor – the ex-Edward VIII and Wallis Simpson – were present. 'A very amusing show and the D. and D. seemed to be enjoying themselves too. He never stopped that nervous rubbing of his jaw and mouth. Everyone very anxious to get sight of them.'

Now Alexander Schneider, formerly the second violin of the Budapest Quartet, came to see her. He was on the committee of Casals' festival. 'Casals wants me to play a Mozart concerto with him (at Perpignan this next time instead of Prades). Perhaps Marj & Saz could go too & we could take the Rover & have a holiday in France?!!'

'Of course I am going,' she wrote in the diary. 'We won't have another Casals in our lifetime……. I have been realising more and more how few great musical experiences there are nowadays.'

After a 'quiet and eerie' Christmas, on Boxing Day Main Bocher took her to 'the best Restaurant "in the world" apparently….and I always enjoy being with him. By the way, he gave Swee 800 cigarettes for Xmas.' Steinways held a lavish lunch party in her honour – 'I couldn't help thinking of the days when I trembled before entering the portals of Steinway Hall, in London.'

She had been missing Toscanini: 'The Maestro has not been conducting since we arrived. Some say that he was furious with NBC because they turned him out of his studio (for television) & others that he has been suffering from Bursitis? Something in the knee? We were also told he will conduct in February & I hope so & that Denis [Matthews] will be able to hear him!' When she returned to New York from Washington DC on 4th January, there awaited 'THREE DOZEN RED ROSES FROM THE MAESTRO with Xmas and New Year wishes in RED INK', and the following day, 'A letter from Casals, not in red ink but equally treasured.'

Myra was living hard and playing hard. She was often up until 1am or later. There was food and company – and more food and company: 'Dined with the Greiners, only one other guest Mr [Nikita] Magalofffff who used to play for Szigeti and is now his son-in-law … there was a hand-cart of drinks, incl. Vodka of course, Caviare and endless layers of smooth smoked salmon. The maid came in continually with hot toast and by the time we went in to dinner S. and I were absolutely choc-a-bloc. Dinner consisted of soup, veal, a large bowl of heavily dressed salad and a chocolate soufflé…'

If not giving a concert herself, she went to other people's. On 20th January she lunched with the soprano Elisabeth Schumann in 'her rather dark but gemütlich flat, with every kind of European furniture' before attending Schnabel's recital. 'He played 4 Beethoven sonatas, Pathetic [Pathétique], 101, 90 and Waldstein. He looks frail and very white, and his hair is snow white, but there were unforgettable and absolutely inspired patches. He was better and better as the evening went on.' Soon afterwards, she and Sidney Griller went to hear Bruno Walter conduct Brahms: 'The 1st Symphony was magnificent and made one sadly conscious of the fact that there are no more Walters and Schnabels coming along as far as one can see.'

Later in January she and Julia Steinway heard Maestro conduct the Verdi Te Deum and Requiem at Carnegie Hall: 'I can't imagine really enjoying the Requiem done by anyone else. He had much too big a choir and a tremendous orchestra which nearly blew us out of the hall, but it was electrifying. The tympanist looked as if he was throwing himself out of a top storey window every time there was a semblance of a climax. We couldn't take our eyes off him. T. looks quite a bit older, but full of fire and vitality…'

As for her own Beethoven: 'I have come to the conclusion that if one has to play in public, it is far better to play the best music possible. … Amused and certainly delighted to find a very, very nice criticism from Mr Olin Downes … Tribune and other papers also v. pleased. Whether one cares one or two hoots what they say, it is much nicer when they say they have enjoyed themselves.'

Brahms with Walter

Myra with Bruno Walter

Myra's live recording of Brahms's Second Piano Concerto with Bruno Walter came from the third of a trilogy of concerts, beginning on 8th February. After the first night, she wrote: 'Thank goodness, my fingers touched quite a lot of the right notes and the nightmare of yesterday [a rehearsal that she felt had not gone well] was dispelled. It was a great experience sharing a Brahms concerto with Walter and the orchestra were really enthusiastic. It was a packed hall and I can only say that my performance was considered to be a good one.'

The next afternoon's was more exciting: 'Things happened, as they can and do, why and how no one can tell….and it was a moving performance with Walter, orchestra and myself metaphorically embracing each other between each movement...... It is an enormous pleasure to please Walter.' A supper party at Julia Steinway's with the conductor, his daughter and son-in-law and others finished a memorable occasion: 'Her table looked as it used to in the days of Paderewski dinners and she looked her best ... It made me feel extremely nostalgic, as things have changed so much and so many artists have gone since I first came here in 1922. When I told Walter how moved I had been by his Symphony I was very touched by his saying that he and I had an affinity in music. What more could I ask?'

Finally the concert on 11th February was recorded live for broadcast on 18th. This became the commercial release. Myra, Saz and Pondie together listened with trepidation to the relay: 'It is quite impossible,' said Myra, 'to listen musically to one's own playing, although there were a few nice surprises...... (I sent Bruno Walter some lovely red roses and had a most touching and "gratifying" letter from him, which has completed the unforgettable experience of playing Brahms with him.)'

The recording captures a Brahms of mountain peaks and craggy rocks, vast musical vistas that cast giant perspective on life and art. Brahms needs gravitas as well as superhuman energy and vitality; Myra and Walter provide lashings of those qualities, in an ideal balance. Myra's comment about hitting 'quite a lot of the right notes' is not without point, because sometimes she splashes; the concerto can be awkward for those without supersized hands. Yet the sense of struggle benefits the music, since there can be no real feeling of triumph without something to triumph over. It is a struggle – and she wins.

The 1950 illness, and maybe the landmark of turning 60, had nevertheless left Myra shaken. She opened up in a November letter to Howard: 'I am going through a deep distaste of my playing and above all of playing in public, but the response has been so touching that I am quite bewildered. Each concert I think must be one of the last and I have talked to Saz seriously of stopping, but ?????????'

She wrote more to him about other people than about herself – asking for news of Nolsie, praising Denis Matthews' US performances, sending encouraging words about the playing of Yfrah Neaman, whose concert had had some unfortunate reviews, and reporting a delightful meeting with a new friend, the Greek pianist Gina Bachauer, who in 1951 married Alec Sherman, Myra's stalwart Mozart conductor. Hearing her for the first time in New York, Myra remarked in her 29th October diary: 'It is virtuosity of a very high order and she is sensitive, dignified and absolutely seriously sincere.... She can do everything that Horowitz can do and so much else...'

'I was absolutely bowled over by Gina – I had no idea she was so terrific!' she told Howard. 'I phoned Gina about 5pm on the day of her concert ... and she said "Maiyra, the only thing to do in this country is to make breeches". I felt it wasn't the moment to cross her in anything so said yes.... We make breeches, she continued, and then we do not have to be nerrrrvous or practise or suffer and we make lots of money. Finally, I said what kind of breeches Gina? "Ah, you know like the George Washington breech........"'

Myra had made a friend that year in a midwestern snowstorm: Edith Frank, who with her husband David Frank was a philanthropist, based at the time in Toledo. She was an accomplished pianist and had a postgraduate degree in journalism. Encountering Myra and Saz arriving at the station in footwear quite unsuitable for snow, Edith gave Myra her own galoshes. In March 1951, back in Britain, Myra was overjoyed when Edith began to send her sumptuously generous food parcels. She and the Mauls rejoiced at the arrival of American butter and plenty of tinned victuals.

'I wish you could have seen the excitement in the kitchen when I opened it, with my housekeeper & her husband!' Myra wrote to Edith on 31st March 1951. 'We took it in turns to unpack all the good things! I only wish that you & your husband could come & share one of the delicious meals with us. My housekeeper unites her gratitude with mine, as it really needs the utmost patience & imagination to produce daily meals of any variety. I complain sometimes of the drudgery of working at programmes year in & year out, but it is nothing compared to that of the English housewife!'

She then revealed: 'I am just beginning a tremendous schedule for our Festival here all spring & summer.'[14] For once, her British summertime was looking almost as exciting as the winter season in the US.

A shadow was cast over the spring, however, when Kathleen Ferrier discovered what she described as 'a bump on my busto'[15]. She underwent a mastectomy for malignant cancer, followed by six weeks of radiotherapy. In a letter to John Newmark on 1st May, Ferrier remarked that she had felt 'ruined with kindness' during her stay in hospital: Emmie Tillett and Myra had waited there throughout her operation and for her to come round afterwards. They visited her almost every day as she recovered, bringing champagne on her birthday – 'a riotous day,' she reported[16]. It was nevertheless the beginning of a long, arduous disease, heartrending for all who knew and loved her.

Meanwhile, in the US on 31st March, Myra's sometime friend Harold Bauer had breathed his last. Moshe Paranov, dean of the Hartt School of Music at the University of Hartford, wrote to tell her the sad news, addressing her as 'Aunty Myra', sending love to 'Cousin Anita' and remarking: '…it is comforting to think of the many wonderful hours you and I spent with him, enjoying his greatness and genius … we can still look back to so many experiences which we shared together and both be forever grateful to our Maker for having given us – to know, to love and be loved by – Harold Bauer.'[17]

So Many Stairs

The Festival of Britain was conceived in 1947 as a 'tonic for the nation'. In the spirit of Myra's National Gallery concerts, its purpose was to boost morale. Postwar Britain was still suffering under austerity and rationing. The bombs had left gouged-out wastelands amid the townscapes; urgent social and economic changes were only crawling in, and the national frame of mind seemed browbeaten.

Churchill, after his 'finest hour' in the war, had been defeated at the 1945 general election and Clement Attlee's new Labour government announced plans for a grand festival to be held in 1951. It would coincide with the centenary of the Great Exhibition of 1851 and celebrate the best of British manufacturing and design. It would also see the opening of a new concert hall for large-scale orchestral music.

The rebuilding of the Queen's Hall had been debated in parliament in May 1949 and a public fundraising campaign for it sourced £70,000, yet the can was sent clattering down the road time and again. Now, on the South Bank of the Thames, a conglomeration of derelict warehouses would be pulled down and, among temporary pavilions and marquees housing festival exhibitions, a permanent concert hall would be built as a lasting legacy. In October 1949, at the site of the demolished Lion Brewery, Attlee laid the foundation stone of the Royal Festival Hall.

Designed by the architects Sir Robert Matthew and Leslie Martin, it went up in 18 months, cost £2m and, with a capacity of 2,900, was bigger than the old Queen's Hall, if smaller than New York's Carnegie. Its terraces looked out over the Thames and the newly cleared riverside areas. In the foyers, an abundance of glass let in natural light, while sleek staircases and bar areas exemplified the streamlined new aesthetic of 1950s modernism.

The surrounding exhibition site was another matter. The King and Queen were expected on the morning of 3rd May and 40,000 visitors that afternoon, but with just three days to go, contractors were struggling to finish in time. Concrete was still being mixed, asphalt laid, paint applied and soil delivered for the planting of hundreds of flowers. The *Evening Standard* was unimpressed: 'And how can the visitor tell which staircase leads where? There are so many stairs in this Exhibition that intending visitors will be well advised to get into condition by climbing up from the bottom of the Hampstead tube without the aid of escalators.'[18] (Hampstead tube station, the deepest in London, has no escalators, only lifts.)

The Manchester Guardian reflected on the contrast between the surge of hope that had accompanied the festival's conception and the time in which it was realised, in the shadow of the Cold War. 'The world into which the Festival is born is a sadder and harder one than we looked for ... In one sense, hard times may even help us to appreciate it more justly.'[19]

The Royal Festival Hall opened on 3rd May with a grand royal gala. After a televised service of dedication in St Paul's Cathedral, King George VI declared the festival open from the steps outside, before proceeding to the South Bank, where he unveiled the new venue's commemorative tablet. At last he and Queen Elizabeth settled down to enjoy a 'British' programme from members of five orchestras and ten choirs, conducted by Boult and Sargent, beginning and ending with Handel.

The first piano soloist to perform in the Royal Festival Hall? Dame Myra Hess. During the week of celebratory concerts, on 7th May she played Beethoven's Piano Concerto No. 4 with the LPO conducted by Boult, who also presented the Berlioz 'Roman Carnival' Overture and Elgar's Symphony No. 1. Other pianists later that week included Moiseiwitsch, who played the Beethoven 'Choral Fantasy' under Sargent, and Denis Matthews, who joined Harry Blech and the London Mozart Players for Mozart's C minor Concerto K491.

The Queen's Hall rebuild, though, had not yet been shelved. Jim Fassett asked Myra about its prospects in their 1952 radio interview. He wanted her opinion of the Royal Festival Hall acoustic, having heard much about it, both pro and con. 'It's something quite new for London,' she responded. 'We've got to get used to it.' She reflected that London's music lovers were sentimentally attached to the Queen's Hall and felt that nothing could take its place; it was supposed to be rebuilt, but the latest budget news 'didn't look very hopeful.'[20] The foundation stone should have been laid during the festival, but it had not happened yet. It was, of course, postponed once again.

That festive summer, Myra's intense schedule took her far and wide around the country. It is a pity that she only kept diaries for her American trips; there would have been fine fodder closer to home.

She had a recital in Derby the day after the Royal Festival Hall opening; the day after that, she went to Wolverhampton to play Beethoven's Third Concerto with the CBSO under George Weldon. On 19th April she had performed the Beethoven 'Emperor' Concerto with Boult and the LPO in a benefit concert for the orchestra at the Royal Albert Hall; and the same concerto ten days later in Manchester with the Hallé and Albert Wolff ('Her approach was masculine in its strength and attack,' said the *Manchester Evening News...*).[21]

She was at Peterborough Cathedral on 24th May appearing in the town's Arts Week, attended by the Duchess of Gloucester and broadcast on the BBC Midland Regional Service. At the Forum Cinema in Bath on 1st June, her all-Beethoven recital rubbed shoulders with a showing of Laurence Olivier's *Henry V*. She stood in for an indisposed Artur Schnabel at the RFH on 25th June, playing the 'Emperor' Concerto with the Philharmonia and Otto Klemperer. A more unusual venue was the Victoria and Albert Museum, where she was soloist in a Sunday series of 12 Mozart piano concertos with the New London Orchestra and Alec Sherman, reprising the success of their series at the National Gallery.

A new international festival had launched in Edinburgh in 1947, under the directorship of Rudolf Bing, who had become general manager of Glyndebourne after arriving in Britain as a refugee from Germany. As so many European festival sites, halls and theatres had been damaged or destroyed, he considered that new venues were desperately needed. Edinburgh seemed a perfect city in which to reconcile people via the refreshing power of art. At the first Edinburgh International Festival, amid the privations of austerity in which floodlighting was not permitted, the castle was floodlit in any case for four nights, using the city's private coal rations.

Myra went there in summer 1951 with the touring New York Philharmonic; the sleek power of the transatlantic orchestra received wild acclaim. She played Beethoven's Fourth Piano Concerto with Walter – and, at short notice, the Schumann with Mitropoulos, when Rudolf Serkin fell ill. 'I stepped in and took his place, or pretended to take his place,' she told Jim Fassett. 'The conductors ... both got ovations, but it was an enormous success for the orchestra.' But *The Times* critic judged the finale 'a grand tour de force … an impassioned diatribe that hardly became the gentle Schumann' and that 'there was some evidence that Dame Myra Hess had not wholly collected herself after her hasty flight from a Prom in London the night before…'[22]

A change of attitude was starting to seep into Myra's reviews. The National Gallery concerts had led to her effective sanctification – but the British press generally has never liked to praise anyone considered over-promoted, too successful or too popular. Add the critics' ingrained distrust of pianists performing from the score; complicate it with the fact that Myra was deeply associated in the public mind with the war years, which everyone wished to put behind them; and the likelihood that she might receive iffy reviews grows incrementally stronger.

A Festival Among Friends

That summer, Myra had one of the most treasured experiences of her musical life: she went to Perpignan to work with Pablo Casals. The cellist was living quietly in the French-Catalan Pyrenean village of Prades, having settled there in 1936 amid the Spanish Civil War. In 1946, after his efforts to enlist British help against Franco had proved fruitless, he gave up public performance in protest against the regime – a powerful symbolic stand in the face of a loathed dictatorship. He refused accolades offered by the Allies after the Second World War; for his own people, the struggle was not yet over.

Casals had an upstairs flat and on his daily errands enjoyed greeting friends and neighbours. When musicians visited, pleading with him to start playing again, he would tell them: 'It is not a matter of money, it is just a matter of morality.'[23]

But then Alexander Schneider came to visit him for three days, bringing a proposal for the year 1950 from the pianist Mieczyslaw Horszowski: 'You can't condemn your art to silence. Since you don't want to leave Prades we shall come there, a group of musicians, in order to celebrate the bicentenary of Bach's death.'[24] At last Casals capitulated, anticipating a one-off event.

The musicians involved would donate their fees to the hospital in Perpignan, which treated Spanish exiles, but substantial finance was still required to bring it about. Schneider set up an American committee to source funding, while local volunteers gave their services.

Such was the mystique around the first festival, however, that in 1951 Schneider made sure it could happen again. This time it would be in nearby Perpignan for the sake of space; Prades had only one hotel. Myra, who adored Casals, needed little persuasion. As she had considered, she, Marj and Saz drove all the way there.

Casals had said, before the 1950 festival, that publicity was unnecessary as it would be only a festival among friends – '*un festival de famille*'. He also refuted the idea that he was coming out of retirement, but was rather performing 'despite' it. Still, his saint-like status was such that the public and the press arrived in droves, some travelling thousands of miles. For 1951, reporters came from as far afield as Australia.

Perpignan – dusty, white-shuttered and dotted with palm trees and oleander, and with many locals speaking Catalan – attracted a strong pull of its own. The concerts were to take place in the open-air courtyard of the citadel, a recently restored palace dating at its earliest from 1285. Concert-goers traversed dark passages in the fortress walls, going up narrow stone stairs, across grassy tracks and through medieval gates to take their seats on chairs or tiers of wooden benches, ready for the concert to begin with the dusk. The orchestral musicians were drawn from devoted pupils, friends and admirers of Casals from around a dozen countries.

Casals opened the concert with Bach's solo Cello Suite No. 1; next he conducted Myra in Mozart's E flat major Concert K271, the young Polish-American violinist Isaac Stern in the Mozart G major Violin Concerto, and finally the Sinfonia Concertante with Stern and the violist William Primrose. When rain disrupted the second concert, it was moved into the cloisters; here the audience sat at the feet of a chamber group consisting of Stern, Primrose, the cellist Paul Tortelier and the oboist Marcel Tabuteau.

Myra's Mozart concerto was recorded and is an exceptional performance. Her empathy for Casals' shaping of phrases makes them perfect partners. Their approach to the conversational element and their affection for the music, which seems shared by the vigorous, tender orchestral playing, allows ensemble and soloist to exchange views in an effervescent type of large-scale chamber music. There is flexibility to the tempi and Myra's touch offers a delicious mix of high spirits and delicacy. The Chicago critic Claudia Cassidy was present and sounded overwhelmed: 'They are twin spirits,' she wrote of Myra and Casals. Their Mozart is intimate and joyous … It is a treasure to hold forever, rich in inflection, mellow in the dappled brilliance of light and shadow. Its spacious splendour fills the whole wide world of the spirit, leaving no empty corner to hunger for more.'[25]

The New York Times reporter Howard Taubman met Myra for lunch at a hotel near the sea. She arrived 'walking briskly and with a bright light in her eye. She had just had a fine swim in the Mediterranean, she observed, and all through it she kept thinking of the piano concertos she would like to play with Pablo Casals. "Was it a long swim?" she was asked. "Yes," she replied, "there were many concertos on my list".'[26]

Behind the scenes, there were grumbles about poor organisation and disarray over the scarce hotel rooms. The critic Irving Kolodin's review suggested that he had experienced one administrative bunfight too many. He thought Casals a has-been: 'It is dismal to be put in the position of saying, "You should have heard him when," but the Casals of this occasion was only a dim likeness of the proudly energetic, masterfully musical, regally technical artist we used to hear…' He grumbled about Myra's 'insecurity attested by the music on the piano (and more than a few wrong notes) that seemed to infect the not too stable orchestra'.

It was a typical misunderstanding of Myra's use of the score; and there's little evidence of insecurity in the recording (admittedly it may have been edited) of a concerto that Myra knew inside out; perhaps two small slips in the finale, but nothing more serious. Kolodin praised Stern's 'native energy and abundance of virtuosity', but he complained about everything else: the 'snob' audience, pricey programmes, expensive local taxis… At least he *had* hotel accommodation, and the two violinists in nearby rooms, Stern and Erica Morini, were not practising at the same time. [27]

Such churlish impressions did not touch Myra's joy in the music-making, nor upset the forming of a valued new partnership with Stern, whose warmth of sound she loved and with whom she collaborated to fine effect thereafter.

The impact of Casals upon her as artist and individual cannot be overestimated. After the festival, she wrote to him:

> …I want to try to tell you what the experience of Perpignan has done for me. The issues of the world today are tremendous & your music is one of the few remaining powers that renew our belief in the ultimate triumph of Truth and Beauty. Everyone who attended your Festival has felt this.
>
> Now you must be patient and hear my own little story. When I left you on that unforgettable Sunday in Prades I told you that I would not write to you until my playing had improved.

> Before every season I suffer agonies of apprehension & this last Autumn I went through one of the darkest & longest tunnels of despair.
>
> It was the memory of your music that brought me back to the Light & now everyone saw that something has been added to my playing. I know it has been inspired by your influence.
>
> No words could be adequate & in your great modesty I know you would ask me not to thank you. The only way I can show my gratitude is to try & understand the revelation of music more & more deeply every time I play.[28]

In June 1952 the festival returned to Prades and its 11th-century abbey of St Michel de Cuxa. Casals was celebrating his 75th birthday; in his honour a day of Catalan folk dancing was held, plus a civic reception. *The Times* reported that 'surrounded by the world's most eminent instrumentalists, Casals made a speech on love and art, in which he thanked the French people for their kindness to him in his exile'.[29]

Myra's performances, most of which were recorded, included the Brahms Piano Trio No. 1 with Isaac Stern and Casals, and No. 2 with Szigeti instead of Stern – more polished and better balanced than her early recording with Jelly and Cassadó, though maybe lacking something of their raw passion. Casals can sound slightly frail, yet the care of detail, the attention to moulding the phrases with all three musicians thinking as one, is remarkable. Myra also played the Schubert A major Duo with Szigeti and the Schumann Piano Quintet with Stern, Schneider, the violist Milton Thomas and Tortelier – a work otherwise absent from her discography, but in which she swims like a fish in a perfect sea. The Quintet is perhaps Schumann's chamber music masterpiece and its combination of intensity, intimacy, energy and transparency bowls out of this generous and sincere recording.

There was one more significant person Myra got to know at the festival: a flautist, Albert Goldberg, who was her page-turner. He was also a music journalist for *The Los Angeles Times*. When he interviewed her in 1955, Myra told him: 'Playing with Casals was a magical experience. It made me feel like going home to really study music. He once said, "We are always beginning. We go backward if we don't go forward." He is a martyr to art like Toscanini, with the same kind of reverence and humility.'[30]

In October 1951 Myra had been reunited with Furtwängler, performing Beethoven's Fourth with him and the Philharmonia at the Royal Albert

Hall. Planning this concert had involved some machinations between Walter Legge, the Philharmonia's founder, and the German conductor; Furtwängler was reluctant to accept Legge's suggested programme, which included a rare piece by Wolf, *Penthesilea*. Legge wrote to him (on 9th July) that box office receipts could not be relied on for a purely orchestral concert, but that a Beethoven concerto would increase attendance ('particularly when you conduct'). Furtwängler had told him, after Myra's concerto with the Berlin Philharmonic, that he was happy with her; she had duly been engaged, since Furtängler's first choice of pianist, Edwin Fischer, was unavailable. 'I should not like to cancel her,' Legge wrote, 'particularly because she is looking forward with great pleasure to playing with you. My motive here was her great influence in America; to play with her can only help you in the USA!'

Furtwängler's reply was less than enthusiastic, judging Legge's programmes as somewhat depressing and the concerts pointless. He even expressed doubt about working with the soprano Kirsten Flagstad. The one positive note he struck, however, was over Myra. 'Myra Hess is, of course, a worthy and charming artist and to create a complete Beethoven or Brahms evening with her help would perhaps have some purpose.'[31] The concert went ahead – no Wolf, just Beethoven and Brahms – with conductor and soloist, according to *The Times*, 'in perfect accord'. The concerto, the report suggested, could go down in history as the 'Myra Hess' as surely as its sibling, No. 5, was the 'Emperor'.[32]

Myra had had other issues with Legge. The story goes that she was once in a taxi with him when he placed a hand on her thigh. She pushed it away, with the inimitable riposte: 'Now, now, Oedipus!'[33]

Myra was 62, playing and travelling full blast. She was on the road more often than not, mainly in the US where there was no rationing and where her numerous friends and colleagues were only too happy to wine and dine her. She loved good food; deprived of this luxury for so long in Britain, in the US she made up for lost time. Photographs show her as rather overweight (once, asked by a photographer to raise her chin, she quipped: 'Which one?'), and in many, a cigarette dangles from her lips – she was a chain-smoker. Exercise was rare, and an American friend who later exhorted Saz to ensure Myra had fresh air every day was given short shrift. This lifestyle, with long hours of practising, concert nerves, social pressures, travel and crazy hours, sometimes driving through the night after a concert, could not help but take a toll.

1 This and subsequent quotes from MH American diaries, Hess Family Collection
2 This and subsequent MH letters to HF from Myra Hess Collection, BL
3 Issued on the APR label
4 N. Hess interview with HF
5 *The Indianapolis Times*, 13 May 1953
6 J. Fassett radio interview with MH, CBS, 1952
7 B. Simonds, 'Myra in America' in *Myra Hess by her Friends*, p50
8 V. Parsonnet, Victor, with B. Glovin, *The Page Turner*, accessed online, https://www.billglovin.com/ghostwriting/ewExternalFiles/The%20Page%20Turner.pdf
9 HF, 9 June 1949, in Myra Hess Collection, BL
10 Speech presented by Public Orator, Keith Guthrie, English version sent to MH. Original in Latin. Honorary Degrees, 9 June 1949
11 MH acceptance speech, script in MHCBL
12 McKenna, op. cit., p198
13 D. Witte, interview with MH, *Milwaukee Journal*, 24 November 1950
14 MH to Edith Frank, 31 March 1951, Wisconsin Historical Society, University of Wisconsin
15 I. Jack, 'Klever Kaff' in *Granta*, accessed online, https://granta.com/klever-kaff/
16 C. Fifield (ed.), *Letters and Diaries of Kathleen Ferrier*, p150
17 Moshe Paranov to MH, undated, Harold Bauer Collection, University of Hartford Archives & Special Collections
18 *Evening Standard*, 1 May 1951
19 *The Manchester Guardian* 3 May 1951
20 J. Fassett, radio interview with MH, CBS, 1952
21 *Manchester Evening News*, 20 April 1951
22 *The Times*, 3 September 1951
23 J. M. Corredor (trans. A. Mangeot), *Conversations with Casals*, p226
24 Ibid.
25 *Chicago Tribune*, 22 July 1951
26 *The New York Times*, 22 July 1951
27 *The Spokesman-Review*, 22 July 1951
28 P. Casals and A. Kahn, *Joys and Sorrows*, p257
29 *The Times*, 5 July 1952
30 *Los Angeles Times*, 3 April 1955
31 W. Legge, *Words and Music*, p139
32 *The Times*, 26 October 1951
33 Author interview with Andrew Keener

'No More Matzah Balls'

(1952–1959)

THE NEXT OBSTACLE Myra had to confront was not her own health, but Annie Friedberg's. Myra had long expressed frustration over her American agent's forgetfulness and neuroses, but it became clear during the 1951-2 tour that Annie was seriously unwell, possibly with dementia. Myra had to face the reality that she could not operate on organisational quicksand; she would have to change managers. She had been with Annie since her first US tour in 1922 and had remained resolutely loyal to her, despite their difficult moments. Who, or what, could ever replace her? To Myra, the 'factories' of big agencies like Columbia (CAMI) and Sol Hurok were anathema – and they had been circling her hungrily for years.

She was, moreover, dealing with this minus the support of Saz, who had a bad back and could not travel. Myra had recruited a temporary new secretary-companion, Louise Orr – a cousin of Ruth Howard who had known Myra all her life, but seems to have been more secretary than companion.

In a further complication, Myra was moving house. She was selling 48 Wildwood Road and heading back to St John's Wood, wishing to be closer to her many friends in the vicinity, among them Marj and Saz, but also Benno Moiseiwitsch, Solomon, Gerald Moore, Kathleen Ferrier and more; the stretch of north London from St John's Wood up to Hampstead village was a popular centre for the musical world's home life. Myra delayed sailing for the States by a week to make the necessary plans.

Her new house, 23 Cavendish Close, was late Georgian, larger and grander than Wildwood Road, and boasted central heating. It stood on a cul-de-sac directly bordering Lord's Cricket Ground, off Cavendish Avenue, one of the suburb's most exclusive streets. By the time Myra returned from the US, the move would be complete; Saz could organise everything, including extensive redecoration, in her absence. The garden lawn was soon shaped like a grand piano.

Myra and Louise reached New York on 27th December, having sailed through Christmas, to be greeted at the docks by Sascha Greiner, Julia and Billy Steinway (Julia's cousin by marriage), and Annie herself, who looked ill and frail. Myra's friends soon flocked round – Pondie, the Parsonnets, Dorothy Shepard – and a contact at a Canasta evening gave her the perfect present for the pianist who has everything: a mechanical card shuffler. 'It is a dream of enjoyment,' Myra enthused. 'You turn a handle and out they come. It is slightly noisy, so I will probably be expelled from the Laurelton.....'[1]

She settled in by practising hard at Steinway's, though she disliked the heat there. She always preferred cooler temperatures and cannot have made herself popular on long train journeys during which she sometimes demanded that the heating be turned down or off; but Saz remained convinced that Myra felt the cold terribly.

She enjoyed concerts by her colleagues, including 'Maestro' on 12th January, when she and Julia Steinway heard him conduct Beethoven, the Leonora No. 2 Overture and the 'Pastoral' Symphony: '...absolutely wonderful. We went to see him afterwards and his face is more beautiful than ever. He stroked mine and called me "Cara", so what more could I ask??????'

At the theatre she saw Katherine Cornell in *The Constant Wife* and visited the actress at her impressive home, Sneads Landing, overlooking the Hudson River. The next day a cellist friend who had played in the orchestra at Perpignan showed her film footage of the Casals Festival: 'I nearly fell off a very low sofa when they first produced the awful picture of me playing the Appass[ionata]...... I don't know how they got hold of it. Some of the pictures of Pau were simply lovely and oh dear, how nostalgic I felt.'

In Baltimore her experiences with Casals resonated: the conductor 'wanted to know all about the Perpignan Festival, as all the musicians had told him how "special" it was ... I ventured the suggestion that Casals has the magic of freedom without seeming to change tempi....... Consequence: quite a different feeling at concert ... The orchestra played con amore and there was terrific life in the last movement.'

Then on 19th January there came a significant encounter: she met Cesar Saerchinger for the first time in years. He went to see her 'about Schnabel Foundation Fund and he wants to write a Profile about me in Saturday Review....a nuisance..... It was extraordinary to see him again ... 30 [years] since he made me come to America.'

The death of King George VI in early February upset Myra deeply. Ever a staunch royalist, and personally acquainted with the Queen, she took it as an almost personal blow.

> February 6th. Oh, what a melancholy day. We heard the sad news at breakfast time. How I wanted to fly home, although I think there was almost as much sympathy and sadness here as in England ... I felt like an exile, having to go to Carnegie Hall and rehearse the two concertos. Even the men 'back stage' spoke so feelingly and affectionately, but it was a cold-blooded thing to sit down and play as if nothing unusual had happened ... one's heart bleeds for the rest of the family, and especially poor young Elizabeth. She will make a wonderful Queen but oh dee dee......

The next day she played Beethoven's Third Concerto with Mitropoulos, running a temperature and with 'pains all over', still feeling moved by Churchill's 'wonderful broadcast'. The temperature turned into a cold and she feared having to cancel her Schumann with the New York Philharmonic on 10th, but by the day she was, she wrote, 'Buch better'.

Even if Myra's breathing was congested, the Schumann Concerto (its broadcast preserved on record) was clear and bright. Myra's tone sings out, and the strongly articulated phrasing which she shares with the woodwind solos in the first movement blends admirably into a unified statement. It is almost as different from her UK studio recording that same year as it would be were another pianist playing it, although the accounts share the nocturnal tempo to begin the first movement's development section.

Myra's radio interview with 'the nice young Mr Fasset' [sic – it was Jim Fassett] was recorded for airing straight after the Schumann. 'The conversation with the microphone between us was the least interesting part of 3 hours' talk and gossip,' she wrote, 'which would not be discreet in blue and white' (she was using a new blue typewriter ribbon). 'Denise wrote about a wonderful recital by Kathleen Ferrier up North. She was quite overwhelmed. Everyone here is so delighted when I tell them that her singing is more beautiful than ever. Fasset said today that there is no one like her here.'

In Chicago, Myra played lavish quantities of Mozart with Kubelik and spent her birthday being fussed over. Louise had ensured the waiters had decorated the breakfast table: 'Bright-coloured birthday paper instead of a cloth, lollipops! stuck into the rolls and all kinds of allusions, polite and otherwise. .... The news of Wildwood was a very pleasant birthday present.' The house had been sold for more than anticipated.

Before her recital, however, she suffered 'a nasty apprehensive morning' in wintery weather, 'and was reduced to taking Yarrow's Funk pills....' She rarely referred to medicine, albeit homeopathic, for pre-concert anxiety, but she had probably had these 'pillies' for a while. Her spirits seemed subdued – 'Relieved to find that the Schubert was going quite nicely and ended by comparatively enjoying playing...' – but she had 'the usual warm Chicago response and played 4 encores, finishing with the Bach Adagio...'

A certain irritability haunts her diaries from the Mid-West, with grumbles about dodgy orchestral standards, dingy hotels, poor sleep and vile weather. Probably she was also missing Saz. Louise's company was altogether more formal. Myra and Saz's old, familiar rituals were not old and familiar to her. Potential stumbling blocks ranged from the complex business of shampooing Myra's hair ('the water went down the plughole,' Myra commented sardonically) to the nonsense-words she and Saz exchanged when surrounded by chatter in a strange language, or the fact that Myra enjoyed Saz's irreverence about her fame. Louise knew Myra little enough to be bemused by the way she would sweat over the small stuff despite dealing so well with greater challenges.

But maybe above all, Myra was not feeling well. It was becoming clear that the 'hippopotamus' might not have been hepatitis at all.

A New Agent

Back in New York in late March, Cesar Saerchinger came to interview Myra as planned for his feature. The meeting took an unexpected turn.

'Most of two hours was spent in discussing my "dead end"!! with poor old A. F.,' she wrote. 'He suggested that he might be my personal representative in Annie's office and taking a long view (how long?????) doing likewise in the office of a Mr Colbert, who has inherited Laberge's Management ... he has a list of REAL musicians. Incidentally, he is bringing the Amadeus 4tet. So Cesar's visit gave me a glimmer of hope for the future...'

The urgent need for new management became clear the next day, 22nd March, when Annie held a party for her in the Wellington Hotel. Flowers, sandwiches and cakes were abundant, and to Myra's delight the Griller Quartet ('the BOYS') were there. But Annie's condition shocked her: 'Poor A. looked like a very, very small ghost, and couldn't remember the people she had to introduce.' She made 'a touching and nervous little speech and I replied likewise..... She was absolutely exhausted and couldn't join us for dinner. I finally took her a ham sandwich.'

Cesar visited Myra again six days later: 'I felt it was necessary to tell him of the situation with A. He was very concerned and very understanding, and we both realise the difficulty of ever making A. see reason…..' On 29th she finally spoke to Annie.

> Without exception, the most appallingly difficult thing I have EVER had to face….. I have made it quite clear that I will not come back in [53]/54 unless we have someone to help us. L. was on the alert, in case A. fainted ….. but I was amazed at her calmness…. The trouble is that she will not, or CANNOT believe how she confuses and forgets everything from one minute to the next … I felt as if I had been put through a dozen mangles, but it was a colossal relief to have got it off my chest…..and I now hope to be also relieved of a headache that has become a constant companion, these last weeks……
>
> … we went to Carnegie to hear the Maestro in Beethoven 1 and 9 … No. 1 was a dream of beauty and perfection. Last mov't of 9 simply terrific, but I felt his tempi were definitely 'driven' in the other mov'ts….I can't forget Furtwängler's 9th in the Albert H….. However, it was a magnificent concert and 'just what we needed'.

Cesar brought Henry Colbert to meet Myra on 31st March. 'I liked him very much,' she wrote, 'and he was absolutely understanding. When I explained my feelings for A. after these 30 years he said "After all, we have to live with ourselves." I was quite touched and there was no question of an argument about my attitude and loyalty to A. … Cesar stayed on for a chat, and I have told him that it will all probably be a case of this time, some time, etc…..but I think my vehicles will wait for me…… in the maelstrom of perfidy, pillarage, profanity, pornography, and pestilency of the managerial world here, these two little men seem pure, peaceful, positive, practical and pleasant moreover…..'

Cesar, learning a whole new job aged 68, became an employee of Annie's company, taking responsibility for Myra's tours, and a second whack of commission on Myra's fees. But Myra was relieved: '… my headache has gone and between now and even one year hence, there must be some development with A!!'

There was. By the time Myra returned for her 1953 tour, Annie Friedberg had passed away.

A Question of Faith

One of the more surprising issues preoccupying Myra was, if not exactly a religious conversion, then a type of spiritual awakening. The catalyst was Reverend Ted Ferris. The rector of Boston's Trinity Episcopal Church, he was a trustee of the Boston Symphony Orchestra and a keen composer and pianist, besides writing prolifically on matters of faith.

He first came backstage to meet her in 1946, on Saz's invitation; a devoted Christian, Saz was overjoyed by the possibility of Myra becoming one too. Ferris used to preach in New York during the Holy Week services at St Bartholemew's on Park Avenue; Myra would go to hear him. According to McKenna, one year she went to the midday services every day for a week. Myra did not mention this in her diaries. She was neither the first Jewish musician, nor the last, to whom a broadly Christian outlook did not seem incompatible with her native religion.

Ferris had had his fair share of adversity. Blind in one eye since birth, he became deaf in one ear due to a childhood illness, though he never let either issue keep him away from his church or his music. Myra would have appreciated his support for admitting women delegates to an Episcopalian General Convention in 1952 (not enough others followed suit) and his open-hearted, down to earth view of theology. His admirers loved him for his lack of dogmatism.

For example, one popular sermon was headed simply: 'When Things Don't Go Well.' Its main points, quoted in *The Preacher's Commentary* (2010), are essentially common sense and it is easy to see how they would have chimed with Myra, after the challenges she had encountered: 'Remember, there are people who became great facing what you must now face. Say, "I don't know how I'm going to handle this, but I can. I know that from sources of which I am not conscious help will come, not necessarily the help I ask for, but help that I know nothing about right now will rise in me, will appear suddenly from all sorts of unexpected places."'[2]

Myra did not wear her faith on her sleeve any more than she wore her heart. She mentioned it only rarely, and then in innocuous comments about providence, or a divine helping hand in a concert that had gone well. Stephen Kovacevich, a committed Catholic when he studied with Myra, recalls just one occasion when she told him quietly that she was glad he was a believer in 'the Lord'.[3]

It was only to Ferris himself that she wrote about it, even if he did not always write back. Around 1958, he began to send her recordings of his sermons, and once made her the topic of an address to the American Guild of Organists ('1400 organists?!!' Myra wrote). She told him that his sermons never failed to give her 'Vision and Faith'.[4] Yet when they met they rarely discussed religious matters. Ferris told McKenna that he could only recall one conversation in which the topic was directly raised.

Saz and Marj encouraged Myra to consider being baptised into the Church of England, but she balked at that, aware of the forced conversions of so many Jewish people across the centuries, and not wishing to appear to desert her own people when their persecution was still so widespread. Ferris encouraged her to be true to herself; that was the advice she needed, and she refrained from formal conversion.

Perhaps it came full circle to the inspiration behind music itself: the religious attitude to art espoused by Bach, Mozart and Beethoven and handed on through their legacy. To them, music was not only as serious as faith, but in some cases indivisible from it. Myra counted Matthay among such people – she once described him as one of the greatest Christians she knew – and her playing was filled with the values she associated with faith. She shared this outlook with fellow artists who might not have espoused organised religion, yet whose music-making resonated with profound devotion. Myra's wholistic stance towards art, spirituality and political issues places her in the select company of Casals, Furtwängler and, of course, 'Maestro' Toscanini.

33 1/3 RPM

The recording industry entered a new era in 1948, when the invention of the Long Playing Record, spinning at 33 1/3 rpm, liberated musicians from squeezing a work onto multiple four-minute sides. One of the first pieces Myra revisited in the new format was her trusty Schumann Piano Concerto. With the Philharmonia Orchestra under Rudolf Schwarz, she recorded it in December 1952; it was released later on Angel Records.

It is a great-hearted performance, displaying Myra's refulgent sound and elegant phrasing. It employs, too, some very relaxed speeds, which she and Schwarz exploit for contrast, offsetting profound introspection with powerful octaves and stormy passagework. The finale is relatively stately, yet never weighty: while it has dignity rather than fire, she keeps her touch light. The orchestra is more assertive than that of her earlier studio recording, while Myra's playing is perhaps more authoritative, with long-spun threads of logical development, expertly balanced inner voices and beautifully smooth trills. There are also a few unintrusive slips. How well or otherwise she was feeling at the time is impossible to gauge; about three months later she was hospitalised for her ongoing gall bladder problem.

That autumn and winter she played all five Beethoven concertos with the LPO and Boult at the RFH. Boult remarked later how well she conveyed the composer's artistic development through the series, and he was touched when she gave him a copy of *The Life of George V* inscribed: 'This book, with my love and gratitude, seals the importance of No. 5.'[5] She also gave a recital in St George's Guildhall, King's Lynn, which the Queen Mother drove up from Sandringham to hear.

Her chief worry was her American visa: the new US McCarran immigration law was holding it up. It stipulated that any person arriving to work in the United States could obtain the necessary permit only after their 'American sponsors' had applied to the local justice department. Myra had been to the US around 30 times and had never had to face such a thing before.

Since the onset of the Cold War, the US had been bristling over the perceived threat of communism. Senator Joseph McCarthy was conducting campaigns of intimidation, which amounted to purges, against prominent figures suspected of being communist party members, having communist sympathies, or being sympathetic to the USSR. Among those targeted, alongside Charlie Chaplin, Orson Welles and the poet Langston Hughes, were contacts of Myra's, including Muriel Draper and Aaron Copland. The FBI also kept an 800-page file on the young conductor Leonard Bernstein.

In practical terms, the implementation of the new law caused serious backlogs. Saz applied to renew Myra's visa a fortnight before their planned departure, but everything was delayed. Among Myra's engagements would be the US premiere of Howard's Piano Concerto; Howard was going too and was similarly affected, but affably told *The Daily Telegraph* paper he assumed that in the end everything would be all right. (No wonder he was such an excellent, calm partner to Myra at the National Gallery.)

When Myra finally reached America on 28th January 1953, most things were all right. She had both the visa and Saz; the only glitch was that Howard had indeed had to postpone his departure – but because he had flu. Besides attending Myra's concerto performance at Carnegie Hall, he was to give some duo concerts and broadcasts with Yfrah Neaman.

At the docks the agent who greeted Myra was not Annie, but Cesar, together with the Steinways; the same day she saw friends including Marjorie Yates, Dorothy Shepard and the Parsonnets, whose son, Victor, had just won a special research grant. Pondie came to lunch. Alec Sherman and Gina Bachauer sent 50 gladioli.

With Cesar taking control, there were structures to be sorted out and plans to be pencilled. Myra wrote home: 'We explored possibilities of the future and we are hopeful.' Cesar wanted to carry on under the name of Friedberg Management and, with Annie's former assistant, Lilian Knapp, would handle all Myra's 'doonings', but 'two seemingly nice young men' who were already established concert managers would share the space and expenses.

Myra writes, rather surprisingly: 'It all looks very hopeful, and I like the idea of ending my career as I began it over here.' But with Bruno Walter calling to ask her to play Mozart, an 'end' seemed unlikely. She was planning the 1954 tour; and further good news arrived that there would be a Casals Festival that summer. Moreover, at dinner Myra and Saz felt 'bewildered with steak'. Nearly eight years after the end of the war, food was still rationed in Britain. 'I had better not describe the meal we had.... it would hardly be fair.'

Not an Outrage

Howard's Concerto for Piano and String Orchestra had been commissioned for the Festival of Britain by CEMA in Northern Ireland; Howard had given the world premiere on 22nd June 1951 and Myra played it at the RFH with the LPO under Boult on 29th May 1952. For Howard, the American premiere by Myra in Carnegie Hall should have been a major career highlight. New York was, to many, the heart of the artistic world, especially while the musical centres of Europe were struggling in the aftermath of the war.

The concerto, in three movements à la Mozart, would not have disgraced 1920s neoclassicism: it is concise, economical and – a word becoming anathema to post-war new music – tuneful. The first rehearsal was on 3rd February, with Efrem Kurtz conducting: 'He had really studied the score and was full of enthusiasm,' Myra wrote. 'At 2.0 we all trooped over to Carnegie H., the orchestra [the New York Philharmonic] gave me a touching welcome, and we had a most enjoyable and constructive rehearsal, in spite of the fact that the orch. was reading it for the first time … Howardie was quite excited, and so was I, especially after all my misgivings.'

On the day of the premiere, 5th February, Kurtz rehearsed Berlioz for so long that only half an hour was left to work on the concerto. 'Everyone did their best, but of course it was somewhat hectic and I didn't attempt to conceal my ANGER….. Poor Yfrah, who was turning pages, turned ashy pale as well…… but was still thrilled to hear the concerto with this orchestra.' But by evening all was well: 'A wonderful audience … a really overwhelming success. There was a real quality of listening in the whole hall and a burst of the warmest spontaneous applause. H. had to come on and bow 3 or 4 times, and I felt quite "teary". The orchestra played it con amore and were so nice to Howard. … The only fly in the ointment was having to stay on through the endless Berlioz in order to see the seething crowds at the end of the concert. I felt it incumbent on me to stay with H. otherwise people would have said "Where's the bride….or perhaps Grandma"????'

After the repeat performance the next afternoon, she noted: 'These two tremendously enthusiastic audiences and the real interest Howard's concerto has aroused cancel out the idiotic critics, who notoriously cannot tolerate any modern work that is not an outrage to the ear.'

The New York Times interviewed Howard and quoted him saying that in England the desire to write 'shocking' music was on the wane. English composers, he suggested, were becoming 'as tradition-conscious as Ralph Vaughan Williams. After a period in which German influence was strong and the most honored names in English music were Handel and Mendelssohn, English composers are rediscovering their national music heritage.' He commented: 'I am a firm believer in tonal music. It is hard to organize a work on a large scale without the help of tonality.'[6]

This ran contrary to the prevailing mood, especially in New York. That same month even William Walton's Violin Concerto, with John Corigliano as soloist, was sniffily dismissed there for 'flightiness'. Olin Downes in *The New York Times* termed Howard's concerto 'an undistinguished composition full of clichés and past periods'[7], although *The Herald Tribune* suggested: 'He has written ecstatically and with wonderfully practised skill.'[8] Myra reported: 'Everyone has been furious about them, but Howard is completely philosophical and says it is exactly what he expected.'

Myra moved straight on to play the Beethoven 'Emperor' Concerto, again with Kurtz. After a rehearsal, a member of the orchestra asked her how she managed to have so much pep in the morning. She replied with poise: 'I am playing with the N. Y. Philharmonic.'

'Pondie asks if I feel "queer" on concert days, and this is one of them...... I hated myself so intensely that I seriously thought everyone would welcome my demise.... My "Pinup" cable [from Ronald Colman] was a great help.' Howard's presence, turning the pages, helped too; and Myra's mood brightened afterwards when Otto Klemperer, who had been listening, called to request a meeting.

The legendary conductor, long exiled from Germany, arrived with his daughter on 11th February; Howard and Myra entertained them together. Klemperer had been in hospital for eight months with a broken hip after slipping on some ice; he was still walking with crutches and was obliged to conduct sitting down. Myra found him 'rather a tragic figure' and was disappointed, too, that visa laws were preventing him from coming to Europe that season. Days later, she also saw Walter, who had given a Mozart performance 'beautiful beyond words' and agreed to perform Myra's favourite K271 with her.

Greiner, with trepidation, asked if she would agree to be televised for the Steinway centenary celebrations that year: 'Apparently, Horowitz, Arthur Rubinstein and I must play our own version of Happy Birthday, fortunately not to last MORE than a minute and a half.' Then Gina Bachauer came down with facial neuralgia and Myra agreed to replace her, playing the 'Emperor' Concerto for the second time in a week, with Alec Sherman conducting.

Devastating news, however, arrived from London. Kathleen Ferrier's cancer had spread. She tried to keep the extent of it concealed from her colleagues, but while she was singing Gluck's *Orfeo ed Euridice* at Covent Garden, horrific pain had struck her as a bone in one leg partially disintegrated. She had struggled on to the end, after which some morphine was administered. It was her last performance.

'This morning,' Myra wrote on 13th February, 'we read in *The Times* of Kathleen and what must have been a heartbreaking scene at Covent Garden, at her 2nd performance of Orpheus. I had not wanted to mention it to Walter, in the middle of his concert, but he already knew about her. He spoke of her in such a deeply moving way, and feels that she is one of the greatest people of our century.' Walter and Ferrier's 1952 recording with the Vienna Philharmonic and tenor Julius Patzak of Mahler's *Das Lied von der Erde* has achieved a rare status, often cited as one of the greatest recordings ever made; many cannot help hearing the last song,

'Das Abschied', as Ferrier's own farewell. Myra found it difficult to concentrate on her last-minute Beethoven: 'With Kathleen on my mind, these days have been rather a nightmare.'

In Chicago, it turned out that Kubelik was unwell and still in Amsterdam, though he later returned ('He is such a dear'). Here Myra found herself faced with a piano bench 'so high that I was almost catapulted into the bowels of the rather small instrument ... its shrieking tone made up for its miniature stature.' It was 'tamed' in time for her to perform Mozart's B flat major Concerto K595, with the assistant conductor, George Schick.

'My, my,' said Myra. '.... Mozart is not easy....but I must own that I have never enjoyed the B. flat so intensely. The slow movement in a large hall is peculiarly and terribly moving, and everyone entered into the gay spirit of the last mov't. ... Mozart is far more exhausting than a couple of Brahms B flats......'

Her Mozart often seems the perfect balance of wit and profundity. She told Albert Goldberg her thoughts on interpreting the composer:

> 'I always make it a point to leave something undone, or unpractised so the performance will be spontaneous and fresh. I try to get it note perfect, but in Mozart one must leave a special margin for improvisation as it were. One must approach each work anew every time one plays it. The beauty in Mozart is so hard to capture because the moods change so quickly. His gaiety is so touching and some of his other moods so poignant that in the gayer moments you have to hear the cork come out of the bottle, as if you absolutely had to be gay or die. A favourite among the concertos? There are two or three which are not quite as great as the others, but all the rest are a revelation. I care least for the popular 'Coronation'. While I was preparing it I was hypnotised by the thought that it was not at all by Mozart. You go on and on with scales in Mozart – always there is something special about them. But this seemed like something you buy by the yard.[9]

Myra spent her birthday on the train to Cincinnati; there, she found the Terrace Plaza Hotel inundated with flowers from Steinways, five dozen yellow roses and four dozen red ('who should count?????') – though the rooms reminded her of the Fritz Lang film *Metropolis*, full of ultra-modern fittings. 'It was all air-conditioned, and we found that it was not allowed to open a window ... There wasn't a bed to be seen until you put on a switch, and then they glided out of the walls in a most sinister fashion.'

Plans for 1954 were in progress, roast beef had been eaten, concerts with Vladimir Golschmann were complete plus a return train trip to Chicago – when on 8th March Myra's diaries abruptly stopped.

Galling Surgery

Tell-tale signs of a gall bladder problem had perhaps loomed when Main Bocher took Myra out for a dinner that she found much too rich. But it was only around 24th March that she revealed to Howard what was going on. After Marj had sent word that he was unwell, Myra wrote to him:

> We have been keeping our evil tidings from each other! I hadn't the heart to phone you the day you left to tell you that my G. B. had assumed the proportions of the Dome of St Paul's & that in spite of much discomfort the Dr thought I could get through my recital the next eve – It was all far too confusing!
>
> I am positively elated this a.m. as the infection has subsided sufficiently for me to go into the Wesley Memorial Hospital … & by the time you receive this, your M. H. will probably have been delivered of a fat unhealthy, cross-eyed G. B. weight 150 pounds.
>
> I am not assuming these good spirits – it is going to be such a blessed relief to be rid of the eternal pain & uncertainty. … Of course, it was a shock to have to abandon the rest of my tour - & Cesar is being extraordinarily nice & good about it all…

She had given her Chicago recital despite considerable pain and a high fever. The hall constructed a special stage entrance so that she did not have to walk up any stairs and her doctor, Gabriel Marquardt, sat in the wings with Saz in case of emergencies. Myra managed to perform a substantial programme culminating in the Schubert B flat Sonata, followed by encores late into the evening.

The operation took place on 25th March; had she left it any longer, Saz commented, the condition could have led to complications like peritonitis. Chicago's radio stations changed their schedules for that morning and played her recordings. The hotel manager, Otto Eitel, insisted that she and Saz should be his guests while she recovered; they stayed until May. 'In all the world,' Myra wrote in a letter to the *Chicago*

Tribune, 'there is no city that could have shown a bigger heart or warmer hospitality to me in an hour of need.'[10]

Recuperation took longer than Myra would have liked. She was scheduled to play at the RFH on 29th May, but when she got home Howard noticed that she was still feeling a bit wobbly; he was further concerned about her because several of her old friends had recently fallen ill or died.

The RFH performance was among eight concerts scheduled there to celebrate the imminent coronation of Queen Elizabeth II, which took place at Westminster Abbey on 2nd June. Myra was to play Beethoven's Third Concerto with the LPO and Boult; in the second half William Walton was conducting his oratorio *Belshazzar's Feast*. She went ahead. *The Telegraph* remarked only that it was 'a restrained performance only occasionally marred by rhythmic instability'[11]. She was not well enough to travel to Prades in mid June; missing the chance to work with Casals again would have been especially galling. Her place was taken by Eugene Istomin. She did, however, play Beethoven's Fourth Concerto at the Proms on 17th September with the BBC Symphony Orchestra under Sargent. Still, she was only playing concertos, entailing about half an hour on stage, and not full-length solo recitals.

It continued to be a tragic year. Annie was dead. On 3rd October Arnold Bax died of heart failure during a visit to County Cork. Just five days later, on 8th October, Kathleen Ferrier died at University College Hospital. She was just 41. Myra attended her memorial service on 25th November, together with 1,500 people including Irene Scharrer, Sir Laurence and Lady Olivier and Benjamin Britten.

Surrounded by times of sorrow and without recitals to provide an outlet, Myra took the opportunity to make some recordings, beginning with Beethoven's Sonata Op. 110 in A flat major, on 1st-2nd October. She followed it with Op. 109 in E major on 17th-19th November. The latter was released on HMV the following October, but Op. 110 not until 1959. Beethoven's final trilogy was becoming ever more important to her; still, she approached it with enormous caution, and regrettably never recorded Op. 111.

These recordings have been described as 'transcendental', with good reason: they are informed by her mix of wisdom, love, faith and a Beethovenian *innerlich* sensibility (introspection – a word she often used when working with Jelly). Pressed by John Amis to pick favourites among her recordings, she reluctantly mentioned Schumann's *Carnaval* and suggested that a few bars of Op. 109 were perhaps acceptable.

But then on 22nd and 23rd October she turned to the Schumann *Etudes symphoniques*, which she had played since her youth. Schumann had dedicated it to Matthay's composition teacher, William Sterndale Bennett; Uncle Tobs had a soft spot for it, which Myra inherited. This is a sedate account – one could wish she had done it 20 years earlier – but something extraordinary happens in the penultimate variation, perhaps the dark before the finale's dawn: a rare moment in which Myra seems to use her velvet touch and unerring balance of voices to reveal her innermost heart, contemplating the depths of the abyss. In the finale the ghosts are banished by high spirits, elegance and poise – but Saz selected the preceding variation as an example of Myra's art at its finest. It is hard to discount the fact that this recording took place just two weeks after Ferrier's death.

Meetings, Greetings and Snow

Myra was back in America by 22nd December. In January she wrote to Howard: 'I don't care for my playing at all, but as Pondie would say 'I am not here for my pleasure'?????' She was facing an internal imperative to change her own approach – not to her profession, but to her actual playing.

On the arriving ship, Myra was woken for morning tea, 'disturbing me in a dream in which Irene (Scharrer) got shut up in a drawer of Swee's desk'. Shades of the strange Madame Pugnati nightmares, perhaps; and Myra would have been aware that new, younger stars were rising to prominence. The Proms season had hosted, for instance, Phyllis Sellick and Livia Rev. Myra, along with Moiseiwitsch, Curzon and Solomon, now represented the old guard and, indeed, a style that was to some beginning to sound old-fashioned – even if, compared with the generation of Cortot, Lhévinne and Friedman, Myra was no romantic, but a resolutely non-wayward, 20th-century performer.

The LP era was heightening a growing reaction against romanticism; some observers felt that pianists were pursuing technical and textual exactitude with an eye on recording for posterity, rather than, for instance, capturing the fleeting poetry of an inspired moment. Pianists known for their perfectionism, such as Arturo Benedetti Michelangeli and Alfred Brendel, were in the ascendant. Horowitz, suffering from depression, withdrew from performing in 1953 and did not return until 1965 – his longest spell away from the stage, if far from the only one. Myra was, in a way, caught in the middle: too modern for the 'golden age', too old-school for some of the younger keyboard lions.

The notion that piano playing was becoming overly clinical, however, was only a broad trend and many artists bucked it. A remarkable group of Russian musicians, notably Sviatoslav Richter and Emil Gilels, transcended all fashions, though their visits to the West were strictly circumscribed by the Soviet authorities. And soon the 1960s would see not only the rise of the coolly magisterial Maurizio Pollini, but also the grand-scale visions of Daniel Barenboim, the mercurial Martha Argerich and the fiery spirit of Stephen Kovacevich, Myra's star pupil.

Myra had left most of her luggage in the Laurelton basement since March. Now she was ready to get back to business. She had a two-hour meeting with Cesar and told Howard that 'as long as we stop him booking me 8 times a week.....all will be well. We like him, and he has a comforting sense of humour.'

She and Saz were reunited with Pondie, whose age and infirmity did not stop her donning blue and gold lamé for the occasion. They spent Christmas with her. Myra managed a little practising and on 27th December spoke to Bruno Walter, telling him that she would like to rehearse every day for a week, for the pleasure of playing with him. Beryl arrived soon afterwards and there ensued many games of Bridge and a sumptuous dinner with Julia Steinway.

She met Walter on 3rd January, 'playing Mozart 271 and talking and talking':

> He was most illuminating and interesting about 'ornaments', calling them the 'spice' of the music, and how man valued spices more than gold. He believes that variety is the spice of life, and that, within certain principles, we must use our own discrimination; all very refreshing. He looks well, and talked of so many interesting things in the world. I was quite pleased that there was no time for 449, which means another visit to him, at his hotel.

That second meeting took place on 10th January: 'His tempi of the last movements were extremely fast, but I hope he will moderate a little, on the platform.... We begin rehearsing with the orchestra tomorrow. He has opened new doors, but oh my! how difficult it is to play Mozart????'

The record company HMV's sluggishness proved an unwelcome contrast; at a meeting, Myra was infuriated to learn, after many months, that her recording of the Schumann Concerto could not fit on one side of an LP:

> It is going to be released some time this Spring by itself, which could have happened a year ago ... At least they are going to announce the Beethoven Sonatas, but they will not come out until September, over here. We parted good friends, but I threatened to leave HMV!!!!! if this kind of thing continues.

The following day brought her first solo recital since Chicago the previous March:

> A funny day, wondering if I could possibly play in public... I practised VERY, VERY SLOWLY and then to my astonished relief, I felt almost AT EASE when I began "delighting"????the public at Paterson, New Jersey. I can't say that I played to my satisfaction, but Saz, Beryl, the P's, Dorothy etc. were all rather excited. I even cooked up a few rusty encores ... And so the first bridge of the tour is crossed.

Her next meeting was with a 'very, very nice young conductor': George Hurst, who had conducted the LPO in London the previous season:

> Saz and I both fell for him, and of course I have promised to play with him, next June (again with L.P.O.). He has dreamt of doing Beethoven 4 with me, since he was in a Norfolk suit, so I agreed. He was born in Edinburgh and was evacuated to Toronto during the War. He is a professor at the Peabody Institute, Baltimore, and longs to rejoin his family, now living in London.

That night she went to Carnegie Hall to hear Stern play the Beethoven Violin Concerto conducted by George Szell. She told Howard:

> He, Isaac, played very beautifully, and gives one the feeling that he may develop into a really great player. S[zell] is VILE..... I intended to listen to Egmont Overture without any prejudice, but it was exactly like trying to cut a tough piece of steak with a completely blunt knife.....INFURIATING......

She also revealed that she had turned down an exotic invitation:

> I have had to decide not to go to Israel...... We have met several people here, some of them keen Zionists, and they all say that I would have to give myself time to have dysentery....... Apparently, most people ARE stricken there. As I have had to say NO again to

> Prades and Pau, it would be just too damnable to go to bed with Dioooooorrrrhhhheeeaaaa..... in Jerusalem..... It is very disappointing, but Gene thinks it is a real risk for me to have such tummy upsets, and I might be ill for months. It just isn't good enough, after these last years??? So that's that.

The Walter concert on 14th January was accompanied by snow flurries, which failed to deter the audience. 'A great experience to play Mozart with Walter ... I was terribly moved by Walter's enthusiasm, and look forward to tomorrow.' It did not disappoint: 'The 2nd performance is always freer and I enjoyed it more than I thought possible ... Walter and I were nearly in tears at the end of the slow movement.' The third, on 17th January, made her lament that these concerts were over: 'They have all been a compensation for all the miseries of a "professional" career.... To play Mozart with him is a glimpse into the better world, and the orchestra again played with such sympathy. It is unexpected to find the quality of real chamber music in a virtuoso orchestra, like the [NY] Philharmonic.'

Despite her health issues, Myra was trying to follow her usual intense schedule. The day after the Walter concert she headed for Washington DC, enduring a stressful train trip and later a piano with a keyboard lid that kept falling down. 'Dismay of Diva' she wrote. The recital on 19th January was in what she called 'Constitutional Hall', which seats about 4,000: 'I felt as if I had gone back more than nine cats' lives playing the Chopin Fune[ral March] Sonata, but everybody seemed to enjoy it, and I was relieved to find I could play it fairly passably... '

In Pittsburgh, her piano for her concerto at Mount Lebanon arrived three hours late. She had been unable to practise, and feared a notoriously snobby audience ('bare fronts and backs were rife, amid a flutter of tulle') – but to her joy, her page-turner was Albert Goldberg, whom she had met in Perpignan. 'I played better than I dared to expect in the circs...inspired by Goldberg and the thought of Pablo.' A giant Country Club reception for 250 people crowned the evening; there, Myra 'made an inspired and vapid little impromptu reply to the sickening eulogies'. All she really wanted was a cup of hot soup.

Back in New York, Myra went with Main Bocher to visit Katherine ('Kit') Cornell; a few days later, Myra and Saz enjoyed her performance in 'a semi-thriller about the United Nations'. They treated themselves to a limousine there and back; afterwards, 'WE SAT ON HIGH STOOLS IN

THE DRUG SHOP AND HAD HOT CHOCOLATE AND FRIED EGG SANDWICHES.'

Another theatre outing reunited Myra with Ruth Draper, who was giving a short season of her one-woman show in New York for the first time since 1947. Myra and Saz went on 30th January and witnessed the monologist holding the audience spellbound for two hours. 'In spite of having heard them [Draper's monologues] all before, I found myself sitting on the edge of my seat all the time. Everything had been amusing until the final Monologue *Vive la France 1940*. We were all reduced to streaming tears and went back stage to see her "in all states"..... She is a very great artist.'

In New Haven Thornton Wilder sent Myra flowers; and she was pleased to see Bruce Simonds and his family. But the red-letter date was 6th February: Myra's return to Carnegie Hall. Thrilled by a giant ovation and pleased to see a large number of young people present, she played the Chopin B flat minor Sonata, the Bach Fantasia in C minor and French Suite in G major, Haydn's Sonata No. 7 in D major and the Schumann *Etudes symphoniques*. Friends crowded in and 'by bed-time, we could hardly move for flowers.....It is all very touching, and people are extremely faithful, and perhaps this mad life is worth while.....' According to *The New York Times*, the tug of the Hess magic was undimmed:

> Part of that magic derives from the fact that Dame Myra plays so personally. Thus one almost sees the music as well as hears it. The joyousness in the two fast movements of Haydn's D major Sonata, for instance, were apparent yesterday, not only in the swift, silvery filigree of the sound, but also in the evident delight that the pianist herself took from the music ... Personal as her style is, however, she nearly always speaks through the music, for she has too much integrity as a musician to impose herself on top of it. Thus, because she is a woman who has clearly experienced life deeply, she brings both the riches of her nature and her individual insights to help in the realization and the projection of everything she plays.[12]

In Detroit she played with Paul Paray – 'very nice and friendly, but I expect I have been spoiled for a long time by having played with Bruno Walter.... It is a case of Alt-wien versus Vive la France.' But Chicago, the city of her operation, brought an 'overwhelming reception'. 'Saz said they gave me a standing ovation, but I thought they were getting up to go home....'

Her surgeon and doctor were there: 'Saz nearly died when the former greeted her with "I am really worried about her". When asked why, he said, "she is MUCH too strong"... Of course, neither of them had ever seen me well, or anything but half dead, and they couldn't believe their eyes.' Dr Marquardt offered her a check-up, but Myra replied that it would not be very convenient – and, as she would have said, that was that. Myra and Saz were 'immensely relieved to have the ghosts of last year happily laid, and a coincidence perhaps that I should play the Funeral March myself, this year'.

About to leave Chicago temporarily, the pair had a brainwave. The piano would stay in Myra's room, locked, until their return the following week and could be a perfect safe deposit box for certain treasures they did not want to take to New York. 'SO....encased in my piano are: one pot of marmalade, two large boxes of chocolates, and a bottle of water-softener ... I only hope that Steinways' won't be moved to think of having the piano tuned while we are away.'

It Shouldn't Happen to a Pianist

On 24th February Myra 'launched' Beethoven's Op. 111 in the relatively safe environment of Jacksonville, Illinois. A lady chauffeur, Janet, drove her and Saz 240 miles from Chicago, which took most of the day – and they spent most of the night driving back afterwards, arriving just before 4am. 'It seemed a mad thing to do, motoring nearly 10 hours, with a concert thrown in, but our insanity was justified when on 25 February we finally woke to a sharp blizzard. The roads would have been frightful...' Another good reason was that the hotel was throwing a birthday party for Myra, complete with 'a marvellous cake, with sugar roses AND leaves, standing on a revolving musical box'.

She had a few days to rest before going to South Bend. But there, her piano failed to show up, 'lost somewhere on a railway siding'. The Chicago branch of Steinways sent a replacement; waiting for it 'nearly gave the tuner nervous prostration'. Part of the town's Notre Dame University, where she was playing, was dedicated to the Naval Reserve Officers' Training Establishment; her dressing room was the Captain's quarters. She played Patience on its desk until it was time to dress. 'It was one of those occasions when one had to enjoy playing. (the piano!)' she wrote.

On 4th March, Myra played in Minneapolis to 4,820 children. This time, the piano turned up, damaged: 'I was quite certain I had gone mad. All the notes sounded normally, but the touch felt so odd that I could hardly control a crotchet, let alone a semiquaver.’ By miraculous coincidence, a technician from Steinway’s in New York was there, working on the university’s pianos. He discovered a crack in the base: ‘…the whole mechanism WAS jumping up and down. Quite obviously, the poor instrument had been dropped by the railway movers. This nice man spent many hours, with glue and nails, and [on 5th March] when I arrived for 2nd rehearsal, he assured me that the piano was in perfect playing order … it was the hand of Heaven that Mr Desche should be in M’appolis, instead of N.Y., especially as he was due to leave the next day.’

In Winnipeg there was a string of interviews, a snowstorm, old friends to entertain and a concert in which Myra made her audience sing while she harmonised ‘God Save the Queen’. In Columbus, she encountered a train that ‘columbed and columbed for 7 hours’ and a hotel ‘seething with Girl Guides, commercial travellers and base-ball players … On account of aforesaid Girl G’s in the concert hall, I couldn’t see my piano or practise until 5.0. … I practised ffffffff while innumerable huskies reorganised the place … and I only once said SHUT UP when they dropped the umpteenth wooden chair…..’ This was a repeat of the concert with Paray; afterwards Myra shot back to the hotel to change, pack, eat a sandwich, and catch the 11.40pm train. The tour, she commented, was ‘rewarding, but extremely strenuous … Why Swee doesn’t burn my clothes, I can’t think.’

Most significantly, she was playing in her programme of the last three Beethoven sonatas. ‘NOT my favourite day,’ she wrote on the morning of the Chicago performance; but her anxiety was rewarded with enthusiasm from her faithful audience. At the end, Myra promised them all the encores they wanted, but next season, saying there was nothing she could add to these three great works. ‘They were musicians enough to have complete, and instant understanding, and they all stood as a final sign of appreciation, and Farewell.’

This explanation became Myra’s habitual (though not universal) way of ending this programme. Many concert-goers on both sides of the Atlantic would hear her explain: ‘What could follow that?’

In Toronto the 3,000-seat auditorium was so full that there was no ticket for Saz, which had never happened before. ‘As at Winnipeg, they all rose to greet the aged Dame … My prog. included Op. 109 and I was glad to give it a 2nd airing before N.Y.’ She lunched with the conductor Boyd Neel, who had performed often at the National Gallery concerts and was now Dean of Music at the university. But back in New York, once again the piano had not arrived…

Her Carnegie Hall Beethoven trilogy was on the afternoon of 27th March. Myra spent the morning on slow practice; after fuelling up on a boiled egg, she donned her best Mainbocher gown, ready for Gene to drive her and Saz to the stage door:

> I shall never know what happened, but instead of being overpoweringly nervous, the Lord seemed to take charge. I can't say that I began to be satisfied, but I know I have never played better in public. There was a wonderful audience, and they seemed to be listening in a very special way, and I was almost overwhelmed by the response and enthusiasm … somehow this one concert has made my whole career more worth while.

A couple of days later, Cesar brought 'VERY gratifying results of Sat's concert (box office…..)'. The net income, $1,961.60, was nevertheless smaller than the amount she had made from the 6th February recital, which had brought in $2,715.17 (equivalent in 2023 to about $30,000).

Meanwhile Cesar had asked her to do an extra concert on 17th April: 'a Schnabel Memorial [Schnabel had died in 1951] … Am going to do Brahms 5tet, with a 4tet called the Juilliard, supposedly v. g. [very good] and will also play Beethoven 109 (by myself).'

One day her friend Marjorie Yates played her a recording from the radio of her Beethoven 'Emperor' Concerto performance the previous year. 'I was really amazed at my pre-gall-bladder vitality,' Myra commented. 'Looking back, I can't believe it could have been me…. I would take exception to some of the things I did; ne'ertheless, I was rather cheered by it.'

The final all-Beethoven concert was in Boston, where she and Saz stayed at the Ritz, in flower-filled rooms where they could enjoy a tureen of scrambled eggs with cream. This city, too, was full of medical ghosts for Myra – 'It seemed a century since I had walked on that platform normally, but all went well…'

On the last page of her diary, following a discussion with Cesar over lunch, Myra articulated her impressions of America in the McCarthy era as the tensions of the Cold War bit:

> It is a terribly disquieting time here, but the majority of serious minded people are only too acutely aware of America's responsibility, and the urgency of international understanding. They are appalled by

> the concentration on the petty Macarthy [sic] squabbles, when there are such terrific issues at stake. Most of them look to England for guidance, in spite of everything one may read in the papers. We do wish everyone at home could realise the balance of public opinion here, as it is probably never reported faithfully, and is really a hopeful sign. Their general anxiety about their Government's behaviour and policy is extreme.

All is Harmony?

Myra was happy to be home – and her new house offered its own encouragements. Earlier that year she had told an interviewer how much she loved living next door to Lord's Cricket Ground: 'I have never had applause when I practise. So now, when I am at the piano and hear people outside clapping their hands, I shall get up from the piano stool, go to the window and take a bow.'[13]

Less welcome was the continuing mend-and-make-do mentality compared to the grand-scale solutions across the ocean. Myra sometimes had to be supremely resourceful. One day in Liverpool she had to insist that the legs of a piano stool were sawn down before she could play, since no adjustable one was available. 'The situation seemed desperate,' *The Daily Express* reported, 'until Dame Myra came out with the bright idea: "Chop a bit off the legs." So the search was switched to a saw and soon the stool was reduced to a convenient height.' A cheery headline declared: 'NOW – ALL IS HARMONY.'[14]

There were joys beyond the cricket in this English summer – notably Mozart's Concerto K271 on 3rd May, and the promised Beethoven No. 4 on 25th June with George Hurst and the LPO, both at the RFH. 'Hers is not every musician's view, but it is entirely consistent with the piano's opening statement,' *The Times* said of the Beethoven, 'and the reading brings balm to the spirit.'[15] The Proms was celebrating its Diamond Jubilee; Myra appeared on 10th September with the LPO and Boult, performing Beethoven plus Howard's concerto. The latter won, again, faint praise.

Myra had stepped back from campaigning, but not from helping charities. She was eager to support a new Kathleen Ferrier Cancer Research Fund at University College Hospital. She, John Barbirolli, Hamish Hamilton, Laurence Olivier, Benjamin Ormerod and Bruno Walter announced it in a joint letter to *The Times*, praising the way Ferrier was loved and admired internationally 'for her greatness as an artist, for her indomitable gallantry and noble spirit'. Walter flew in to conduct part of the charity's inaugural concert at the RFH. Eventually the funds raised were transmuted into a singing scholarship in Ferrier's name. This was the genesis of the Kathleen Ferrier Award, which grew to be one of Britain's most significant singing competitions.

Myra did not perform at the Ferrier event, but she did appear in a Florence Nightingale Centenary Concert on 3rd June, playing the Schumann Concerto, with HRH The Princess Royal [Princess Mary] present. In addition, she, along with Vaughan Williams, agreed to join a committee set up by the pianist Yolanda Mero, executive director of the Hospital Veterans Fund, which in the US had organised 165,000 music lessons in American hospitals, mainly for long-staying patients: disabled ex-servicemen, or those with polio, tuberculosis or mental illnesses. Mero hoped to set up a similar scheme in Britain.

Having become adept at writing letters to newspapers, Myra had not quite lost the habit. She penned one to *The Daily Telegraph* on 6th September, this time about homeopathy, which had been in the news with the Boyd Medical Research Institute's discovery of 'potency energy', which was thought to vindicate the system:

> … For many years I have been a confirmed believer in homeopathy and was glad to pay tribute to the great work being done by Dr Boyd when I gave a concert, a few years ago, in aid of the Institute.
>
> I am sure it is vital to the interests of medical science that homeopathy should win even more worldwide recognition.

She was about to take her programme of the final three Beethoven sonatas to the RFH for the first time – on 10th October. The date's significance would not have escaped her: it was the 16th anniversary of her first National Gallery concert.

'London concert tradition demands that before we can declare the autumn recital season well and truly opened we must hear a piano recital by Dame Myra Hess,' *The Times* opined. The review went on somewhat equivocally: 'The earth did not yawn before us, nor the heavens open; we saw these things, but as if reflected in a glass …. Yet the recital was deeply enjoyable … Dame Myra's *mezza voce*, high on the keyboard, had a crystalline beauty, the mysterious trills were of surpassing eloquence, and the slow variations of Op. 109 and 111 lapped us with warm, loving tone.'[16]

But when, on 31st October, she played Beethoven's Concerto No. 3 with the LSO under Anthony Collins, a chirpy reviewer had to say that her 'characteristic suavity and feminine lightness of touch were much appreciated by the large audience'[17]. One could almost picture her, Saz and Marj, after nearly half a century of critics seeking feminine charm and lightness in music that needed other qualities, ceremoniously ripping the paper to shreds. When she had played the same work with the CBSO and Rudolf Schwarz in September, a review said that her 'superb' performance could 'still wipe any junior streamlined technique right out of the picture'.[18]

One of her last UK concerts that year, on 1st December, brought her together with Harry Blech and his London Mozart Players for the first time – an orchestra founded in 1949 which had largely grown out of the National Gallery series. Blech had been a violinist in the RAF orchestra when Myra had asked him to conduct one of the concerts; he never looked back. Now she played two Mozart concertos, K467 and K449.

Perhaps the most important thing she did in Britain in 1954, however, was a short recital on television for the BBC. This seems to be the only extant footage of her beyond Humphrey Jennings's wartime films. It is simply Myra and a piano in a studio, with no audience and no extraneous distractions.

The film, directed by Patricia Foy and screened on 20th October, was part of a series of TV recitals that also included Claudio Arrau, Gregor Piatigorsky, Gioconda de Vito, Moiseiwitsch, Stern and Menuhin. Anticipating it, *The Guardian*'s reporter hoped that the producer would realise 'that viewers do not generally like constant camera movement, but prefer to see the performer without frequent alterations of angle'.[19]

Sure enough, the camera angles are limited, showing Myra and her hands clearly at all times, without too much cutting in and out. Myra's stillness and focus would please the most stringent teacher of yogic meditation. She performs *Jesu Joy*, the second half of Beethoven Op. 110 (the arioso and fugue) and her transcription of the Adagio from the Bach Toccata, Adagio and Fugue in C major. She wears a plain black gown with lace sleeves, her jade amulet around her neck, the soft wings of her hair greying at her temples.

The sound has suffered with the years and the pitch fluctuates, but still Myra's mix of introspection and heroism, of searching and empathy, exerts an irresistible pull. In the Beethoven fugue, the stentorian climb of the left hand octaves near the climax offsets the tragic ariosos with granite-like certitude. The only sign that Myra is maybe less than comfortable is that after the last chord of the sonata she sits back abruptly, as if in relief.

After the Bach Adagio, she stands, faces the camera and, twisting a handkerchief between her fingers, announces: 'Bonsoir, or good night, to all my friends here and abroad' – banishing any vestigial anxiety with a smile away from the screen. Why she used a French greeting for a BBC broadcast is not clear, but this remains the only readily available film of her speaking to her audience.

Blood on the Keys

The ups and downs of Myra's 1955 American tour were worthy of the finest of Californian roller-coaster rides – but this was the last of her US visits that went without serious mishap.

Myra and Saz sailed into New York on 23rd December 1954 to find Rose Parsonnet, Sascha Greiner and Billy Steinway at the docks, with Cesar 'looking exactly like Arthur Askey'. The crossing had been smooth, their favourite restaurant had scattered rose petals on their table in welcome, and Main Bocher had made Myra a new dress, 'a most beautiful, simple and dignified creation of black crepe with satin panels at side', though its fit proved problematic and had to be redone ('Poor Main, "in all states")'.

Myra's diary involved much shorter entries than usual, perhaps because she was pacing herself. Fortunately Cesar had built in more days off for her between performances; she could relax and enjoy, for instance, a visit from the nonagenarian Pondie. She also sharpened up her card games: she and her friends decided to play Canasta for money, besides enjoying 'riotous cut-throat Bridge' chez Julia Steinway. (The typical winnings were under $2.)

On 8th January Myra swallowed some toast and coffee, then set out for Carnegie Hall. Throughout her recital she felt that 'the gods' were with her. 'In spite of my apprehension re familiar programme, the largest audience I have ever had. The whole hall, including standing room, sold out. Masses of young people and the serious attention throughout was most moving and inspiring. I cracked a finger in Paganini (Carnaval) and had to wipe the blood off the keyboard and lick my finger clean.'

The skin of Myra's hands tended to crack rather easily, with painful results that sometimes hindered her practising. It puzzled her friends and pupils, who had some bizarre theories about it, but there is probably a simple explanation: it was the middle of winter and her hands could have been painfully chapped. Perhaps she was inured to the cold after the wartime deprivations in London.

She was thrilled to see Pondie in the hall, 'holding court with friends and strangers', and Julia Steinway, who was 83 and still came back to the flower-filled hotel. The evening finished with a dinner party and Bridge: 'So that's that, and Saz says it could not be thatter.'

Next she could enjoy working with a new ensemble. The Budapest String Quartet's current members were not remotely Hungarian: they were four Russian-Jewish musicians, several from Odessa, who had been through many trials and tribulations individually and together, but had made dozens of recordings that cumulatively sold two million copies. They were at the peak of their considerable powers and Myra, playing with them for the first time, was singularly impressed. 'My, my, what a quartet. Had a wonderful afternoon,' she wrote after the rehearsal. They played Mozart's G minor Piano Quartet and the Brahms Quintet, with Beethoven's String Quartet Op. 59 No. 2 in between. For Myra the Brahms was a revelation: 'I don't think I have ever enjoyed a chamber work so much.'

Planning ahead, however, was a headache. There were rumours that the New York Philharmonic had cancelled its tours abroad; a manager from Georgia wanted Myra to 'travel and play every day for a week or two next year, and apparently my tour has got inextricably mixed with a ballet'; and 'we are being badgered about 1956, 7, 8, 9, ad infinitum'. She was thrilled by a new 'marvellous double-drive highway, with no crossroads, all the way to Boston'. There her recital turned out well, despite what Saz cryptically called 'murder most foul' beforehand – though the hotel, amid a January snowstorm, was too hot for Myra's liking, 'even turning off heat, opening windows and discarding blankets'.

In Washington DC, in brilliant sunshine, the White House looked whiter than ever. Myra was guest of honour at the city's Bohemians' Club, which ran a musicians' charity resembling the MBF at home. She was dreading the dinner – for more than 500 people at the Hotel Plaza – but she made a speech, then played Scarlatti, Brahms, Schubert and *Jesu, Joy* to crown the night's musical offerings (which also included the Saint-Saëns Septet and a performance by the tap-dancer Paul Draper, Muriel's son). Here Myra mentioned she had told 'the story of dear old Richard Aldrich ([New York] Times critic in 1922) being responsible for my ever having played *Jesu, Joy* in public'. The next day she headed for Baltimore to play the Brahms D minor Concerto – and was delighted to find George Hurst turning her pages.

In New York, she was to play the same concerto with the NY Philharmonic and Mitropoulos, in three concerts, one of which would be broadcast; back in town, she had a session on it with the unsinkable Carl Friedberg. 'As he knew Brahms, of course, it is always exciting to make music with him. He is 83, had been teaching all day, and left us at 7.15 to give yet one more lesson...'

Myra woke on the day of the first concert, 10th February, with a fever, feeling like 'mild death'. She remained 'in a kind of trance all day, struggling to the piano for an odd hour..... However, a Temp[erature] of 100 usually brings me luck, and although I hadn't the faintest idea whether I could play until I sat at the keyboard, all was well ... a terrific reception.' The repeat concert went better still, with Myra's temperature normal again. All she cancelled was a dinner out in favour of a quiet evening and Bridge with Benno and his wife.

On 13th February the concert was broadcast, and was then made into a record. 'Felt better, pretending to look forward to 3rd performance...... but somewhat dreading the fact that the Microphone AND Benno would both be there.....' Mitropoulos was eager to perform the concerto with her in London in October, if the date of Myra's recital at the RFH could be changed.

He was principal conductor at the Metropolitan Opera; the drama and passion he brought to operatic work was often reflected in his orchestral performances. The D minor Concerto blazes out of the recording huge and fiery, an epic poem in musical form. Yet Harold C. Schonberg's review for *The New York Times* trundled down well-worn tram lines:

> She played it as though she hadn't heard or read that the concerto is supposed to be for men only.
>
> She addressed herself to the music with considerable force, sounding out the heroic themes with a strongly assertive quality. There was nothing 'womanly' about her playing.
>
> Except that Dame Myra did not pound. She never does. Last night she drew a rich tone from the piano that was a superb vehicle for the rich keyboard writing. Her interpretation was that of an experienced artist and in the second movement, wondrously lyrical.[20]

Schonberg was probably being ironic; nobody had ever heard or read anywhere (at least, not anywhere trustworthy) that Brahms's First Concerto is for men only. And if Myra's Brahms does not reflect elements somehow expected in a female artist's playing, there was no reason it should.

In Madison, Wisconsin, Myra and Saz stayed with Edith Frank. It was a cold, damp February day and Edith, thinking that a cheery fire would provide a warm welcome, built one, but forgot to open the 'damper'. When Myra, Saz and their driver Janet arrived, the house was full of smoke. Myra responded cheerfully, 'Just as long as I'm not a singer.'

'It is "once in a blue moon" that I accept an invitation to stay in a private home during a tour,' Myra wrote in her letter thanking Edith, 'as so few people understand the stress & strain & concentration of public performing. But we knew you would be the perfect hostess with complete understanding, & I only hope we did not exhaust you with demands for soup, & more soup, & meals at all times of day & night! Our triumphant Canasta was the crowning point!!'[21]

She gave two recitals on consecutive days: first Op. 110 with the Schumann *Etudes symphoniques* and Bach, Mozart and Scarlatti – here she felt 'they look upon me as an old friend by now, and I felt exactly like one'. The next day was the Beethoven 'Moonlight' Sonata and Schumann's *Carnaval*, plus the same shorter works.

In Chicago she enjoyed an unexpected meeting with Wilhelm Backhaus and his wife, who were friendly with the Eitels of the Bismarck Hotel. 'It is years since we had met. He is having enormous successes with Beethoven recitals, after an absence of 30 years. He is 70, and looks 50.' She was impressed, too, by the Eitels' means of communicating with their son in Britain, recording conversations to send via airmail: 'We think we'll have to invest in machines, here, there, everywhere ????' More machines greeted her in East Lansing on 23rd February in the University Union Club: 'Beds came trundling out from the walls, and the air-conditioning sucked up sacks of dust on my concert dress.'

She celebrated her 65th birthday in Chicago. Breakfast appeared with a vase of red roses from the Eitels, plus a birthday cake set with her name and, tactfully, 18 candles, on a revolving plate that played 'Happy Birthday'. 'Apparently, the whole kitchen had been in an uproar of excitement, waiting for me to wake up...' That afternoon she held a hotel 'at home' for her friends, with white wine and cake.

It was a welcome respite before the arduous drive, around 240 miles, to Bloomington, Indiana, where she played at the university, the music school of which was gaining enviable repute: 'They have one of the most beautiful concert halls imaginable, of which they are duly proud but not boastful.'

Her Chicago recital, on 1st March, was disrupted by what she took to be a camera flash in the second row. It was in fact a silver pendant worn by her friend the philanthropist Judith Waller. 'It caught the light, and my eye, every time she breathed. Someone must have sat in front of it for the 'Moonlight', which was a relief.' Fortunately Judith had asked to see Myra in the interval as she would have to leave quickly at the end. Myra, true to form, spoke up: 'I am afraid she was very embarrassed, but the first thing I did was to make her put her ornament inside her dress.'

The train to California was a treat for Myra and Saz: 'WHAT A LAZY DAY..... We didn't even get dressed, but played games, and watched the wonderful scenery through the Rocky Mountains. Brilliant sunshine and snow, and a marvellous sunset.' On arrival, the manager of the San Francisco Symphony Orchestra, Howard Skinner, drove them to their hotel across the Golden Gate Bridge. After dinner, 'There was an almost full moon, and we made [Mr Skinner] drive us on the hills.' It was a welcome return to a favourite city and its balmy climate.

During this visit, friends introduced the 'Pilgrims' to Scrabble, which at first they found overly laborious. This quickly changed. According to Joyce Grenfell, 'Myra played Scrabble with the malice aforethought of a Russian chess champion and was very hard to beat. She even hissed a little in a villainous way as she planned her next relentless move.'[22]

The vogue for one-composer concerts, especially Beethoven, was on the rise and took Myra somewhat by surprise. 'Schemozzles and debates about my recital programme here. MOST unfortunately, Backhaus recently gave a Beethoven recital, with FIVE sonatas, and that wretched Gieseking played Op. 110. Also, there have been other orgies of Beethoven. After much heart-searching rage and thought, I have decided to change the 2nd half, playing Op. 109 and 110 before 'Intermission' and then Scarlatti and the Schumann Symph. Studies. It is disappointing not to do the 'last three', but I am quite sure it was a wise decision.'

She played the Schumann Concerto three times to warm receptions; then went from Sacramento to Fresno, where she met friends who had driven several hundred miles for the occasion. The return drive to San

Francisco allowed them to have supper by the roadside and to arrive at 2.30am.

Three days of well-earned rest ensued. On 19th March Myra's friends Albert and Elizabeth Elkus took her and Saz to see some ancient redwood trees, including one '1,800 years old, and over 200 feet high, with a girth of 17 feet'. Her recital on 21st March at the San Francisco Opera House, proved enjoyable: 'With room for improvement, (cela va sans dire) Op. 109 was the best I have done, I think. Op. 110 was made slightly uncomfortable by the gradual lowering of piano stool....but especially last movement "came off"... Back about 1.30am and now I feel the most important concert of tour is over, and I feel like the horse smelling the hay, going back to his stable.'

Los Angeles still lay ahead. There, Myra's hotel suite filled with bouquets, 'including magnificent red roses, and violets, from my 'Pin-up' Ronald Colman (AND his wife...)'. The first rehearsal of her Schumann with the Los Angeles Philharmonic under Alfred Wallenstein was only hours after her arrival. Wallenstein had been first cello in the New York Philharmonic and had played the solo in the Brahms B flat Concerto with Myra and Walter, 'MOST memorably beautifully,' Myra wrote. 'A member of orch. took an unexpected photo of soloist and conductor in a close embrace.'

With Albert Goldberg, Myra felt comfortable; and when he interviewed her for the *Los Angeles Times*, she opened up more then usual, on matters ranging from the challenges of Mozart to some uncharacteristically critical comments about her studies with Matthay.

Of the first, she commented: 'In Mozart one must leave a special margin for improvisation, as it were. One must approach each work anew every time one plays it. But the discovery of beauty in Mozart is so difficult, partly because the moods change so quickly. When he laughs he cries.' She was playing the A minor Sonata K310: 'I never dared to do it before. I have listened to so many play it and have been so disappointed... But I thought if I am ever going to play it, I had better begin.'

Over Matthay, she offered praise, but also recalled:

> Before we played at student recitals he would pat us on the shoulder and say, 'Enjoy the music!' I resented it then and inwardly retorted, 'But it is not you who has to go out and play'.
>
> That thought has helped me through many terrible moments. I have walked on the stage in such a state that I couldn't remember

> where to put my hands on the piano, and I would repeat to myself in desperation, 'Enjoy the music!'
>
> That covers a multitude of sins. When I think I have played my worst I sometimes have been supposed to play my best. I suppose the more uncomfortable one is the more one concentrates. The only thing is to concentrate on the spirit of the music.
>
> Once when I had been going through a bad phase of nervousness and apprehension Harold Bauer said to me, 'Don't you ever enjoy a recital?' 'Enjoy it!' I gasped. 'In all my life I have only enjoyed maybe five or six.' 'But that's a lot!' he exclaimed.

She praised the way that Matthay would not impose interpretations on his students if they had original ideas, only showing them his own concepts if they brought something 'half-baked'. 'He never let us forget the purpose of all the striving and straining,' she said. Then she added: 'But Matthay made too many people play the piano who should never have played. Tremendous facility can be a dangerous thing. … Nowadays you can make the appearance of being a pianist much too easily.' One wonders whom she was thinking of…

> It has become too easy to play the piano. A cat can walk across the keyboard and make sounds. It is great fun to go out and enjoy the crash bang – but then what? To make the piano a musical instrument takes more than one lifetime.

Finally she talked about a recital in Pasadena for a seemingly bronchitis-laden audience. She had been so annoyed by the noise that she broke off in the middle of a Beethoven sonata and said: 'May we have a good cough now and get it over?'

> I have dared to do that several times … And on some occasions I have been quite naughty about it. An audience … [thinks] we are above such things. But the more we concentrate the more easily we are distracted. Everyone thinks his little cough does not matter, but when there are 15 or 20 coughs it means we are disturbed 15 or 20 times. It is an element of modesty on the part of the audience. They do not realize how much it disturbs us.[23]

Around her Pasadena recital, she and Saz stayed in a 'very cosy little cottage' in the grounds of some friends' sizeable house. Myra likened

Pasadena to an American Cheltenham, marred only by the sound of jets breaking the sound barrier 'and distant explosions of mysterious gasses from experimental stations in these lovely valleys'.

On 26th March, basking in Californian sunshine, the pair went to Beverly Hills for lunch with Bruno Walter and his surviving daughter, Lotte (his elder daughter, Gretchen, had been murdered by her jealous husband in 1939 after falling in love with the baritone Ezio Pinza; her mother, deeply depressed thereafter, had died in 1945). Walter's career in Germany had ended with the rise of Hitler; he remained in Vienna until the 1938 Anschluss, when Hitler annexed Austria, but was fortunate to be away conducting in the Netherlands at the time. He emigrated to Los Angeles just before the outbreak of the Second World War.

By now Walter and Lotte had lived in Beverly Hills for ten years, close to numerous fellow refugees from Hitler who had found sanctuary in California, among them Thomas Mann, Alma Mahler-Werfel, Arnold Schoenberg and Erich Wolfgang Korngold. Myra was touched 'to find Europe so near to Hollywood'. Intriguingly, in his later years, Walter became a committed follower of Rudolf Steiner's anthroposophy, to which Myra's former housemates, the Compton-Burnetts, were so devoted.

> We were greeted by an enormous Dalmatian, who barked hoarsely and unbrokenly, even while we were playing Mozart concertos, which we were choosing for next season, in New York. We changed our minds so often, but finally decided on G major and D minor. A really lovely house, where our Kathy [Ferrier] had stayed. A delicious lunch, and then they both showed us every room, and the books they had managed to collect since they lost everything to the Nazis. He looks so well, and we all talked so happily and easily. His daughter has taken a beautiful photograph of him and he has put a lovely inscription on one for me. Two and a half unforgettable hours.

Last but not least, 'WE FLEW.....literally.... to San F. as it only took 1 ½ hours, instead of spending whole night in train. A beautiful, steady flight, in perfect weather, with champagne served FREE with an extremely large lunch. The Coast looked so beautiful.' The following day, 31st March, was Myra's final concert, in Berkeley; April began with a lengthy train trip back to New York, punctuated only by a stop in Chicago for a bath.

Bidding a temporary farewell to New York, Myra was saddened by news of Churchill's resignation at home – he was stepping down as prime minister due to ill health – and in Manhattan, news came that Pondie had

had a second small stroke. Nevertheless, Myra enjoyed a drive through Central Park on the hottest Easter Day in 60 years, with magnolias in full bloom, and was pleased to find her 'pet' concert Steinway repaired and ready for her use next time. Meanwhile, as she had told Goldberg, she intended to take the entire summer off and play the piano only for her own pleasure.

A sound apart

Alone at home, Myra was aiming at more than that. She had decided she disliked her own playing and was attempting to change the core of it: her personal sound.

In general, Myra's sound was warm, clear and mellow: if reimagined on other instruments, it could be scored as clarinets, cellos and French horns, rather than the strident brilliance of violins and trumpets. When she had had singing lessons at the Academy, she was a contralto; and the singers she loved the most were also contraltos or mezzo-sopranos, such as Ferrier and Gerhardt.

Sometimes non-pianists find it strange to think that pianists can have their own sounds. Yet they do, through an alchemy of physics, physique, mechanics and imagination. One theory suggests that one note alone cannot determine the quality of someone's sound; it depends on how the pianist moves *between* the notes. Even one note, however, can sound quite different depending on the position of the attack, the speed and the weight behind it. A page-turner to the great pianists, Mike Oldham, relates that when Clifford Curzon played a single A for the Amadeus Quartet to tune to, he could identify his sound at once.

The golden-age performers who surrounded Myra in her youth – Rachmaninoff, Cortot, Friedman, et al – valued a unique, recognisable approach. Even in the 21st century, often there is no division between the personalities and performances of the finest pianists; if you talk to them, then hear them play, the same 'voice' permeates both mediums. Some musicians, moreover, believe that personal sound is like DNA, something that you are born with; while it can be developed, polished and perfected, it cannot be actively changed.

Myra nevertheless told Howard that this was what she wanted to do. 'I am enjoying this marvellous space for work,' she wrote to him on 8th August, '& I really believe I am establishing a new sound. Whether it is less or more Semitic I don't know, but I am sick & tired of sounding like matzah balls in soup. … It is heavenly not to mind how badly I play for yet another few weeks!'

She was referring to a traditional Jewish dish: 'matzah balls', *kneidlach*, are dumplings made of the matzah flour used in unleavened bread for Passover. Served in chicken broth, *kneidlach* soak up the flavour and complement it with a soft, doughy texture.

Myra did not explain the analogy. Rounded, soft, lacking in edge? Was she, at 65, finally being seduced by the extrovert dazzle of Rubinstein, or the vast, aurora-like colours of Richter and Gilels? She certainly does not sound *kneidlach*-esque in the Schumann Concerto with Mitropoulos; it has an impassioned forcefulness. Perhaps she was fed up with being expected to sound 'womanly' and associated qualities of roundness and softness with that. Still, her comment about 'more or less Semitic' is puzzling. Had some unnamed contact made blanket assumptions about the way Jewish musicians were presumed to sound?

The only evidence of her efforts is in her subsequent recordings; but there, if her sound seems slightly different, it is unclear how much might be attributed to the technological set-up. On the one hand, it seems an extraordinary direction to take at this stage of a career, at which most pianists might instead be mellowing. On the other hand, this is Myra.

1 This and following quotations unless otherwise marked, MH Diaries, Hess Family Collection
2 See also https://notoriouslyepiscopalian.com/2020/04/15/and-if-i-am-to-do-nothing-let-me-do-it-gallantly/
3 Author interview with SK
4 McKenna, op. cit., p267
5 Sir Adrian Boult, 'Conducting for Myra' in *Myra Hess by her Friends*, p26
6 *The New York Times*, 5 February 1953
7 *The New York Times*, 6 February 1953
8 *The Herald Tribune*, 6 February 1953
9 *Los Angeles Times*, 3 April 1955
10 *Chicago Tribune*, 27 April 1953
11 *The Daily Telegraph*, 30 May 1953
12 *The New York Times*, 7 February 1954
13 *Chicago Tribune*, 23 February 1954
14 *The Daily Express*, undated clipping October 1954, Hess Family Collection
15 *The Times*, 26 June 1954
16 *The Times*, 11 October 1954
17 *The Daily Telegraph*, 1 November 1954
18 *Birmingham Post*, 24 September 1954
19 *The Guardian*, 15 September 1954
20 *The New York Times*, 11 February 1955
21 E. Frank, manuscript intended for but not included in *Myra Hess by her Friends*, Wisconsin Historical Society
22 J. Grenfell, 'Julia M.' in *Myra Hess by her Friends*, p64
23 *Los Angeles Times*, 3 April 1955

Studies with Dame Myra
(1959–1965)

After 1955 Myra's American diaries stop. Perhaps she was beginning to run out of time and steam. From here on, her tours are traced chiefly via her letters and the newspaper reports; and later, in diaries by Saz and letters from her to Marj, or from Beryl to Howard.

Early in 1956, Myra was ready to test out her 'new sound'. She reported to Howard from Chicago, on 8th February:

> Everything has been very worth while so far, everyone thinking I have improved - I was afraid all I had worked for this summer would slide away with the Am.[erican] piano action - but many hours at Steinways helped to adjust me!
>
> My piano is travelling with me & thank Heaven it has just arrived here - from Knoxville, Tennessee - having heard that 3 coaches of a freight train fell into the river!!! (No one hurt, apparently.)
>
> Had a marvellous audience at Carnegie - & they have been most responsive everywhere. The plight of the coloured people in the South made us feel sick and furious - & we were so thankful to have Janet, who drove us everywhere - including a 13 hour drive from Knoxville on Sunday![1]

On 20th March she played Mozart's 'little' A major Concerto K414 with Robert Scholz & his 'excellent little orch. with enthusiastic young players [the American Chamber Orchestra]'. The performance was recorded, which affords the first chance to assess whether Myra had succeeded in changing her sound. The piano is closely miked compared to the orchestra, but Myra's tone, while bright and open, does seem to have a more rapidly articulated attack than usual; perhaps seamless legato has less priority than before, though it is judiciously applied. There is a certain crystalline brilliance of touch, even in this treacherously transparent, gemlike concerto.

'It was v. enjoyable & colossal enthusiasm,' Myra wrote, 'but of course THE experience was the week with Walter.' With him, she worked for six days out of eight on two Mozart concertos:

> G maj. delightful & lovely - & then the D. min for the Sunday broadcast. As is usual after a dose of special apprehension, 'something seemed to happen' at the performance - & it was an experience to remember, in fact an inspiration that will last for a very long time … Altogether it has been a marvellous time of heartening appreciation & my returning date is again postponed!

Myra and her last duo partner, Isaac Stern

She had three recitals ahead, playing Schubert *Moments musicaux*, Beethoven Op. 111 and the Schumann *Etudes Symphoniques* at the Metropolitan Museum on 5th April; then another concert there on 16th with Isaac Stern, including Brahms's G major Sonata and a solo performance of Beethoven Op. 110. It celebrated the 90th birthday of David Mannes and profits would go to the music school he had founded in Manhattan. 'Tickets $100 EACH!!!!!' the astounded Myra noted.

But the letter was full of signs of anxiety over friends' well-being – and her own. She mentions James Friskin, Rebecca Clarke's husband, giving a recital for his 70th birthday including the Bach Goldberg Variations ('A touching afternoon !!! but you know what I feel about the "Variations"'). Julia Steinway had had two heart attacks; Janet had had a major operation; Benno, too, had been undergoing surgery.

Myra herself had an alarming new problem: 'my B[loody]..... hand'. Developing osteoarthritis has nothing to do with playing the piano, but can seriously hamper it. Here Myra was simply unlucky. By the middle of the summer she was telling Howard (17th August) that 'it doesn't hurt my B..... hand to type... [it] has been pretty depressing, and I have ... been thinking seriously if I dare to play in public, but yest. and today it is a bit more comfortable, and I am going to try both progs. at Denise's this weekend.' She was planning to test them further in private, before heading up to Scotland.

The Edinburgh Festival was a high-profile ground on which to unleash both a new sound and a painful hand. That year's line-up of pianists was impressive, while the programming exploited the trend for one-composer recitals. Myra was giving two all-Beethoven concerts. The American pianist Rosalyn Tureck would play all the Bach Partitas, Nina Milkina was playing Mozart, Clifford Curzon would perform Schubert, Robert Casadesus Schumann and Louis Kentner Liszt.

Tureck, from Chicago and of Ukrainian-Jewish background, associated herself chiefly with Bach, following a bizarre mystical experience aged 14 that she said had left her with an absolute certainty about how to play his music. Her expertise extended across various keyboard instruments, the electronic Theremin and conducting. Oddly, Myra commented more on Tureck's presentation than her musicianship. 'I was so interested in your report of R. T.,' she wrote to Howard (rather later, in 1958). 'She is an enigma...' But then (10th Feb) she noted, 'I am afraid I shall not hear from you about R. T's backside-to-the-audience, conducting and playing. B.....'

Myra also played an all-Beethoven recital at the RFH on 7th October – the now traditional opening of her season and London's. This time she chose the Variations in F major Op. 34, the D major Sonata Op. 10 No. 3, the 'Appassionata' and Op. 110, representing all three phases of the composer's creative life. *The Times* judged: 'It is the humanity of Beethoven which is the key to her interpretation: she catches the serious warmheartedness of the first period, the greater ardour of the middle period ... and the more intense brooding, the intellectual effort, which issue in the visionary message of the late A flat sonata...' [2]

Among concertos, she played the Mozart D minor at a Prom with Sargent and the BBC Symphony Orchestra (13th September) and Brahms D minor Concerto with the LSO and Josef Krips at the RFH (16th October), then on 13th December two Mozarts, K414 and K595, with Blech and his London Mozart Players. On 8th May 1957, back from the US, she produced her beloved Beethoven Fourth again, with Boult and the Royal Philharmonic.

None of these are small orders, but there was a certain retrenchment in Myra's outlook. Benno, bouncing back after illness, was performing the likes of Mussorgsky's *Pictures at an Exhibition* and Chopin's B minor Sonata. Kentner was playing Tippett's new Piano Concerto. Gilels was coming to town, playing Prokofiev's Third Concerto, and Shura Cherkassky was starting to shine across eclectic repertoire. Myra – even if playing works she did not often perform, such as Beethoven's Op. 10 No. 3 – was sticking to her trusty Viennese classics.

Perhaps familiar programmes enabled her to keep going at the required pace. When in Britain she was giving between four and seven concerts per month, but on overseas tours, many more: in the US, up to ten. November 1956 found her in Holland: she visited Amsterdam, Hilversum, Eindhoven, Utrecht, Maastricht and The Hague between 9th and 30th November, playing the Schumann and the Brahms Second Concerto with the Concertgebouw, Beethoven's Third in Utrecht and six recitals. That schedule would not have disgraced her at half her age.

A Time of Farewells

The American tour of 1957 found Myra mourning and afraid of mourning further.

'Everything as usual here, excepting the going of so many friends,' she wrote to Howard (21st January 1957). 'I can't believe we won't see Ruth [Draper] again.' The actress had died in her sleep the night after a performance just before Christmas. Toscanini, too, was dead. Myra could not bear to attend his memorial service:

> And now the Maestro. That was also merciful, as he was getting tired of being idle….and had told his doctor recently that he intended to conduct again! He was unconscious for several days, so did not suffer. Walter sent me an Admission to the Centre Aisle of the Cathedral….. for the Memorial Service, but I didn't go!! The Maestro would have run a million miles to get away from all the Rites and Rituals ????

She was distressed by Pondie's condition. Her venerable friend, who could scarcely walk, was insisting on attending her recital; Myra hoped she would agree to use a wheelchair.

'I am unforgivably tired of trying to play the piano,' she wrote, 'partly on account of my hand being painful. … Also, I have had to choose a new Concert Grand. … We have had terrific pow-wows with Cesar about the future, and at last he and Marion realise that this must be the last of such strenuous tours……'

The prospect of going coast to coast, with a good month in California, was more daunting than it used to be. Still, she looked forward to playing with Stern at the Metropolitan Museum and mooted with Howard the idea that they might perform his Second Violin Sonata. 'I am rather afraid that he won't have time to learn [it] for our London recital, although he said he would order it immediately…..'

In Los Angeles, Goldberg wrote a more than glowing review of her Op. 111: 'The eloquence and beauty of that finale as Miss Hess played it simply preclude any attempt at description. It was searching to the ultimate degree and it left the audience in a deeply moved moment of silent awe before the thunders of applause broke loose. It was something that no one who heard it will ever be likely to forget.' He termed the recital 'a revelation of such beauty as one encounters only infrequently in a lifetime.'[3]

Most unusually, Myra phoned the office to thank him. 'You know at my age press notices don't mean much any more,' she said. 'I usually look at them hastily and throw them away. But I have cut out your review of that recital and I am putting it away where I will know where to find it. I am saving it to take out and read again on days when I am discouraged.'[4]

Musical experiences awaited that were far from discouraging. Notably, she played in Chicago with the Hungarian conductor Fritz Reiner, whose reputation for ferocity preceded him. 'The concerts here with Reiner have been a most pleasant surprise,' she told Howard (9th March 1957). 'A really beautiful accomp. for Beethoven 3 – extremely sensitive – the last thing I expected - & nothing but friendliness, which is a great relief!'

Walter, however, was 78 and reaching the end of his career. 'It was a deeply moving occasion, being his last "official" appearance with the [New York] Philharmonic,' Myra wrote (28th February).

> I was suddenly asked to make their Presentation, a first edition score of the Pastoral Symph. (which he gave at the end of the programme) AND I had to say a few words. ... and there were touching ovations for all of us. ... he took the 1st M'vt MUCH faster than I ever play it... ..I was rather devastated at rehearsal, and had to rethink it all during the afternoon (as well as learning my little speech....) but there was quite a LITTLE compromise, in the evening, and only Saz and Rose seem to have noticed that I had to 'change my spots'..... However, he was happy about it and said 'Not too bad' when we came off the platform, as he used to say to Kath [Ferrier] when he was pleased with her..... But you can imagine what an 'emotion' it was.....and I had to manage NOT to be 'in all states'.

Boult had asked her to accept the Gold Medal of the Royal Philharmonic Society on Walter's behalf, in London on 8th May. 'I have begged him to send me a little message that I can read, and we have put a few sentences down already,' she wrote (28th April 1957), but she was anxious about the tight timing of her return voyage: 'We are due to arrive in the evening on the 6th and I only pray for NO FOGS.

> It seems a million years since I left home, and at the moment I feel that much older....These are rather melancholy last days in N. Y. We have just come back from lunching and saying Goodbye to our Pondie ... She hates our going, as we hate to leave her but her realisation of Time becomes more and more vague and therefore one can only hope that she is beyond really fretting about anything.

The year saw the deaths of Vaughan Williams and Albert Sammons. The previous year, Solomon had suffered a stroke that left him unable to play the piano. He lived on for 30 years at his St John's Wood home, 16 Blenheim Road; Myra and Benno, who were both nearby (Benno lived at 46 Avenue Road) visited him regularly to play card games. Howard's mother passed away; and Myra was anxious about her brother, Herbert, who had been in hospital. Finally the telephone rang with the long-dreaded news that

Pondie was gone. Myra told Howard on 18th August: 'She just went to sleep, with no pain or discomfort (possibly with my last letter in her hand…).'

Myra needed a relatively quiet summer and was not particularly happy that Howard was off to South Africa. On 9th July she wrote to him:

> The bulk of *Falstaff* [at Glyndebourne] was a happy diversion on the day of your departure, which as you know, I resented deeply!! What a brilliant, and bewitching opera it is, with such endless wit and invention, and poetry? I thought it was exceedingly well done, on the whole, and it was a marvellous night. What a lovely picture by the water, with the reflections of evening dresses. I managed to avoid any glaring faux pas', which was a relief!!
>
> Then last night I went to *Titus [Andronicus]* with Phyllis Carrington [the actress], looking like every painting of Charles First… She listed the horrors to me beforehand, (which was all to the good?) and I was enthralled by Olivier's magnificent acting. It is a wonderful production, and I am glad I went!! As P. has had connections with O. and Viv. Leigh, we were admitted to their dressing room afterwards. They were most warmly friendly, and I quite lost my heart to him. He was very interesting and amusing about his performance, but told us that they couldn't possibly do it much longer.

Besides that, she enjoyed a chance to relax, with dinner parties, a heat wave and tennis from Wimbledon on TV. Ted Ferris and the Parsonnets travelled from the US, planning to hear her play with Stern. Myra and Saz took Ferris to the Keats House museum in Hampstead; Myra had lived nearby all her life, but had never before been inside. She found the poet's home deeply moving.

In the States, plans were brewing for the Golden Jubilee that November of Myra's official debut. Sascha Greiner wanted to hold 'a Mammoth reception' at Steinway's in New York and Myra craved Howard's opinion:

> Saz and Marj would gladly have me celebrate it here, there and everywhere, but I am utterly 'agin' it. As you know, I loathe publicity of any kind, and I think the ramifications might be frightful? Wouldn't hundreds of people write, thinking they ought to congratulate, or condole??? Or do I over-estimate my position???? I would feel exactly like [Adelina] De-Lara-Boomdeay….retiring one day, and reappearing the next, and being a trouble to everyone…. I think if

> anyone has been misguided and idiotic enough to play in public for fifty years, the less said about it the better? That's all, and tell me what you feel????

She was missing Howard. Her letters sound unusually tetchy and needy, grumbling about her new American neighbour with four screaming children, while her hand was suffering 'from rain, rain & rain'. She wanted his response to her suggested programme of Mozart's Rondo, Adagio and Gigue, Schubert's 'little' A minor Sonata, Bach's Partita No. 1 in B flat and Beethoven Op. 111; she even asked his advice on ornamentations for the Bach. She remarked, too, that she had been to hear 'little Allan Schiller' play Mozart's A major Concerto at the Proms with the National Youth Orchestra – 'really very moving'.

Ultimately she decided against jubilee celebrations, telling Howard (23rd Aug) 'I have just written to dear Sascha, hoping he will understand even if he does not agree with me!!! I have said that I want to finish my career with as few sforzandos as possible, and enjoy a jubilant celebration when I retire, and cease to be a public person... So that is that, and couldn't be thatter...'

On 12th October 1957, she made a recording that proved her last. It was of nine short pieces, including some of her favourite encores: two Scarlatti sonatas, the C minor Kk11 and G major Kk14; Beethoven's *Für Elise* and Bagatelle Op. 126 No. 3; Mendelssohn's *Song without Words* in A major; Granados's 'The Maiden and the Nightingale' from *Goyescas*; Brahms's A flat Waltz and C major Intermezzo Op. 119 No. 3; and to close, *Jesu, Joy*. Her choice of the last piece suggests that perhaps she really did have retirement in mind.

Throughout, she surpassed herself. The Granados has been termed (by Stephen Siek) 'the jewel in the crown' and 'one of the greatest recordings of her career'. 'When you hear Myra's nightingale sing on this recording,' Denise wrote, 'you begin to get a sense of what she could actually do...'[5] The pieces formed the second side of an LP together with the Schumann *Etudes symphoniques*. Myra was gratified, in America the following year, to learn that the first pressing had sold out.

Decades earlier, Myra had earned her living primarily through giving lessons for the Matthay School, while struggling to build a performing career. In the years of intense touring, she lacked the time and energy for regular teaching, but frequently young pianists would seek her advice, including Denis Matthews, during the National Gallery

Concerts days, and Clive Lythgoe, whom she had met when he turned pages for her. But with her inevitable slowing down, now there came more pupils: musicians who carried her advice and methods on into a new generation.

'Not The Queen Mother': Stephen Kovacevich[6]

The San Francisco piano student Stephen Bishop first met Myra when he was about 15 years old. He changed his name later because Bishop was his stepfather's surname; ultimately, after a spell as 'Bishop-Kovacevich', he settled on Kovacevich alone.

He first met Myra through Sidney Griller: his high-school girlfriend was Griller's daughter. 'I think he [Griller] wanted me out of California!' he remembers. 'So he introduced me to Myra while she was there. I played Op. 109 for her.'

He had to choose between a scholarship to the Juilliard School in New York and studying with Myra in London. 'I knew I'd never survive Juilliard because of the competition – people playing Chopin études while they're eating chocolate biscuits. Also I hadn't liked Beethoven until I heard the Diabelli Variations and I suddenly fell in love with the piece. I'd never played Beethoven until I was 17 or 18. I knew that with Myra that was her world, whereas in Juilliard it wouldn't be so central.'

In London, Kovacevich lived in a bedsit in Chalk Farm and would go to practise at Emmie Tillett's St John's Wood home, close to Myra's. He was given a scholarship for his living expenses by a young would-be musical agent who was then working for a bank: Terry Harrison (who later co-founded Harrison Parrott Artists Management). Myra charged him £14 per lesson: 'She used to say that she had to charge, otherwise she would be very unpopular with other teachers – but sometimes she did give me a free lesson.' Occasionally he turned pages for her, including for a rehearsal with Stern, during which the violinist dropped a lighted cigarette into Myra's piano. Myra reprimanded him: 'Naughty boy!' Afterwards, Stern said to Kovacevich: 'Young man, never forget what you heard today at the start of the slow movement,' so much did he admire Myra's quality of sound.

Kovacevich found 23 Cavendish Close sombrely beautiful. 'The piano room was simple but elegant: two pianos, a desk, a couch. Of the two pianos, the smaller one was horrible to play, with a very slow action; then there was a very good Model D concert grand. Occasionally you were allowed to play on the D, but occasionally I would be extreme on it and that was not popular. But if you were playing Liszt and you played the small piano, it was doomsville because it was so slow.

'My first lesson was on the Brahms Handel Variations. We must have spent at least 50 minutes on the theme alone. I'd never worked on anything in that detail and with that possibility of variety of style, attack, timing. I'd never done anything in my life like that. I suppose we got through the whole piece, but I remember clearly the matter of establishing the beginning with enough gravitas but without being heavy; the kind of trill to use, the kind of sound, the tempo in relation to the variation that came afterwards.

'Myra was never doctrinaire; I never felt "You must do *this*". She might demonstrate the way she thought was *in*appropriate. You didn't feel free to say to her, "I believe I should do it like *this*", but still there were no shackles.' He recalls that Myra complimented him on his Diabelli Variations, 'but she said: "The critics will never understand you". I'd been trying to play the fugue; maybe I do play it too fast, but it would have been much faster then! She probably convinced me that it would be more exciting at a different sort of tempo.

'In the opening of Beethoven's Fourth, we were trying to make the first chord expressive, with the top singing a little bit, but not lumpen, and not with a Brahmsy sound. She showed me how to practise the chord, which involved playing it silently. You press the keys down a little, then a little bit more each time, and if the piano is in perfect condition, though it rarely is, eventually you hear a sound. In that way you stop being paranoid about how soft it can be – the fear is that nothing happens, or only one note sounds. Instead of being terrified by that, or being forced to play too loud, you start to look forward to it. That took months of attention to something I'd never much considered before.

'We studied the 'Emperor' Concerto and the D minor Brahms; the B flat Brahms I studied with Howard once while she was away. In Mozart she had marvellous articulation, both expressive and very brilliant at the same time. During or soon after my training with her, I played all the Mozart concertos in London; many of them I studied with her. Of Schubert, I remember studying the *Moments Musicaux*; as for Brahms, Malcolm Frager [another pupil, the first American pianist to win the Queen Elisabeth Competition in Brussels] told me that he would have given a lot to be able to play the intermezzos with a sound like hers.'

Kovacevich felt that Myra was 'one of just a handful of musicians who understood in their gut how to play Beethoven. There are people who play it and you know that they don't understand a bar! But it was her world. And Schnabel's, Serkin's, and Backhaus's. These people really got it.' Myra had not performed the Diabelli Variations herself: 'She adored getting to know it better. I couldn't imagine studying it with anyone who had more intuition.'

Kovacevich's technique was already strong, so Myra spoke little about such matters. 'One wonderful thing she did say was that you have to feel the weight of the key. I think that is a Matthay concept. When I came to her, I could play quickly and I wasn't unmusical. But it was a rather monotonous sound, without many levels of variety, and the spectrum of pianissimo was a concept of which I had no idea. She said: "If you want to weigh a postage stamp, you hold it between your fingers very lightly, because you can't weigh it otherwise." This transfers to how she wanted a person to approach the keyboard. A whole world opened up.

'She insisted strongly that speed was sometimes the enemy of excitement, and although I was sceptical at the time, she convinced me of it. Around then I was hearing Klemperer giving numerous concerts: some were dull, but some I'll never forget. It was the only time in all my years of hearing Beethoven that I'd ever felt Beethoven himself was on the stage. It was slow, but he understood it and he got the orchestra to achieve the perfect sonority. Myra was right: articulation and ferocity of expression is sometimes more exciting than just a loud, fast playthrough.

'The only thing we ever disagreed about was Chopin. In passages of a cadenza-like nature, those small notes with indeterminate speed, I would sometimes play very fast and she was sarcastic about that. It was the only time she was ever sarcastic to me. We agreed, without saying anything, not to study Chopin any more! But I did do some nocturnes with her and she was great about those; there was no temptation to play them too quickly.'

Stephen's Wigmore Hall debut on 12th November 1961 was a triumph. *The Times* reviewed it: 'It was in Beethoven's Diabelli Variations … that Mr. Bishop really showed his mettle. It was no surprise to find that he understood the music as a developing entity and not merely as a series of technical hurdles, but he now began to convey a more active identification with it … Mr. Bishop may make a remarkable Beethoven pianist.'

'Unfortunately,' Kovacevich reflects, 'the English started treating Myra like the Queen Mother, and she started playing accordingly. In America she did *not* play like the Queen Mother. She admitted she loved the American Steinways. It released something in her. I never heard her play in Britain the way she played in America.' In Britain, he thought she was taken for granted and could sound repressed.

'The English dried her up. She had a demoniac side, which you can hear in the "Appassionata" – a performance Martha Argerich adores – and in the Chopin F minor Fantasy. She was not the girl next door. And the English turned her into that, and possibly the claustrophobic life she led.'

The one thing that puzzled him about Myra was her attitude to his personal life. As a devoutly Catholic youth of 20, he told her he intended to get married (to Bernardine Wall, a novelist and therapist). 'She said that she would have to consider very hard whether she could carry on teaching me.' He never knew if her objection was that he was too young, or if she was opposed to the entire idea of a musician being married, becoming distracted from their vocation. He and Bernardine married in any case; and Myra relented, inviting them to dinner and paying for a tank of petrol for their car, 'which was extremely kind'.

Later, when Kovacevich's career was taking off and he had been accepted for management by Emmie Tillett, Bernardine fell pregnant. He rang Myra to tell her. 'There was a startled silence. And then she said: "Oh! *But what would Mrs Tillett say*?"'

'Such Intensity': Ann Schein[7]

Ann Schein was born in 1939 in White Plains, New York. Her grandfather, a brilliant violinist, had come to the US with his family orchestra from Austro-Hungarian Galicia to perform at the Columbia Exposition in Chicago in 1886, then stayed in the US. When Ann was four, the family moved to Washington DC; here she first heard Myra play, 'in one of those gorgeous Sunday afternoon concerts at Constitution Hall,' she says. 'She came every year post-war and she and Arthur Rubinstein became my great loves.

'When she entered the stage, something about her aura – knowing about her history in the war, one could understand it – made me feel, even as a young child, completely safe. She sat authoritatively there in her black dress and made the most beautiful music possible.' Ann was ten when her father took her to the Bohemian Club to hear Myra play and speak about her experiences: 'That was my first personal view of her and I remember she was very funny and witty. She played the Brahms Op. 119.

I loved everything that came out of the music and I got to meet her briefly because my father wanted me to have that gift.'

Schein made her debut in Mexico City aged 17 and was 18 when she played in London for the first time. 'Somehow, here was a young American girl that they totally accepted. Not that all the reviews were good, but I played there every year. Then I auditioned for the BBC and failed the first time, which did not surprise me. A week later, I had a letter from them saying they had suddenly learned how old I was and would accept me after all.' Yearly BBC broadcasts then led to six Proms, including two Last Nights, 'treasured memories which I can never forget'.

She had extensive coaching with Rubinstein. Then in 1961 she got to know Kovacevich, who brought her to meet Myra. 'I went to play to her and she accepted me. I said, "I'm having coaching also with Mr Rubinstein – is that all right with you?" She said: "Oh, Arthur – a bit of a show-off, isn't he? But it's fine."' Schein posed the equivalent question to Rubinstein. 'He said: "Myra? A little bit boring. But it's fine."'

By the time Schein started studying with her, Myra was suffering in the aftermath of life-threatening illness. 'You could feel the darkness about her. However, she wanted you there. She wanted people to come and play, and to help them. Rubinstein was the opposite: to me he was like the sun. You just entered his home and the sun shone, whether it was raining or not.

'I remember I brought Myra a bouquet of flowers and she was very sweet about it. Then she would sit in the chair, and say, "What would you like to play?" I remember hearing that she had to feel comfortable with the student – and she didn't have many, because she didn't have time. Stephen was one of her loves and Yonty Solomon around then.'

Ann once undertook a romantic concerto tour for the BBC. She was taking three works respectively to three different towns: Rachmaninoff's Third, Schumann, and Chopin's Second. Myra had coached her on the Schumann. The concerts were broadcast live: 'I was eager to know if she thought I had done what she wanted, so I telephoned her after the Schumann. All she said was: "Don't you have another concert tomorrow? Isn't it Chopin F minor? Then we won't speak until you're through with your tour." That was the first time any teacher had approached me with that kind of seriousness. It really resonated. That's how she approached her own musical life and discipline.'

In solo repertoire, Ann remembers working on Schumann, Brahms and Beethoven with Myra. She felt most influenced by her in Beethoven's

'Les Adieux' Sonata: 'I opened my Carnegie Hall debut recital with it, and that was the beginning of my adulation of the way she played that beautiful work.' A less happy experience involved playing the Schubert 'Wanderer' Fantasy at the Wigmore Hall; afterwards, she took it to Myra. 'Like most pianists, I had trouble with this piece and on her piano I probably made a mess of it. She had her head in her hands. At the end she simply said, "Not quite perfect, was it?". That was all! But I worked hard on it and tried to clean it up…'

Myra was famous for 'a pace that was not hurried,' Schein says. 'She slowed me down – and so did Rubinstein, because I had studied with one of the greatest virtuosos of the time, Mieczyslaw Muncz, who loved speed! In my Schumann Concerto Myra slowed everything down, saying: "You must love every note." There was time; there was the aura of her depth.

'And that darkness. I didn't mind it, because I knew that she had suffered terribly, both in the experience of the war, and then in the illnesses afterward, but she persevered, which inspired me.'

The ultimate inspiration, Schein says, was Myra's broadcast of the Brahms B flat Concerto with Walter: 'It absolutely floored me! Of course it made me attempt to play it.'

'I'll Pray with You': Richard Contiguglia[8]

The identical twins Richard and John Contiguglia, who have devoted their careers to their piano duo, were among Myra's last students. They first met her at Yale University, where from 1956 they were pupils of Bruce Simonds. 'She used to perform there every season,' Richard says. 'We were transfixed by her incredible artistry. I can still hear the sound of her playing: for instance, the start of the slow movement of Beethoven's Third Piano Concerto. She played an E major chord and it just rang through the hall, but without any sense of forced tone. That was the only time I ever heard Myra perform without a score.'

Simonds asked the Contiguglias if they would turn pages for Myra. At Yale, for her last three Beethoven sonatas, 'John turned for Op. 109 and Op. 110. I turned for Op. 111, after intermission. As we were walking onstage, Myra turned to me and said, "Pray for me." I responded, "I'll pray *with* you." She squeezed my hand and ended the recital as only she could. I have never forgotten the exchange or the playing.

'We heard her in Carnegie Hall in 1959 when again she played the last three Beethoven sonatas. About 3,000 people were there and when she finished, there wasn't a sound in the hall. All at once the entire audience stood up and paid tribute as if it were a kind of religious experience. Finally it just erupted in applause. I still remember Dame Myra in the midst of this turning to the audience and saying that when she played the same programme in Holland and got a similar response, she asked the audience, "What can one play after Op 111?" and they screamed back "Nothing!" Then she sat down at the piano and played seven encores!'

After their first encounter in Yale, Myra said to the twins: 'If you ever get to London, look me up'. 'It was an incentive to go,' says Richard, 'because you don't turn down an invitation like that. In 1961 we received a small stipend to go abroad and we immediately decided on London.

'We arrived there late in the fall of 1961. The first concert we attended was at Wigmore Hall. Joel Ryce and Yaltah Menuhin were giving a four-hand recital – and we saw Myra Hess, Howard Ferguson and Beryl Davis enter the auditorium through the artists' door. Our hearts were pumping and I don't think I could even listen to much of the playing. During intermission, we went up to her. She said "Ohhhh, it's the Twins!" She invited us to go round, play to her and have tea.'

The Contiguglias were preparing for their own Wigmore debut and had intended to study with Hilda Dederich, but she was away in Italy: 'Myra had said to her, "Don't worry, I'll hear them." It was an awesome experience for two young neophytes from New York who had an absolutely exalted impression of her.'

On and off across several years, the twins would spend at least a couple of hours per session with her (though it was only on the first visit, Richard remarks, that she gave them a cup of tea). Playing to her in her music room was a challenge: 'She would sit right in the middle, between two pianos that were quite a distance apart - one was a concert Steinway and the other was the Model B. She would be sitting in her chair following the music and John and I could hardly even communicate with each other because all we could see when we looked up was Myra Hess!'

Like Stephen, they found the smaller, heavy-actioned piano problematic. 'I remember Saz telling us that when Myra picked out pianos in America for her tours, she would always choose ones that had a heavy action. She never liked pianos that were too easy, because it made her feel as if she were skating on ice. Her concert grand at home had a perfect action, but initially she would only let us play on the model B.'

'When we first played for her, we had the use of only one piano where we were living. Consequently, when we decided to make our Wigmore

Hall debut, we did so playing duets at one piano. Playing to her on her Model B strengthened us. I don't know whether she got the same benefit from practising on it, but it made us aware of the relationship between strength and tone production. Later, when we performed two-piano music for her, the person playing the B had to work a little harder.

'She completely transformed our piano technique, emphasising the use of our arms. We came to realise that to get tone from the arms, you had to strengthen the fingers, the wrists and the forearms, and we set about doing that in our practice. It changed everything about our playing. Once, when we were leaving, she stood at the door of her house and said, "Don't forget playing with your arms" – she was moving her arms like a giant bird.

'I had never had a teacher who emphasised that. They had talked about loose wrists, dropping weights and so on. Myra never talked like that. She would say, "My wrists don't collapse when I play". And they didn't. She played right from the surface, she got her weight from her arms and she produced a sound that nobody else I ever heard could replicate. Her most frequent comment was "It does not sing", if she needed more tone, and we would have to think again about how to use the pressure of our arms to make the piano obey.

'Early in our visits, Myra occasionally would come to the piano to illustrate an aspect of tone production. In later visits she would mostly remain seated in an armchair while criticising a performance. Once when I was trying to project the theme of the Andante of Mozart's four-hand Sonata in D, she showed me how to do so with pressure from the arm and from the key surface, transferring the weight from note to note. After watching her and imitating her delivery, I turned to her and said, "It's so easy." Her unforgettable response was, "Yes, and it took me a lifetime to learn." This was so different from what I had been told by other Matthay pupils (who often talked about "dropping arm weight") that I realized that this approach to tone production was "pure Hess". It also confirms that she was not a product of an "English School", as many critics have alleged, but of a self-defined technique that I have rarely seen in other pianists.

'Once we were playing the Mozart Sonata for Two Pianos and we got to one of the broken arpeggios in the first movement where we made an agogic accent. She rose out of her chair and exclaimed "*No!*" That was the last time we ever thought of gratuitous gestures to try to make something sound expressive. She never accepted that in her playing or anybody else's.

A friend of mine, a British pianist, went to play the Chopin Barcarolle for her. He got no further than the low octave and the upper chord before she stopped him and said, "It has no conviction". Her idea of conviction had a lot to do with sound quality. After he had been repeating it for half an hour, finally she said, "It still doesn't have any conviction, but go on…"

'We never resented criticisms like that of our playing. Once when we played the Brahms Haydn Variations for her, we had thought it was wonderful, but she said, "That wasn't very good, was it? Would you like to play it again?" We did. Then she said, "Would you like to play it again?" We played it three times for her. The following week we went to Holland for a recital and got the best reviews we ever received in our lives for playing that piece.

'When we were playing Mozart's little D major four-hand sonata, she spent half an hour on the theme. After we got a sound that pleased her, she said: "Now let's work on the accompaniment." That was the kind of advice that we took with us all of our lives.' The twins also felt much aided by Myra's instinct for tempi. 'We were trying to learn the Schubert Variations on an Original Theme. Her remark was "It doesn't sound important" – because it was too fast.'

Richard insists that Myra never spoke to them about Matthay's teaching. 'The only person she ever talked about was Casals. I think he's the one who was responsible for showing her more forcefully how to use her arms like a bow, because that's what she kept telling us to do. That's not Matthay. But it's the most profitable advice she ever gave us. I think that her advice really to listen to the sound and to find a way to capture it is what gave us our piano technique.'

The twins often beat a path to 56 Abbey Road to study violin sonatas with Marj. 'Marjorie had a studio in their back yard and she let us go there to practise and to play with her. She was a remarkable violinist and had studied with a pupil of Joachim. She gave us so much help in building our sound. Dame Myra would talk to her and tell her that too much of our playing was pianissimo. Marjorie would keep telling us, "Play with more tone!" I thought we were overpowering her violin, but I realised she had a role in strengthening our tone.' Marjorie he remembers as 'indomitable' and Saz as 'businesslike': 'They were remarkable women, straight out of the 19th century.

'One of the last instructions Myra gave us was: "You must devote your lives to educating audiences to the beauty of the Schubert four-hand repertoire." I wish we could have done it, but sadly we found no wide enthusiasm for four-hand recitals. We had to worry about earning a living.'

'That Time, It Worked': John Contiguglia[9]

John's first memories of Myra are from turning pages for her in Yale. At the piano, he says, 'She was motionless. She sat so peacefully – she had all this power, but never through any excess contortion of her body. She was the most peaceful-looking performer I've ever known. At one point she turned to me and said, "Oh, my hands are so cold". I started rubbing them to warm them up.

'When a performance really "worked", as she said, it was something special. It meant everything "worked": the shapes, the pedalling, the nuances, the silences. She could mesmerise an audience with her sound. Everything came through her command of the instrument.

'Before she began a performance, she would test the key resistance. It was her subtle feeling for the sound mechanism of the piano. After she finished, she turned to me and said, "How was it?" Can you imagine? I could barely get up to turn her page because it was so moving to listen. When she performed K271 at Yale, when I was turning, she said to the audience: "This slow movement is one of the most beautiful pieces Mozart ever wrote and I would like to repeat it." She did so – and at the end she said to me, "That time, it worked…"'

The twins' determination to come to London was all the stronger after Myra could no longer travel to the US: 'We arrived in the year that she had cancelled a special performance of ten Mozart concertos in New York.' They had lodgings in the London Visitors' Club. 'I had sent her a Christmas card of the Winged Victory, which Saz had said was her favourite sculpture. The club had a communal phone in the hall and if it rang, anybody picked up and yelled for whomever it was for. So when it rang, I ran out there. And a voice said: "Is this my John?" I almost fainted! Dame Myra's voice was so singular that I knew exactly who it was. She said she would call us as soon as a performance was over that she was preparing, and we would go to see her.

'The experience was devastating, because the most praise she gave was that it was "promising". She said: "All your playing is double piano and all I hear is accents." We, who had graduated from Yale School of Music with a Master of Music degree, were absolutely cut down to size. We went back to our apartment and practised like we'd never practised before.

'She taught us that to create a beautiful sound, you had to use the muscles of your fingers, wrists, arms and back and nothing in this continuum could collapse on you. Our muscles were so undeveloped that we started practising endlessly to build up a real piano technique and a real sound. We practised five or six hours a day, sometimes nothing but Hanon or Czerny exercises.

'Often she told us, "You must play as if you're playing to the last seat in the last row of the hall," and that's what we did. She never complained about our sound after that. She taught us to keep close to the surface of the key and mould the sound: "Use your arm like a bow". That's something I never got from any other Matthay teacher – we studied with two or three others and all they talked about was total relaxation.

'I discovered that when you "used your arm like a bow", you were physically involved in playing more than one note at a time: you played whole groups of notes, whole phrases, giving shape to every single note, whether melody, counterpoint or accompaniment. To me it was revolutionary. I remember going back to our London Visitors Club and adopting what she had said. I tried to play the Adagio of Beethoven Op. 110, thinking of moulding my sound and playing from the key surface, as if I were bowing a group of notes. It was amazing how different it sounded. Suddenly she had given me a key to doing something I never would have thought of before. Then I played the slow movement of the Beethoven "Spring" Sonata with Marjorie and I'll never forget how expressive it was when for the first time I moulded the sound trying to apply that advice. Marj knew it. She told her sister, Saz told Dame Myra, and the news spread!'

Ultimately, he says, hearing Myra play was like experiencing a type of Platonic ideal in music. 'I've sometimes likened Myra's performances to Platonic forms, to ideal representations of whatever music she was recreating. When Dame Myra finished a piece, you felt as if the whole composition lay before you as a perfect representation of itself.'

'Simplicity, Simplicity': Yonty Solomon[10]

Coming to Britain from South Africa to study with Myra, Yonty Solomon had made contact via Howard's friend Nolsie. Solomon was an important inheritor of her open, singing tone, variety of colour and sense of cherishing the music; as a professor at the Royal College of Music, he passed this on to many students (including Piers Lane, who for some years in the 2000s ran an annual Myra Hess Day at the National Gallery).

After gaining a degree from Cape Town University, he joined the small coterie of devoted students at Cavendish Close.

He first visited Myra soon after she had returned from a US tour. 'I played the Schumann Concerto and she played the orchestral part on the second piano,' he recalled (in an interview with the screenwriter Judy Meewezen). 'I was terrified – so nervous of someone of that ilk – but she was absolutely wonderful to me. I doted on her and after every lesson I used to go home and write everything down.'

He recalled Myra talking about 'the balance of the arm, like a suspension bridge, and she used the analogy of a tennis racket, never forcing the key. She was very much for playing on the cushion of the finger, and the paper-thin weight of the key. I remember in Beethoven's Fourth she spoke about getting the shape of the chord into the hand; the weight from the shoulder would permeate right down into the cushions of the fingers, reach into the piano and draw the sound out.'

One day he took her Schumann's *Carnaval*. 'She wanted simplicity; she wanted the rhythms to spring along; and she had a mania about being true to the text. If you didn't do that - ! And what was fascinating about it was, in a way, not being emotionally involved: the emotion was in the music, but the message wasn't about *you*.

'She was at her best in Schumann, which engendered a spark in her. She had marvellous ideas about pedalling, dissonances and simplicity: her basic message to me was, "Simplicity, simplicity!" This took me years to understand fully. I had the most wonderful lesson on the Schumann Piano Concerto, and one on Beethoven's Fourth – there was a very personal approach to the way she shaped the opening. Her voicing of the chords was part of a chamber music approach, bringing out inner voices. It was never for effect. Whatever she did had an overall simplicity and truthfulness. She would always say, "You have to get nearer to the truth…"'

Yonty, who was homosexual, was sometimes puzzled by Myra's attitude towards personal life, which centred on her priest-like vocation. 'She was leaning on the piano,' he related, 'and said, "You cannot have a life: this is everything. I made that decision too."'

And there were blind spots – including, it seems, Howard. While Myra was touring, she often asked Howard to coach her students in her absence. Once, Yonty said, he thought that Howard was making a pass at him. Intensely uncomfortable, he decided not to consult him again. Myra, who did not know about the incident, was not happy. 'I had several lessons with her after that and she was very tight-lipped,' he recalled. 'She was furious.' Unable to continue with Howard, but equally unable to tell Myra exactly what the problem was, Yonty felt he had made 'two very big faux-pas … it was a side of Myra I had never seen before.'

He felt that Myra was never the same towards him after this; the shift extended even to some destructive comments about his playing. 'I played the Beethoven "Pastoral" Sonata at a competition at the Royal Over-Seas League, and she was horrendous to me: I played the slow movement and she said: "That's not a scherzo". Everything I did seemed to be wrong. After all these wonderful lessons, on everything from the Bach Goldberg Variations to the Brahms D minor Concerto, it was a complete volte-face. I was innocent! I came from South Africa! I lost confidence and it took me years to recover.'

The somewhat possessive, absolutist side of Myra reared up again when he praised a recording of Clara Haskil playing the Schubert B flat major Sonata. 'She said, "Oh, maybe you should go and play to *her*!"' Yet Myra's generosity was legendary too. She was fond of Yonty's South African Jewish mother and when she came to visit, they spent a whole day together. He remembered Myra once asking her what it was like to give birth.

'Later she loaned me the piano that she had lent to Kathleen Ferrier, for two years. She was a great human being – I learned so much from her. And I've tried to promulgate her ideas on music and spirituality.'

'She Tore Me to Shreds': Myra's Other Students

Myra's students were notable, overall, for their very different, strongly defined musical characters. She seems to have given them the necessary tools to build individuality; it would be difficult to mistake Yonty Solomon's playing for Stephen Kovacevich's, for instance. Among Myra's other charges were the duo of Joel Ryce and Yaltah Menuhin; Malcolm Frager, a former Juilliard student of Carl Friedberg, who left an impressive discography, primarily of Viennese classics; and Clive Lythgoe, who after a high-profile career decided to leave behind the performance nerves that had plagued him and devoted himself instead to bringing music to underprivileged communities in the US.

The American pianist John Kenneth Adams did not become Myra's pupil but gained insights into her approach and attitudes while he was studying with Hilda Dederich at the Academy on a Fulbright Scholarship.

For experience accompanying, Hilda sent him to Marj, which he valued tremendously. His teacher in America, Virginia French Mackie, had given him a letter of introduction to Myra, encouraging him to offer to turn her pages. When he plucked up the courage to do so, he was invited to Cavendish Close for tea:

> I had in my mind the picture of Myra Hess on stage, tall and majestic with long black dress and short train. Imagine my surprise when I found her to be quite short, moving around the house with a lively step. She was so relaxed and so funny I soon forgot I was in the presence of one of the world's greatest artists.
>
> I asked her how she enjoyed teaching, as I had already heard several of her pupils. She grew rather serious and said she sometimes had to steel herself before coming downstairs for a lesson, saying she felt they played everything so fast. She was very frank in her comments, saying some students played things in public before they were ready, and that upset her.[11]

The British pianist Peter Katin played to Myra when he was 17. 'She was the first person who actually criticised me,' he said, laughing, in an interview long afterwards.

> I was there for about three hours and she tore me to shreds. It wasn't until months later that I realised she wouldn't have kept me there for three hours if she hadn't thought it was worth doing. All the criticisms she made were in fact quite right. The way she set about it was rather brutal, but I'm not sure she wasn't right to do that too.
>
> I was a very inhibited player. I couldn't even talk about music and she said I was 'playing to myself', as it were, and I had to learn to project: not in terms of noise, but in terms of feeling the projection, playing *to* something. She went to the other end of the room and said: 'Now play the beginning of the Chopin Scherzo again. Play it to me. Don't just make a noise. Speak up and play it to me.' And I did and she said: 'That's better. That's what you must do.' Myra's abrasive manner aside, I learned more in three long afternoons than I ever learned anywhere else.[12]

If Myra's very different pupils inherited anything in common, perhaps it was the range of colour in the touch; an open, singing tone quality; the ability to play very softly while keeping real substance in the sound; a dedication to extremely hard work; and the transcendental, no-nonsense, all-or-nothing embrace of the music.

1 This and subsequent letters MH to HF, Myra Hess Collection, BL
2 *The Times*, 8 October 1956
3 *Los Angeles Times*, 26 March 1957
4 *Los Angeles Times*, 19 December 1965
5 S. Siek booklet notes to *Myra Hess, The Complete Solo and Concerto Studio Recordings*, APR 7504
6 Author interviews with Stephen Kovacevich
7 Author interview with Ann Schein
8 Author interview with Richard Contiguglia
9 Author interview with John Contiguglia
10 J. Meewezen interview with Yonty Solomon, by kind permission
11 J. K. Adams, 'Myra Hess in America', *Women in Music* 2011
12 Sue Stevens filmed interview with Peter Katin, *Spectrum*, Swindon Viewpoint

Final Years
(1958-1965)

Myra might have talked about retiring, but she was in no hurry to do it. If a musician is happy with her schedule, plays well and is booked for concerts, she need never stop if she does not want to. In the US in 1958, Myra was busy planning 1959. 'It will mean being over here for about four months again, but I don't think that can be avoided,' she told Howard, with impersonal wording to sidestep any sense of choice in the matter.

Saz now wrote most of the diaries and letters; Myra was tired and, with her arthritic hand, often in pain. Yet the rewards were still strong enough to keep her on the road. Maybe she drove herself too hard – but as her latest recording proved, she still had much to give and, indeed, to experience.

One such moment was when Helen Keller came to visit her. Keller, who had lost both her sight and her hearing during a childhood illness aged 19 months, had become an author, lecturer and disability rights campaigner, triumphing over her situation and travelling as far afield as New Zealand. She was ten years Myra's senior. The visit took place despite a blinding snow-storm. Saz wrote:

> Helen Keller motored in from the country with her wonderful friend Polly....and after lunch Nancy Hamilton [Katherine Cornell's companion] brought them to hear M play. It was one of the most poignant things that has ever happened to us. We thought she would just sit with her hand on the piano and get perhaps, the feeling of the rhythm. But it was one of the greatest manifestations of the power of the unseen that can be imagined. Helen didn't even touch the piano for most of the time; she just seemed caught up into the essence of the music, so that she apprehended and anticipated the whole of it. More than anything else, she reminded me, who could see her better than M could, of Toscanini conducting. Her hands moved with the music and you could see her preparing for what was about to come. M could see

> a lot too and had the same impression. Myra first played the Bach Gigue from the French Suite, then some variations of the slow movement of the Appassionata and ended with the Bach Adagio. We shall neither of us ever forget the transfiguration of H's face and the radiance. We are quite sure that she got more from the music than 99% of the people who have ears. Nancy, who knows her so well, stood there with tears running down her face, as even she had never seen Helen so inspired.[1]

The musical world around Myra was changing faster than ever. One can only imagine what she made of the runaway rise of rock'n'roll, or the sweeping popularity of Elvis Presley. As for new classical music, Shostakovich, Britten, Poulenc, Messiaen and the elderly Stravinsky continued writing in their own inimitable languages; but elsewhere composition was entering a strange, ghettoised period in which, as Myra had noted, critics seemed only to approve of sounds that were painful to the ear.

The traditional means of musical construction were being jettisoned by a generation of composers who associated regular rhythms and melody with military marches. The traumas of World War II seemed to demand a clean break with the past, but as a new approach took shape, public appetite for it was never considered necessary. 'Total serialism', as advocated by Pierre Boulez (one of a tiny handful of composers who created masterpieces with this system) meant the equalisation of all notes, regardless of tonal affinities or the human need for orientation in the sound. Ultimately it had the opposite effect to what was intended. Pursued, often fanatically, by professors who insisted their composition students must follow it at all costs, it gave the impression that new classical music was only for an initiated elite that could 'understand' such noises. Even many of them could not.

Countless composers, for around half a century after 1950, felt alienated or creatively destroyed. Howard, who had valiantly declared that the fad was passing, was among those who seem to have admitted defeat. He remarked that he was retiring from composing because he had nothing more to say. He turned instead to editing music for The Associated Board of the Royal Schools of Music. His Violin Sonata No. 2 was the last new work that Myra performed.

Asked by John Amis why she did not play more contemporary music, Myra remarked that in her youth, new music was more romantic and melodic. 'Now composers use the piano mainly as a percussive instrument ... and this percussive business is something I've spent my life trying to avoid,' she said. 'To me, music should sing. And if it does not sing, it eventually makes one, or makes *me*, cross and irritable.'[2]

Carnegie Hall was crammed full for Myra's afternoon recital on 8th February 1958, at which she played the last three Beethoven sonatas. Saz felt overwhelmed: 'From the first note till the last, the glory of the Lord was evident.' Perhaps the best was Op. 111, particularly the second of its two movements: 'There was a transcendental quality which was beyond description and when she had finished, there was complete silence for what seemed an eternity, but was probably half a minute, before that huge audience gave her a perfect ovation.' [3]

Myra made her speech explaining that nothing could follow that sonata; New York acquiesced. 'The evening papers said that no-one else could have done such a thing,' Saz added, 'but how right it was and the audience's acceptance was the greatest tribute she could have had. It was all shockingly moving and upsetting.'

On 15th February, Steinway's held a giant party for Myra. In the showrooms, the pianos were replaced by great vases of flowers and tables laden with fine food and drink. For two and a half hours Myra stood and received the guests, flanked by Henry and Polly Steinway, the company's new president and his wife. Among the guests were the Danish pianist-comedian Victor Borge and Katherine Cornell. 'It was an extremely exhausting affair, but almost worth it to see the love and affection that so many people had for M., of every age, sort and kind,' Saz wrote.

She and Myra struggled on with the tour through the dead of winter. On the way to Providence, all the water on the train was frozen, the journey took six hours instead of three and the two venerable lady 'pilgrims' sat in their fur coats throughout before arriving and stepping into a snow drift several feet deep. Myra just had time to swallow some coffee at the hotel before rushing off to give a Schubert and Beethoven recital, including the 'Appassionata'. 'It is typical of M that she gave a staggering performance throughout!' Saz reported.

The next day, 19th February, was Matthay's centenary. Myra was to mark the occasion in an anniversary concert with Bruce and Rosalind Simonds. They were rehearsing Bach's Concerto for Three Keyboards together when from New York there came tragic news: Julia Steinway had suffered a heart attack on the afternoon of the party.

Myra and the Simondses had to press on with the performance regardless; friends had come all the way from Kansas City and Chicago, Thornton Wilder included. But on 21st February Greiner rang Myra to tell her that Julia had passed away. Myra wrote a tribute for *The New York Times*; the funeral took place at St Thomas's Church on 24th February.

Myra spent her birthday mourning her old friend while on the train to St Paul, Minnesota. There Beryl joined her and Saz. A litany ensued of missing pianos, a coughing audience and, in Chicago, 'air conditioning ...[that] works through old radiators, which make a noise like a dyspectic dragon'. But Myra's Chicago recital Saz considered even finer than Carnegie Hall. In Detroit, she broke her rule of not playing an encore after Op. 111, having received a letter from a 13-year-old girl pleading for the Bach Adagio from the C major Toccata as it was her favourite piece.

Myra and Saz then encountered a startling new piano star: Glenn Gould, from Canada, who had not yet abandoned the concert platform for the recording studio, as would later be his choice. He was playing in New York with Mitropoulos; they gatecrashed what they hoped would be his rehearsal. Saz wrote on 12th March:

> He is extremely eccentric and the whole rehearsal was rather like a dream... Mitropoulos was rehearsing the orchestra in the Schoenberg, when Gould arrived, had the piano raised on blocks and then brought in a very low chair to sit on. It was the most incredible position, with the keyboard almost on a level with his chin. We had no means of judging about his playing, as Mitropoulos rehearsed the orchestra all the time, singing the piano part instead of letting Gould play. He meanwhile beetled on and off the stage fetching himself glasses of water, etc. I went home ... but M stayed and finally went up and talked to Mitropoulos and Gould. In spite of his antics, he seemed a nice simple chap and M was very sorry not to hear him properly.

Saz's sharp eye captured everything from a fuss about a hedgehoggy loofah to the 'hooha going on in all the papers about the accidental dropping of the un-charged atomic bomb in Carolina ... Anyhow, it has very much justified our objections in England to having aircraft flying about loaded up with the things.' She also recorded that 'a very touching coloured girl, who is blind, came to play for M'.

Myra meanwhile was performing with the NY Philharmonic conducted by Ernest Ansermet – 'very "sweet and gentle", but a little "vieux jeu,"'[4] she told Howard. The Carnegie Hall concert – the Beethoven C minor Concerto – filled up despite a snowstorm that had left much of New Jersey without heat and light.

Her Washington DC recital at Constitution Hall on 16th March left Saz positively staggered. 'It made us sad, but me specially, that this was the last concert with the Mozart, Schubert, Bach and Op. 111 programme. It has been probably the most exacting programme M has ever played, not only physically but more still from an emotional and musical point of view and each time she has reached greater heights and more profound revelation.'

At the Metropolitan Museum, Stern 'had forgotten to bring his part of the Brahms D minor, which of course he knows by heart, but to keep up appearances, he put the music of the Mozart Sonata on the stand and turned over, most convincingly! We thought afterwards, of all the people who wondered what edition he was using…' But for Myra, Saz noted, it was a great joy to be playing chamber music again.

The stresses of the 1958 tour did not stop Myra returning in 1959, which carried her as far as three Mozart concertos in San Francisco. She wrote from New York to Howard that she was trying to refuse 'exasperating demands for 1960', but had enjoyed the chance to see John Gielgud in 'a tremendous evening of Shakespeare … I had to send him a telegram in order to get a seat…' and was pleased to hear that her student Clive Lythgoe was standing in for 'poor Gary Graffman', who was unwell. She also gave a recital with Pierre Fournier: 'I don't think I have heard such lovely cello playing since Casals, and it was a sublimely easy ensemble.'[5]

But then she came down with bronchitis. Victor Parsonnet, one of the few people she would listen to on health issues, advised her to cancel ('Thank goodness she will listen to someone!' wrote Rose. 'Quite a gal, all in all.')

To Howard on 8th March, Myra described herself as 'a frustrated Virgin of the Bronx!'[6] She had not cancelled Toronto and Toledo gladly, she wrote, but needed a week off since she was suffering 'a recurrence of our dear little Virus … and this time it has caught me in the bronchial, or bronxial toobs…' Victor advised her against going to Canada 'where there may be innumerable inches of snow'.

At her Chicago recital, she wrote on 18th March, she was not only well enough to go ahead, but played six encores, rather to Dr Marquardt's alarm. She was pleased to find him less gloomy about her arthritis than the doctors at home, but accepted his view from the previous year that she was taking on too much. 'He says I can play for years IF I am sensible.... He doesn't quite appreciate how I have to twists round on my behind to play certain chords....but while you all think I am playing better, I will "hand on".'

She agreed to tour again in 1960, 'but for a very limited number of concerts, yes...really! The H[and] has been as unaccountable as ever, hurting like H[ell] and then recovering for no reason..... This respite is all to the good, I know, and I am sure it will see me through the rest of the tour.' A publisher had approached her about writing her autobiography: 'I sent regrets... A. that I had already promised it to several publishers, and B. that I had no intention of ever writing one!!!!!'[7]

Despite Myra's upbeat tone, Rose told a different story. Writing on 15th April to Howard – who had just received an honorary doctorate in Belfast – she called Myra 'Julia'. She feared Saz and Beryl were not making Myra's life easier, whether because of Saz's own shaky health or their incessant worrying. 'Sometimes,' she wrote, 'we look at that little triangle and throw up our hands in despair ... we have confidence in Julia's great wisdom and her ability to evaluate a situation correctly.'

The Parsonnets had always promised Myra that if the time came when her playing went downhill, they would tell her. Rose, reporting successful recitals in Los Angeles, considered that this was not the time, especially as Myra knew that longer periods of rest between concerts was key to her continuation. Rose was convinced that she was not planning much after the next season, that she understood the limits imposed by her condition and that her increasing number of interesting students signalled her future direction.

Attempting to deny her 'the very breath of life' would be cruel and futile, Rose thought. As long as she felt physically capable and nobody was telling her that she was not playing well enough, nothing in the world was going to stop her. Myra had admitted that she should not have taken on so much that season, but that she saw red when she felt people were trying to run her life. Rose concluded: 'She is not an easy handful!!'[8]

Farewell to Carnegie Hall

Myra's home life was not an easy handful either. The Mauls had retired in 1953; the couple who had replaced them, the Newnhams, had issues with an elderly, infirm mother. But it turned out that the situation was considerably worse. The pair horrified Myra by resigning the day before she returned from the US. She got back to find her car stinking of alcohol and the house 'in the most indescribable state of dirt, and an accumulation of rubbish that had to be taken away in truck loads!!! … I think I would have been less shocked if I had been knocked down by a taxi.'[9]

After a careful recruitment process, she hired a Scottish couple: Andrew and Williamina Christie, with their daughter Carolyn. They were interviewed at length by Myra, Marj and Saz; McKenna relates that Myra remarked that she could at times be 'up in the air' with nerves before a concert, to which Mrs Christie responded that she felt exactly the same when making a soufflé. This sealed the deal – and Mrs Christie was a superb cook. Her husband served as butler and also driver when Myra bought a new black Austin Princess, a luxurious limousine with red seats.

In the US, her services as campaigner were needed. Back in 1955 Robert Simon, owner of Carnegie Hall, had put the building up for sale. New York City was soon awash with rumours that the concert hall was to be demolished and replaced with a skyscraper. Isaac Stern formed a Committee to Save Carnegie Hall in 1956 and initially managed to block the sale. Now the issue was rearing up again. Lincoln Center was being built and the New York Philharmonic would move there when it was ready. Support for Carnegie Hall was gathering, however, thanks to a roll-call of philanthropists, senators and celebrities including Eleanor Roosevelt, Kreisler, Heifetz, Rubinstein, Stokowski, Reiner, Marian Anderson, Van Cliburn and, of course, Myra. In 1960 Stern persuaded civic leaders to organise a Citizens Committee for Carnegie Hall, creating a not-for-profit organisation to save it.

He asked Myra to make a point of this in her recital on 13th February 1960. 'I should have to say that I was the Prima Donna giving her first Farewell ?????' Myra wrote to Howard. 'Isaac is the prime mover, and apparently has telephoned everyone, including God….' [10]

She gave the concert, less than two weeks before her 70th birthday: again, the last three Beethoven sonatas. In her speech she remarked:

'Let us hope that a miracle will happen and that I may be able to play for you again in this great hall.' To that end, she provided a string of encores.

New York City finally saved the building, purchasing it for $5m. Stern remained president of the Carnegie Hall Corporation until his death; in 1997 the main auditorium was renamed after him. Yet, with bitter irony, Myra's own failing health meant that that recital was indeed her farewell to it.

Myra had been enjoying 'jetting' from place to place instead of spending hours on trains. When the news of Carnegie Hall's rescue arrived in the spring, she had jetted off again – this time, on holiday with two men, as she gleefully told Ted Ferris afterwards.

She, Howard and Frank Mannheimer went to Sicily in mid April for three weeks; she relished the fact that her gentlemen were helping to unpack her dresses. They motored to see ruined temples and through the mountains to rural trattorias and a marionette theatre. From her hotel room, she had a view of the sea and Mount Etna. A card table was moved in for her use. But on hearing the news from New York, she at once began to plan her return to that hallowed stage, wondering whether to play the last three Beethoven sonatas again.

In Britain she was driving herself hard as ever, with performances at Southwark Cathedral with Boult and a charity concert for the World Refugee Cause (the Bach D minor Concerto). At the Edinburgh Festival, now an annual highlight, she and Stern gave a recital of varied and demanding violin and piano repertoire: the Brahms A major Sonata, Beethoven's last Sonata Op. 96 in G major, the Schubert D major Sonatina and Howard's Sonata No. 2.

First broadcast, then issued on LP, the recital reveals a spontaneous, conversational, engagingly natural partnership. There is some occasional insecurity in Myra's touch, but, to be fair, in Stern's too. The sense of love for the music is as vivid as ever; perhaps working with him was a welcome return to repertoire she had loved performing with Jelly for two decades before World War II – and with Aldo Antonietti before World War I. Since the Gallery concerts, she had only given occasional duo concerts with violinists.

By some miracle, when the heart attack finally struck in September, Myra was not travelling or performing, but sitting at home by her own fireside. It was fortunately a mild one, but her doctors ordered complete rest, a cessation of smoking and the cancellation of all concerts for the rest of the year.

Myra was not a compliant patient. She disliked conventional medicine (which to some extent was just as well, as she had proved allergic to penicillin) and had no intention of relinquishing either her cigarettes or her American tour. She shared a consultant, Lord Evans, with the Queen – but even he could not keep her away from the piano, the planning calendar or her January embarkation for the US.

Recovering, Myra had had more time than usual to listen to the radio, and before heading for the US she penned some strong opinions to the Pilkington Committee on Broadcasting (chaired by the industrialist Sir Harry Pilkington, it aimed to consider the future of broadcasting, especially TV). Myra's letter is not a grumble, but offers real insights into her dislike of machines and her preference for live performance. She wrote on 9th January that she was distressed by the growing amount of pre-recorded music on the radio.

Her view was that ideally all music should be heard at first hand. 'A live radio performance is the next best thing. But a pre-recorded radio performance removes the listener twice from the live original and much is bound to be lost in transit.' Even in a live transmission, the engineer added interference between musician and listener, and a repeat broadcasting meant a further compromise: 'May I therefore, in the interest of music, beg for as little mechanical reproduction as possible and ask for more live broadcasts to allow for the most direct communication possible between artist and listener.'[11]

Not that the committee took much notice; it was focusing on the creation of local radio channels and colour TV licences. Live concert broadcasts do not seem even to have crossed its radar.

The Last US Trip

When Myra left for the US, Saz and Beryl both went with her; and Howard took over teaching Stephen, her star pupil, while she was gone. But on the Queen Mary, she was plagued by headaches and Beryl worried desperately about what to do if she had another heart attack at sea.

She arrived at the Simonds's house before her first concert at New Haven, but while practising complained of numbness and stiffness in her left arm, which briefly made her consider cancelling. Yet the concert – her Beethoven trilogy – was a gratifying experience that gave her confidence.

At Hunter College, New York, on 28th January, she was playing the Schubert B flat Sonata, and a heap of Schumann – the *Etudes symphoniques*, *Papillons* and some of the *Bunte Blätter*. During the *Etudes symphoniques*, she lost some sense of coordination. Nobody realised exactly what was happening, though *The New York Times* was baffled by wrong notes, blurred passages and apparently inconsistent musical ideas. Beryl, in the wings, knew something was seriously amiss.

Myra told Howard a few days later that 'it was not happy hunting', but she blamed the dry acoustic, exacerbated by 100 people in chairs on the stage, for an experience she found 'nightmarish'. She managed a snipe at Harriet, after whom Stern had enquired, following a conversation with one of Harriet's admirers. Myra had 'put him wise', reporting that her old nemesis had been 'making a fool of herself' giving lectures about the composers who loved her and wrote for her. Meanwhile, she herself was planning a 'Mozart Fest' – ten piano concertos – for the following winter's US visit, plus recitals in the autumn. 'It is astonishing how optimistic old hags can be??!!' she joked.[12]

Amid 'annihilating cold', Myra, Saz and Beryl were preparing to fly to Toronto. Saz told Marj that she had to stand her bottle of milk on the radiator to prevent it freezing overnight. Before they could leave, however, the disaster they had feared took place. Beryl came into Myra's room in the Laurelton to find her lying immobile but for frantic twitches on the left side of her body.

Saz told Marj everything on 10th February, discouraging her from hastening to Myra's side. 'Missie' had to be kept 'quiet' and Marj would not be able to see her even if she were to travel over. 'The excitement would send her off like a rocket,' Saz wrote. 'She can't think of you without bursting into tears.' She remarked, pragmatic as ever, that if Myra got better, they would soon be home; and that if she did not, she would prefer Marj not to see her in such a state.

By 16th February the papers were announcing the smokescreen excuse that Myra had cancelled the rest of her tour due to a viral infection. Saz told Howard on 23rd February that Myra's symptoms were confusing. As far as she understood it, Myra had had a blood clot, not in the brain but in an artery, which disrupted the flow of blood to the part of the brain that controls the motor nerves on the left. The resulting spasm had made the left of her face, left arm and left leg twitch, also affecting her ability to speak:

> There is no apparent reason why she should not make a complete recovery and be able to play in public again, but the doctors all say that they cannot be sure at this juncture. It is really a matter of the amount of control she gets back in the arm; as you know, it has bothered her for some time, feeling it was not under control. Play again, she certainly will and it will be up to her to decide the rest.

It seems extraordinary that Myra was not hospitalised – but she loathed hospitals and it seems to have been virtually impossible for anybody to stand up to her, even in circumstances that threatened her life. Surgery was not an option: vascular surgery was only just being developed and neurosurgery, which was suggested, was regarded by Saz, Beryl and Myra's 'personal physician' as 'unpromising'[13]. Myra had been given an anti-coagulant after her heart attack the previous year and had the same again now.

The trio holed up in the Laurelton with a nurse for Myra, and complete muzzling of the truth to the outside world beyond Howard and Marj. They were afraid people would associate what had happened to Myra with the fate of Solomon. 'Nothing could be more different,' Saz wrote. 'No paralysis, no loss of strength and her mind and memory have been crystal clear all the time. Also, her sense of humour has been very much to the fore!'[14] She told Marj that Myra was doing better at *The Times* Crossword than she, Saz, was.

Beryl wrote that Myra was 'as brave as a lion'[15]. She and Saz were making such efforts to keep her calm that they vetted and rationed her post, even tearing up some letters and instructing Howard not to let Stephen send her mail marked 'private'. Myra loved Howard's missives and enjoyed what news from home her assistants let through, including ecstatic reviews for the young cellist Jacqueline du Pré's Wigmore Hall debut. But Saz judiciously kept back the news that all was not well with Myra's 'boys' of the Griller Quartet. That year the violist Philip Burton took his own life. The remaining ensemble limped on, trying out new violists, but ultimately disbanded in 1963.

Myra was up one day, down the next. For therapeutic work on her hand, she had a small red rubber ball to squeeze, intended to strengthen her fingers. She kept it in an ashtray beside the bed, as she had not smoked for two weeks. Through February she improved slowly, but, Saz said, she could maintain her act just so long and no longer.

At first, according to Saz, one doctor thought Myra was heading for complete paralysis, because she considered the symptoms were caused by a haemorrhage, but the result of the lumbar puncture showed it was not. She had had a 'vascular disturbance' caused by a clot, which stopped the circulation of blood: if it dispersed without causing irreversible damage, all would be well. The quantity of damage would be determined by how quickly the symptoms cleared. Myra's were going reassuringly fast.

One doctor told Saz that Myra should not contemplate performing again until the end of October. Another said – to Beryl, but not to Myra – that she should wait a whole year from the end of January. But no doctor wanted to be the one to tell Dame Myra Hess that her career was over.

By late March, Myra was able to write letters, heading one to Howard 'March 27th – so they tell me! 1961, I believe'. She wrote: 'It has been a nightmare & for several days I did hope it was the end. Apparently it is going to be very difficult to get rid of me & I have to learn quite a new kind of Patience to get me through these next weeks (or months?). Two ½ hours a day at the piano are beginning to bring my hands back to life.' Steinway's had promised to send her a piano for the return voyage so that she could continue 'therapeutics' at sea. Dr Marquardt had come from Chicago 'and was amazed at my progress - & gave me untold hope for the future, even possibly my Prom in Sept – between ourselves! I had virtually resigned myself to no more playing…'

Arriving home at Cavendish Close at long last, she burst into tears.

Crisis Point

A notice in *The Times* on 3rd April broke the news that Myra would be unable to perform in the near future…because of 'a rheumatic condition in her hands'. She had to cancel a concert at the Royal Festival Hall on 4th May; the Hungarian pianist Annie Fischer stepped in. Yet by summer, she was well enough to contemplate a return; and, remarkably, she was back on stage in time for the new season. She played Beethoven's Fourth Concerto with her old friends Boult and the LPO at the Proms on 8th September, which Saz described as her 'best ever'.

At the RFH on 28th September she played Mozart's concertos K414 and K453 with Blech and the London Mozart Players, and on 31st October the Mozart A major Concerto K488 with the LPO, the RAF Central Band and Boult at the RFH. This was a gala concert to mark the 21st anniversary of the Battle of Britain – and the 21st anniversary of Myra's performance of the same work at the Gallery concerts with the RAF Symphony Orchestra. Her great admirer, the Queen Mother, was in the audience. Myra told *The*

Daily Telegraph that she still practised every day 'for as long as I can think constructively'; the paper explained that this could amount to six hours. [16]

This concert turned out to be her last public performance.

Crisis point arrived on 10th December. Myra was giving a radio broadcast from a BBC studio of Schubert's B flat Sonata D960 and the second of the Klavierstücke D946. The sonata, Schubert's last, written weeks before his death aged 31, has acquired a mystical status; the notion exists, whether imagined or actual, that the composer has sensed life drawing towards a close. It has an aura of wisdom, beauty, regret and tragedy. In the first movement shuddering bass trills are left hanging in mid air like unanswered questions; the finale hovers between major and minor, laughter and tears, with pauses that freeze on bleak octaves, and a jubilant coda that can feel like a forced smile.

Suffering both physically and in terms of confidence, Myra wanted the opinions of Frank Mannheimer and Howard on the broadcast. With difficulty, Frank admitted to her over dinner that it had had serious problems and that he would advise against broadcasting it again. Myra was upset, and well she might be, as Frank was one of her oldest friends and a musician who always inspired confidence. But the coup de grâce came when Howard, away at the time of the transmission, went with her, Saz and Marj to listen back to it in a BBC control room. He echoed Frank's opinion. The first two movements were beautiful, but they thought the scherzo lacked adequate control and had too many mistakes. Both men were suggesting, clear as crystal, that it was time Myra should retire. 'Poor Myra believed them,' John Continguglia says.

The Contiguglia twins were horrified. They felt, as Saz did, that Howard and Frank had somehow set out to destroy Myra's confidence; they could not understand why anyone should do such a thing. They called Myra to say that they had both had goosebumps in the minor episodes of the Klavierstück, to which she replied with satisfaction that that was exactly what ought to happen. John remembered Saz being 'indignant' and saying that if Myra played one beautiful phrase then it was worth hearing her – 'and she played many beautiful phrases,' he adds.

The twins had missed the broadcast except for the Klavierstück, but later acquired a rare copy of the recording. John comments: 'I've heard every pianist under the sun play the Schubert B flat Sonata, and they don't come close to that. Of course there were a few smudged notes, but the quality of her playing for most of the piece is breathtakingly beautiful... It moves me to tears.'[17]

Nevertheless, Stephen Siek, who was close to Denise and Frank, recalls that many in Myra's inner circle knew it was time for her to stop, including Denise: 'She said it broke her heart when Myra came backstage floating on air after a performance, convinced that she had done a wonderful job. Denise, listening, thought she had not at all, but of course she didn't know how to tell her.'[18]

Who was right? Possibly everyone, each in their own way. The Schubert sonata performance, which survives privately, comes across as a profound, raw, exposed emotional experience. Myra seems to make Schubert's existential angst the outlet for her own. Her exquisite phrasing, voicing and eloquent warmth of tone are wholly intact. There are a few wrong notes, chiefly in the scherzo, which is indeed slightly unsteady at times. Yet plenty of pianists have given more error-strewn performances, and few play this work with a fraction of Myra's wisdom and poetry. Is it up to her usual standard? Technically, maybe not, to those who knew her in her glory days. Musically, yes – and more than. But is that enough?

Myra at the end of her career was in direct competition with younger, stronger pianists hungry for opportunity. Would promoters still book her if her health was uncertain and she might have to cancel? A further BBC broadcast recording of Haydn's late E flat major Sonata went ahead in January 1962, but Beryl reported that it was heavily edited by the sound engineer. When Ibbs and Tillett requested a Prom date for Myra, the concerts manager told them that the position was 'very complicated'. They nevertheless pencilled her in for Beethoven's Fourth with Klemperer on 7th August.

It was not even Myra's heart problem that stopped her, but the agonising arthritis in her hands. Her appearance was cancelled; Stephen played instead. She went along to listen: 'I was proud of him & he had a great reception,' she wrote[19]. The Contiguglias attended with Myra and remembered her whispering 'Nice' at the rehearsal when Stephen played the concerto's opening phrase. From her, that was high praise. Next, her plans for ten Mozart concertos in New York in the new year evaporated.

Sadly, her nearest and dearest seem not to have handled the situation in a helpful enough way: everyone was rather scared of her. Saz could not abide the notion that Myra should retire. Howard and Frank were being loyal by suggesting she should quit, yet perhaps came across as destructive because they felt so awkward. Beryl thought the doctors should tell Myra she should stop, but they did not. Everybody wanted someone else to take responsibility.

Eventually the person who had to do the deed was Myra's agent, Emmie Tillett. Having known Myra since World War I, she found it unspeakably painful to face her and tell her she could no longer perform in public. She tried to suggest a grand retirement occasion, but Saz insisted that they could not possibly do that when Myra might yet recover.

And so a press release on 2nd April 1962 stated: 'Dame Myra Hess, internationally known concert pianist, has cancelled all engagements today because of rheumatism in her hands. The British pianist, seventy-two years old, said she was undergoing physiotherapy treatment, but would not need to enter a hospital.'

That was Myra's only official farewell.

A Time for Everything

Myra wrote to Edith Frank the day after she should have begun her Mozart marathon in New York, saying that she was making the best of the situation. 'It would have been extremely strenuous and I had to bide by my doctors' tiresome decision. I am filling in a good many hours hearing young players – hoping to help them along the right road. It is very interesting and also exhausting as I never seem able to give a lesson that does not last for at least two hours!'[20] The upside of her time to rest was that she was free to spend three weeks in early summer escaping to San Giorgio, Italy, with Beryl and the Parsonnets.

Just as the fifth lion of Trafalgar Square was bowing out, Britain was starting to boom. Young people were at last free of conscription. Mary Quant invented the mini-skirt. The contraceptive pill was being developed and would be legalised in 1967. Rock'n'roll was sweeping the world and in Liverpool a new band called The Beatles was making its first recordings. The bleak postwar era was over and the fruits of recovery were ripening, ready for the new generation to pluck and tuck in.

London was a magnet to the finest young musicians in the world: life was affordable and the artistic scene replete with top-notch concerts, theatres, opera and ballet, available at low ticket prices thanks to the subsidy system. At the Royal Opera House, ballet lovers could relish Margot Fonteyn at her finest, soon joined by a young defector from the

USSR, Rudolf Nureyev. Operagoers could hear Maria Callas and Joan Sutherland. The conductor's podium was dominated by such towering figures as Klemperer, Georg Solti and Carlos Kleiber.

The piano world was welcoming a generation of virtuosi, their flames fanned by the growing significance of international competitions. Martha Argerich had won the Chopin Competition in Warsaw in 1960; the American Van Cliburn had startled the USSR by triumphing at the Tchaikovsky Competition in Moscow in 1958 at the height of the Cold War; and in Britain, a Yorkshire piano teacher, Fanny Waterman, in 1961 started an equivalent contest in her home city of Leeds.

'Our first abode in London was in Belsize Park, just below Hampstead Heath,' John Contiguglia recalls, 'and we used to walk across the Heath to go to concerts in the grounds of Kenwood House. I remember how beautiful it was. Those were golden years for us, because everything that we loved doing was so unbelievably inexpensive! We could go to the theatre and concerts for a few shillings. We saw great performances of Shakespeare. I remember seeing Laurence Olivier and paying ten shillings. If you wanted to go to a concert by a celebrity in New York, you could pay hundreds of dollars. In London, for Dame Myra we paid a few dollars and got the choicest seats in the house.'[21]

Myra, having had to give up performing, did as much teaching as her reduced stamina allowed. Accounts vary of her mental and physical state. One doctor thought she had manic depression and should have psychological treatment, but this sounds potentially like the latest in a long history of dodgy diagnoses. It was perfectly rational that Myra would feel depressed when deprived of her life's purpose. She had other sorrows to deal with, too; her brother Herbert died in 1963.

The litany of Myra's ailments extended beyond arthritis, heart trouble and depression, to diabetes and emphysema. Even so, she only gave up smoking in her last year. She responded well to anti-depressants and tranquillisers, but that did not stop speculation that she might have suffered damage to the brain from a lack of oxygen during her heart attack. Howard presented this theory in his essay for *Myra Hess by her Friends*: 'the medical evidence, hitherto little known outside her immediate circle, showed that the cause was physical'. He added that after her 'second thrombosis' in 1961 the doctors knew there had been brain damage and that this would become clearer over time. He was convinced that Myra, who he considered had never lacked courage or the ability to face facts, simply could not have been her normal self, otherwise she would have willingly accepted the necessity of retirement.

This, with hindsight, looks extremely dubious. Refusing to accept the situation was perhaps only the third irrational thing Myra had ever done – the first was falling for Arnold Bax, the second refusing to accept the end of the Gallery concerts – but she had form in this respect.

That belief would have gone some way towards explaining Howard's response to her Schubert broadcast – if the recording of that occasion did not seem fine enough to allay such fears. Could anyone suffering brain damage have played such a lengthy, powerful work hampered only by minor unsteadiness and a few wrong notes? It seems unlikely. Besides, none of Myra's family members and surviving pupils thought she was anything but her normal self, even if she was occasionally 'down'.

The interview that John Amis recorded with her for his 1963 radio series *Talking About Music* shows her intellect, humour, memory and charm all intact. Although she is older and speaks more slowly than in Jim Fassett's 1952 interview, she has lost none of her oratory skill. Indeed, in the leafy surroundings of Cavendish Close, where Amis noticed birdsong in the trees and the gentle thwacks of cricket balls at Lord's, Myra wraps her former Gallery concerts assistant round her proverbial little finger.

He asks if her style of playing Mozart has changed. 'Oh, I *hope* so,' Myra exclaims, with a chuckle. Pushed on Mozartian style in other performers, she insists, 'That's a terrible question!' but goes on to offer genuine insights: 'Mozart is more often played badly than almost any other composer ... because it lacks spontaneity. I would say if Mozart isn't spontaneous, it's dead, and the public doesn't have a chance to realise the endless inspiration.'

Reminiscing about the Gallery concerts, she paid tribute to her friends in the US: 'We should never have been able to carry on if it hadn't been for America and Canada. ... they sent us thousands of dollars.' She added: 'It was a profound sorrow to me that the concerts had to stop after six and a half years, and I would willingly have given up my playing career to continue organising them, for the sake of the younger artists if for nothing else. It is so hard nowadays to make a start...'

She opened up on her views of the new generation of performers and the 'terrible competition' they faced. She considered that too many people who were not necessarily great musicians had achieved excessive facility on the piano and could play 'much too well, and much too fast! In fact, one day, when these young people take these exaggerated tempi, I'm going to get up in the audience and I'm going to say "*Vive le sport!*" I tell them, when I'm teaching and they play so ridiculously fast, that it isn't music anymore. I'd just as soon watch skating, or a hockey competition.'

The winter of 1963 was the coldest in Britain for 200 years. The capital was muffled repeatedly by blankets of snow and the Gunns were not alone in finding their gas and electricity cut off. The Contiguglias had a call from Saz: 'She asked if we would go over and shovel Dame Myra's snow for her,' John says. 'I would have swept it off with a toothbrush if I had to! But we went round and she produced a coal shovel for us to clear the snow with. We made sure there was not one bit left on her walk.' [22]

In 1964 she had surgery to clear her right-hand carotid artery, but due to her weak heart it had to be done under only a local anaesthetic. After that she was too weak, and too self-conscious about the scar, to accept many visitors except Saz, Beryl and Howard. Under duress, she spent time with friends who had travelled from America to see her. The Parsonnets took her and Beryl to Wales for a short but challenging break.

Stephen, meanwhile, was heading for stardom, hailed as Myra's heir. On 26th August 1965 he played the Beethoven 'Emperor' Concerto at the Proms with the LSO and Colin Davis. *The Guardian*'s Edward Greenfield termed him the new 'standard-bearer of the European tradition' and praised him as 'a pianist magician, a man for whom argument comes first and display a long way behind, a potential master and thinker… This was a performance such as I have rarely if ever heard from great masters.' He regarded the young musician as 'the exact opposite of an American steam-hammer virtuoso… This, I am sure, is something he owes not merely to his inborn qualities, but to his studies with Dame Myra Hess.'[23]

When her arthritis allowed, Myra would go to the piano and practise one piece that she had always wanted to play, yet never quite dared to: Beethoven's 'Hammerklavier' Sonata, Op. 106, or at least its slow movement. That is the heart of the work, a vast musical canvas that seems to travel into the darkest reaches of faith, doubt and isolation.

Howard would visit most evenings and play Scrabble with her; otherwise, she played Patience, did *The Times* Crossword and watched tennis and show-jumping on TV. Sometimes a friend or pupil would be with her during a test match over at Lord's. Applause would drift over to Myra's house. Jack O'Brien of the former Griller Quartet came to visit and recalled that the pianist's eyes would fill with misty remembrance as she commented: 'What a wonderful sound.'[24]

Edith Frank saw her for the last time in August 1965, at Cavendish Close, with Saz and Beryl; the little group spent the afternoon reminiscing together. 'Myra was all dressed up for our "tea" in her music room with doorway leading into a delightful garden,' Edith recalled. 'Beryl brought out the beautifully bound in red leather volumes she had compiled herself of all the programs of the National Gallery Concerts, with the pencilled notations made by her of what had occurred on each date. The first page I opened at random was that of the day of the Battle of Britain. She also read me the letter from the Queen, acknowledging with deep thanks the gift of these volumes to be presented to the nation as a bequest. The letter concluded with the hope "that this would be at a very distant date".'[25]

When close friends came to see her – Vera and Judy one day, Clare another – Myra bade them farewell by playing them Beethoven's Sonata Op. 109. Clare watched, moved beyond measure, as afterwards Myra closed the piano lid and kissed it. By then, many of Myra's other friends had died, including Benno, while Marj seems to have developed dementia. Once, deep in the night, the chandelier in Myra's music room crashed to the floor.

Myra went into hospital on Saz's birthday, 24th October 1965. After ten days she returned, with two nurses, who were intermittently relieved by Saz; but in November everything deteriorated, with a catalogue of calamities including pneumonia and failing kidneys. Beryl was unable to help much, preoccupied with her own family after her mother Irene's death a few weeks earlier. Howard was too upset by Myra's state to continue visiting so often. The Christies, the nurses and Saz did the best they could for her. In her last three days, Myra knew mercifully little about what was happening. Except for the night nurse, she was alone when the end came, on 25th November after dusk.

Tributes flooded in. Sir Arthur Bliss, as Master of the Queen's Musick, was called upon for quotes: 'Dame Myra's [National Gallery] concerts were the most positive thing that music could do in those days,' he said.

'She performed a great service to the country.'[26] Sir Malcolm Sargent, described by the *Evening Standard* as 'distressed', said: 'Her profound musicianship sprang from an inner humanity which was exemplified by those wartime concerts.'[27] *The Times* obituary noted: 'She was not in the least a solemn person, though she had a proper appreciation of music's significance and social value. There emanated from her presence on the platform as from her actual performances a combination of integrity and geniality.'[28]

Harriet Cohen, responding to a commemorative piece in *The Daily Telegraph*, wrote an effusive letter describing how she, Harriet, had refused a request from Sir Henry Wood to perform Beethoven's Piano Concerto No. 4 because it would seem 'like sacrilege' compared to Myra, and mentioning that to her mind Myra had only ever been equalled by .... Harold Bauer, to whom Myra had told her she was 'deeply indebted'[29]. The number of ancient wounds, veiled attacks and double meanings within those few lines scarcely bore consideration.

As for Saz, she wrote: 'With her passing, a light has gone in the world.'[30]

Myra was cremated at Golders Green, but on 13th December at noon, a memorial service was held for her at St Paul's Cathedral. It was filled with music: the Allegri Quartet performed the slow movements of Schubert's A minor String Quartet and, with Gervase de Peyer, Mozart's Clarinet Quintet. Among a reported 350 people present were Bliss, Boult, Solomon, Leon Goossens, Gerald Moore, Jacqueline du Pré, the composer Nicholas Maw, and Miss Harriet Cohen. They were joined by the Minister for the Arts, Jennie Lee, and the Prime Minister's personal representative John Hughett. Canon Collins, who had organised the Berlin Philharmonic tour with Furtwängler, gave an address recalling the occasion and Myra's unforgettable performance of Beethoven's Fourth Concerto: 'It was a gesture of reconciliation.' There were readings by Dame Sybil Thorndike. Finally Dr John Dykes Bower, the cathedral's organist, played *Jesu, Joy.*

British writers recalled Myra as 'a gracious lady' and the vast majority called her 'the greatest *female* pianist of her time' [our italics]. Yet it was the American critics who had truly got the measure of her. And it was Albert Goldberg who wrote the most personal, substantial and heartfelt tribute, in the faraway *Los Angeles Times*:

> For everyone who loves great music played with selfless devotion and illuminating insight, a light went out with the death of Dame Myra Hess ... She was more than a great pianist, although she certainly was all of that. She was also a unique personality, a woman and an artist of tremendous dignity yet of infinite charm. To hear her play on stage, or to know her off-stage, was to love her; she was irresistible as an artist and as a human being.

He concluded: 'The memory of Myra Hess will always remain vivid to those who heard her and knew her. She was one of the chosen.'[31]

Coda

Myra's will grossed £64,768 – equivalent to over £1m in the 2020s. She left the income from her residuary estate to Saz and Marj. They also received £5,000 and the income from her OUP royalties, pianos, papers and other effects.

The rest was to go to her nephews and nieces after the Gunns' decease. They each were left £1,000, as were her brothers John and Herbert (though Herbert had by then passed away). To Beryl, she left her letter from the Queen Mother for the 1,000th National Gallery concert, as well as all the records and programmes from the series, instructing that after Beryl's death they should go to the British Museum. She bequeathed the Epstein bust to the Royal Academy of Music, her complete Bach edition to Denis Matthews and the rest of her music collection to Howard Ferguson. She left the Christies £1,000 plus £50 for each year of service after their first five, and £500 to the Musicians Benevolent Fund. Myra's house was sold to a London solicitor in March 1966, with seven years left on its lease.

One of Myra's delights had been helping young professional musicians; in 1966 Bliss formed, with Boult, Sir Kenneth Clark, Joyce Grenfell, Malcolm Sargent and Nicholas Sekers, a Myra Hess Trust to carry on where she had had to leave off. They intended to support young performers in the critical time immediately following graduation. The fund, as they wrote in *The Telegraph*'s letters page, had been established by one very generous gift and the trustees would seek further contributions in the UK and US. Performances in its aid were given by artists including Jacqueline du Pré and Stephen Kovacevich in duo, as well as Joyce Grenfell, raising over £12,000 within two months.

A memorial concert in Myra's honour was given at the City Music Society by Yfrah Neaman and Howard on 4th January 1966, with proceeds going to the MBF. After that, concert series sprang up in Myra's memory in many and varied locations. Chicago University's Myra Hess Memorial Concerts are still running in the 2020s. The National Gallery hosted an annual Myra Hess Day, run by Piers Lane, for several years in the 2000s; it continues to hold an annual commemorative recital each 10th October. The City Music Society, which was inspired by the National Gallery Concerts, owned one of Myra's pianos until 1997: a beautiful Rosewood grand of 1927. When CMS acquired a new Steinway Model D, the 1927 piano was sold to the Bishopsgate Institute, where it still resides and is used. A smaller rosewood Steinway of hers, built in 1904, was owned by Wells Cathedral School before being acquired by Myra's great-nephew, the composer Nigel Hess.

Howard moved to Cambridge, where he continued editing music for The Associated Board and in 1995 published a book called *Entertaining Solo*. He died at home on 31st October 1999, aged 91. Jelly d'Arányi died in Florence in April 1966, a few months after Myra's demise. Marjorie Gunn died in 1967 and Saz around 1976. Irene Scharrer and Beryl Davis both died in 1971, Harriet Cohen in 1973. Denise Lassimonne, who was made a fellow of the Royal Academy of Music in 1957, died in 1994.

Myra was survived by her elder brother John and her nieces and nephews. Her talents had included not only music, but public speaking and writing; and many family members went into these fields. Nigel Hess, Herbert's grandson, is celebrated for the film score for *Ladies in Lavender* and was chosen by King Charles III as one of 12 composers to write new works for his coronation in 2023. One of Nigel's cousins, Louise Barder, became a music PR consultant. Irene Davis's grandchildren included Nigel Lawson, Chancellor of the Exchequer under Margaret Thatcher; his son Dominic became a political journalist and his daughter Nigella a celebrity chef. That was one skill Myra had never acquired, though she certainly loved good food.

Myra deserves a reassessment, stripped of the myths, prejudices and assumptions that the 20th century dumped on her shoulders, both during and after her lifetime. She exemplified the confluence of musical standards and philosophies, spiritual faith and moral stance: in her, as in the colleagues she loved best, Toscanini and Casals, they become indivisible. It is otherwise known as integrity.

Over time, the music world's attention turned to more superficial matters. The industry became desperate to make music 'fun' and 'accessible'. With a scarcity of high-quality new compositions that engaged audiences, the canon of famous works sometimes became dulled by overfamiliarity and distorted by half-truths about historical practices, its essential structures semi-understood or ignored. Prejudices about classical music's supposed 'elitism' have ridden roughshod over Myra's humane, all-embracing ideals – despite the latter's veracity being demonstrated by the National Gallery concerts. Those concerts stand as a reminder of music's profound human significance, with which the composers Myra played invested their works whether we like it or not. The Gallery concerts would never have been possible if, to Myra, striving to get 'nearer the truth' in music had not been a matter of life and death.

What really drove her? The little Victorian girl from Boundary Road grew up to be a national heroine, the fifth lion of Trafalgar Square. The pianist once deemed 'not of British origin' had become a symbol of British wartime identity perhaps comparable to nobody except Vera Lynn. Shaped by her times, she shaped in turn those that followed. But what is it that induces somebody to sacrifice her whole self to music for 75 years?

The last word must go to Sir Kenneth Clark, who with Sir Stafford Cripps and other close friends used to listen to Myra playing the piano at home late into the evening during the fearsome nights of World War II. 'How she loved to play,' he wrote simply. 'Nothing could stop her.'[32]

1 A. Gunn diary, 14 March 1958, Hess Family Collection
2 J. Amis interview with MH, op. cit., 1962
3 This and subsequent quotations from A. Gunn diary, as above
4 MH to HF, 24 March 1958, this and subsequent letters BL
5 MH to HF, 8 March 1959
6 MH is referencing the incident in October 1945 when a small boy in the Bronx claimed to have seen a vision of the Virgin Mary
7 MH to HF, 29 March 1959
8 RP to HF, 15 April 1959, BL
9 MH to Ted Ferris, 9 August 1959, see McKenna op. cit., p258
10 MH to HF, 8 Feb 1960
11 MH to Pilkington Committee, 9 January 1961, National Archives
12 MH to HF, 2 February 1961
13 McKenna op. cit., p257
14 AG to HF, 23 Feb 1961, BL
15 Beryl Davis to HF, 17 February 1961
16 *The Daily Telegraph*, 31 October 1961
17 Author interview with John Contiguglia
18 Author interview with Stephen Siek
19 MH to Judy Felton, 18 August 1962, see McKenna op. cit., p264
20 MH to EF, 4 March 1962
21 Author interview with JC
22 Ibid.
23 *The Guardian*, 27 August 1965
24 McKenna op. cit., p273
25 E. Frank, manuscript op. cit.
26 *Evening Standard*, 26 November 1965
27 Ibid.
28 *The Times*, 27 November 1965
29 *The Daily Telegraph*, 3 December 1965
30 A. Gunn, 'American Pilgrimage' in *Myra Hess by her Friends*, p37
31 *Los Angeles Times*, 19 December 1965
32 K. Clark, op. cit., p29

Selected Bibliography

Books

Allen, Roger, *Wilhelm Furtwängler: Art and the Politics of the Unpolitical*, Boydell & Brewer, Woodbridge, 2018

Amis, John, *Amiscellany*, Faber & Faber, London, 1985

Baldock, Robert, *Pablo Casals*, Gollancz, London, 1992

Banfield, Stephen, *Gerald Finzi: An English Composer*, Faber and Faber, London, 1997

Bauer, Harold, *Harold Bauer: His Book*, W.W. Norton, New York, 1948

Bax, Arnold, *Farewell My Youth*, Longmans, Green & Co, London; New York, 1943

Bosman, Suzanne, *The National Gallery in Wartime*, National Gallery Company, London, 2008

Boult, Sir Adrian, *My Own Trumpet*, Hamish Hamilton, London, 1973

Bratby, Richard, *Forward: 100 Years of the City of Birmingham Symphony Orchestra*, Elliott & Thompson, London, 2019

Broad, Leah, *Quartet*, Faber & Faber, London, 2023

Brooks, Christopher A., and Sim, Robert, *Roland Hayes: The Legacy of an American Tenor*, Indiana University Press, Bloomington; Indianapolis, 2014

Cardus, Neville (Ed.), *Kathleen Ferrier 1912-1953: A Memoir*, Hamish Hamilton, London, 1954

Corredor, Josep M., and Casals, Pablo, *Conversations with Casals*, Dutton, New York, 1957

Casals, Pablo, and Kahn, Albert E., *Joys and Sorrows: Pablo Casals, His Own Story as Told to Albert E. Kahn*, Simon and Schuster, New York, 1970

Clark, Kenneth, *The Other Half: A Self-Portrait*, John Murray, London, 1977

Coates, Eric, *Suite in Four Movem*ents, Thames, London 1953, revised edition 1986

Cohen, Harriet, *A Bundle of Time: The Memoirs of Harriet Cohen*, Faber & Faber, London, 1969

Cohen, Harriet, *Music's Handmaid*, Faber & Faber, London, 1936

Cooper, Artemis, *Elizabeth Jane Howard: A Dangerous Innocence*, John Murray, London, 2016

Curtis, Liane, *A Rebecca Clarke Reader*, Rebecca Clarke Society, Title 9 Music, Massachussetts, 2005

Draper, Muriel, *Music at Midnight*, Harper & Brothers, New York, 1929

Farjeon, Annabel, *Morning Has Broken: A Biography of Eleanor Farjeon*, Julia McRae, London, 1986

Farjeon, Eleanor, *Edward Thomas: The Last Four Years*, Oxford University Press, Oxford, 1958

Ferguson, Howard, *Music, Friends and Places*, Thames Publishing, London, 1997

Fifield, Christopher, *Ibbs & Tillett: The Rise and Fall of a Musical Empire*, Ashgate Publishing, London, 2005

Fifield, Christopher, *Letters and Diaries of Kathleen Ferrier*, Boydell Press, Woodbridge, 2004; revised and enlarged edition, 2011

Foreman, Lewis and Susan, *Felix Aprahamian: Diaries and Selected Writings on Music*, Boydell Press, Woodbridge, 2015

Foreman, Lewis, *Bax: A Composer and his Times*, Scolar Press, London, 1983; revised edition, 2007

Frank, Mortimer H., *Toscanini: The NBC Years*, Amadeus Press, Lanham, 2002

Fry, Helen, *Music and Men: The Life and Loves of Harriet Cohen*, The History Press, Cheltenham, 2008

Gál, Hans, trs Anthony Fox and Eva Fox-Gál, *Music Behind Barbed Wire: A Diary of Summer 1940*, Toccata Press, London, 2014

Gardiner, Juliet, *The Thirties: An Intimate History of Britain*, Harper Press, London, 2011

Gelatt, Roland, *Music Makers: Some Outstanding Musical Performers of Our Day*, Knopf, New York, 1953

Gerhardt, Elena, *Recital*, Methuen & Co, London, 1953

Haas, Michael, *Forbidden Music: The Jewish Composers Banned by the Nazis*, Yale University Press, New Haven and London, 2013

Hampton, Janie, *Joyce Grenfell: A Biography*, John Murray, London, 2002

Hayter-Menzies, Grant, *Charlotte Greenwood: The Life and Career of the Comic Star of Vaudeville, Radio and Film*, McFarland & Co, Jefferson, 2007

Howard, Elizabeth Jane, *Slipstream: A Memoir*, Pan Macmillan, London, 2003

Howard, Elizabeth Jane, *The Light Years (The Cazalet Chronicles 1)*, Macmillan, London, 1990

Hurd, Michael (Ed.) and Ferguson, Howard (Ed.), *Letters of Gerald Finzi and Howard Ferguson*, Boydell Press, Rochester, 2001,

Jacobs, Arthur, *Henry Wood: Maker of the Proms*, Methuen, London, 1994

Kennedy, Michael, *Adrian Boult*, Hamish Hamilton, London, 1987

Lassimonne, Denise, and Ferguson, Howard (Ed.), *Myra Hess by her Friends*, Hamish Hamilton, London, 1966

Legge, Walter, *Words and Music*, Duckworth, London, 1998

Lieberman, Richard K, *Steinway & Sons*, Yale University Press, New Haven and London, 1995

Lympany, Moura, and Strickland, Margot, *Moura: Her Autobiography*, Peter Owen, London and Chester Springs, 1991

MacLeod, Joseph, *The Sisters d'Arányi*, Allen & Unwin, London, 1969

Maddocks, Fiona, *Goodbye Russia: Rachmaninoff in Exile*, Faber & Faber, London, 2023

Matthay, Jessie Henderson, *The Life and Works of Tobias Matthay*, Boosey and Hawkes, London, 1945

Matthay, Tobias, *The Act of Touch*, Bosworth & Co, London, 1903

Matthews, Denis, *In Pursuit of Music*, Victor Gollancz, London, 1966

McGee, Tim, *Barely Clare: The Little-Known Life of Clare Mackail*, Angela Thirkell Society of North America, Southeastern, PA, 2020

McKenna, Marian, *Myra Hess: A Portrait*, Hamish Hamilton, London, 1976

McVeagh, Diana (Ed.), *Gerald Finzi's Letters, 1915-1956*, Boydell Press, Woodbridge, 2021

McVeagh, Diana, *Gerald Finzi: His Life and Music*, Boydell & Brewer, Woodbridge, 2005

McVeigh, Simon, *Music in Edwardian London*, Boydell & Brewer, Woodbridge, 2024

Moiseiwitsch, Maurice, *Moiseiwitsch: Biography of a Concert Pianist*, Frederick Muller, London, 1965

Moore, Gerald, *Am I Too Loud? Memoirs of an Accompanist*, Hamish Hamilton, London, 1962

Moore, Gerald, *Furthermoore*, Hamish Hamilton, London, 1983

Monteux, Doris, *It's All in the Music*, Farrar, Straus & Giroux, New York, 1965

Morris, John, *Culture and Propaganda in World War II: Music, Film and the Battle for National Identity*, I.B. Tauris, London, 2014

Morris, John, *Music and Politics in Thirties Britain: Raise the Standard High*, Bloomsbury, London, 2011

Neel, Boyd, *My Orchestras and Other Adventures: The Memoirs of Boyd Neel*, University of Toronto Press, Toronto, Buffalo, London, 1985

Nicholas, Roger, *Ravel*, Yale University Press, New Haven and London, 2013

Nicholson, Virginia, *Singled Out: How Two Million Women Survived Without Men After the First World War*, Penguin, London, 2008

Ponsonby, Robert, *In and Out of Tune: Personal and Public Memoirs*, Lulu.com, 2016

Ponsonby, Robert, *Musical Heroes*, Gilles de la Mare, London, 2009

Reynolds, Mabel Edith, *Memories of John Galsworthy: By his Sister M. E. Reynolds*, Robert Hale & Co, London, 1936

Roose-Evans, James (Ed.), *Darling Ma: Joyce Grenfell Letters to her Mother*, 1932-44, Hodder & Stoughton, London, 1988

Rubinstein, Arthur, *My Many Years*, Jonathan Cape, London, 1980

Rubinstein, Arthur, *My Young Years*, Jonathan Cape, London, 1973

Ryding, Erik, and Pechevsky, Rebecca, *Bruno Walter: A World Elsewhere*, Yale University Press, New Haven and London, 2001

Sachs, Harvey, *Arthur Rubinstein: A Life*, Grove Press, New York, 1995

Sachs, Harvey, *Toscanini: Musician of Conscience*, Liveright, New York and London, 2017

Shore, Bernard, *The Orchestra Speaks*, Longman, Green & Co, London, New York and Toronto, 1944

Siek, Stephen, *England's Piano Sage: The Life and Teachings of Tobias Matthay*, Scarecrow Press, Lanham Maryland, Toronto and Plymouth, illustrated edition, 2012

Smith, Julia, with introduction by Hess, Myra, *Master Pianist: The Career and Teaching of Carl Friedberg*, Philosophical Library, New York, 1963

Spurling, Hilary, *Ivy: The Life of Ivy Compton-Burnett*, Richard Cohen Books, Omnibus Edition, London, 1995

Steiner, Rudolf, trs and foreword by Vera and Juliet Compton-Burnett, *Foundations of Esotericism*, Rudolf Steiner Press, Forest Row, 1983

Steiner, Rudolf, trs Vera and Juliet Compton-Burnett, *Eurythmy as Visible Music*, Rudolf Steiner Press, Forest Row, revised edition, 1977

Steinway, Theodore E., *People and Pianos: A Pictorial History of Steinway and Sons*, Amadeus Press, New Jersey, 1953

Szigeti, Joseph, *With Strings Attached*, Alfred A. Knopf, New York, 1947

Tertis, Lionel, *My Viola and I*, Elek Books, London, 1974

Vaughan Williams, Ursula, *R.V.W.: A Biography of Ralph Vaughan Williams*, Oxford University Press, Oxford, 1964

Walter, Bruno, *Theme and Variations: An Autobiography*, Hamish Hamilton, London, 1948

White, Jerry, *London in the 19th Century: A Human Awful Wonder of God*, Jonathan Cape, London, 2007

White, Jerry, *London in the 20th Century: A City and Its People*, Viking, London, 2001

White, Jerry, *Zeppelin Nights: London in the First World War*, Vintage, London, 2015

White, John, *Lionel Tertis: The First Great Virtuoso of the Viola*, Boydell Press, Woodbridge, 2006

Wood, Henry, *My Life of Music*, Gollancz, London, 1949

Articles

Adams, John K., 'Bruce Simonds and the Power of Words', American Matthay Association website, https://www.matthay.org/Bruce.htm

Adams, John K., 'Myra Hess in America', *Signature: Women in Music*, Spring/Summer 2011

Bernath, Victoria, 'Jelly d'Arányi - The recorded legacy and career of a virtuoso violinist in the roaring twenties.' British Library *Sound and Vision* blog, 24 February 2023 https://blogs.bl.uk/sound-and-vision/2023/02/jelly-darányi-the-recorded-legacy-and-career-of-a-virtuoso-violinist-in-the-roaring-twenties.html

Burgoyne, Elizabeth, 'Dame Myra Hess – A Personality Sketch', *The Queen*, 18 June 1941, p12

Cahill, Garret, 'Howard Ferguson (1908-1999): The life and work of an Irish composer', *The Journal of Music*, 1 May 2003 https://journalofmusic.com/focus/howard-ferguson-1908-1999

Glovin, Bill, and Parsonnet, Victor: The Page Turner https://www.billglovin.com/ewExternalFiles/The%20Page%20Turner.pdf

Haas, Michael, 'Exiled Austrian and German Musicians in Great Britain', Orel Foundation, 26 October 2014 http://orelfoundation.org/journal/journalArticle/exiled_austr039_great_britain

Hudlow, Kelley, 'Notoriously Episcopalian' https://notoriouslyepiscopalian com/2020/04/15/and-if-i-am-to-do-nothing-let-me-do-it-gallantly/

Jack, Ian, 'Klever Kaff', *Granta*, accessed online, https://granta.com/klever-kaff/

Levi, Erik, 'How the London Philharmonic became a Pawn in a Nazi Propaganda Scheme', BBC Music Magazine, accessed online 19 October 2021, https://www.classical-music.com/articles/how-the-royal-philharmonic-orchestra-became-a-pawn-in-a-nazi-propaganda-scheme

Mahler Foundation, 'Carl Friedberg (1872-1955)' https://mahlerfoundation.org/mahler/contemporaries/carl-friedberg/

Mendoza, Joe, 'How Humphrey Jennings Saved My Life', *The Veteran*, no. 94, 2001, pp.18–27

Nicholas, Jeremy, 'The Lady Vanishes', *International Piano*, Jul/Aug 2016, p67ff

Parsonnet, Victor, with Glovin, Bill, *The Page Turner*, https://www.billglovin.com/ghostwriting/ewExternalFiles/The%20Page%20Turner.pdf

Potter, Tully, 'Farewell to Academia' (Interview with Sidney Griller), *The Strad*, January 1986

Potter, Tully, Interview with Watson Forbes, *The Strad*, July 1991

Settle, Mary Lee, 'London – 1944', *The Virginia Quarterly Review*, Vol. 64, Autumn 1987, No. 4

Woolsey, F.W., and Roland Hayes. 'Roland Hayes.' *The Black Perspective in Music*, vol. 2, no. 2, 1974, pp. 179–85. JSTOR, https://doi.org/10.2307/1214234.

York, John, 'Into the Light – Rebecca Clarke's Rhapsody for Cello and Piano', *The Strad*, December 2019

CD Notes

Izen, Marshall, for *Myra Hess, Live Recordings from the University of Illinois*, 1949, APR 7308

Siek, Stephen, for *Myra Hess, The Complete Solo and Concerto Studio Recordings*, APR 7504

Siek, Stephen, for *Irene Scharrer, The Complete Electric and Selected Acoustic Recordings*, APR 6010

Online Resources

American Matthay Association Summer Festival 2022, 'Celebrating the legacies of two great teachers, Tobias Matthay and Frank Mannheimer, at the College of St. Scholastica, Duluth, Minnesota, June 22-25, 2022' https://www.youtube.com/watch?v=Z0FMF67-4eg

John Amis interview with MH, BBC Radio 3, 'Talking About Music', 1963, available on Youtube

Sir Arnold Bax: https://www.arnoldbax.com/

Arthur Bloomfield, *More than the Notes*, http://www.morethanthenotes.com

BBC Genome Programme Index https://genome.ch.bbc.co.uk/search/0/20?order=first&q=Myra+Hess

Carnegie Hall, Performance History Search https://www.carnegiehall.org/About/History/Performance-History-Search?q=Myra%20Hess&dex=prod_PHS

Willa Cather – Letters https://cather.unl.edu/writings/letters/let1869

Rebecca Clarke Society https://www.rebeccaclarke.org

Jim Fassett interview with MH, 1952, available on Youtube

Friends of Medway Archive, Newsletter February 2021 https://foma-lsc.org/Downloads/Issue%2061A5.pdf

Hallé Orchestra, Online Archive https://archive.halle.co.uk/performer/hess-myra;-dame

Holman, Hannah, Influential British Cellists, Episode 8: May Mukle https://www.youtube.com/watch?v=ORHvtEqj_Xc

Tobias Matthay http://www.pianosage.net/index.html https://www.matthay.org

The Pianola Institute – Reproducing Pianos https://www.pianola.org/reproducing/reproducing_duo-art.cfm

Marie Brockway Pond (1862-1957), Sibley Watson Digital Library https://dslab.lib.rochester.edu/esw/mbpo

Royal College of Music Oral History: Andrea Rauter, interviewed by Norbert Meyn https://www.rcm.ac.uk/singingasong/oralhistorycategory3/andrearauter/

RWJBarnabas Health: A Tribute to Victor Parsonnet https://www.youtube.com/watch?v=GrhXmoEWdG4&t=3s

Ralph Vaughan Williams – Letters https://vaughanwilliamsfoundation.org

Nicholas Winton, Kindertransport List https://www.nicholaswinton.com/the-list

The Times Archive

The New York Times Archive

Newspapers.com

The Musical Times and others via JSTOR

Primary Sources and Archives

BBC Archives

Edwin Evans Collection, Westminster Music Library

Hartt School of Music, University of Hartford

Myra Hess's letters to Jelly d'Arányi – private archive, d'Arányi family

Myra Hess's letters to Sidney Griller – private archive, Arnold Griller

Myra Hess Collection, British Library

Hess Family Collection

Marjorie Gunn diaries, Medway Archives Centre

National Archives

National Gallery Archives

Oxford University Press Archives

Wisconsin Historical Society, University of Wisconsin

Myra Hess Genealogy by Duncan Honeybourne

Myra Hess 78rpm discography by Mike Spring

Interviews by the author with John Contiguglia, Richard Contiguglia, Libbie Foster, Fiona Fraser, Arnold Griller, Nigel Hess, Andrew Keener, Diana King, Stephen Kovacevich, Nadia Lasserson, Nicholas Logie, Diana McVeagh, Michael Oldham, Ann Schein, Stephen Siek.

Interview by Nigel Hess with Howard Ferguson.

Interviews by Judy Meewezen with Yonty Solomon and Colin Hess.

Selected Discography

Duo-Art Piano Roll Recordings, 1922-1927

Debussy: La Cathédrale engloutie – 69270

Brahms: Klavierstücke Op. 119: III Intermezzo in C major – 69119

Brahms: Klavierstücke Op. 119: IV Rhapsody in E flat major – 69119

Attrib. Paradis: Toccata in A major – 70599

Scarlatti: Sonata in G major – 70590

Bach: Toccata in G major – 7236

Bach/Busoni: Whitsuntide Chorale Prelude – A-93

Beethoven: Sonata in G major, Op. 79 – A-109

British Productions of the Aeolian Company

Debussy: Préludes, Book 1: No. 2, Voiles – 061

Szymanowski: Etude, Op. 4 No. 3

Beethoven: Sonata in G major, Op. 79

Grieg: Piano Concerto, Op. 16

With Harold Bauer, 1926:

Burgmein: The Story of Pierrot and Pierrette (piano duet) – 7069-4

Pierné: March of the Little Lead Soldiers, Op. 14 No. 6 (two pianos) – 7329

Unissued: Liadov: Gigue

Studio Recordings

Myra Hess's complete solo and concerto studio recordings are available in remastered editions on Appian Publications and Recordings's set APR7504

28-30 December 1927, New York – Columbia (US) 67436/9-D (in set M91)

Schubert: Piano Trio No. 1 in B flat major, D898 (with Jelly d'Arányi, violin, and Felix Salmond, cello)

17 January 1928, New York – Columbia (US) 2063-M

Bach: French Suite No. 5 in G major, BWV816: VII Gigue

Bach/Myra Hess: Jesu, joy of man's desiring (from Cantata BWV147)

19 January 1928, New York – Columbia (US) 175-M

Ravel: Pavane pour une infante défunte

16-17 February 1928, New York – Columbia (US) 67417/9D (in set 87)

Schubert: Piano Sonata in A major, D664

17 February 1928, New York – Columbia (US) 7151-M

Debussy: Images, Book 2: III Poissons d'or

Debussy: Préludes, Book 1: No. 8, La fille aux cheveux de lin; No. 12, Minstrels

Columbia (US) 67419

Schubert/Rudolf Ganz: Ballet Music from Rosamunde D797 No. 9

14 March 1928, New York – Columbia (US) 168-M:

Beethoven: Bagatelles, Op. 119: No. 11 in B flat major, Andante ma non troppo

Brahms: Klavierstücke Op. 119: III Intermezzo in C major

Scarlatti: Sonata in C major, K159 (L104); Sonata in C minor, K11 (L352)

23 April 1929, New York – Columbia (US) 1951-D

Bach: The Well-Tempered Clavier, Book 1: No. 3 in C sharp major, BWV848

Bach: Toccata in G major, BWV916: I Allegro

26 April 1929, New York,.Columbia (US) 2512-D

Palmgren: 24 Preludes, Op. 17: No. 9 Cradle Song

29 April 1929, New York – Columbia (US) 50199-D

Brahms: Klavierstücke Op. 76: II Capriccio in B minor

3 May 1929, New York – Columbia (US) 50149-D

Falla: El amor brujo: Ritual Fire Dance

Griffes: Roman Sketches, Op. 7: No. 1 The White Peacock

– Columbia (US) 50199-D

Mendelssohn: Songs without Words, Op. 38: VI, No. 18 in A flat major, 'Duetto'

Mendelssohn: Songs without Words, Op. 67: IV, No. 24 in C major, 'Spinning Song'

23 March 1931, New York, Columbia (US) 2512-D

Schumann: Waldszenen Op. 82: VII Vogel als Prophet

17 October 1933, London, Abbey Road, Columbia (UK) D81232

Chopin: Nocturne No. 5 in F sharp major, Op. 15 No. 2

Dvořák: Slavonic Dances, Op. 46: No. 1 in C major, Furiant (with Hamilton Harty, piano)

Field: Nocturne No. 4 in A major, H36

Columbia (UK) D81235

MacDowell: Sea Pieces, Op. 55: III AD MDCXX

25 & 27 October 1935, London, Abbey Road, Columbia (UK) LX497/500

Brahms: Piano Trio No. 2 in C major, Op. 87 (with Jelly d'Arányi, violin, and Gaspar Cassadó, cello)

28 June 1936, London, Abbey Road, Columbia (UK) LX641/3

Beethoven: Cello Sonata No. 3 in A major, Op. 69 (with Emmanuel Feuermann, cello)

5 October 1937, London, Abbey Road, HMV C2942/5

Schumann: Piano Concerto in A minor, Op. 54 (with un-named studio orchestra and Walter Goehr, conductor)

25 April 1938, London, Abbey Road, HMV B8758

Matthay: Elves, Op. 17

8 June 1938, London, Abbey Road, HMV B8758

Matthay: Album Leaf Op.22

25 April & 3 May 1938, London, Abbey Road, HMV C3008/10

Schumann: Carnaval, Op. 9

9 January 1940, London, Abbey Road, HMV B9035

Bach/Myra Hess: Jesu, joy of man's desiring (from Cantata BWV147)

Scarlatti: Sonata in G major, K14 (L387)

8 April 1941, London, Abbey Road, HMV C3226

Brahms: Fantasies, Op. 116: VII Capriccio in D minor

Brahms: Intermezzos, Op. 117: I in E flat major

Brahms: Klavierstücke, Op. 119: III Intermezzo in C major

29 April 1941, London, Abbey Road, HMV B9189

Brahms: Klavierstücke, Op. 76: II Capriccio in B minor; III Intermezzo in A flat major

24 June 1941, Wolverhampton, Civic Hall, HMV C3237/8

Franck: Symphonic Variations (with City of Birmingham Orchestra and Basil Cameron, conductor)

2 & 4 March 1942, Manchester, Houldsworth Hall, HMV – unissued on 78s

Mozart: Piano Concerto in C major, K467 (with Hallé Orchestra and Leslie Heward, conductor)

19 November 1942, London, Abbey Road, HMV C3335/7

Ferguson: Piano Sonata in F minor, Op. 8

1 February 1943, London, Abbey Road, HMV C3337

Purcell/Myra Hess: Sarabande, Minuet and Air – from Suite Z661 (Sarabande), Z660 (Minuet), Air ZT693/2 (Air)

12 January 1945, London, Abbey Road, HMV C3423

Ferguson: Five Bagatelles, Op. 9

Haydn: Piano Sonata in D major, Hob XVI:37: 1 Allegro con brio (unissued on 78s)

17 November 1949, London, Abbey Road, HMV C3960

Bach: Six Little Preludes: 4 Prelude in D major, BWV936

Bach/Myra Hess: Adagio (from Toccata, Adagio & Fugue in C major, BWV564)

22 December 1952, London, HMV BLP 1039

Schumann: Piano Concerto in A minor, Op. 54 (with Philharmonic Orchestra and Rudolf Schwarz, conductor)

1-2 October 1953, London, Abbey Road, HMV ALP 1169

Beethoven: Piano Sonata in A flat major, Op. 110

22-23 October 1953, London, HMV BLP 1061

Schumann: Etudes symphoniques, Op. 13

17-19 November 1953, London, Abbey Road, HMV ALP 1169

Beethoven: Piano Sonata in E major, Op. 109

12 October 1957, London, Abbey Road, HMV BLP 1103

Bach/Myra Hess: Jesu, joy of man's desiring (from Cantata BWV147)

Beethoven: Klavierstück in A minor, 'Für Elise', WoO59

Beethoven: Bagatelle in E flat major, Op. 126 No. 3

Brahms: Waltz in A flat, Op. 39 No. 15

Brahms: Klavierstücke, Op. 119: III Intermezzo in C major

Granados: The Maiden and the Nightingale (from Goyescas)

Mendelssohn: Song without Words in A major, Op. 102 No. 5

Scarlatti: Sonata in C minor, K11 (L352)

Scarlatti: Sonata in G major, K14 (L387)

Live Concert and Broadcast Recordings

Current remastered CD and streaming editions are listed when available

7 March 1937, Masonic Temple Auditorium, Detroit, from Ford Sunday Evening Hour, APR 7306

Grieg: Piano Concerto in A minor, Op. 16, first movement (with Detroit Symphony and Victor Kolar, conductor)

Chopin: Etudes, Op. 25: No. 1 in A flat major; No. 3 in F major

Bach: French Suite No. 5 in G major, BWV816: VII Gigue

25 August 1942, London, live in the National Gallery, APR5646

Brahms: Piano Quintet (with the Griller String Quartet)

24 November 1946, New York, Naxos 8110804

Beethoven: Piano Concerto No. 3 in C minor, Op. 37 (with NBC Symphony Orchestra and Arturo Toscanini, conductor)

2 November 1947, New York,

Mozart: Piano Concerto No. 14 in E flat major, K449 (with New York Philharmonic and Leopold Stokowski, conductor)

February 1948, radio broadcast, authenticity uncertain

Chopin: Nocturne in C minor, Op. 48 No. 1, Heritage Records HTGCD260

6 February 1949, New York, Music & Arts, MACD0779

Mozart: Piano Concerto No. 21 in C major, K467 (with New York Philharmonic and Leopold Stokowski, conductor)

4 March 1949, New York

Brahms: Piano Concerto No. 1 in D minor, Op. 15 (with Boston Symphony Orchestra and Serge Koussevitzky, conductor)

17-18 March 1949, Live recordings from Auditorium of the University of Illinois, APR 7306

17 March 1949

Chopin: Fantasy in F minor, Op. 49

Schubert: Piano Sonata in B flat major, D960

Schubert: Dances for Piano (with spoken introduction), Myra Hess's own selection, given as encores on 17 and 18 March 1949

Brahms: Klavierstücke, Op. 119: III Intermezzo in C major

Scarlatti: Sonata in G major, K14 (L387)

Chopin: Waltz in E flat major, Op. 18

Mozart: Piano Concerto in C major, K467 (with University of Illinois Sinfonietta and John M. Kuypers, Conductor)

18 March 1949

Bach: Partita No. 4 in D major, BWV828

Beethoven: Piano Sonata in D minor, Op. 31 No. 2, 'Tempest'

Mozart: Piano Concerto in E flat maor, K271 (with University of Illinois Sinfonietta and John M. Kuypers, Conductor), with closing speech

13 October 1950, BBC studio

Bach/Ferguson: Sarabande from Lute Suite in C minor, BWV997 (unissued)

Bach: Toccata in G, BWV916 – ICA Classics, BBC Legends Vol. 2 ICAB5141

Schumann: Carnaval, Op. 9 – APR 5646

11 March 1951, New York, Music & Arts MACD0779

Brahms: Piano Concerto No. 2 in B flat major, Op. 15 (with New York Philharmonic Orchestra and Bruno Walter, conductor)

July 1951, live recording from the Casals Festival, Perpignan

Mozart: Piano Concerto in E flat major, K271 (with Perpignan Festival Orchestra and Pablo Casals, conductor)

10 February 1952, New York, AS 627

Schumann: Piano Concerto in A minor, Op. 54 (with New York Philharmonic Orchestra and Dimitri Mitropoulos, conductor)

June 1952, live recordings from the Casals Festival, Prades

Schubert: Duo Sonata in A major, D574 (with Joseph Szigeti) – Sony G010004475771M

Brahms: Piano Trio No. 1 in B major, Op. 8 (with Isaac Stern, violin, and Pablo Casals, cello) – Sony G010004265748Z

Brahms: Piano Trio No. 2 in C major, Op. 87 (with Joseph Szigeti, violin, and Pablo Casals, cello) – BNF Collection, 3610156348016

Brahms: Piano Quartet No. 3 in C minor, Op. 60 (with Joseph Szigeti, violin, Milton Katims, viola, and Paul Tortelier, cello) – Sony G010004475773I

Schumann: Piano Quintet in E flat major, Op. 44 (with Isaac Stern and Alexander Schneider, violins, Milton Thomas, viola, Paul Tortelier, cello) – Sony, G0100042657368

9 December 1952, Music & Arts MACD0779

Beethoven: Piano Concerto No. 4 in G major, Op. 58 (with BBC Symphony Orchestra and Sir Adrian Boult, conductor)

8 February 1953, Music & Arts MACD0779

Beethoven: Piano Concerto No. 5 in E flat major, Op. 73 (with New York Philharmonic Orchestra and Efrem Kurtz, conductor)

17 January 1954, New York, Music and Arts MACD0275

Mozart: Piano Concerto No. 14 in E flat major, K449 (with New York Philharmonic and Bruno Walter, conductor)

13 February 1955

Brahms: Piano Concerto No. 1 in D minor, Op. 15 (with New York Philharmonic Orchestra and Dimitri Mitropoulos, conductor)

Available on Youtube

4 March 1956, New York, Music and Arts MACD0275

Mozart: Piano Concerto No. 20 in D minor, K466 (with New York Philharmonic and Bruno Walter, conductor)

20 March 1956, Music & Arts MACD0779

Mozart: Piano Concerto No. 12 in A major, K414, and No. 27 in B flat major, K595 (with American Chamber Orchestra and Robert Scholz, conductor)

2 November 1956, BBC Studios, BBC Legends Vol 2 ICAB5141

Bach: Prelude in G major from BWV902; English Suite No. 2 in A minor

12 September 1957, BBC Promenade Concerts, Royal Albert Hall, London

Beethoven: Piano Concerto No. 5 in E flat major, Op. 73, 'Emperor' (with BBC Symphony Orchestra and Sir Malcolm Sargent, conductor)

23 March 1958, New York

Beethoven: Piano Concerto No. 3 in C minor, Op. 37 (with New York Philharmonic Orchestra and Ernest Ansermet, conductor)

18 September 1958, London, ICA Classics, BBC Legends Vol 2 ICAB5141

Schumann: Piano Concerto in A minor, Op. 54 (with BBC Symphony Orchestra and Sir Malcolm Sargent, conductor)

12 October 1958, London, BBC Studio recital

Mozart: Rondo in D major, K485; Gigue in G major, K574; Sonata in C minor, K457

11 September 1959

Beethoven: Piano Concerto No. 3 in C minor, Op. 37 (with London Symphony Orchestra and Sir Adrian Boult, conductor)

19 December 1959

Mozart: Piano Concerto No. 27 in B flat major, K595 (with Philharmonia Orchestra and Rudolf Schwarz, conductor)

12 July 1960

Beethoven: Piano Concerto No. 2 in B flat major, Op. 19 (with BBC Symphony Orchestra and Sir Malcolm Sargent, conductor)

28 August 1960, live recordings from the Edinburgh Festival, with Isaac Stern, violin, Testament SBT1458

Brahms: Violin Sonata No. 2 in A major, Op. 100

Schubert: Violin Sonata in D major, D384

Ferguson: Violin Sonata No. 2, Op. 10

Beethoven: Violin Sonata No. 10 in G major, Op. 96

30 August 1960, live recording from the Usher Hall, Edinburgh Festival, BBC Legends, BBCL 4178-2

Beethoven: Piano Concerto No. 2 in B flat major, Op. 19 (with Royal Scottish National Orchestra and Sir Alexander Gibson, conductor)

8 September, 1961

Beethoven: Piano Concerto No. 4 in G major, Op. 58 (with London Philharmonic Orchestra and Sir Adrian Boult, conductor)

31 October 1961, London

Mozart: Piano Concerto No. 23 in A major, K488 (with London Philharmonic and Sir Adrian Boult, conductor)

3 January 1962, London, BBC Broadcasting House

Haydn: Sonata No. 52 in E flat major

Other Unissued Recordings

31 May 1938, broadcast concert

Beethoven: Piano Concerto No. 4 in G major, Op. 58 (with BBC Empire Orchestra and E. Fogg, conductor); Franz Schubert: Dances

15 June 1958, Jubilee Hall, Downe House School

Bach: Concerto in D minor (with Downe House Chamber Orchestra and Marjorie Gunn, conductor)

10 December 1961, London, BBC Broadcasting House

Schubert: Piano Sonata in B flat major, D960, and Klavierstück in E flat major, D946 No. 2

Index

Publisher's Acknowledgements

The publisher would like to thank the following whose help and encouragement contributed to bringing the story of this fascinating life into print:

The author, Jessica Duchen, who has such passion for her subject.

Stephen Kovacevich for writing the Foreword.

The Hess Family for allowing access to their private archives and photographs.

Many others who provided source material for giving their time so willingly.

The Society of Authors as the Literary Representative of the Estate of John Masefield for their kind permission to reproduce *When Death Came Near*.

The editorial team of Sidney Buckland and Leslie East OBE for their vigilance, enthusiasm and patience.

Økvik Design for the book jacket design.

The production team at Halstan especially Ric Topping for his skills in layout and typesetting.

Louise Barder and Victoria Bevan for their valuable assistance with promotion.

The National Gallery for its enthusiasm for this project.

Photographic Credits

We are grateful to the following for supplying photographs:

The Hess Family Collection: Front cover (Florence Vandamm), frontispiece, pages 3, 7, 13, 31, 42, 48, 65, 78, 101, 118, 144, 151, 166 (*The Times*, News International), 170 (The National Gallery, London), 177 (Howard Coster), 182, 184, 190 (Ronald Proctor, London), 201 (© National Portait Gallery, London), 211, 214, 219, 227, 241, 244 (Florence Vandamm), 275, 289, 338.

American Matthay Association: pages 11, 17, 21, 25

Jessica Duchen: Front cover flap (Corinna Desch)

All possible efforts have been made to contact the owners of copyright material. The publisher would be pleased to hear from any person who can assist in tracing the identity of any owners of image rights who have not been correctly identified and acknowledged.